Broken Sword

Broken Sword

The Tumultuous Life of
General Frank Crozier 1879–1937

Charles Messenger

PEN & SWORD
PRAETORIAN PRESS

First published in Great Britain in 2013 by
The Praetorian Press
an imprint of
Pen & Sword Books Ltd
47 Church Street
Barnsley
South Yorkshire S70 2AS

Copyright © Charles Messenger 2013

ISBN 978 1 84884 897 9

Typeset in Ehrhardt by
Mac Style, Bridlington, East Yorkshire
Printed and bound in the UK by CPI Group (UK) Ltd, Croydon,
CRO 4YY

Pen & Sword Books Ltd incorporates the Imprints of Pen & Sword
Aviation, Pen & Sword Maritime, Pen & Sword Military, Wharncliffe
Local History, Pen and Sword Select, Pen and Sword Military Classics,
Leo Cooper, The Praetorian Press, Remember When, Seaforth
Publishing and Frontline Publishing.

For a complete list of Pen & Sword titles please contact
PEN & SWORD BOOKS LIMITED
47 Church Street, Barnsley, South Yorkshire, S70 2AS, England
E-mail: enquiries@pen-and-sword.co.uk
Website: www.pen-and-sword.co.uk

Contents

List of Illustrations

List of Maps

Introduction

I first came across Brigadier General Frank Crozier in an Oxford second-hand bookshop some fifty years ago, when I purchased his *A Brass Hat in No Man's Land*. I found it an entertaining read, and a surprising one. This was not the usual way in which a general wrote about his war experiences, but it did contain some nuggets. His name cropped up in other books and gradually I developed an interest in him as a person. It was when I discovered his Army personal file at the National Archives, Kew, that I realised quite what an intriguing character he was. Compared to the average slim officer's file, Crozier's is the largest that I have seen and goes into detail about some of his misdemeanours. It confirmed that he was a colourful character and one who saw much active service – South Africa, West Africa, Ireland before and after the Great War, three years and more on the Western Front, and in the struggles of the Baltic States to preserve the independence granted to them by the Treaty of Versailles. There are, too, the interludes in Ceylon and Canada. Finally, there was his conversion to pacifism. Thus, one can argue that Crozier was a child of his time, who played a greater or lesser role in many of the events that shaped the first third of the twentieth century for Britain. His, as the subtitle indicates, was a turbulent life.

In terms of sources, and apart from his Army personal file, there are the books he wrote. Most of these have to be treated with caution, since Crozier was prone to exaggeration or to glossing over the truth. His autobiography *Impressions and Recollections*, which was published in 1930, is more truthful, but there are significant omissions and unanswered questions. Much of this concerns his personal life. I hoped that some of the answers might be provided by an unpublished biography written by his second wife. Alas, the typescript is incomplete, with those chapters relating to the years 1905–14 and 1919–21 missing. It was precisely during these years that Crozier's life did undergo changes, some controversial, and the suspicion is that these were destroyed at some stage, together with his personal papers. Scouring archives, books, and newspapers has helped to complete much of the jigsaw, but it is still incomplete in some respects. Even so, I consider that I have been able to add considerably to what is generally known about him, as well as throwing fresh light on numerous historical incidents, some better known than others.

I have addressed Crozier by his first name, Frank, throughout the book. Some may accuse me of over-familiarity, but it has made it easier to get under his skin and to provide a more balanced portrait.

I owe much to numerous individuals and institutions for their help. Ian Bailey, Curator of the Adjutant General's Corps Museum, Winchester, gave me information on Burrard Crozier's service as a paymaster. David Biggins and his Anglo-Boer War website produced useful information. Old friends colonels Bob Caldwell and Jack

English in Canada were most helpful on aspects of life in Canada when Crozier was there. Likewise, Brent Holloway of the Directorate of History and Heritage, National Defence, Canada, obtained transcripts of Tom MacFie's court-martial. Mark Cook, formerly of the London Branch of the Western Front Association but now in Australia, shared information gleaned during his BA studies on Crozier. Sarah Cox of the British Red Cross Society Museum & Archive investigated whether Ethel Crozier was a VAD during 1914–18. Catherine Boylan shared her research on Crozier. Steve Chamberlain of the Parliamentary Archives, London, provided copies of Crozier's correspondence with David Lloyd George and Lynne Chapman of the Tameside Local Studies and Archive Centre produced material from the Manchester Regiment archive. Lorraine Coghlan of the John Rylands University Library, University of Manchester, obtained copies of Crozier's correspondence with T.P. Scott, Editor of the *Manchester Guardian*. Dr Robin Drooglever, of Bulleen, Victoria, Australia and author of the history of Thorneycroft's Mounted Rifles, gave me his views on Crozier.

In Sri Lanka Major Anton Edema checked on Crozier's claimed service with the Ceylon Light Infantry, while Aled F. Jones checked out mentions of Crozier in the *Ceylon Observer*. Dick Flory provided information on Ormonde Winter, while Mandy Fyfe, Archivist of the Royal School Bath, gave me details of Mary Crozier's time there. David Grant was most generous in passing information about Ireland during 1920–21 and his two websites, on the Cairo Gang and Auxiliary Division of the Royal Irish Constabulary, proved very valuable sources. James Harte of the National Library of Ireland, Dublin, provided me with copies of Crozier's letters to Erskine Childers.

In Northern Ireland Jennifer White, Isaac Hall and Jim Bowan of the Royal Ulster Rifles Museum, Belfast, dug out information on Crozier and his time with the 9th Royal Irish Rifles, as well as looking after me very well when I visited. I also received guidance from Mrs Carol Walker, Director of The Somme Association & Somme Heritage Centre, Newtownards, as well as from my former comrade-in-arms Alan McFarland.

Peter Hart, who runs the Oral History Department at the Imperial War Museum and is now a very well-known Great War historian, kindly produced material for me. Bill Hethrington, the Peace Pledge Union's archivist, both produced material on Crozier and discussed the early history of the PPU when I visited. Frances Jeens, Curator of the Alderney Museum, kindly looked for information on the 2nd Manchesters' time on the island in the 1900s. Halima Khanom of the Royal Geographical Society produced Crozier's Fellow's application form and Colin MacInnes of Busy Hive Family History sent me copies of the minutes of Officers' Mess meetings of the 2nd Manchesters 1906–07.

I am grateful to Peter Maasz and Derek Marsh of the Oxfordshire Yeomanry Trust for their efforts to locate information on Anthony Muirhead, Crozier's Brigade Major in 1918 and his Chief of Staff in Lithuania. In Lithuania itself I had much help from Lt Col Dr Gintautas Surgailis, Director of the Vytautas Museum in Vilnius and also Dalius Zizys, Director of the Lithuanian Central State Archives, also in Vilnius, in shedding light on Crozier's period in the country.

Dr Patrick Mileham, Archive Project Manager at Wellington College and another former comrade-in-arms, generously gave of his time to provide me with a feel for Crozier's time at the school. Peter Robinson supplied me with details of Rifleman Crozier's court-martial. Keith Steward kindly read and commented on my West Africa chapter in draft. Alexander Thorneycroft gave information on his great-uncle, who married Crozier's mother. Richard van Emden, the author of a number of highly praised books on 1914–18, gave me quotes from two officers who served under Crozier in 119 Brigade. Dorothy Williams of the Museum of the Queen's Lancashire Regiment checked through the archives for information on Crozier's time with the 3rd Loyals.

I am also very grateful to the staffs of the British Library, Imperial War Museum, especially the Department of Documents, the Liddell Hart Centre for Military Archives, the London Metropolitan Archives, the National Archives, Kew, London, and the Public Record Office Northern Ireland.

As ever, I am very appreciative of the many informal discussions on Crozier that I have had with fellow members of the British Commission for Military History (BCMH) and the Western Front Association, especially the London branch. Once more I would like to pay my respects to my fellow forumites in the Great War Forum, now well over a decade old and flourishing ever more vibrantly. I am also grateful to fellow BCMH member Barbara Taylor for her excellent maps.

As for Pen & Sword, I am very grateful to Jamie Wilson, who accepted the idea for the book and steered the project through the contract phase. Rupert Harding marshalled the project through to publication and Susan Last was meticulous in her editing.

In terms of Crozier descendants, I would like to very much thank Mrs Carol Germa, whose mother was Crozier's elder daughter Mary, for the sight of correspondence between Mary and a Canadian researcher, Brett Taylor, and Crozier's erstwhile batman, David Starrett, in the 1970s. The same goes to Des Rees, Grace Crozier's great-nephew, for the sight of her papers, including an incomplete manuscript copy of her biography of her husband *Guns and God*.

Finally, I am very deeply indebted to Mike Taylor. It was not until after I had signed the contract that I learnt that he was doing a PhD on Crozier as a brigade commander. He had already done much research into Crozier's life as a whole and it was through his good offices that I was able to see the material held by Carol Germa and Des Rees. He also very generously shared archival research that he had done, thus saving me much time and effort. In this respect I do hope that I have been able to repay him, at least partially, through sharing my own research. Even though he lives in Scotland, we have been able to meet on a number of occasions and exchange views on our subject. I like to feel that he has become a good friend.

Charles Messenger
London, June 2013

Chapter One

The Early Years: 1879–1899

Francis Percy Crozier was born on 9 January 1879 on the island of Bermuda in the West Indies, but his name was soon shortened to Frank, after his grandfather. His father was Lieutenant Burrard Rawson Crozier of the 46th Regiment (soon to become 2nd Battalion The Duke of Cornwall's Light Infantry under the Cardwell reforms), which was stationed on the island. His mother, Rebecca Frances Crozier, was born a Percy and this was their first child. The two had met and married two years before when Burrard had been stationed at Birr in Ireland. He himself had been born in India in 1850, his father Frank Crozier being an Indian civil servant, while his mother was a Burrard. The family did have a house on the Isle of Wight and it was to here that Frank's grandfather retired. Rebecca came from a military family, her father having been an officer in the 9th Foot (later Royal Norfolk Regiment) who had fought in the Crimean War. Her family were also proud to be members of the historic Northumberland Percy clan. After retiring from the Army, Rebecca's father became a resident magistrate in Ireland, which explains how she met Frank's father.

In 1880 the 46th Regiment moved to Gibraltar and the infant Frank accompanied his parents there. The following year Burrard managed to gain promotion by obtaining a captaincy in the 79th Highlanders, who were also based at Gibraltar, but within a few months had exchanged with a captain in the 2nd Royal Scots Fusiliers, who were in South Africa and had taken part in the Zulu War and the disastrous first campaign against the Boers. Then, at the end of 1881, the battalion sailed to India and came to rest at Secunderabad. While at home and staying with Burrard's parents in Hampshire, in September 1881, Frances had given birth to another boy, but he was premature and died very quickly. Another brother for Frank, Pearson William, arrived in July 1883. Sadly, the family was again unlucky and Pearson died within a year. This highlighted the vulnerability of young children to disease in India and, following the custom of the day, Frank was sent back to Britain in 1884. That same year, however, Burrard and Rebecca were blessed with a baby girl, Evelyn, who survived.

Frank spent this time in Ireland, living with Rebecca's sister Helen, who was married to Captain Leslie Martin, a former 12th Lancer. (Two of Rebecca's other sisters also married former 12th Lancer officers.) He then died and she married Peter Fitzgerald, a resident magistrate in County Limerick, but Frank continued to stay with them while his parents were abroad. It was this that caused him to develop a deep interest in Irish affairs. Curiously, though, during all the time he spent in Ireland as a boy he was never taught to ride, in spite of having cavalrymen as uncles by marriage. The most likely explanation is that Rebecca, having lost her two other sons, did not want to expose Frank to any unnecessary risk to his life.

In June 1885 Burrard was detached to the Army Pay Department (APD). This had been formed in 1877. Prior to that time paymasters had had separate commissions, but did not have their own corps. The APD recruited from captains with combatant commissions, who were under the age of forty-five. Normally they served a year's probation before becoming fully-fledged members of the department. In Burrard's case it is likely that the extra pay attracted him. He served his probation and returned to the 2nd Royal Scots Fusiliers as their paymaster in June 1886, by which time they were in Burma.[1] For Frank, the most memorable event of this period was when his father came home to take part in Queen Victoria's Golden Jubilee celebrations in 1887. Frank recalled travelling over from Ireland on his own, initially under the charge of the stewardess on the ship and then from Holyhead in the care of the guard on the train. His father, whom he had not seen for three years, met him at Euston station and they repaired to the United Services Hotel in Haymarket, nowadays Her Majesty's Theatre. Frank recalled attending a levée with his father and grandfather and then, on 15 July, Frank was also present for the main purpose of Burrard's visit, escorting representatives of the women of Burma who, together with similar delegations from elsewhere in the Empire and Britain, made an offering of gifts to the Queen in Windsor Great Park.[2]

Early in 1890 there was a radical change in policy with regard to the Army Pay Department. To save money, it was decided that regimental paymasters would no longer operate and that adjutants would take over most of their duties, albeit with additional pay, and would be overseen by Station Paymasters. As a result, all those who had been accepted in the APD since 1 April 1884 were to revert to their combatant commissions.[3] Burrard, however, later in the same year, was offered a permanent appointment in the APD and returned to England at the end of 1890 to take up the appointment of Station Paymaster Colchester Garrison. He set up house there with Frances and Evelyn early in 1891.[4]

Frank now rejoined his family and attended a preparatory school on the outskirts of Hove in Sussex. It was known as Brunswick School, from the street on which it stood, and was run by two spinster sisters in their mid-forties, Charlotte and Catherine Thomson.* Although the 1891 Census shows the school as having just thirty-four pupils, including one American, it had already had one boy who would soon become famous. This was Winston Churchill, who attended the school from 1883–85. His parents had sent him there after unhappy experiences at previous schools and also because they thought him frail, believing that the sea air would do him good. Winston appears to have been happy at the school, and so too does Frank. He recalled that among his friends were Donough O'Brien, son of Lord Inchiquin, and one of the Earl of Leicester's sons, Tommy Coke, although neither is shown as being at the school in the 1891 Census.

---

* The school later moved to Haywards Heath, but was evacuated to Cornwall during World War Two. It moved again in 1958, this time to a large country house in Ashurst Wood, West Sussex. Stoke School joined it from Seaford in 1963 and the combined school became known as Stoke Brunswick. This survived right up until 2009, when it was forced to close because of lack of pupils.

Frank spent two years at Brunswick School and in January 1893 he was sent to Wellington College. It seems certain that he had set his heart on following his father into the Army and the College had a strong military tradition, being founded in the memory of the Duke of Wellington with the original intention of providing an education for the sons of deceased Army officers, although when it opened in January 1859 sons of serving officers and civilians were also admitted. By the 1890s, nigh on half the boys went on to join the Armed Forces. Burrard may also have been influenced by a close friend of his in the Royal Scots Fusiliers, Captain Alexander ('Alec') Thorneycroft, an old boy of the school and also a great admirer of Frank's mother. As it was, Burrard was now in Cairo and shortly to be posted once more to Gibraltar.

In *Impressions and Recollections*, his autobiography, Frank makes only one mention of Wellington, the fact that he was there. Like most other public schools of the day, life at the College was tough, with very few comforts. After visiting the school many years later to give a talk, Frank commented in a newspaper article entitled 'Are We Too Kind to the Modern Schoolboy?': 'The food, the cooking, the sleeping accommodation, the baths [apart, of course, from the swimming bath, which had always been a feature], reading-rooms, tuck-shops, and restaurant – every one of these had either been introduced since I was there or so completely changed as to be hardly recognisable.'[5] This gives an indication of how spartan it was in Frank's day. Wellington itself was organised in dormitories, as opposed to the houses of other schools, and these were named after the leading lights among the Duke of Wellington's subordinates. Frank's dormitory was Hopetoun, after John Hope, Earl of Hopetoun, who was a divisional commander in the Peninsular War. Each dormitory contained some thirty boys but, unusually for the day, each had his own cubicle from the outset, a policy instituted by the first headmaster of Wellington. A search of the school magazines and the Hopetoun Dormitory Book reveals that Frank clearly did not shine at sport, being in none of the dormitory teams throughout his time. He also does not appear to have taken an active part in any other activities, such as the Debating Society, although he was in the College choir during his first year. The overall conclusion must be that he did not enjoy his time at Wellington, perhaps partly because his small stature and angelic features made him look very young for his age.

Scholastically, Frank was no more than average. At the time, Wellington offered two streams of study. The Classical School, as its title implies, placed emphasis on the Classics, but included maths, French, history, geography and English and some science. It was primarily for those boys aspiring to go on to university. The other was the Mathematical School, which meant less Latin and no Greek, with more emphasis on maths, languages and science. It was this stream which attracted those bent on joining the Army, with some ending up in a special Army Class to prepare for the entrance exams to Sandhurst and Woolwich. It is not surprising, therefore, that Frank chose the Mathematical School. As for precisely what he studied, his first form was known as Lower III, and in his first term his textbooks were Ransome's *History of England*, Chambers' *Geography of Europe*, and, for English, Sir Walter Scott's *Lady of the Lake*. In addition, for French he used Somerville's *Primer* and *Grammar*, and Bertenshaw's *Exercises*, and for Latin, Moore's *Latin Primer* and

Mansfield's *Exercises*. He also did much English dictation and for Divinity had to study portions of the books of Kings and St Matthew, as well as *Notes on Catechism*. His form placing for that first term is not recorded, but he did sufficiently well to be promoted to the Upper Third for the summer term and was ranked fifteenth out of twenty-four pupils at the end of that term.

The winter term of 1893 saw Frank rise to fifth in his class, which earned him promotion to Lower IIA. He now found himself tackling Caesar's *Invasion of Britain*, but continued to wrestle with Ransome in History and Chambers in Geography. He spent a year in this form, working his way up to second in the class at the end of the winter term of 1894. He then moved up to Middle IIA. This gave him the option of studying German as a second language or natural science. Frank chose the latter and showed some aptitude for it, being placed second out of eighteen at the end of the Easter term in 1895. His maths, though, was somewhat shaky, and he was bottom of his set, although it was one of the top ones.

While at Wellington Frank spent his summer holidays in Ireland and winter holidays on the isle of Lewis in the Outer Hebrides. The latter was very much thanks to Mrs Jessie Platt, one of Alec Thorneycroft's sisters. She and her husband Joseph owned Eishken Lodge on the shores of Loch Snell and Frank clearly fell in love with it, making visits throughout much of his life. It was especially the sport on offer which attracted him:

> There [at Eishken Lodge] more mixed sport can be obtained than in most places. I suppose that the trout fishing is the best in Scotland. It must be good, as even I can catch a heavy basket of fish there. Over a hundred stags a year are killed, while the hind stalking is equally as good. Though the grouse shooting is not as good as when I was a boy, the woodcock shooting is first class. Wildfowl, snipe, plover, seals are all apt to show up suddenly to add to a mixed bag, while for real excitement I commend the local otter pack.[6]

While Joseph Platt died in 1907, Jessie lived on to the ripe old age of eighty-seven, continuing to spend her winters at the Lodge and dying there in February 1935.*

At the end of the summer term 1895, and still in Middle II, Frank left Wellington, now aged sixteen and a half.[7] The reason is not clear, since the majority of boys stayed on at the College until they were at least seventeen and often longer. One reason may have been that the College had a rule that no boy could stay in the Middle School beyond the age of sixteen. Frank still had to pass through the Upper Second before he could enter the Upper School and, with only one term left before he became seventeen, it could be that his masters considered that he was unlikely to achieve this, although he was placed seventh out of thirty-one boys in his form at the end of that term. Another possibility may have been that Burrard, who was still in Gibraltar, simply could not afford to pay the fees, which were £95 per annum, any longer. In 1892 he had had to borrow a total of £1,800 from his father and during 1898–99

---

* Eishken Lodge continues to exist as a sporting base. See http://www.sportinglets.co.uk/eishken/eishken-int.htm

he would borrow a further £700 – not inconsiderable sums in those days. These monies were to be deducted from the legacy he would receive on his father's death.[8] There may also have been concerns that Frank's slight and small frame might make it difficult for him to secure a place at the Royal Military College at Sandhurst. Since Frank's leaving address was given as that of his Uncle Peter Fitzgerald in County Limerick, it is likely that he went to Ireland in the hope that the air and good food would help him put on weight and gain a little in height.[9]

According to Frank himself he attended a military crammer in Earl's Court Square – a Mr Watson, according to Frank's second wife[10] – to prepare for the Sandhurst entrance exam; a common practice in those days.[11] But his hopes of a military career were seemingly dashed when he learned that his height of 5ft 4ins was half an inch below the minimum height for a regular commission for a seventeen-year-old,[12] and his weight and chest measurements also apparently let him down. According to one of his obituary writers, Frank then took a job in a stockbroker's office.[13] Yet, in spite of his disappointment at being barred from the Royal Military College at Sandhurst, the main stepping stone to a regular commission, Frank still wanted to be a soldier. Accordingly, he eventually obtained a commission as a Second Lieutenant in the 4th Middlesex Rifle Volunteer Corps (more commonly known as the West London Rifles), dated 6 June 1897. This unit recruited in the Kensington area and had its headquarters just off Kensington High Street. As it happened, Burrard and the remainder of Frank's family had returned home from Gibraltar that February. Burrard had been posted to Hounslow, on the outskirts of London, and the family settled in Scarsdale Villas, Kensington, where Frank joined them.[14] It so happened that the 2nd Royal Scots Fusiliers were now stationed at Chatham, which enabled Alec Thorneycroft to resume paying court to Frank's mother.

Two weeks after Frank was commissioned Queen Victoria celebrated her Diamond Jubilee. After a banquet at Buckingham Palace on the evening of 20 June, the Queen proceeded to a service at Westminster Abbey on the following day. Among the troops who lined the streets was a contingent of six officers, eight sergeants, two buglers and 100 rank and file from the 4th Middlesex. Frank wore the Diamond Jubilee Medal thereafter, although his name does not appear on the medal roll.[15] Also, unlike the Queen's 1887 Jubilee celebrations, he makes no mention of 1897 in *Impressions and Recollections*, although he does imply elsewhere that he was a member of the 4th Middlesex street-lining contingent.[16] A question mark therefore hangs over his entitlement to the medal and, as we shall see, it was to become a habit of his to wear medals to which he was not entitled. This aside, Frank proved himself a keen soldier. The West London Rifles was an apparently thriving organisation, with a strength of around 800 all ranks and organised in the conventional eight companies of the day. Frank himself was posted to F Company, which had just one other officer at the time, its company commander. The training emphasis was on drill and musketry and everyone attended at least one evening a week (recruits were expected to drill three evenings per week). Shooting on the open range was carried out at Staines, but, thanks to the Morris tube, which was inserted in the barrel of the rifle, sub-calibre shooting could take place on the miniature ranges at Hyde Park Barracks, where much of the training took place, and at the Regimental HQ. There were also

Adjutant's parades, which were done by half battalion, and a monthly or fortnightly Commanding Officer's parade. Frank would therefore have had many evenings, as well as Saturdays, taken up with the Rifle Volunteers. The culmination of the training year was the Annual Inspection, which usually took place in July.[17] In 1898 Frank also attended a course of instruction at Chelsea Barracks, which gained him a certificate of proficiency.

An office job was clearly not what Frank wanted out of life. On 21 September 1898 he embarked at Liverpool on the SS *Cheshire* bound for Colombo. He was doing what many young middle-class men of his generation did: having a stint in the Empire. In his case he was to learn tea-planting. He had already made arrangements to be apprenticed to Keith Rollo, a Scot and one of the leading planters in Ceylon. His Wanarajah estate was situated at Dikoya in the hills some sixty miles east of Colombo and comprised some 1,000 acres of tea planting, with a further seventy acres in forest. Unfortunately, Frank fell ill with typhoid during the voyage and on arrival at Colombo had to be rushed to hospital, where he spent some weeks.[18] When he did reach the estate he soon got into the ways of a 'creeper', as an apprentice planter was nicknamed:

A 'lick and a promise,' followed by a dash into one's clothes and a rush down to 'muster', when the duties of the day were told off rather on the Army system, began the day's work at dawn. While the coolies were getting their ground the 'creeper' had returned to this bungalow for breakfast, after which he went out, generally to the 'plucking'. It is rather a long time ago since I supervised a gang, but I believe we used to 'pick out', that is to say, get rid of coarse leaf and 'weigh up' three times a day, after which the leaf was carried down to the factory. We came in about midday for tiffin, and woe betide him who drank beer at the meal, as, if he did, he surely went to sleep afterwards and had the greatest difficulty in waking up again, for work had to be started once more soon after two o'clock. By about five o'clock work was over for the day, after which a game of tennis concluded the hours of daylight.[19]

Frank certainly seemed to enjoy his tennis and the *Ceylon Observer* notes him taking part in competitions.[20] He is also reported as being at a fancy dress party as Tweedle Dum, with a friend dressed as Tweedle Dee.[21] Indeed, when he could, Frank continued the exuberant living that he had enjoyed in London. Apparently, on one occasion, after a football match, there was the usual junketing. Next day, Frank woke up to discover that he had a butterfly tattooed on his arm, but had no idea how it had got there.[22] He was also enrolled as a Freemason at a meeting in a hotel in the nearest town to the estate, Hatton.[23] After learning the rudiments of tea planting, Frank then moved to an undefined post in Kandy.[24] He also claimed to have joined the Ceylon Light Infantry, but his name does not appear on the regiment's rolls.[25] However, events across the Indian Ocean in South Africa during autumn 1899 would soon satisfy Frank's martial desires.

Chapter 2

Regular Soldier At Last: South Africa 1900

It was the outbreak of the war in South Africa which had drawn Frank's attention. The conflict came about as a result of growing tension in Transvaal, the independent (in all but name) Boer republic in otherwise British South Africa. The immediate cause was the discovery of gold in the Witwaters Rand in 1886. While within a decade it made Transvaal the richest state in Africa, it also brought about an influx of foreigners, three-quarters of them British, whom the Boers termed *Uitlanders*. The behaviour of many of these adventurers horrified the Calvinist Boers, who introduced increasingly restrictive legislation, both to ensure that the state was not drained of its wealth and to prevent the *Uitlanders* from usurping power. Matters came to a head in November 1898, when an *Uitlander* was shot dead by a Boer policeman, who, at his trial, was not only acquitted, but commended by the judge. The *Uitlanders* petitioned the Queen to reassert her sovereignty over Transvaal. Consequently, the British Government instructed Sir Alfred Milner, the High Commissioner in South Africa, to approach the Boers. The negotiations that followed made little progress and the two sides grew ever further apart. As the tension grew, the Boers slowly mobilised, while in August 1899 2,000 additional troops were sent out from Britain, followed by a further 10,000 from India.

Matters came to a head on 8 October when the Transvaal government issued an ultimatum. The British were to withdraw their troops from the Transvaal and Orange Free State borders and turn back their reinforcements still at sea; otherwise a state of war would exist. The ultimatum was rejected and war broke out on 11 October. Some 20,000 Boers advanced into Natal, aiming for Dundee and Ladysmith. They were faced by just 12,000 British under Sir George White. The first significant clash came on 20 October, when the British drove the Boers off Talana Hill overlooking Dundee. Two days later, at Elandslaagte, the occupation of which by the Boers had cut communications between Dundee and Ladysmith, White scored another success by recapturing the village. But, operating on the false intelligence that the Boers were both advancing once more on Elandslaagte and encircling Ladysmith, he promptly gave up the former and Dundee. Now the Boers did turn their attention to Ladysmith and began to occupy the hills which surrounded the town. White attacked the Boer positions on 30 October, was repulsed and withdrew into Ladysmith.

What had become clear to White from the outset was his lack of mounted troops against a highly mobile enemy. He was also aware that many of the *Uitlanders* wanted to join the fight. Accordingly, on 16 October he had authorised two of his officers, both veterans of the 1881 campaign against the Boers, to each raise an indigenous mounted infantry regiment. One of these officers was Edward Bethune of the 16th Lancers, who formed Bethune's Mounted Infantry and later, during 1914–18, was Director-

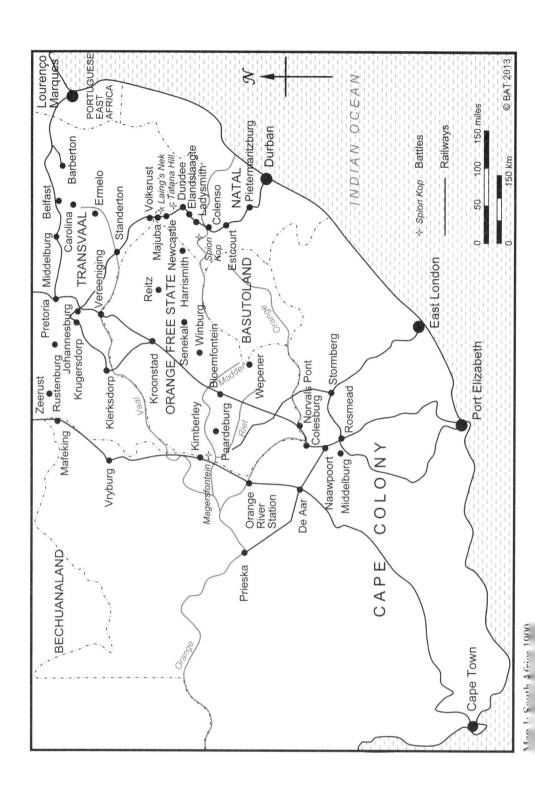

Map 1: South Africa 1900

General of the Territorial Force. The other was Alec Thorneycroft. He was serving with the 2nd Royal Scots Fusiliers in Aldershot when he finally received his majority in July 1899. Shortly after this he was summoned to South Africa, presumably as a result of his previous experience there, and was made Deputy Assistant Adjutant General under White in Natal. He had an established reputation as an organiser[1] and was an obvious choice to raise a new regiment. It was to Thorneycroft's regiment that Frank would be drawn.

Both Bethune's Mounted Infantry and Thorneycroft's Mounted Infantry were to have a strength of 500 men. Thorneycroft established a tented camp on the Race Course at Pietermaritzburg and the recruits started to pour in. The enlistments were of good quality – men who could both ride and shoot, although they had to take an initial test in both before being accepted. Only refugees from Transvaal were forbidden to join. Thorneycroft selected his own officers. They were a wide mix – serving and ex-serving regular officers, civilians with military experience, Yeomanry officers who had come out to South Africa in the hope of employment and members of the Indian Army who had brought remounts from India. The horses themselves were indigenous, small but tough. The saddlery, on the other hand, was of poor quality, and had had to be obtained locally. Each man was given two uniforms, which were worn with boots and puttees, and infantry accoutrements, which Thorneycroft found generally unsatisfactory. They were paid at so-called colonial rates – five shillings a day, considerably more than the British private soldier – although there was initially a struggle to get this agreed by the War Office. They were initially equipped with Martini-Enfield rifles, obtained from the Natal Volunteers Armoury, then Lee Metfords, and finally Lee Enfields. Thorneycroft also managed to obtain two Maxim machine-guns from his brother back in England and later borrowed machine-guns from the Colt Gun Company.[2]

Thorneycroft left Pietermaritzburg on 8 November, his men organised as four companies, and set up another camp three miles away. This allowed another few days' training before they moved to the front, which they did on the 14th, joining General George Barton's 6th Infantry Brigade at Mooi River, some thirty-five miles north-west of Pietermaritzburg and on the Durban-Johannesburg railway. On 19 November came their first skirmish with the Boers when they clashed with Commandos under David Joubert near Mooi River.

By now significant reinforcements had arrived from Britain and Sir Redvers Buller, in overall command, had conceived a plan which would involve dividing his force into three. One element, under Lord Methuen, was to advance along the Western Railway and relieve Kimberley, which, like Ladysmith, was now under siege. A second element was to secure the key junctions on the Central Railway, while the bulk, under Buller himself, was to relieve Ladysmith. Methuen fought two successful battles against the Boers before being rebuffed at Modder River on 28 November. With most of the reinforcements being sent round by sea from the Cape to Durban, Buller established himself at Frere, ten miles south of Colenso, where the Boers had created a blocking position. There now occurred what became known as Black Week, when the British suffered three defeats in the space of five days. First, General Sir William Gatacre, operating on the Central Railway, was bested by the Boers at Stormberg on 10 December. On the following day, Methuen, who had resumed his advance on Kimberley, was repulsed at Magersfontein and withdrew to the Modder River. Finally, on 15 December, Buller himself failed to shift the Boers from Colenso. Although the Boers did little to exploit their victories, Black Week sent a tremor through not just Britain, but the Empire as a whole. The result was a massive increase in volunteers wanting to fight in South Africa.

In Ceylon, Frank had been following events and certainly knew that his parents' friend Alec Thorneycroft was in South Africa and that he had raised his own regiment. He also apparently learnt in November that the former occupant of his job in Kandy was returning.[3] Black Week was clearly the tipping point and shortly afterwards he embarked on a steamer bound for South Africa. Others had the same intention and he was only able to obtain a berth by a signing on as a cook, 'for the privilege of which I paid a first-class fare, slept on deck and washed out of a bucket.'[4]

Landing at Durban, Frank noted that Thorneycroft was looking for new recruits and immediately sent a telegram to Thorneycroft himself, announcing his arrival.[5] As it happened, Thorneycroft's men had taken part at Colenso and suffered some thirty-five men killed and wounded. A further thirty-two men had been struck off strength by the end of December and the regiment had also received authority to expand to 600 men. Consequently, two new companies, E and F, were being recruited.[6] Frank first had to go through the riding test, which was held on the Durban Racecourse. Having never been taught to ride, this was obviously an ordeal, but somehow he managed to bluff his way through it. Consequently, on 8 January 1900 he was signed on as 2753 Private Crozier, F.P., and allocated to F Company. This consisted largely of Australians, but Frank claims to have brought in some twenty men with him, including planters from Ceylon who had travelled in the same ship as himself, and people who had been friends of his at the Earls Court crammer and whom he met again in Durban.[7] Frank's own account of his time with Thorneycroft's Mounted Infantry, *Angels on Horseback*, which he wrote thirty years later, leads one to conclude that his enlistment date was actually when he joined the regiment at Frere. After passing into the TMI, he spent another night in Durban before moving up to Frere and he records the day after this, 9 January, as being his twenty-first birthday. As it was, Alec Thorneycroft, who stood nearly a foot taller, welcomed Frank in person when he arrived in the regiment's camp. He asked whether Frank had informed his mother that he was in South Africa and, receiving a negative answer, said that he would let her know. He also promoted Frank to corporal. Whether it was to protect him from some of the private soldier's more arduous fatigues – Frank himself recalled in *Angels on Horseback* that the first time he was ordered to carry a sack of oats he collapsed after just a few yards[8] – or in recognition of that fact that he held a commission in the volunteers, is not clear. As for his birthday, one of his friends apparently managed to 'liberate' champagne, whisky and beer from the officers' mess and there was also a reinforced daily rum ration. The result was that the twelve-man tent, which Frank now had charge of, had a party which lasted long into the night.

At this time, Thorneycroft's and other mounted elements were probing the Boer defences along the Tugela River. Buller now decided that he would move westwards twenty-five miles to Potgeiter's Drift, cross the Tugela there, and then make a flanking march on Ladysmith. The move began on 10 January, the day after Frank's birthday celebrations. Thorneycroft's were now under the Earl of Dundonald's Cavalry

Brigade. This formation led the way, with overall control of the advance being in the hands of Sir Charles Warren. Dundonald first secured a bridge at Springfield on the Little Tugela, a tributary of the main river, and then advanced to Potgeiter's Drift, where, although under fire, his men managed to seize the ferry which crossed the Tugela at this point. He also advanced to Trichardt's Drift, some five miles further west, and was intending to outflank the Boer defences along the river. On 17 January Warren's infantry crossed the Tugela at these two points. Dundonald now moved further west to begin his outflanking move, but Warren then ordered him to detach almost a third of his men to protect the infantry camps. He did this and also diverted Thorneycroft's to Venter's Spruit, another tributary of the Tugela which ran into it from the north. Dundonald then advanced along the Spruit to Acton Homes, taking the Boers here by surprise. It seemed that his outflanking move was working.

By now it was 19 January. As his troops were crossing Venter's Spruit, Warren summoned Dundonald and told him that he was not to go off on his own. He also ordered Dundonald to hand over Thorneycroft's. Rather than take advantage of Dundonald's success in having seemingly turned the Boer flank, Warren's plan was to force his way northwards along the road which ran between two hills, Spion Kop and Thabanyama. Dundonald used his initiative for a final time, seizing Bastion Hill, which dominated the Boer positions on Thabanyama, especially if artillery was positioned on it. The following day, Warren's infantry secured Three Tree Hill, at the foot of Thabanyama, but they were not able to seize the latter. In the meantime, Thorneycroft's, which had been deployed to Bastion Hill, was relieved by infantry and returned to Venter's Spruit Drift. Warren now concluded that he could not get any further without capturing Spion Kop, but since no one knew anything about this feature there was now a pause while reconnaissances were carried out. The attack itself was to be mounted by Major General Sir Edgar Woodgate's brigade, but this was to include Thorneycroft's, who were now deployed to a ridge one and a half miles south of Three Tree Hill and two miles from Spion Kop. The attack was to be by night and a silent one.

In the early evening of 23 January, Thorneycroft and some 200 of his officers and men, mainly from A–D companies, set off, leaving the remainder of the regiment to hold the ridge and, with the rest of Dundonald's brigade, be prepared to counter any Boer threat to the left flank of the attack. In *Angels on Horseback* Frank claims that he was one of the 200.* He described the ascent of Spion Kop: 'After half an hour spent in crossing dongas and rough ground the ascent begins … Stumbling, jumping stretching, in silence, save for the swearing, continues for what seems like hours.'[9] By 3.30am they were closing on the summit and some ten minutes later they were challenged by a Boer picquet, which then opened fire. Thorneycroft himself remembered: 'I had ordered the men to lie down when challenged; they did so. The Boers opened fire from magazines. When I thought that they had emptied their magazines I gave the order to charge. An officer on my left gave the order to charge

---

* There is no evidence to support Frank's claim and in *Impressions and Recollections*, which is reasonably truthful, he makes no mention that he fought on the crest of Spion Kop. In fact, he does not describe the battle and merely discusses Thorneycroft's actions.

also, and the whole line advanced at the double and carried the crest line at 4am when I halted and re-formed the line.'[10]

At this stage there were three units on the hill – Thorneycroft's, the 2nd Lancashire Fusiliers, and the 2nd King's Own (Royal Lancaster) – together with some sappers, who were there to help prepare defensive positions. The 1st South Lancashires were about to arrive on the crest. It was now a question of digging in, but the ground was too hard and so they had to resort to using pieces of rock to construct sangars. Luckily, not only was it still dark, but there was also a thick fog to provide cover. As dawn broke, Woodgate sent a message to Warren, entrusting it to Colonel Charles a'Court, one of Buller's staff, whom he had ordered to accompany Woodgate.* It stated that Spion Kop was secure. Warren received the message at 9.15am, but by this time the situation had changed. Louis Botha, the Boer commander, had heard the shouts of the British and had been told that Spion Kop was in their hands. He deployed his artillery to engage the hill and was soon inflicting casualties, since the low sangars offered little protection from artillery fire. As the fog lifted, Boer riflemen also opened fire. Woodgate himself was hit in the head, a wound from which he died some eight weeks later. The Boers began to creep ever closer. A panicky message, purportedly from Woodgate, was received by Warren's HQ at 10am: 'Am exposed to terrible crossfire, especially near the first dressing station; can hardly hold my own; water badly needed; help us. Woodgate.'[11] Shortly afterwards, Lt Col Malby Crofton of the King's Own, who had taken command after Woodgate's wounding, sent a further signal stating that Woodgate was dead and demanding reinforcements. Warren had already sent up the Imperial Light Infantry, but now he ordered Major General Talbot Coke to take charge of Spion Kop, bringing with him further reinforcements in the shape of the 2nd Dorsets and 2nd Middlesex. In the meantime, Buller, who had seen the signal from Crofton, concluded that he was not fit to be in command and sent a message that Thorneycroft was to take over.

By now the Boer pressure was increasing. Indeed, they had reached the crest of the hill and were engaged in virtually hand-to-hand fighting. Thorneycroft's men were at the forefront and suffering casualties. The 2nd Scottish Rifles were also sent up to join the fray by General Neville Lyttleton, commanding the 4th Brigade. Lyttleton also saw the Boer guns on Twin Peaks and on his own initiative sent the 3rd King's Royal Rifle Corps to seize the feature, which they did. But the situation on top of Spion Kop was becoming parlous, especially through lack of water. Thorneycroft himself recounted:

> The Boers closed in on the right and centre. Some men of mixed regiments at the right end of the trench got up and put up their hands; three or four Boers came out and signalled to their comrades to advance. I was the only officer in the trench on the left, and I got up and shouted at the leader of the Boers that I was the commandant and that there was no surrender.[12]

---

* Having been forced to resign from the Army on account of being involved in a divorce case, as 'á Court Repington' he became military correspondent of the London *Times* from 1903–18.

Frank's memory of the event was Thorneycroft shouting: 'Get back to your trenches, you men. No surrender ... I'm commandant here, get to hell and be damned to you ... I command. Get back to your _____ lines or I'll open fire on you. Put that damned flag down or I'll shoot.'[13] Yet there was some confusion as to who was actually in command on the hill. Buller may have appointed Thorneycroft and, indeed, made him a local Brigadier General, but Coke, although had he had not reached the summit, believed he was in charge and had told the Dorsets to withdraw, since he thought there was too much congestion. He also intercepted a message timed at 2.30pm from Thorneycroft to Warren describing the seriousness of the situation and stressing the need for artillery to engage the Boer guns. He also asked for infantry reinforcements and water. Coke added a postscript that he had seen Thorneycroft, which was untrue, and that reinforcements were on their way.

By now the King's Royal Rifle Corps (KRRC) were making their way up Twin Peaks, albeit under British artillery fire, an indication of the lack of coordination. They reached the top and the Boers fled, but after receiving a message from a member of his staff who was with the Scottish Rifles that the situation on Spion Kop was not good, Lyttleton began to send a series of messages to the KRRC ordering them to withdraw. Their commanding officer, Robert Buchanan Riddell, turned a blind eye, but was then shot dead. A final message from Buller warned that it was not possible to support the KRRC overnight and that they must withdraw, which they did once darkness had fallen. On Spion Kop itself, General Coke's previous optimism had now evaporated. Just before 6pm he sent a message to Warren hinting that withdrawing from the hill might be the only remaining viable option. Independently of this, Thorneycroft, who had just received news of his promotion to local Brigadier General, also sent a message to Warren timed at 6.30pm: 'The troops which marched up here last night are quite done up. They have had no water, and ammunition is running short. I consider that even with the reinforcements which have arrived that it is impossible to permanently hold this place so long as the enemy's guns can play on the hill.' He went on to state that the Boers had six artillery pieces, together with a Pom-Pom heavy machine-gun, and that he was under heavy fire both in front and on his flanks. He concluded: 'The situation is critical.'[14] After discussion with the CO of the Scottish Rifles, he also sent a note to General Coke asking for a discussion with him and stressing that the hill could not be held unless something was done about the Boer artillery. Coke, however, later stated that he never received this message.[15]

Another who told Warren of the critical situation was Winston Churchill, who had lately escaped Boer captivity and was serving as a subaltern in the South African Light Horse, as well as acting as war correspondent for the *Morning Post*. He had been up the hill with another officer and described it as a 'bloody reeking shambles.' Warren ordered Churchill to go up the hill again and consult with Thorneycroft, but the latter had now decided to withdraw and had begun to put this into effect when Churchill reached him. Frank recalled that he had fallen asleep when he was alerted by a Cockney soldier that the withdrawal was underway.[16] By dawn Spion Kop had been vacated by the British. They had suffered some 1,450 casualties, while the Boers had lost 200. Thorneycroft's share was seven officers and twenty-one other ranks killed, four and forty-three wounded, and sixteen missing.[17] In other words, some 45 per cent of those members of the regiment involved in the attack became casualties. Frank was lucky, if he had been on the hill, to have come out unscathed.

In the days following Spion Kop there was an intense debate. Some faulted Thorneycroft for giving up the hill. They included Lord Roberts, who had recently arrived in South Africa to take overall charge of the British forces. He claimed that Thorneycroft 'issued an order, without reference to superior authority, which upset the whole plan of operations, and rendered unavailing the sacrifices which had already been made to carry it into effect.'[18] Others, including Buller and Lyttleton, defended him. In his own report Thorneycroft gave clear reasons for his decision to withdraw – the superiority of the Boer artillery and his lack of information on what his superiors were intending to do about it, lack of food and water, and his inability to construct defences which could provide protection against artillery fire.[19] His men supported him, but in later life Frank condemned Thorneycroft. While he acknowledged his bravery in stopping some of the men from surrendering, 'he flagrantly and deliberately disobeyed the orders of the Divisional and Brigade Commanders (Sir Charles Warren and Major General Talbot Coke) by evacuating the position at the very time when the battle was won, for the Boers left the hill …'[20] This was true, although they quickly reoccupied Spion Kop when they realised that the British had gone. In the event, Thorneycroft was not harmed by the incident, earning the brevets of Lt Col and full Colonel and being made a CB by the end of the war.

After licking his wounds, Buller tried again to force his way through to Ladysmith, attacking the Boers at Vaal Krantz on 5 February. Again he failed, but this time Thorneycroft's were not involved. Meanwhile, Roberts had formulated a plan to launch a major offensive from the west and designed to lift the sieges of Kimberley and Mafeking. This began on 10 February and during the second half of the month the British managed to trap a sizeable Boer force under Piet Cronje and bring about its surrender. Buller made another attempt to get through to Ladysmith, striking at the hills astride the Tugela immediately north of Colenso. During a reconnaissance across the Tugela before the operation was launched Frank had a lucky escape. He and his fellows had to swim the river under fire on their horses. On the far bank they dismounted, climbed a small kopje and then opened fire on some Boers. They, in turn, engaged Thorneycroft's men from 'an unexpected quarter'. Their company commander ordered them to return to their horses and remount. 'I was riding a grey pony and was weighed down with accoutrements, rifle and ammunition. The reins being thrown to me I fumbled them, off went the grey and with it, I thought, my chances of getting away to safety.' Frank was in the open and being fired at, but found an ant-heap from behind which he began to fire back. Shortly afterwards, one of Frank's officers, Lieutenant Arthur Green* of the Essex Regiment, galloped up with his mount, helped Frank into the saddle and away they went. But Frank's troubles were not yet over. While re-crossing the Tugela he became separated from his horse

---

* Green was awarded the DSO for his performance in South Africa. He had previously served in West Africa and attended the Army Staff College. He returned to West Africa in 1903 and in 1914 was Brigade Major to 17th Infantry Brigade. He was killed by a German sniper in September 1914, while carrying out a reconnaissance with his brigade commander.

once more, but one of his fellows grabbed him by the bandolier and got him to the home bank.[21]

Buller's attacks on the kopjes were again costly and achieved little apart from successfully crossing the Tugela. On 25 February, after eight days' fighting, he proposed a truce, to which the Boers agreed, so that both sides could bury their dead. The Boers expected the British to withdraw during the twenty-four-hour truce, but they did not and resumed their attacks. This, and the news of the British victory at Paardeburg, caused the Boers to withdraw from the whole area, including lifting their siege of Ladysmith, which Buller entered on the 28th. Thorneycroft's had hoped that they would be the first to enter the town, but Lord Dundonald gave that honour to the Composite Regiment, which was made up of a squadron of the Imperial Light Horse (ILH), one of the Natal Carbineers, and mounted infantry companies of the Royal Dublin Fusiliers and 2nd King's Royal Rifle Corps, on the grounds that another ILH squadron had been besieged in Ladysmith. Indeed, Thorneycroft's did not enter until 4 March.* Thomas Mansbridge, an Australian serving with D Company, described in a letter written a few days earlier just how tough the last few weeks had been:

> We are all in a filthy state. I have only slept under canvas four nights since I left Frere four weeks ago. This is the rainy season here, and it is horrible. All we have to sleep in is a waterproof and a blanket. It is wretched having to sleep in wet clothes, yet it has to be done. We are out before daylight each morning and back in camp after dark nearly every night. We have tea and breakfast (when they give us time for any) always in the dark. We sleep nearly always with our spurs on, our accoutrements by our side, and use our saddles for pillows. I have been over a week at a time without a wash, and a bath would be a luxury.[22]

Thus, the chance to recuperate was warmly welcomed, especially the prospect of ten days' leave in Durban, which Frank described as 'late up, late to bed, making merry at all times.'[23] He also attended riding school and thus finally learned to ride properly. This stood him in good stead when Buller resumed his advance into Transvaal in May.

Buller began his movement on 7 May, heading north-east towards Dundee. Initially Thorneycroft's were used to scout and they expected to be engaged by the Boers at any time. Not until 13 May, however, did they have a significant brush, when they were temporarily held at Helpmekaar until the remainder of Dundonald's brigade forced a Boer withdrawal by outflanking their position. Thereafter Thorneycroft's escorted the Royal Horse Artillery (RHA) until reaching Dundee on the 15th. Then it was a thirty-seven-mile dash to Newcastle by some seventy men of Thorneycroft's, including Frank, during the night of 17/18 May. He described it as follows:

> We trot-gallop for most of the night on the top of boiled lamb and onions. And as we near the objective we hear a terrific explosion. The [railway] bridge [at

---

* In *Angels on Horseback* Frank gives the impression that Thorneycroft's did enter Ladysmith on 28 February, but this is not so.

Newcastle] has not been saved, but under the orders of Captain Shea [actually Molyneux*, since Shea did not join until 10 June] we push on across the drift, securing the approaches to the square in the centre of the little town and culverts on the northern side as the last Boer train steams out towards Ingogo.[24]

Thorneycroft's then went into camp at Ingogo, which was close by the scene of the disaster that befell the British at Majuba during the First Boer War. Roberts had given Buller orders to continue his advance to Belfast, but the latter needed time to repair the railway bridges that the Boers had destroyed so as to maintain his supply line.

Not until 6 June did Buller begin to move again. Initially facing him was a well-entrenched force of some 500 Boers on Laings Nek. Buller decided to outflank them by going through Botha's Pass in the Drakensberg. The main assault was to be carried out by the infantry, with Dundonald's brigade being prepared to protect their right flank. In the event it was Dundonald's men, supported by machine-guns, a Pom Pom, and the guns of the RHA who won the day, climbing onto a ridge and enfilading the Boers, thus forcing them to withdraw. This enabled Buller to get through Botha's Pass. Frank recalled spending a night at the top of it in 'extreme cold', an occasion he would never forget. 'Our blankets and greatcoats had gone astray, while tents we had none. We made fires out of cow dung and walked about to keep the circulation going, but it was not till the advent of hot coffee and the sun that we got relief.'[25] Now Buller had finally entered Transvaal and the next objective was Volksrust.

The next Boer resistance came at Alleman's Nek, twelve miles west of Volksrust. Dundonald's brigade, supported by an RHA battery, closed on this feature on the morning of 11 June and began to engage it. Infantry closed up and an attempt was made to outflank the Boer defences using Dundonald's brigade. This included E and F companies of Thorneycroft's, the remainder of the regiment being deployed to guard the baggage train. Again, Dundonald used his guns to discomfit the Boers, who eventually withdrew, using a grassland fire for concealment. F Company suffered two killed, one being Captain Horace Mann, a former regular soldier and veteran of the 1884–85 Nile campaign who, according to Frank, was killed at long range by a sniper.[26] On arrival at Volksrust Frank was the recipient of some good news.

During the Alleman's Nek action Frank had apparently received a cable from his father. It read 'Commissioned Winchester', which made no sense. However, Thorneycroft had some time earlier contacted Frank's commanding officer in the 4th Middlesex Volunteers, recommending Frank strongly for a regular commission. This clearly did the trick, for Thorneycroft now summoned Frank and informed him that he had been commissioned into the Manchester Regiment with effect from 19 May. Burrard's cable now made sense, in that 'Manchester' had been scrambled

---

* Edward Molyneux was a member of the Indian Staff Corps. He served with Thorneycroft's February–October 1900 and won the DSO, but was severely wounded. He was an accomplished artist, who was three times shown at the Royal Academy. He died in 1913 when a squadron commander in the 12th Bengal Cavalry.

during transmission. That night Frank dined with Thorneycroft and his officers and he left the regiment the following day, 16 June:

> I said good-bye to T.M.I with great regret. There I had received my baptism of fire; there I had learnt to ride under difficult and even, at times, dangerous circumstances; there I had made many friends in all walks of life, united for the time in the common bond of service; and there I had not only become a man but, for the first time in my life, actually been commanded by *men*[sic].[27]

On his way back to Pietermaritzburg, Frank stopped off to look at the battlefields of Spion Kop and Colenso, especially from the Boer perspective. On arrival at Pietermaritzburg, he managed to persuade the base commandant there to grant him some leave so that he could kit himself out as an officer. Thereafter he went to Durban and enjoyed donning plain clothes, which he had brought with him from Ceylon. He then was ordered to proceed by mail-boat to East London and thence to Bloemfontein by rail. He was told that he was to join the 2nd Battalion, The Manchester Regiment. At Bloemfontein he ran across another recent member of Thorneycroft's, William Murphy, an Assam tea planter who had been a sergeant with the machine-gun section and had now been commissioned into the Leinsters. Frank and Murphy were told that they were to take a draft of some 200 men up to Senekal and for this purpose they would be attached to the 2nd Battalion Grenadier Guards, who were commanded by Francis Lloyd (later GOC London District for most of 1914–18). Unlike Murphy, Frank had a 'feel' for the Guards as a result of the course of instruction he had attended at Chelsea Barracks. This was as well, especially since he found himself deploying the advance guard on the second day out. On arrival at Senekal Frank, with a small draft of Manchesters, acted as escort to a supply convoy bound for Harmonia on the border with Basutoland (present-day Lesotho). Here lay the 2nd Manchesters.

One might have thought that Frank would have been commissioned into the Royal Scots Fusiliers, his father's and Thorneycroft's old regiment. He had also seen quite a bit of the 2nd Battalion in South Africa. It is most likely that the regiment simply did not have a regular vacancy for him at the time. Certainly, a study of the *London Gazette* reveals that during the period April–May 1900 the two regular battalions of the Royal Scots Fusiliers had no fewer than eleven men granted regular commissions as 2nd Lieutenants. They came mainly from the militia and volunteer battalions. Whatever the reason, it does not appear that Frank had any choice in the matter. As for the Manchesters, they certainly had vacancies, especially as in March 1900 they had been authorised to raise two additional battalions.* It is probably for this reason that Frank found himself a member of the regiment.

The 2nd Manchesters themselves had only arrived in South Africa from Aldershot in April 1900. They formed part of the 8th Division under Sir Leslie Rundle. This was deployed to the Orange Free State and was initially involved in operations to relieve Wepener, which had been attacked by Christian de Wet as part of a raid to cut off

---

* See footnote on p37.

Bloemfontein from its water supplies. The battalion had arrived at Harmonia on 1 July and Frank joined a couple of days later. He recalled that the colonel, Charles Reay,* 'was very kind to me on arrival, and at mess that night I sat next to him, in accordance with the usual custom on first joining, and at his invitation split a bottle of champagne with him, and recounted in a modest way my experiences in Natal.'[28] Indeed, Frank had seen considerably more action than his brother officers had, which may well have caused them to regard him with a certain amount of suspicion, especially since he had been serving with an irregular unit. Nevertheless, Colonel Reay recognised his mounted infantry experience and posted him to H Company, which had this role.

In line with other infantry battalions departing for South Africa, The Manchesters had formed their mounted infantry company prior to leaving Britain, the men being given training by the Army Service Corps at Aldershot. They were issued with fifty mounts just two weeks before they left England and collected a further fifty, albeit only half broken in, after they reached South Africa. When Frank joined H Company half of it was away on escort duty under the company commander, Brevet Major W.H. Goldfinch, a veteran of the 1898 Sudan campaign, as a result of which he had been awarded his brevet, and who was known as 'Dickey'. One of the other subalterns in the company, Charles Mytton Thornycroft (a distant kinsman of Alec Thorneycroft),[29] had succumbed to dysentery and Frank found himself in charge of the remaining half company.

Soon after Frank arrived and H Company was reunited, the Manchesters found themselves involved in a major operation designed to run Marthinus Prinsloo and his commandos to earth. Three divisions, including the 8th, took part, creating a huge cordon. After two weeks Prinsloo was trapped and forced to surrender, with over 4,000 of his men and the same number of ponies, which enabled the company to be remounted. Frank himself acquired 'three very good-looking Basuto ponies for my personal use, which carried me for the rest of the war.'[30] It had, however, been tough on the infantry. Colour Sergeant Cordon of the 2nd Manchesters wrote:

> ... the men were and had been having a very rough and hard time of it, short rations (¾lb flour daily), no warm clothing & what they had was in a very bad state; many of the men were without trousers & were marching with their blanket or w[water]proof shirt round them like a kilt; others marched in their drawers or wore their greatcoats. It was not until the end of the cold season that we received an extra blanket; in fact many of the men were without one at all.[31]

Frank also mentioned the flour, which his men didn't know how to cook, some mixing it with water and drinking it. Otherwise 'we existed at this time on very tough fresh beef, which was driven along with the column day after day and killed, cooked and eaten during a halt.'[32]

---

* Frank refers to him as 'Tom', but Charles was how he signed his letters (see, for instance, letter dated 11 July 1900 to Major J.H. Abbot-Anderson, Manchester Regt Archives MR1/16/5/16). Although Reay made mention of other young officers joining the Battalion at this time, Frank's name does not appear in his letters to Abbot-Anderson.

Thereafter the Manchesters found themselves trekking backwards and forwards across the Orange Free State, often returning to towns that the Boers had re-entered. Eventually a new tactic was employed. The towns were now permanently occupied and the Manchesters spent much time escorting supply convoys to their garrisons. At the end of September the battalion was at Reitz, where it remained for two weeks before moving to Harrismith. H Company remained behind for a time, attached to the Imperial Yeomanry. Frank recalled being under the Hampshire Yeomanry, one of whose members was Captain Jack Seely, who had just been elected a Member of Parliament. They were escorting a supply convoy when they came under Boer attack. Seely was commanding the rearguard and immediately deployed the four troops of his squadron in defensive positions on a nearby hill. Seely's commanding officer then arrived and ordered him to take two troops further up the convoy and leave the other two in place. Seely chose to remain himself, telling his second-in-command to take off the two troops. With shot and shell flying, a furious CO demanded to know why he had disobeyed an order and said that he must do as he was told. Seely declared that he would not obey. The colonel withdrew and Seely conducted a highly successful rearguard action, which kept the Boers at bay. Frank witnessed this exchange and never forgot it. He commented: 'As my men were Regulars I was glad they were out of earshot.'[33]*

By now Frank had a feeling that the war against the Boers was drawing to a close and that it was merely a question of mopping up. This was reinforced by a signal he had seen from Lord Roberts that implied the same. It so happened that a call had gone out for young officers to volunteer for service with the West African Frontier Force (WAFF). Maybe, too, he was influenced by a brother officer, Wilfred Hastings, who had served a tour in West Africa prior to joining the 2nd Manchesters in South Africa. In any event, Frank put his name in for the WAFF, but Colonel Reay was apparently furious when he heard about it, feeling that Frank had no business leaving the battalion after such a short sojourn. Consequently, he transferred Frank to an ordinary infantry company. The brigade commander got to hear of it and Frank was restored to H Company.[34]

In mid-November Charles Thornycroft rejoined the Mounted Infantry Company, which was then at Standerton. The trekking continued. By the end of the month they were at Harrismith and two days before Christmas had arrived at Winburg. Thornycroft wrote of this trek:

We have had rather a bad trek as it has rained a good deal. We went in Reitz and Senekal and although the Boers sniped us every day almost we only had about a dozen casualties in the Brigade. My company had three men missing the day before we got to Reitz. The day before yesterday we got into a very tight place as

---

* Seely was subsequently court-martialled, with General Rundle presiding. He was reprimanded, but restored to command of his squadron. Later he was awarded the DSO for his services in South Africa and rose to be Secretary of State for War, but was forced to resign in the aftermath of the March 1914 Curragh Mutiny. He subsequently commanded the Canadian Cavalry Brigade with distinction on the Western Front, 1915–18.

about a thousand Boers suddenly attacked us when we were the advance-guard and we had to retire in a hurry. One Yeoman was killed and one wounded. They let us get within 30 yards of them.[35]

Christmas, too, became an ordinary day. They were ordered out on the 23rd, just after Thornycroft had finished the letter quoted above.

I never want to pass another Xmas week like it. On Xmas Eve I was in the saddle from 6 in the morning to 7.30 in the evening, and on Xmas Day from 4.30 to 4. What we were supposed to be doing goodness only knows, but we never saw any Boers.[36]

Frank's new posting had come through, however, and on 3 January 1901 he left Cape Town on board the SS *Dungevin Castle*, bound for a new land and fresh adventures. South Africa had taught him much. 'Thinking on horseback' had accustomed him to 'the making of rapid decisions and bold strokes.' He had also gained 'a great imperial experience, and had had my eyes opened to the greatness of England.' Furthermore, he was hardened and very fit.[37] He was therefore well prepared for the next challenge.

Chapter Three

Bushwacking in West Africa: 1901–1905

British trading charters in West Africa were originally granted by Queen Elizabeth I. The establishment of the Royal Africa Company in the reign of Charles II brought the first military presence, with the establishment of forts on the Gold Coast to protect the 'factories', as the trading stations were called, against hostile natives. In 1822 the Crown took over the Gold Coast settlements as part of the process of eradicating slavery and Sierra Leone became a home for freed slaves. The main threat was now the Ashanti kingdom, which lay in the centre of present-day Ghana. Indeed, during the first half of the nineteenth century there were no fewer than five wars against the Ashantis, with locally raised militias defending British interests, although elements of the West India Regiment were also deployed. In 1873

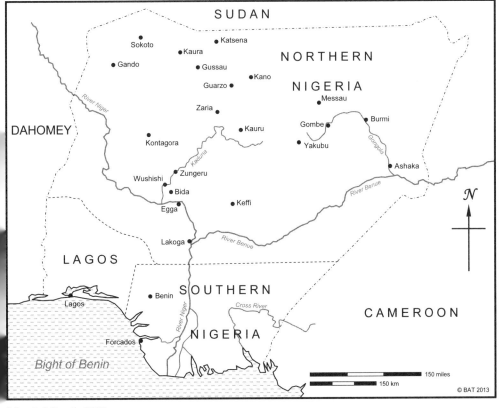

Map 2: Nigeria 1905.

such was the threat that 10,000 British troops under Garnet Wolseley were deployed. While Wolseley subjugated the Ashanti capital Kumasi, the Ashanti flame was still not extinguished.

In the aftermath of this war a number of regional British officered constabularies were formed – the Gold Coast Constabulary, the Sierra Leone Frontier Police (although the Sierra Leone Police Corps had been in existence since 1829), and the Royal Niger Company's Constabulary. During the late 1880s and 1890s the French were increasingly seen as a threat to British expansion north of the River Niger. Consequently, it was decided to put the various constabularies on a more organised footing, with the ability to move from one territory to another when required. The result was the formation of the West African Frontier Force (WAFF) by Colonel Frederick Lugard, Commissioner for the Nigerian and Lagos hinterland. It was initially built round the 1st, 2nd and 3rd Special Corps Battalions of the WAFF, the first two having been the Royal Niger Company's Constabulary and the third the Niger Coast Constabulary. In January 1900 the 1st and 2nd Battalions became the Northern Nigeria Regiment and the 3rd Battalion the Southern Nigeria Regiment. The Sierra Leone Frontier Police became the Sierra Leone Battalion of the WAFF and additionally there was the Gambia Company.

A report dated 2 January 1899 by Lt Col T.S. Pilcher* of the Northumberland Fusiliers, and commanding the 1st Special Corps Battalion, reviewed the first year of the WAFF's existence. Perhaps the most telling paragraph was that dealing with the climate:

> The climate of West Africa has for long had the reputation of being the worst in the world, and the last year's experience has gone far to prove that the climate of the Middle Niger is rather worse than better than that of the coast. For of the 70 officers and non-commissioned officers who landed in Nigeria in December 1897, 18 per cent died and 22 per cent were invalided before completing a year in West Africa. As far as can be gathered at present it seems that this high percentage of loss will be maintained in the case of those who have not yet completed their year in the West African Frontier Force.

He pointed out that there was no cold season and that 'all seasons of the year are unhealthy.' Other discomforts included the shortage of good servants and the lack of beef, fresh milk and butter. Unless actually campaigning, life could be very dreary.[1] For these reasons every officer and NCO was entitled to two months' leave at full pay and a further four months at half pay, together with free passage home, for every year of service.[2]

Frank's voyage to West Africa took him first to Las Palmas, where he transferred to the *Accra*, 'a mere cockleshell, which was stuffy and uncomfortable.' But he fell in with an old WAFF hand, Captain A.B. Molesworth of the West India Regiment, who

---

* He later commanded the Burma Division just prior to the Great War and then 17th (Northern) Division, but was sacked for poor performance on the Somme in July 1916. He was the author of *A General's Letters to His Son on Obtaining His Commission* (1917).

was commanding the Northern Nigeria contingent engineer company and doubtless told him much of what to expect. His next stop was Freetown, Sierra Leone, and thereafter to Forcados at the mouth of a tributary of the river Niger of that name and which Frank described as a 'hot hell-hole'. Frank and fellow passengers were put up in an old hulk, which acted as temporary accommodation for travellers. To reach it required a four-hour voyage in a vessel with a small deck cabin. During it Frank learned a salutary lesson. One of the other passengers died of sunstroke and, as he recounted in a letter to his father:

> His dead body, covered in a sheet, was laid out at one end of the saloon, which was only about fifteen feet long, while we were supposed to sit down to 'chop' (in West Africa all food is 'chop'), ten of us in all, at a long table, the end of which almost touched the corpse. I couldn't do it, yet I was afraid to go out in the heat of the intense sun, as it was just twelve o'clock, and the iron and steel work on the deck added to the high temperature… The dead man, it appears, had been drinking heavily on board and had been up the Coast and back for his health's sake, which accounts for his sudden end, when exposed to the sun on the top of whisky. But it did, and still does, make me think and shudder. Life is apparently very cheap out here.

It was going to be at least a week before the next government stern-wheeler set off up the Niger to Lokoga (present-day Lokoja), the WAFF headquarters. But an acquaintance of Frank's from South Africa, Captain Neville Dickinson of the Leinster Regiment, who was due to join the 1st Battalion, while Frank was bound for the 2nd Battalion, arranged passage for them both on a Royal Niger Company boat, which was leaving earlier.

Frank described the journey upriver in a thirty-page letter home. The boat's engines continually broke down, but Dickinson was also a competent engineer and able to repair them. They halted each night and every meal consisted of sardines and chicken cutlets. He noted how the river was initially 'a raging torrent, from a mile to two miles wide' and gradually began to be narrower and less frenetic until it became 'almost a trickle, just wide enough for a stern-wheeler to plough through a winding course, not unlike an unlimited number of 'S' springs piled one on top of another.' This was the dry season, and on either side of the meandering water there were sand flats stretching up to the river banks proper. Frank recounted that he often walked along the sand flats and easily outpaced the boat. Otherwise the passengers amused themselves by taking 'pot shots' at crocodiles and shooting guinea-fowl for the pot.[3]

During his journey Frank would have also learned that the regiment's main role was to secure northern Nigeria against the Muslim Fulani, who had dominated the region for centuries and strongly resented it being taken over by unbelievers. In particular, the main threat came from Attahiru Ahgmadu, the Emir of Sokoto, and it was only in the previous year, 1900, that the first steps had been taken to clip his wings. The aim had been to abolish the slave trade, a cornerstone of the Fulani culture, and to ensure the safe passage of caravans. To this end, each year the WAFF carried out a number of operations to reduce Fulani power. The Northern Nigeria Regiment itself consisted of the two infantry battalions, each 1,200 strong, two artillery batteries, each with six 75mm guns, and the engineer company. But as far as the British officers and NCOs were concerned, the going could be tough. For example, Colonel Sir James Willcocks,* the Commandant of the WAFF (Lugard had been made High Commissioner of northern Nigeria), stated in his report on operations in Ashanti in 1900 that of twenty-four officers of the two infantry battalions involved two had been killed, five severely wounded, and nine had been invalided back to Britain.[4]

On arrival at Lokoga, Frank was impressed by the 'affability and complete lack of side' of his new colonel, Lt Col Augustus McClintock of the Seaforth Highlanders, who had just been appointed to command the 2nd Battalion. He was then surprised to be told that he was to play polo, of which he had no experience, that afternoon. He survived his initiation, but that evening he was amazed by the amount of drinking that went on: '… after mess everyone sat on at the table till a very late hour, sang songs and drank a great deal, many being carried off to bed for a brief sleep and a cold bath before going on to early morning parade.'[5] Living was clearly expensive there and it was with relief that Frank, accompanied by Dickinson, then took to the river again for his final destination of Wushishi, where C Company of the 2nd Battalion was based. This involved a journey by stern-wheeler to Egga, some seventy miles upstream, and then by canoe and on foot to Wushishi, a further 120 miles or so. 'Thank heavens we are off to the unexpected once more. New people, new country, new life, new experiences are in front of me,' he wrote home.[6] At Egga Frank dropped off his friend Dickinson, and then he was on his own. He had with him his servant, a houseboy, cook, and pony, with twenty-five porters to carry his own baggage and stores. He also had small arms ammunition, and engineer and telegraph equipment for Wushishi. This necessitated a flotilla of some twenty canoes and a seven-day voyage, during which Frank had nothing to do but shoot for the pot. Then followed the trek through land which had only recently been pacified. Frank had no map and did not yet speak the Hausa language and so had to rely entirely on the native lance corporal commanding his escort of three men. 'The inhabitants are completely hostile to us and entirely dominated by Fulani slave-traders who have ruled on tyranny and robbery for centuries. But I have a Union Jack to carry in front of us as we penetrate to an outpost where one white man – Porter – rules.' Yet, 'I have ammunition, a rifle, a gun, a camera, plenty of food and drink, a new kind of life and an almost unknown people to explore; I am indeed in luck!'[7]

Eventually, on 20 March 1901, Frank arrived at his destination to be greeted by Captain Herbert Porter of the 19th Hussars, who had been with the WAFF for three years. He had been at Wushishi for a year and was due home leave. 'Porter and his company are in rags,' as Frank wrote in a letter home.[8] A fort was their base:

> Made of sun-dried mud, it is surrounded by a wall high enough to shoot over. In front is a deep ditch filled with sharp spikes pointing 'towards the enemy'. Made some eighteen months ago, before the subjugation of Bida and Kontagora, it had been an outpost in rear of the enemy, isolated, self-contained and nominally held by a company of infantry and two Maxim guns …

---

* He later commanded the Indian Corps in France during 1914–15.

The Fort, I see, is well chosen for the defence. On the edge of a steep cliff which juts out into a nose, overlooking the Kaduna river, it is, in fact, absolutely secure on three sides, while the southern face, although exposed, dominates a natural glacis running down to the old town wall some three hundred yards away....

Oblong in shape and containing an adequate supply of water, food, and ammunition, it is impregnable, provided relief arrives within thirty-five days, the margin of safety governed by considerations of water and food.[9]

As for accommodation, the men were housed in grass huts situated between the cliff and the river. Porter had a mud hut within the fort itself, while Frank was given one of two just outside it.

Within a short time Porter's company was relieved by C Company under Captain F.F.W. Hall of the Suffolk Regiment. It was now that Frank's role became clear. Porter had acquired some thirty Fulani ponies and had formed a mounted section. The ponies were handed over to C Company and Frank, with his extensive mounted infantry experience, was to take command of the section. A section of 75mm guns under an artillery subaltern also arrived, as did a civil Resident. Since C Company also had a subaltern with it, Frank noted: '... we shall be six men, including the doctor, in addition to a British colour-sergeant and all kinds of railway construction people who will make the station a second Lokoga. But it is still the bush.'[10] The mention of 'railway construction people' referred to steps being taken to develop a railway system in northern Nigeria. In charge of the project was John Eaglesome, recently appointed Director of Public Works for northern Nigeria. The reason was that Wushishi represented the highest navigable point of the Kaduna River, but it had been decided to establish Zungeru as the administrative headquarters for northern Nigeria and this lay a further ten miles upstream. Hence, the communications gap was to be bridged by a light railway.

Frank was quickly nicknamed 'The Bull Pup' by his brother officers,[11] certainly on account of his small size, but perhaps also because he displayed a degree of pugnacity. Now he was to have the chance of his first independent operation and the reason was the railway. Eaglesome needed labourers and food. The Resident had been found wanting in this respect, according to Frank, and so he turned to the WAFF. Frank was given orders to patrol the Gwari region, which lay to the north of Wushishi. He was to obtain 200 labourers and food for 500 men and the horses from the villages he visited, payment for them being cloth.

At 8am next day my party, headed by a Union Jack and a bugler, starts off from the parade ground. Next in order rides my orderly, carrying my sporting rifle as well as his own carbine, followed by my spear carrier carrying my gun and ammunition. Next march a sub-section of M.I. in single file, mounted, followed by my cook who is in charge of the five carriers (two for the tent, one for bath and kit inside bath in wicker carrier, one for cooking pots, etc., one for 'chop') and a spare horse, led. The remaining forty mounted men bring up the rear.[12]

Frank was away for three weeks. At first he found it difficult to get what he wanted, especially since each village appeared to be an entity on its own and there was no overall ruler whom he could approach. He did eventually succeed, partially thanks to the loan by a brother officer of a musical box, gramophone and records, which enabled him to entertain the villagers.

In June 1901 Frank's family suffered a shock. His father had been posted as the Station Paymaster in Leicester in autumn 1899. Rebecca and Evelyn had remained in London and Burrard took up residence in a hotel. It may have been to do with his drink problem, but in June 1901 he was found to have misappropriated public funds and was removed from the Army, 'His Majesty having no further use for his services', as the *London Gazette* put it.[13] From his writings it would seem that Frank had always been close to his father and so he must have been deeply upset when he learned of it. Understandably, he makes no mention of his father's fall from grace in his books. It also may have turned Rebecca further against her husband and deeper into the arms of Alec Thorneycroft, who was still in South Africa. But life for Frank had to go on.

The British were constantly nibbling away at northern Nigeria, bringing one region after another under their sway. During December 1900 and January 1901 a force had secured Bida, some forty miles south-south-west of Wushishi and Konagora, sixty miles to the north-west. Frank was ordered to take a half company to Bida to relieve a fellow Manchester, Captain E.M. Baker, and his company, who were required for another expedition. Baker had taken part in the operation to subdue Bida and had constructed the mud fort which he and his men now occupied. En route, Frank spent three days with his friend Major Dickinson, who was constructing the administrative capital of Zunguru out of virgin bush. Having relieved Baker, Frank found himself in command of a half company of infantry, two Maxim guns, and some mounted scouts. More important than this independent command was his first opportunity to learn something of the civil side, since Bida, which was an emirate in its own right, was accorded not just a Resident, Major Alder Burdon, but an assistant as well. Frank got to know both men well. Indeed, Burdon tried to persuade him to transfer to the civil side, something which he regretted in later life not doing.[14] At the end of three months it was time for Frank to take his first home leave. Thus it was back down the river to Forcados, where he boarded a ship for England.

His time in England was not all pleasure. For a start, it was Coronation Year, although matters were complicated by the fact that the King was taken ill with appendicitis two days before the event, which was scheduled for 26 June. Prior to this Frank had attended a levée at St James's Palace on 2 June, something which all young regular officers were expected to do.[15] Now it was clear that the Coronation had to be postponed. In the meantime, numerous military contingents from the Empire had arrived in London to take part in it. They included a party of thirty-two men from the Northern Nigeria Regiment under the command of Captain C.R.G. Mayne of the Highland Light Infantry and a British sergeant-major.[16] The detachment took part in a parade of the Colonial Forces held on Horse Guards in the presence of Queen Alexandra and the Prince of Wales on 1 July, very soon after the King had been declared to be on the road to recovery. It was, however, Frank, and not Mayne, who was in command, and he was able to sport his Queen's South Africa Medal with its six clasps.* It was an occasion which *The Times* described as 'one of the most brilliant and significant displays ever held in this country.'[17] The Coronation itself eventually took place on 9 August, but it was clearly Mayne who commanded the contingent for it, since it is his name that appears on the Coronation Medal roll for the Northern Nigeria Regiment and not Frank's. The King himself was also very strict when it came to awarding the medals (silver for officers, bronze for other ranks). Only those who had actually taken part or had had a key role in the planning and preparation would receive it. Frank claimed to have helped administer the contingent at Alexandra Palace, where it was quartered, but his name does not appear on the roll for the staff of the camp there.[18] Yet he wore the Coronation Medal. Whether he did this when he was serving in Nigeria, where it would have been questioned if he was not entitled to it, or merely later on, cannot be established.

Frank had other military duties to perform besides those connected with the Coronation. As every infantry officer was expected to do, he attended a musketry course at the Army's School of Musketry at Hythe, Kent. It was during this that he committed his first serious military crime, when he wrote a cheque for his accommodation that was subsequently dishonoured. He could have easily been court-martialled for this, since it was viewed as a very grave offence by the military authorities. It would appear, though, that Frank claimed mitigating circumstances and avoided any significant punishment, but the incident was officially noted.[19] Frank also spent two weeks learning about the intricacies of machine-guns at the Maxim works at Erith in the south-eastern outskirts of London. In addition, he was elected as a fellow of the Royal Geographical Society. He described his residence as 'Junior Naval & Military Club, Piccadilly & Bida, Nigeria' on his application form. He was proposed and seconded by two Fellows of the Society, the former being F.G. Aflalo, a noted author and sportsman, who had spent time in Africa.[20] He took advantage of his membership to attend a course on the prismatic compass and sextant at the Society's headquarters. This reflected the fact that there was little in the way of maps of northern Nigeria at the time and, when on trek, officers were expected to carry out basic surveys of the country they passed through.

On 12 September 1902, towards the end of Frank's leave, his father died. His address was given as at St Leonards-on-Sea on the south coast. From this it can be inferred that he and Rebecca had been living apart, since she was still in London. Even so, he left her his estate, which was valued at £630. It was thus a saddened Frank who returned to Nigeria on 29 September.[21] He did, however, have a companion, a fox terrier bitch, which he had acquired and called Bee. On his return he rejoined his company, still under the command of Capt F.F.W. Byng-Hall (he had now added Byng to his name). The company was now based at Lokoga, which Frank stated he did not enjoy, mainly because it was expensive. Even though WAFF officers received handsome allowances, mess bills at Lokoga were very high. As Frank wrote: 'Thirty pounds a month for a mess bill was a small amount, in addition to which there were polo ponies and poker debts. I saw an adjutant part with six months'

---

* The clasps were Cape Colony, Tugela Heights, Relief of Ladysmith, Transvaal, Laing's Nek and Wittebergen, although Frank always claimed that he had seven bars.

pay and his ponies, his gramophone, guns and spare saddlery, everything par his shirt, in fact, in one night at poker after mess.'[22] The routine, as Frank described it, certainly encouraged heavy drinking – 6.30am parade, 7.45am breakfast, 9am orderly room, company duties, parades, 12pm lunch and then siestas, 4pm polo or parades, 5.30pm–7.30pm cocktails, 8pm dinner and then 'sing-songs or poker until 1am'. On the other hand, he did accept that Lokoga had excellent training facilities and was run very efficiently, especially when it came to mounting an operation at short notice after, say, the murder of a European.[23]

Frank, however, was in eager anticipation of a larger operation which was being planned. It had been triggered in October 1902, when one of the emirs, the Magaji of Keffi, murdered the British Resident, a Captain Maloney. The Magaji then sought refuge with the Emir of Kano, who refused to surrender him. Lugard, with Colonial Office permission, decided to march on Kano. A force based on a composite infantry battalion was assembled under Colonel Thomas Morland, who later commanded a corps on the Western Front, with Major Tom Cubitt of the Royal Artillery as his staff officer. The advanced base for the operation was to be Zaria. Also included in the force was the Mounted Infantry Company under Bertie Porter. He had just one subaltern under him, Wallace Wright of the Royal West Surreys, and so it was decided to increase the company's establishment by two further subalterns. These were to be Charles Wells of the 3rd Hampshires and Frank. He himself marched to Zaria with Byng-Hall's company and joined his new company on arrival. Little opposition was met on the way to Kano and the generally open and scrubby terrain was good for mounted infantry.

Kano itself was, even in those days, a sizeable city protected by a thick mud wall. When Morland arrived in front of its gates on 3 February 1903 he first formed his men into a large square, expecting an assault by Hausa horsemen. This did not materialise and so he used his artillery to blast open the gates (it had had little effect on Kano's walls) and then the attack went in. By nightfall the city was in British hands at a cost of two British officers and twelve rank and file wounded. According to Frank himself, his part had been small, covering the left flank against possible attack. Yet the official despatch states that the Mounted Infantry did 'great execution' of those warriors trying to flee the city and that their pursuit 'turned the defeat into a rout.'[24] The Emir of Kano, however, had been away at Sokoto when his city was attacked.

Overall command of the operation had been given to Brigadier General G.V. Kemball, the Inspector-General of the WAFF, on the grounds that troops from southern Nigeria had also been deployed. He arrived at Kano on 13 February, having given Morland orders to make no further moves until he had done so. Kemball in turn was given orders by Lugard, who had arrived at Zaria, that he must ensure the security of both Kano and the Zaria-Kano road. Kemball, however, learned that warriors from all parts of Kano district were gathering some sixty miles to the north-west of Kano. Satisfied that, with the contingent from the Southern Nigeria Regiment now deployed, he had more than sufficient forces to carry out Lugard's orders, he decided to move against this force. He ordered Morland to move against the tribesmen gathering to the north-west of Kano. The force, accompanied by

Kemball, set out on 16 February.* They were spurred on by news that the Emir of Kano was moving to join the force. This turned out to be untrue and the Fulani force gradually withdrew in front of the British.

The Mounted Infantry were kept very busy. The main problem, according to Frank, was water; '… we were completely tied to the wells, water-holes, and occasional river-beds, in which we had to dig for water. The process of watering the horses was sometimes almost unending, and lasted for hours.'[25] Porter's company did provide valuable information, including that the Emir was now making his way to Sokoto. It was also detached for a time and joined up with the main body on 25 February at Modamawa, some 150 miles from Kano, after marching sixty miles in thirty-one hours. They brought news of the Fulanis advancing towards Kano. Meanwhile, Wallace Wright and Charles Wells were still out and detached with forty-five men. On the 25th they had come in contact with the Fulani advance guard, which they routed, and continued to move forward. They were then ambushed by another thirty horsemen, whom they also repulsed. They camped for the night in a ruined village and the following morning continued the advance cautiously. After a short time Wright's scouts informed him that the enemy's main body was approaching. Wright's men hastily formed a square, with the horses in the middle. The Fulani horsemen charged repeatedly, but failed to break into the square and after two hours drew off, leaving sixty-five of their number, including several chiefs, dead on the ground. Wright then resumed his advance and soon sighted the main army, consisting of some 1,000 horsemen and 2,000 foot, which was now slowly withdrawing. Now low on ammunition, Wright decided merely to keep them under observation and sent word back to Morland. He despatched the remainder of the MI company under Porter, but Frank did not take part as he was running a high temperature. Porter caught up with the majority of Fulani horsemen when they were watering their horses and scattered them. This removed the threat to Kano. Wright's performance earned him the Victoria Cross, but Frank felt that it was very unjust that Wells, who seems to have been Frank's closest friend in the WAFF, received no award, even though Wright singled him out for praise in his report.

The general advance continued to Kaura, 140 miles north-west of Kano, which Morland reached on 27 February. Attention now turned to Sokoto, 100 miles further north-west from Kauru and whose Sultan was an ally of the Emir of Kano. Consequently, Morland set out from Kauru on 3 March and reached Bakura, thirty miles further west, three days later. Learning that the chiefs and their warriors had been summoned to Sokoto, Kemball ordered a small column of two companies and an artillery piece under Captain G.C. Merrick RA to join Morland at Shagali, thirty miles south of Sokoto. Morland arrived at Shagali on 10 March and Merrick joined him the following day. By then it was clear that the Sultan of Sokoto was bent on war and so Kemball gave Morland orders to attack Sokoto. He carried out a reconnaissance with the Mounted Infantry and noted that the enemy were clearly determined to fight outside the town rather than defend the walls.

---

* This caused considerable friction and such was Morland's resentment of Kemball's presence that he attempted to resign as soon as the campaign was over (TNA CO 445/15). Frank also noted the friction (*Impressions and Recollections* p103).

The following day, 15 March, Morland mounted his attack. He formed his men into a square, with the Mounted Infantry dismounted and leading their horses inside it. Frank described what happened:

> As we approached close to the city hordes of horsemen and footmen armed with swords, spears, old guns and bows and arrows appeared, charging the square over and over again, only to be mown down by machine-gun and carbine fire. These men faced certain death with fanatic bravery to the beating of drums and tom-toms, the sounding of shrill blasts on horns, and the chanting of extracts from the Koran. The horsemen urged their horses right up to the bayonet points of the kneeling Hausa soldiers.

He went on to relate that eventually there was merely a group of men under a large flag with Arabic writing on it. All of the party were gunned down and Porter then rushed out of the square and grabbed the flag. His company was now ordered to pursue the beaten enemy, so he tore the flag from its staff and tucked it about his person. The pursuit itself did not go on for long, since it was across open country and against widely scattered fugitives. In *Five Years Hard* Frank describes how he and Charles Wells wandered about the battlefield looting the dead, even to the extent of cutting off ankles and arms in order to obtain gold anklets and arm bands, something which would cause an outcry when the book was published.[26] Returning to camp, Frank spotted the flag that Porter had seized lying in the dust and picked it up, securing it to his saddle. Later Morland asked Porter for the Emir of Sokoto's battle standard and the latter had to admit that he had lost it. Frank went to check the flag he had and, to his horror, found that it was missing from his saddle and that his horse boy was lying dead with a dagger in his heart. He kept quiet about it.[27]

On 19 March Lugard himself arrived at Sokoto, with Frank having the privilege of escorting him into the camp. He oversaw the installation of a new Emir of Sokoto and the campaign was officially wound up on 31 March. Those who took part, including Frank, were later awarded the African General Service medal with the Northern Nigeria 1903 bar.* The Mounted Infantry then withdrew to Kano and then Zaria, where a new third battalion of the Northern Nigeria Regiment was being formed. The rainy season was approaching and the expectation was for a quiet time, but this was not to be.

The former Emir of Sokoto was not prepared to accept defeat after initially fleeing to Gussau, 100 miles east of Sokoto. A detachment was sent to apprehend him in mid-April, but he fled further to the east on its approach. The British Resident of Kano also caught wind of the ex-Emir while on trek and sent out a party of troops from Kano. On the same day, 22 April, and on the Resident's orders, Major Eustace Crawley, commanding at Zaria, sent out a detachment of twenty-five mounted infantry under Frank to apprehend him and Magaji of Keffi, who had murdered

---

* Frank claimed that his dog Bee also received the medal and clasp as 'Private Bhee Kalhm' *Five Years Hard* p199) but this is not reflected in the actual medal rolls (TNA WO 100/391).

Captain Maloney the previous October. Frank and his men travelled light, taking no tents and just fifty rounds of ammunition each. Frank recalled:

> For four days I followed, overtaking, overtaking, all the time, and then I came to burnt villages, which was serious for me, as we were living on the country. The fugitive rebel crowd must have covered in time and space four days or sixty miles. Suddenly, one morning at 11am, I struck a fighting bunch of fanatics (it had been impossible to tell which was which), who rounded on us when resting. I had taken all the necessary precautions against surprise, but the whole population was against us, thanks to the presence of the Emir's flag in their midst. I lost two men, hit by poisonous arrows, their subsequent and speedy deaths being too agonising for words, and over a dozen horses from the same cause.

They beat off their attackers, but were having great difficulty in obtaining food. They were attacked again and again repulsed their assailants. By now they were now short of ammunition and Frank himself went down with fever. The party therefore made its way back to Zaria with Frank on a stretcher.[28]

The Kano group under Captain W.D. Sword of the North Staffords was almost twice the strength of Frank's party and had a Maxim gun. On the evening of 25 April he closed on the Emir at Gala, but his approach was spotted and his prey fled. Sword had a number of clashes with the ex-Emir's rearguard and eventually reached the town of Messau. He discovered that its emir was besieging it because it had been seized by a usurper. The siege was immediately raised and Sword resumed his pursuit, leaving a much gratified emir. On 9 May he linked up with another force of seventy men, with a further Maxim, under Major W.F.G. Plummer of the Royal Munster Fusiliers. In addition, on 8 May Major Crawley had despatched Major C.W. Barlow, Essex Regiment, with two other officers (but not Frank) and sixty mounted infantry to also join up with Sword, who was now pursuing the ex-Emir of Sokoto along the line of the River Gongola. On 13 May he arrived at the town of Burmi and asked its Mallam (religious leader) to meet him outside its walls. The Mallam refused and so Sword sent a section into the town. It was fired on and withdrew, followed by many of the populace. Sword now formed a square, which was attacked. Major Plummer then led an attack on the gates which was repulsed by heavy arrow fire. The townspeople, led by the Mallam himself, assaulted the square again and were beaten back with heavy losses. Plummer made another attempt on the gates, but was again forced to withdraw. Sword had by now suffered two killed and nearly sixty wounded and decided to pull back to Bautchi. Meanwhile, the ex-Emir of Sokoto had reached Gwoni, thirty miles south of Burmi. On learning of this, another detachment set out from Gujiba on 12 May. It reached Gwoni five days later and took the ex-Emir by surprise. He and his followers fled to Burmi, leaving behind their entire baggage and much livestock. Captain W. Hamilton-Browne, Royal Fusiliers, the officer commanding, not being strong enough to tackle Burmi withdrew to Gujiba, but left a patrol covering the Gongola.

The spotlight now turned on Major Barlow and his mounted infantrymen. They had left Zaria on 8 May and, having learned that the ex-Emir had arrived at Burmi, reached the village of Ashaka, on the Gongola and just two miles east of town, on the 31st. On the following day he managed to entice a number of tribesmen out of Burmi and inflicted heavy casualties on them. He tried to do the same on the 4th, but the ex-Emir and his followers did not rise to the bait. During the next two weeks Barlow harassed the enemy by cutting off their food supplies. This drove the ex-Emir to mount a night attack on Barlow's base at Ashaka, but he flung the attackers back. He was now reinforced by Sword and Hamilton-Browne. This brought Barlow's force up to 270 men and three Maxims, but the commandant of the Northern Nigeria Regiment, Colonel Morland, ordered him not to attack Burmi again until further reinforcements, with guns, reached him.

While waiting for the reinforcements, Major Barlow, on the orders of the Resident, carried out a tour of the other towns in the area. Those which proved to be hostile he attacked. Simultaneously, Captain Sword continued to harry Burmi from Ashaka. Barlow met up with the reinforcements in the shape of eight Europeans, 165 rank and file and a 75mm gun under the command of Major F.C. Marsh, Royal West Kents, at Nafada, twenty miles north of Burmi, on 23 July. Four days later this combined force linked up with Captain Sword and a fresh assault on Burmi was launched, with Major Marsh in command. The 75mm gun made a breach in the gates. A storming party under Major Plummer made for the breach, but the men were temporarily nonplussed by fire coming from a ditch in front of the walls. Marsh came up with reinforcements, but was mortally wounded by a poisoned arrow in his knee. After a stiff fight the attackers entered the town and gradually subdued it. There was a final stand inside the Mallam's house before resistance finally ceased. Among the dead was Attahiru Ahgmadu, the former Emir of Sokoto who had finally been brought to bay. As for Barlow and his mounted infantry, they prevented any fugitives from escaping. Burmi itself was burnt to the ground and within a few days the various detachments returned to their bases.[29]* Frank, however, remained at Zaria and must have been very envious, especially since all three Mounted Infantry officers who took part in the campaign were awarded the DSO. But an event at home in Britain would have provided some distraction.

It was perhaps inevitable that Rebecca would marry her long-time admirer, Alexander Thorneycroft, and she did so at St Mary's Bryanston Square, London, on 20 June 1903, nine months after Burrard's death. Interestingly, rather than a London address, she gave her residence as Adara, County Limerick, her ancestral home. Thorneycroft himself was now home from South Africa and a national hero. He had been made a Commander of the Order of Bath for his services and had received the brevets of lieutenant colonel and colonel. At the time of the marriage he was serving

---

* The ex-Emir's flag, which Frank apparently had for a few hours after the fall of Sokoto, was found, it is related, by a Captain Mundy lying by the ex-Emir's corpse. Mundy presented it to the officers of the 1st Leicesters (his regiment) in June 1904, but at some later stage it was handed over to 1st Battalion Queen's Own Nigeria Regiment. It was, however, very tattered and bloodstained and was sent back to London to be repaired in time for the Nigerian independence celebrations in 1960. (Haywood & Clarke, *The History of the Royal West African Frontier Force*, p47).

on the staff of the 7th Division in Ireland. It is thus possible that Rebecca had moved to Ireland prior their wedding in order to be close to Alec.

With campaigning over for the time being and still based at Zaria, Frank was able to enjoy sport, which was primarily polo, shooting and racing. He was also the station staff officer, which taught him about administration, and for a time was the acting Resident, which put him in close touch with the Emir of Zaria. Come the autumn it was time for his annual home leave. He spent part of it with his friend, and now step-aunt, Jessie Platt on Lewis. He was also in Ireland, presumably staying with his mother and stepfather, and did some hunting. Probably arranged through his stepfather, Frank also passed the practical examination for promotion to captain at the Curragh. In addition, he attended a veterinary course at Aldershot.[30]

While he was in England, Frank met a girl and fell deeply in love with her. Her name was Ethel Cobb and she was the daughter of Robert, a lieutenant colonel in the Indian Medical Service, and Elizabeth (known as Lilian or Lily), who had married her husband when she was just sixteen. Ethel herself was aged nineteen and described as being about the same height as Frank, with strawberry coloured hair and large, dark eyes. She was romantic by nature and had run away from school and gone on the stage. Chaperoned by her mother, she joined a touring company and during the first half of 1901 was, under the stage name of Ethel Romney, playing the part of Amy Sperrigue in the popular farce *Charley's Aunt*. Also appearing in the play was Edith Heron-Brown, who became Ethel's closest friend. Ethel was always called Babbie by her family and close friends, including Edith. In return, Ethel called Edith Ela.[31] She appears to have been a reasonable actress, picking up the odd complimentary review in *The Stage*. The issue of 21 March 1901 comments on the play as performed at the Royalty, Glasgow, that 'the three girls having charming representatives in Misses Ethel Romney, Isla Glynn and Edith Heron'. During the second half of 1902 she was with the same company, this time playing Annie in *Are You a Mason?*, another comedy. Thereafter there are no further mentions of her in *The Stage* and one assumes that she gave up acting and settled down in London with her mother, while her father, who had been having a long-standing affair with another woman, continued in India.

In the normal course of events Frank would have become formally engaged to Ethel, but, probably fearing that this might not last his next tour in West Africa, he took the bull by the horns and married her in the Kensington Registry Office in West London on 6 February 1904. Frank gave his address as 3 Alma Terrace, which is in Wandsworth, while Ethel's was 15 Iverna Gardens off Kensington High Street. It is likely that Ethel did not have her parents' consent, which, being under the age of twenty-one, she needed to obtain to be legally married. Instead, she lied to the registrar, claiming that she was indeed twenty-one. That the two witnesses were unknown names is another indication that her parents were unaware of what had taken place. Frank, too, kept quiet about the wedding, not least because married officers were not wanted in the West African Frontier Force. Indeed, it seems to have remained a secret between him and Ethel until, as we shall see, he felt forced to come clean about it a few years later. On 24 March, seven weeks after his wedding, Frank left Liverpool bound once more for Forcados.[32] One piece of good news was that three days earlier he had been granted the rank of local captain by the WAFF.

The reason for Frank's elevation in rank was that the Mounted Infantry had been expanding. By the end of 1903 it had grown to four companies and a further expansion was carried out in 1904, with three further companies being raised. Frank was given command of one of these new companies. His arrival back at Zaria coincided with a change in overall command of the Mounted Infantry. Crawley had been sent home sick and in his place came Tom Cubitt, who had been Morland's staff officer during the Kano/Sokoto campaign and who now was elevated to the rank of lieutenant colonel. Frank had a very high regard for Cubitt, who appears to have instilled much greater discipline among the officers, especially in terms of them drinking during the day. Unlike the previous year, though, the Mounted Infantry were engaged in no significant operations and Frank was mostly concerned with training his company. He also passed the written part of his promotion to captain exam. Although in his autobiography Frank states that he remained at Zaria, this was not so. Because of the incidence of tetse fly, fatal for the horses, and poor watering, it was decided to move the MI base from Zaria to Gwarzo near Kano. Three companies lived there, while the others covered some 600 miles of Nigeria's northern frontier, operating from company bases. In December 1904 Cubitt returned to Britain, his place being taken by Major C.W. Barlow, who had commanded the mounted infantry during the Burmi operation.[33] In Frank's words: ' … with his [Cubitt's] departure came a crash. The station went to pieces. Some of us drank all day, formed ourselves into clicques and became demoralised.' His last months with the WAFF were therefore not very rewarding and he left for England in the early summer 1905 'full of fever and cocktails, supported by sips of champagne instead of food, and was [to be] in the doctor's hands for months.'[34]

Chapter Four

Rolling Stone: 1905–1911

Frank's final return from West Africa may have seen him somewhat sick in mind and body, but there were compensations to be had. In February 1905 his paternal grandfather had died, leaving an estate worth in excess of £34,000, a considerable sum in those days. Frank's share of this came to £4,300 plus some pictures and would have been much more if it had not been for his late father's borrowings against the estate during the last decade or so of his life. Then, on 10 July, Frank married Ethel for a second time, and in church. It is most likely that now he was home for good from West Africa he wanted to make his marriage official in the eyes of the Army, perhaps fearing that if he revealed his original marriage he might be accused of being in West Africa under false pretences. This time the wedding took place at St Mary's Church, The Boltons, West Brompton, with the Reverend J. Cobb, Ethel's grandfather, officiating. Frank gave his address as 19 Half Moon Street, just off Piccadilly and in a very fashionable part of London. He merely noted in *Impressions and Recollections* that the wedding 'was noticeable for the fact that it was packed with men, most of whom were killed, or did well, in the Great War.' Indeed, this time the witnesses were not called off the street and were five in number – Frank's stepfather, his uncle W.F. Percy, Tom Cubitt (his erstwhile commanding officer in Nigeria), Ethel's mother, and her great friend Edith Heron-Brown. Where he and Ethel spent their honeymoon is not recorded.

Frank remained on the books of the WAFF until mid-September, when he reverted to the British service. Now he found himself a subaltern again and without the allowances he had enjoyed in West Africa. As he later wrote, it 'meant serving on six shillings and sixpence a day instead of £600 a year'.[1] Another sadness was that his little dog Bee died when in quarantine. It was not, however, until early December 1905 that he rejoined the Manchesters, possibly because he had been unwell. He served initially with the 4th Battalion, which had been in Ireland, but moved to Aldershot in October 1905. He enjoyed his time at Aldershot. He found the training programmes 'progressive', with emphasis on putting into effect the lessons learned from South Africa. He also began to prepare himself for the Staff College, which was now finally beginning to be recognised as an essential step for promotion to the higher ranks. The following year Frank rejoined the 2nd Manchesters, who were now based in the Channel Islands. The battalion was split in two, with one half under Battalion HQ on Guernsey and the remainder on Alderney.

Although the *Entente Cordiale* with France had been signed in April 1904, thus resolving differences between the two countries over their burgeoning empires in Africa, the French were still seen as the principal threat when it came to the Channel Islands. It was envisaged that the most likely form of attack would be a naval raid, possibly accompanied by a landing of up to 2,000 troops. The 2nd Manchesters were the only regular battalion on the two islands and while there were the two militia battalions of the Royal Guernsey Light Infantry available for the defence of Guernsey, there were no other infantry on Alderney, apart from the Manchesters. The Royal Navy, however, saw its port as 'a port of refuge, a strategic port, and a base of communication for cruisers.' This was the reason why four companies of Manchesters, with Frank included in their number, were based there. On both islands there were Royal Garrison Artillery (RGA) detachments and RGA militia to man the coastal guns, which were housed in forts, but otherwise there were no combat troops.[2]

What Frank got up to on Alderney is not related. It is also not clear whether Ethel accompanied him. Suffice to say that the four companies of the battalion were based in Fort Albert and Chateau le Etoc and there is one recorded incident of the troops being called out to prevent the pilfering of a wrecked vessel called *Petit Raymond*.[3] Yet it was on Alderney that the first step was taken that would lead Frank to financial ruin. It concerned a bill for five pounds and three shillings for a dinner he had hosted at the Aldershot Officers' Club when he was still with the 4th Manchesters, which had not been settled. The matter was officially raised in summer 1906. Colonel Shaw, the honorary secretary of the Officers' Club, apparently wrote to Frank several times, but received no reply. Consequently, on 14 August he wrote to Frank's commanding officer. Frank wrote in explanation that he had now settled the account and that letters must have crossed in the post. He stated that since he was not presented with a bill after the dinner he had arranged for it to be sent to the 4th Manchesters. He also said that he had sent a letter to his bank and assumed that all was well. Unfortunately, his bank refused to honour the cheque. The matter was referred to the General Officer Commanding (GOC) Guernsey & Alderney District, who wondered if Messrs Cox & Co., Frank's bank, had informed him that his cheque had been dishonoured. The bank replied that they had warned him of the state of his account before he issued the cheque, but that they had not told him that they had returned the cheque unpaid. They had, however, written to Frank for funds to meet the cheque. These apparently were forthcoming and no further action was taken. The matter did not, however, do Frank's standing much good in the eyes of his colonel. What is puzzling, though, is that Frank had received his inheritance and had assets of over £3,500 in March 1906.[4]

Probably realising that his reputation with the 2nd Manchesters was poor, Frank wrote to the War Office asking to be re-employed in the West African Frontier Force or King's African Rifles. The War Office wrote to the Colonial Office in January 1907, pointing out that although Frank was married and therefore technically ineligible, his previous service with the WAFF counted in his favour. The Colonial Office stated, however, that while the rule against married officers could be waived if the officer was 'especially well reported on', this was not so in Frank's case. His application was therefore rejected.[5]* In the meantime, in December 1906, he went

---

* In *Impressions and Recollections* pp132–3 Frank states that he had volunteered to return to West Africa after learning of the death in action of one of his fellow Mounted Infantry officers, Lt Blackwood, in February 1906, and that he was placed on a day's notice to ship out, but that in the end his services were not needed. He makes no mention of applying to rejoin the WAFF later in the year.

on leave. Unfortunately, Ethel was taken ill and had to undergo an operation, which was performed by an Irish surgeon, Mr Cowen of Half Moon Street, London. After Christmas Frank wrote to his colonel asking for an extension of leave, but this was turned down because of a shortage of officers on Guernsey. This is odd, because both the 3rd and 4th Manchesters had just been posted to the Channel Islands prior to being disbanded and on 1 December 1906 the 2nd Battalion had absorbed the remaining strength of both and could boast of no fewer than sixty-three officers on its books.[6]* On the other hand, it could have been because Frank had spent only a limited length of time on regimental duty since being commissioned into the Manchesters in May 1900. He therefore applied to go on half pay as a captain. He was told that he could do so for six months as a subaltern and then there would be no guarantee of a return to full pay because he had not been well reported on. Frank himself later stated that the reason he went on half pay was that he had been offered the choice of remaining with the Manchesters, transferring to another regiment, or going on half pay. He chose the last because of ill-health. Indeed, he mentioned that while at Aldershot he had suffered from bouts of malaria and had taken recourse to nips of spirits to keep him going.[7]

Frank stated that he then sailed to South Africa. He had been invited by a friend to raise a mounted company in Natal to deal with Zulu unrest, which had plagued the province during 1906. He had put a proposal to the Colonial Office, but received no reply. His doctor recommended a sea voyage and Frank took the opportunity to go to Natal, where apparently he received a cable stating that the War Office required him back in England.[8] There is no evidence from surviving passenger lists that he did go out to South Africa during the first part of 1907. There was, however, further trouble with his regiment. In early April 1907 the CO of the 2nd Manchesters wrote to the GOC Guernsey and Alderney District informing him that Frank had issued another bad cheque, this time in settlement of a mess bill. He had also received several letters from tradesmen stating that Frank owed them money and requesting Frank's address. Colonel Watson, the CO, said that he had sent Frank several letters, but could do little else since he was no longer under his command. The reply was that Frank should be given an ultimatum to settle his mess bill by the end of April. Colonel Watson duly did this and money arrived from Frank's solicitors before the deadline. Reporting this to the GOC, Colonel Watson stated: 'I have the honour to request that in the event of that officer being brought back from half pay, steps may be taken to prevent his being posted to the Battalion under my command, as after his grave conduct I have no wish to have, under my command, an officer who has brought discredit to the Regiment.' The GOC, in turn, recommended to the War Office that Frank not be brought back to full pay and that his services be dispensed with.

Nothing more appears to have happened until July 1907, when the War Office wrote to Frank complaining of his failure to reply to letters. On 1 August 1907 he

---

* The Manchester Regiment, along with five others (Northumberland Fusiliers, King's (Liverpool Regiment), Worcestershire Regiment, Middlesex Regiment, Royal Munster Fusiliers), had its strength increased by two regular battalions in March 1900 as a result of the demands of the war in South Africa. All these extra battalions were disbanded at the end of 1906.

replied from a Chelsea address. He explained that he had had to take Ethel abroad to convalesce; presumably she had accompanied him on his supposed trip to South Africa. Now he wanted to return to active duty, but in a regiment other than the Manchesters. Failing that, he wished to remain on half pay, but as a captain. He enclosed letters of support from, among others, Major General Pilcher, with whom he had served in West Africa, and his stepfather, now Brigadier General Thorneycroft and commanding the 14th Infantry Brigade in Ireland. The War Office immediately replied that nothing could be done until he responded to the letters sent to him by his former colonel. There followed a further letter from Maj Gen B.B.D. Campbell CB, GOC Guernsey and Alderney District, concluding that Frank's 'retention in the service is now only an expense to the public'. In reply, the War Office stated that steps were being taken to terminate Frank's half pay. This duly happened. On 27 September Frank wrote to the War Office, explaining that he had been sailing in the north of Scotland and had discovered from his solicitors that his half pay had been stopped from the end of July. In reply, the War Office stated on 4 October that this was because Frank had failed to reply to their letters requesting an explanation for the dishonoured cheque. He replied to this on 8 October, giving his solicitors' address. He claimed that he had been on leave at the time the mess bill was raised, but had sent the President of the Mess Committee (PMC) a blank cheque. He then heard that the mess bill was still outstanding and arranged for his solicitor to telegraph fifty pounds to the Commanding Officer, 2nd Manchesters. For some reason, Frank, still not knowing the amount of the mess bill, told his solicitor to send a second tranche of money. Twenty-five pounds was apparently returned, but the original cheque, which presumably the solicitor had instructed the PMC to fill in, bounced. Frank stated that this was 'in the complete belief that the money was there to meet it, otherwise I would not have troubled to meet my mess bill at the moment. It was the result of a business delay, which might happen to anyone.' He also explained that he had given the Paymaster-General his address as a flat in Chelsea, where he had taken up residence while attending a crammer as part of his preparation for Staff College. He had to give it up when Ethel fell ill. As for his 1 August letter, he had sent this from another London address the day before he departed for Scotland and it was only when his solicitor informed him of the termination of his half pay that he learned about the mess bill cheque. He concluded: 'I trust that the Army Council will not think that I have either attempted to defraud the 2nd Manchester Mess or to deceive the War Office as to my whereabouts.'[9] It would seem that the matter was settled and once more Frank was given the benefit of the doubt. His half pay was restored.

Frank set sail with Ethel from Dover for Monrovia on 11 December 1907, describing himself on the passenger list as Captain Crozier. Frank stated that this was on behalf of a timber merchant who was keen to acquire a concession in West Africa. It proved to be a disaster, both Croziers falling ill and the firm refusing to pay their return passage because Frank had been unable to complete the work. However, according to Tom Cubitt, Frank was 'mentioned in a very discreditable incident with his wife and coloured people.'[10] This may have contributed to or been the actual reason for their early return to England, although the details of the incident cannot be established. Frank said that they landed at Plymouth, but in fact it was Liverpool, at the end of March 1908. In the meantime, Frank had, the previous December, borrowed £500 from his sister, who had married Lieutenant William ('Bill') Allan of the 1st Black Watch, then stationed at the Curragh in Ireland. The security for this loan was a policy on the life of Ethel's father. This indicates that Frank and Ethel had got through the inheritance from his grandfather, and four shillings per diem half pay was simply not enough to maintain their lifestyle. Frank, however, now saw another opening. On 21 April 1908 he wrote to the War Office requesting permission to resign his commission and be granted a captain's commission in the Special Reserve, specifically in the 3rd Battalion, the King's Own (Royal Lancaster) Regiment. He was also hopeful that he might be entitled to a gratuity for his regular Army service.

The War Office, probably with some relief, duly sanctioned Frank's request, but informed him that since he did not have eight years' service he was not entitled to a gratuity. Accordingly, on 17 June 1908 he resigned his regular commission and was appointed a captain and given command of a company in the 3rd Loyal North Lancashire Regiment. The fact that he was posted to the Loyals, rather than the King's Own, seems to have been because the former had for some time been suffering from a severe shortage of officers.[11] The battalion itself had originally been a Militia unit, with two roles. One was home defence and the other was supplying reinforcements to the two regular Loyals battalions in time of war. The problem with this, as had been recognised during the South African War, was that the Militia battalions were unable to perform both roles, since sending out reinforcements to South Africa denuded them of trained soldiers. To overcome the problem, at the end of 1907, and as part of Lord Haldane's reforms of the Army, the Special Reserve was created. The bulk of the Militia battalions were absorbed by this, with the remainder being disbanded. Infantry regiments with four regular battalions were provided with a reserve and an extra reserve battalion, while the remainder, including the Loyals, had just a reserve battalion. They originally had just one role, that of providing regular reinforcements. As for home defence, this was given over to the newly-created Territorial Force. Militia members were given the option of joining the Special Reserve, remaining in the Militia, or obtaining their discharge. As far as the 1st Lancashire Militia, which became the 3rd Loyals, was concerned, all the officers chose to join the Special Reserve and just under 70 per cent of the Other Ranks. Of the remainder, 45 per cent chose to remain in the Militia and the rest took their discharge.[12] The 3rd Loyals were based at Preston and this necessitated a move north for Frank. He had, however, just begun to rent a house at Looe in west Cornwall and also had a flat in London. Life would therefore continue to be just as expensive for him and Ethel and they soon began to run up unpaid bills. This was in spite of the fact that Frank was now earning over £200 annual army pay, instead of the mere £73 he had received on half pay, and that his mother gave him an allowance of some £350 per annum, with Ethel's family providing her with approximately £150 per year.

Initially the debts were for small amounts – a tailor in Winchester, a butcher in London, and a Plymouth draper being among the creditors. A further debt was to Spinks of London for mounting a 1906 Zulu Uprising in Natal Medal on Frank's set of miniatures. Whether he was entitled to this medal is questionable, to say the least. It was issued by the Natal government in 1908 and presented to all those who had taken part in crushing the unrest during 1906. Frank was certainly not in Natal in 1906 and if he had been there in 1907 it would have been too late to qualify for the medal. In any event, the only Crozier appearing on the Natal medal roll is a Capt G.R. Crozier of the Natal Medical Corps.[13] By the same token, Frank also wore the King's South Africa Medal, which was granted to those who were serving in South Africa on or after 1 January 1902 and had done so for a minimum of eighteen months or had completed that period before 1 June 1902. Since Frank only served in South Africa from January 1900–January 1901 he could not possibly have qualified for it. In addition, he sported the Ashanti Medal awarded to those serving in the Ashanti Field Force used to quell native unrest during the period March–December 1900. Frank, of course, was in South Africa throughout this time and could surely not have been in two places at once.

Be that as it may, Frank sank ever more steadily into debt. He had managed to borrow £30 from his mother-in-law in October 1908, but this was a mere drop in the ocean, and he had no other option but to put himself in the hands of the moneylenders. That November he answered a moneylender's advertisement in the *Western Morning News*. A woman then met Frank at the Royal Hotel, Plymouth. She put him in touch with the representative of a London moneylender and Frank signed a promissory note to the effect that in return for an immediate loan of £150 he would pay back £100 on 7 January 1909 and a further £100 six months later. On 1 January, responding to another newspaper advertisement, he borrowed an additional £50, which cost him £20, to be paid back in two instalments at three and six months. Four weeks later he borrowed a further £100 from yet another moneylender. This time he had to pay back £160 in twelve instalments. In the meantime, Frank had failed to pay back the £100 due to the first moneylender on 7 January. Consequently, on 17 February 1909 the first moneylender filed a petition against Frank on the grounds of non-compliance. He gave Frank's address as a flat in Powis Square, Bayswater, but stated that he had been unable to ascertain precisely where Frank was currently living. The other moneylenders took the same action and on 23 March a receiving order was made.[14]

If Frank had hoped to keep his financial troubles from the military authorities, he was to be sorely mistaken. On 17 March Major C.E.A. Jourdain DSO,* then second-in-command of the 3rd Loyals, was made aware that Frank had issued dud cheques locally in Preston. He wrote asking for an explanation and Frank replied that he had given Ethel a blank cheque which she had made out for more money than expected, thus presumably leaving his account with insufficient funds to meet his cheques when they were presented. He himself was now staying at the Crown Hotel, Preston, but said that he was too ill to go into barracks. Major Jourdain therefore wrote to him again giving him an ultimatum to settle the amounts owed by midday on 20 March. Frank duly settled his debt in time, apart from fifteen shillings from a hotel bill. He said that he had paid this at 1.30pm on that same day, 20 March. The hotel proprietor then said that this outstanding amount had not been paid until after 1.30pm. Major Jourdain, observing that this was not the first time that there had been this sort of trouble, recommended to the commanding officer, Colonel T. Cowper-

---

* Later killed on the Aisne in July 1918 while commanding the 2nd Loyals.

Essex, that Frank be removed from the Special Reserve. Major Jourdain subsequently discovered three more dishonoured cheques. Frank initially denied two of them and would not give an answer on the third. Furthermore, he had vacated a flat owing rent and a gas bill. Then, in a letter addressed to the adjutant of the 3rd Loyals and dated 12 April, he accepted that he had stopped one of the cheques because he was uncertain of the state of his bank account, but would settle it in due course. As for the other two, he had issued them in good faith, but he thought they had not been cashed because he had written them to friends of his as loans on the understanding that they not be cashed without his express permission. He assured the adjutant that these two individuals were now being pursued through the courts. It was an unlikely story, and Colonel Cowper-Essex considered that he had no option but to refer the matter to HQ Western Command, whose GOC recommended that Frank be given the opportunity to resign his commission. If he did not, he should be removed. This was passed to the War Office, which also noted the publication in the *London Gazette* of the receiving order in bankruptcy being issued. The upshot was that Frank did resign his commission on 22 May 1909.[15]

With regard to his impending bankruptcy, Frank was summoned to a public examination on 5 May, but pleaded illness and so it was postponed until 15 June. He had to answer a long list of questions, beginning with where he was living. He stated that for the past three days he had been staying at a hotel in Euston and for the two months prior to that in a flat in Blackpool. He described himself as 'a Captain in the Army without pay', although this was not strictly true, since he had resigned his commission and hence was no longer in the Army. He believed that his unsecured debts amounted to some £400, but disputed some of the claims made against him. In terms of assets, he claimed to have some £700 worth of furniture. In terms of rented property, apart from the Looe house, he had entered an agreement for the rent of a flat in Charing Cross Road, but had never occupied it and thought he had a letter absolving him of the agreement. There was also the Powis Square flat, which he stated that he had vacated on 20 March, having stayed there for just three weeks. He had to give the date of his marriage and the clerk noting down his answers originally put down the date of 10 July 1905, but then amended it to read 8 February 1904. It would seem that, as part of making a clean breast of his affairs, Frank decided that he must officially reveal the original date of his marriage. As for the reasons for his insolvency, Frank gave them as 'heavy interest on borrowed money and my Army pay proving insufficient for my household and personal expenses, including heavy Doctor's fees.' The last referred to Ethel's illnesses, which Frank estimated had cost him £600.

Some of Frank's answers were vague and he was called back for a second examination on 29 June. He had clearly thought carefully since the previous examination and now agreed that his unsecured debts actually totalled some £570 and this was taking into account the fact that his sister was no longer pursuing repayment of the £500 loan she had made to him. He no longer disputed any of his debts, which apart from the three moneylenders, were for dishonoured cheques and miscellaneous bills to tradesmen. All were for relatively small amounts and even included three pounds in wages owed to a domestic servant in London. He now accepted that his insolvency had been brought about by extravagant living and it is highly likely that drink was at the bottom of it. The result was inevitable. On 26 July 1909 Frank was made bankrupt and his financial affairs were handed over to a trustee appointed by the Official Receiver. His fellowship of the Royal Geographical Society was also cancelled, presumably because he had failed to keep up to date with his subscriptions. Frank himself later dismissed the whole business as a 'stupid, silly, senseless scrape, which, had I had a sane soul to turn to at the time, need never have been.'[16]

Frank was not one to throw his hands in the air, however. He had been planning a new life for Ethel and himself and decided to emigrate to Canada. With the western part of the country now being opened up and plots of land available at cheap prices, Frank saw himself setting up as a farmer. Indeed, the Canadian government was actively encouraging Britons to settle in the country, even to the extent of paying agents to arrange for them to emigrate and offering assisted passages. As a result, the number arriving in Canada from Britain increased from some 87,000 for the year ending 31 March 1906 to 142,500 for that ending 31 March 1914. Frank set sail from Liverpool, arriving in Quebec on board the SS *Lake Manitoba* on 2 August 1909, a mere week after he had been declared bankrupt. He described himself as a retired army captain and tourist and expressed no intention of obtaining work in Canada.[17] Curiously, Ethel sailed on a different vessel and arrived three days later, explaining that she was joining her farmer husband. One presumes that the family had rallied round to provide the necessary money to give them a fresh start.

In any event, the Croziers headed west and it looks as though Frank might have purchased a farm in the Red River area of Alberta. A brief item in *The Red Deer News* of 2 February 1910 stated: 'Frank Crozier, who recently purchased Hovenan Farm, has left for High River.' This could have indicated the beginning of a trapping expedition that he said he made towards Hudson Bay, leaving Ethel installed in a flat in Winnipeg.* He apparently returned to her on the day that King Edward VII died, 6 May 1910. That night, he says, he took Ethel out to one of Winnipeg's best restaurants. While she was in the ladies cloakroom, he had a drink with two friends and became involved in a punch-up with some strangers, who had insulted the new king. The result was a night in the cells and a court appearance next day. The charges against Frank and his two friends were dismissed, but the three men they fought with were found guilty. Frank also said that members of the newly formed Canadian Veterans Association were present at the hearing and he certainly became involved with this organisation.[18] A report in the *Manitoba Free Press* of 16 May 1910 reported his arrival in Winnipeg and the likelihood that he would be attending a parade of veterans. It also gave an account of his military career, which is worth quoting in full:

Capt. Crozier retired from the active list last June and has since been in Saskatchewan. He joined the army in 1896 and served in the South African War 1899–1902 with 18th Hussars and Manchester Regiment as lieutenant, for which he received the Queen's medal and six clasps and the King's medal and two clasps. Subsequently he saw service in Ashanti with the West African Frontier Force (medal) and in Northern Nigeria and Central Africa with the

---

* In *Impressions and Recollections*, p136, he states that the trapping expedition lasted six months.

Northern Nigeria Mounted Infantry (medal and two clasps). In 1906 he was attached to Royston's Horse* in Zululand; as captain in the operations against Dinizulu (medal and clasp). He holds the late Queen's Diamond Jubilee medal and King Edward's Coronation medal. Captain Crozier served for some time in India, Hong Kong, and Ceylon.

This shows how Frank was embroidering his military exploits. He also later claimed to have helped raised a squadron of the Saskatchewan Light Horse (today the North Saskatchewan Regiment),[19] but a trawl of the Canadian archives has revealed no evidence that he served in any capacity with the Canadian Forces.[20] What is true is that he did become actively involved in veteran affairs, representing Lloydminster on the Alberta-Saskatchewan border.[21]

On 4 December 1910, while in Winnipeg, Ethel gave birth to a daughter, Mary Elizabeth, but according to Mary herself she was known as Baba (Hindi for 'baby') up to the age of thirteen, although David Starrett, Frank's batman during 1914–18, called her Babs.[22] If, however, Frank had carried out his trapping expedition when he said he did, it throws doubt on him being Mary's natural father. Notwithstanding this, he also took a momentous decision. In *Impressions and Recollections* he recounts that he attended a St Patrick's Day dinner in Winnipeg. He states that this was in 1912, but, as we shall see, it must have been 1911. The wine flowed freely:

> Next morning, waking up with a most perfect headache I have ever had to endure, I decided to call for a brandy and soda to put matters right, which, as a matter of fact, has exactly the opposite effect. Changing my mind, however, I had a cup of tea instead, after which I felt decidedly better. I certainly could not have felt worse, as I was 'ill all over.' Later, I decided not to have a drink till lunch-time, while I thought things over.

The upshot was that he concluded that he felt much better when operating in an environment in which alcohol was not available and resolved there and then to give up drink for good. True, it was a struggle for the first six months, but Frank stuck to his resolution and never touched alcohol again.[23]

Frank says that he decided to send Ethel and Mary back to England in spring 1911,** while he worked as a labourer on a government scheme to extend the telephone system in Manitoba. Certainly, he appears as such in the 1911 Canadian Census, which was conducted that June, and residing at Telephone Camp, Township 8.11 W, Macdonald, which lies south-west of and close to Winnipeg. Ethel and Mary cannot be found in the 1911 British Census, which was conducted in April, so they had not yet returned to England, but must have done so before the Canadian Census, since they do not appear on that either. Their names cannot be found on surviving ship's passenger lists and so it is impossible to pin down an actual date for their

---

*   Raised by a well-known Natal character, Lt Col 'Galloping Jack' Royston, specifically to help put down the unrest.
** In *Impressions and Recollections*, p139, he states that it was 1912.

return. Frank himself later wrote that he went home in autumn 1912 because of the worsening situation in Ulster.[24] In actual fact, he arrived back in Liverpool on 15 September 1911, having travelled 3rd Class on board the *Empress of Britain* from Quebec and describing himself on the passenger lists as a farmer. Tom Cubitt, his erstwhile commander in the WAFF, later stated that Frank got into trouble in Canada and that Walter Besant, who was married to Frank's mother's sister Maria, helped him to leave the country.[25] Frank did, however, subsequently register his name with the Canadian High Commission, a sign that he planned to go back to Canada, indicating that the trouble he had found himself in was not criminal.[26] As for why he did return to Britain, it is likely that he had run up further debts in Canada and this was why he had in the end to become a labourer. As far as his bankruptcy was concerned, he had, in May 1910, unsuccessfully appealed through his solicitor to be discharged, but in February 1912 his discharge did come through.[27] How his debts were paid off is not recorded, but it is more likely that his and Ethel's relations put their hands in their pockets, than that Frank settled them himself from money earned in Canada.

Chapter Five

Ulster Will Fight Rather than Unite: 1912–1914

What Frank's immediate intentions were on arrival back in Britain are not known. It is also not clear how he occupied himself for the next eighteen months or so. His stepfather had just been promoted to major general and given command of the South Midland Division (which became 46th Division during the Great War) of the Territorial Force after almost two years on half pay. He was forced to retire through ill-health in July 1912 and settled in a house outside Reading. Frank, Ethel and Mary would have certainly spent time with his mother and Alec. Frank, too, would have visited Jessie Platt on Lewis. Ethel's mother also needed her daughter's support. Robert Cobb had now retired from the Indian Medical Service and returned to London, but not to reside with Lilian in Hammersmith. Instead, he chose to live in Belsize Road, Hampstead, with his mistress of some years standing. In October 1912, Lilian finally took the first step towards divorcing him, placing a petition before the courts asking that Robert return to her.[1] This did not have the desired effect and a year later she filed for divorce, but her husband appears to have created difficulties and it is not clear whether she was eventually successful.[2] It is therefore more than probable that Ethel spent a good deal of time with her mother, who would have found her new granddaughter a welcome distraction.

Ireland, however, was about to dominate Frank's life for the next few years. For the past twenty-five years and more one of the major political topics in Britain had been Irish Home Rule. Matters initially came to a head with the 1885 General Election, which was won by William Gladstone and his Liberals, but the only way in which they could achieve an overall majority over the Conservatives was by allying themselves to eighty-five Irish MPs under the leadership of Charles Stuart Parnell, who had been elected on a Home Rule platform. To placate them, Gladstone introduced a Home Rule bill the following year. It was implacably opposed by the Conservatives. They stirred up an already suspicious and largely Protestant Ulster, renewing fears of a new Ireland entirely dominated by Catholicism. Indeed, Ulstermen began to drill with arms and, fearing a civil war, many of Gladstone's supporters deserted him and the bill was lost. Parnell, too, lost support when it became known that he had been having an affair with the wife of a fellow Irish MP. Gladstone tried again after being re-elected in 1892, but although the bill got through the Commons, it was blocked by the staunchly Conservative House of Lords. There matters rested for the next few years, but the desire for home rule was still as strong as ever in many Irish hearts. The establishment of the Gaelic League reflected a desire to reinvigorate the Irish language and culture, while Arthur Griffith founded Sinn Fein ('Ourselves Alone') to work for an entirely Irish parliament with no MPs sent to Westminster. More extreme was another political group, the Irish Socialist Republican Party, which advocated a socialist revolution. On the other side of the fence, the Ulster Unionist Council was established in 1905 to ensure that at least the Protestant-dominated north of Ireland remained part of Britain.

In 1911, however, Home Rule once more came right to the forefront of British politics. The General Election of the previous year had seen the Liberals returned to power with a narrow majority over the Conservatives and meant that Nationalist MPs could once more influence the government. Indeed, their situation was even better than it had been seventeen years before, because the passing of the Parliament Act meant that the House of Lords could no longer veto a bill permanently. Consequently, Asquith's government introduced another Home Rule bill in April 1912. Even before this happened Sir Edward Carson, leader of the Ulster Unionists, had addressed some 50,000 people at Craigavon, just outside Belfast and the home of Captain James Craig, a place which Frank would soon come to know well. Ulstermen had also begun drilling, as they had done twenty years before. They also once more received support from the Conservatives. Then, that September, Carson drew up a 'Solemn League and Covenant' pledging resistance to Home Rule, which was signed by almost half a million people. Yet the bill itself was not very drastic. It called for an Irish parliament, which would merely legislate on Irish affairs and would not be allowed control of the Royal Irish Constabulary until six years had elapsed. Even so, at the beginning of 1913 the Ulster Unionist Council formally established the Ulster Volunteer Force (UVF) under General Sir George Richardson, a distinguished retired Indian Army officer, who, although an Englishman, had been recommended by Lord Roberts. The plan was to recruit 100,000 men aged seventeen to sixty-five who had signed the Covenant and were prepared to defend Ulster. Simultaneously, Carson came up with a compromise. He proposed that the six counties at the heart of Ulster be excluded. By now prime minister Herbert Asquith was becoming concerned and eagerly seized on this proposal, obtaining Conservative agreement not to block the bill in the Lords if it was suitably amended.

It was at this time that Frank became actively involved in Irish affairs when he joined the British League for the Support of Ulster and the Union. This was established in late March 1913 by 100 Unionist peers and 120 MPs and its aim was to 'support the men of Ulster in the great struggle that lies before them.'[3] A few days later, Frank apparently received a mysterious parcel, which turned out to contain a 0.303in carbine, which he was told he might need in Ulster one day. He became an 'honorary delegate' and recalled attending a meeting of delegates at Londonderry House in Park Lane, followed by a luncheon at the Hotel Cecil, 'during the season of 1913'.*

It was probably late in 1913 that Frank travelled to Ulster to join the UVF – he wrote that it was six months after the Londonderry house meeting.[4] He claimed that he was sponsored by Tom Cubitt and Julian Hasler, who also served in West

---

* A report in *The Times* of 6 June 1913 on the intention of Sir Edward Carson and other Irish Unionists to address various meetings around the United Kingdom mentioned that a meeting of 'honorary delegates' had recently taken place at Londonderry House, with Lord Willoughby de Broke in the chair. The impetus for all this was likely to have been the second reading of the Home Rule bill, which also occurred in June 1913.

Africa and would be killed in April 1915 while commanding a brigade during the Second Battle of Ypres.[5] Neither of these two seems to have had any close connection with Ireland, although Cubitt had served as a staff officer there. It is also especially surprising that Cubitt would have supported him in this way, given what he knew about Frank and Ethel's visit to West Africa after he left the Manchesters. Frank, of course, had not signed the Covenant, and never did, but his Irish family connections and his military experience were clearly attractive to the UVF. It would seem, however, that he actually travelled to Belfast under the auspices of the British League for the Support of Ulster and the Union.[6] How Frank supported himself financially is not clear, but since the UVF paid Sir George Richardson an annual stipend of £1,500, it is quite likely that Frank received one as well, although for a much lesser amount.[7] As for Ethel and Mary, Frank makes no mention of what happened to them while he was in Ireland and one can only assume that they stayed with Ethel's mother.

The UVF itself was organised on a county basis. It included not just the hardcore Ulster counties of Londonderry, Antrim, Tyrone, Down, Armagh and Fermanagh, but also Donegal, Monaghan and Cavan. Belfast itself was divided into four regiments (North, East, South, West), each containing a number of battalions and whose recruiting areas reflected those of the parliamentary constituencies. Frank joined the West Belfast Regiment, which was commanded by Captain the Hon. Arthur Chichester, who had served with the Royal Fusiliers in the Boer War. The overall commander in Belfast was Colonel George Couchman DSO, a veteran of the Burma campaigns and who had recently retired from the Army after commanding a territorial brigade. Frank's specific task was to organise a Special Service unit of some 300 men of the West Belfast Regiment which could be called out in the event of an emergency. In his books Frank implies that this was a unique element of the UVF, but each Belfast regiment had a Special Service section and others were formed elsewhere in Ulster. The authorities were fully aware of the UVF's activities, with both military intelligence and the Royal Irish Constabulary monitoring them. They also knew the names of all the senior officers. Frank, however, appears to have kept his name hidden – certainly it is not mentioned in any of the intelligence reports.[8] Much of the reason may have been that although he was offered an office at the UVF HQ in Belfast Old City Hall, he declined, since he did not want to be caught up in 'red tape'.[9] As it was:

> Immediately after arrival in Belfast I was given three hundred blank attestation forms (documents very like the army form), three hundred names of men, clothing, arms and ammunition and a place to parade in and told to get on with the job of producing the finished article in as short a time as possible.[10]

Frank seems to have created an immediate impression. Edmund Malone, former regular Royal Fusilier and now a member of the regiment's Special Reserve, had, like Frank, been sent to Ulster by the British League, and had been appointed second-in-command of the North Belfast Regiment. In a letter to a friend, he mistakenly mentioned Frank as a regimental commander, but commented that he 'improved on acquaintance – a regular soldier of fortune, I think.'[11] This was probably the impression that Frank wanted to give, but it would not be long before his men were called out.

March 1914 proved to be a time of crisis in Ireland. To placate John Redmond, the Nationalist leader, the British government had decided that Ulster could only be excluded from Home Rule for six years, but on 9 March Carson rejected this. He and the other Ulster Unionists began to fear that they might be arrested and on 16 March the chief administrative officer at HQ UVF, Lt Col T.V.P. McCammon, issued an instruction to all senior officers of the force warning that they, too, might be arrested and that they should make arrangements for another officer to receive communications for HQ in the event of this happening.[12] Three days later Carson declared that he was leaving London to be among his own people. The first Frank heard of what was happening was when Colonel Couchman told him that night that he must sleep 'at a certain address, where I would be on the telephone' and that he was to register under the assumed name of Percy. Presumably this was a hotel. The reason for the secrecy was fear that even Frank might be arrested. Couchman told him to be at the Belfast quayside early the following morning to escort Carson to Craigavon. Frank recalled that he met Carson, who set off in a car with Craig and drove through Belfast, followed by Frank and his men and a crowd of supporters. On arrival at Craigavon, Frank's men relieved the UVF men who had been guarding the house overnight. But if Frank hoped to keep his anonymity, it was not to be. *The Times* of 21 March 1914, the following day, described how Carson's arrival was 'awaited by two companies of the West Belfast Regiment of the Ulster Volunteer Force, under the command of Captain Crozier, equipped with bandoliers, cartridge belts, and water bottles.' Craigavon itself was now placed under siege, with Frank's men guarding the two entrances. Within the house itself were Carson, Craig and his wife, and, among others, Lords Londonderry and Castlereagh, General Richardson, his chief-of-staff Colonel Hackett Pain, Colonel McCammon and Captain Wilfrid Spender. Spender was an interesting character. He had been among the youngest to attend the Army Staff College before leaving the Army and joining the staff of the UVF. He, Frank, and Colonel McCammon slept in the nursery of the house.[13]

That weekend, however, the attention of those at Craigavon and elsewhere in the British Isles was directed on events at Curragh Camp outside Dublin. Fearing that they might be sent north to bring Ulster under control, sixty out of seventy-two officers of the 3rd Cavalry Brigade, including its commander Brigadier General Hubert Gough, declared that they would rather be dismissed than obey such an order.[14] This declaraion was made on Friday 20 March. Orders issued on the same day by Major General Sir Charles Fergusson, commanding the 5th Division, made it clear that in the event of 'active operations in Ulster' officers who had their homes there would be allowed to 'disappear'. Any other officers refusing to obey the order would be dismissed from the service.[15] This was in line with instructions supposedly given by the Secretary of State for War, Jack Seely, to the commander-in-chief of Ireland, Sir Arthur Paget. The fact, too, that British warships had sailed into Belfast Lough also served to increase the pressure on Carson and his followers, as did movements of troops within Ireland. The media became focussed on what was happening and Frank even had a photograph of himself using a field telephone on the front page of *The Daily Mirror* on Monday 23 March. He was mentioned by name in the caption, an indication that he might well have enjoyed the publicity.

In the meantime, the King had become concerned and had summoned Seely, who told him that Lord Roberts was the root cause, through his encouragement of the Unionist movement. Roberts himself was very agitated about the whole affair and requested an audience with the King, at which he denied influencing Gough and his officers in any way. Roberts also made the same denials to Seely. As for Gough, he had sent a telegram to his brother Johnnie, who was Douglas Haig's chief of staff at Aldershot Command. In support of his brother, Johnnie offered his resignation to Haig, who refused it and went up to London to try to get a solution to the problem. Johnnie himself also went to London and to his mother's flat, where he based himself. Hubert crossed from Ireland on the Saturday night. Johnnie had meanwhile visited the War Office and saw Henry Wilson, Director of Military Operations, who indicated that he might also resign. Hubert and Johnnie then went to the War Office, where Hubert was joined by his three commanding officers. He was summoned to see the Adjutant General, Sir John Ewart, who had Sir Nevil Macready, the Director of Personal Services, with him to take notes. Hubert Gough related what had happened and then Ewart asked him whether he felt he had any right to question an order to act in support of the civil power. Gough responded that if he had been given an order to take his brigade to Belfast he would have done so, but he had been given no order by Fergusson, merely asked whether he was prepared to serve in Ulster or leave the Army. Prime minister Herbert Asquith had also realised that matters had got out of control. He ordered that no further naval reinforcement of the waters around Ireland should take place and that Gough and his officers must be reinstated. On the following day, Monday 23 March, he was called to the War Office once more and saw not just Ewart, but Sir John French, the CIGS, as well. Sir John took the lead, telling Gough that there had been a misunderstanding and asking him to return to his command. The latter, however, wanted a written assurance that the Army would not be called upon to enforce the Home Rule bill on Ulster. French was only prepared to give a verbal assurance and so Gough was taken to see Seely. A written assurance was now hammered out and approved by the Cabinet. In essence, the whole affair had been a misunderstanding, but Gough and his officers were reminded that orders, once issued, had to be obeyed. The document was then passed to Seely, who added two further clauses, which emphasised that the Government had a right to employ the armed forces in support of the civil power, but that it had no intention of using this right to crush opposition in Ireland to Home Rule. It was then passed to Sir John French, who handed it to Gough. He conferred with his colonels and added a further sentence to the effect that he understood that Seely's last clause meant that the Army would not be used to enforce Home Rule on Ulster and signed it. The CIGS noted underneath: 'That is how I read it. J.F.'[16] Gough then pocketed the document and returned to the Curragh. Once Asquith heard of the additions which had been made, he instructed a message to be sent to Dublin stating that Seely's additions were not to be considered as 'operative'. Gough, however, stood his ground and also refused to return the document.

In the meantime there had been furious debates in Parliament, during which the truth of what had happened was slowly dragged out of the Government. All this was watched with bated breath by Unionists and Nationalists alike in Ireland. At Craigavon the Unionist leadership made plans in the event of Ulster being forced to break away from the remainder of Ireland. It had been agreed that Carson should form a 'provisional' government in the province, but now it was clear that the UVF must be properly armed. It would also have to act as both army and police force and, according to Frank, he was to be the 'chief executive officer' in Belfast in this respect. The conclusion was that martial law would have to be imposed in the city to protect life and property, and Frank was asked to draw up a plan as to how this could be put into effect. He also considered the problem of Victoria Barracks in Belfast. This was usually occupied by the 1st Dorsets, but this battalion was now moved out of the city to Holywood on Belfast Lough, since it was considered to be too isolated, and had left just a small rear party in the barracks. Even so, Frank carried out reconnaissance of the barracks and worked out how to 'bottle up' those troops remaining inside them without having to fire a shot.[17] Once, however, it became clear that Westminster was not going to use force to implement Home Rule or arrest the Unionist leaders, the atmosphere became more relaxed. Carson himself returned to London on the night of 27 March, but it was to be another week before Frank and his men were stood down.

Frank was very pleased with the way that his section had performed at Craigavon, but once the crisis was over reaction set in. A number of his men over-imbibed and failed to turn up to parades. Consequently, he issued an order on 15 April reminding everyone that the title 'Special' denoted 'that special efforts are required of its members. It is impossible for those who do not attend parades, etc, regularly to be efficient for war.' In future, any man not making the necessary effort to make himself fit for 'active service' would be struck off strength and returned to his parent company in the West Belfast Regiment. Frank also reminded his men that parade nights were every Monday, Tuesday, and Wednesday at 8pm at the Forth River Football Ground, which lay in the Shankhill area, with Frank giving his address at the bottom of the order as 222 Shankhill Road.[18] It would not be long, though, before Frank and his men were called out again.

Although the UVF did have some weapons, mainly obsolete Italian rifles, obtained from various sources, the decision taken at Craigavon during the 'siege', to obtain more, in a better-organised way, soon bore fruit. The architect was Major Fred Crawford, businessman, traveller, and part-time soldier. Indeed, as the UVF's Director of Ordnance, he had already procured some weaponry, as had others. In February 1914, well over a month before the Craigavon discussion, he had purchased 20,000 rifles and two million rounds of ammunition in Hamburg, in what was to be the most audacious of the UVF's gun-running operations. He obtained the Norwegian-registered but British-owned SS *Fanny* to transport his purchases and this sailed from Hamburg on 2 April. Just under three weeks later, and to cover his tracks, Crawford transferred the cargo to a coaling vessel, which he had purchased in Glasgow. This was the SS *Clyde Valley*, but Crawford disguised her as the *Mountjoy II* and the transfer took place off the coast of Wexford. Four days later, on the night of 24/25 April, the munitions were landed. For this the whole of the UVF was called out under the guise of a practice mobilisation.

The plan was for the *Mountjoy II* to first of all sail to Larne and land some arms there, as well as cross-shipping others to two smaller craft, which would take them to Donaghadee. The *Mountjoy II* would then sail on to Bangor, where it would deliver the remainder of its cargo. The UVF had numerous tasks to perform. It needed to secure the three ports prior to the arms being landed. Its Motor Corps was to provide the transport for delivering the arms and other elements were to secure the major routes along which the arms were to be carried. Telephone and telegraph links were also interfered with, especially those connecting the battalion stationed at Holywood. Finally, an elaborate deception was put into effect. Crawford had arranged for another coaling vessel to enter Belfast harbour at much the same time that *Mountjoy II* was entering Larne. Some 2,500 UVF men, under the command of Colonel Couchman, provided the reception party in an attempt to make the police and customs officials believe that arms were on board. When the UVF did allow the authorities to open the hatches they found only coal. Frank does not relate what part his men played, but he wrote that Colonel Couchman told him the details of the plan on the evening of 24 April. Thereafter he dined at the Ulster Club with some Royal Irish Constabulary (RIC) officers and others whose job it was to keep the former entertained until midnight. A car arranged by Lt Col McCammon collected him from the club at 10pm and took him to Bangor. On arrival, 'I found all approaches to the town picketed, the telephone temporarily out of action, the Coast Guard office in the hands of the gun-runners, reserves of the UVF ready at hand, motor-cars waiting, ready to drive off with their loads to known destinations, and Colonel McCammon all expectant.' The *Mountjoy II* was late arriving at Bangor, not until just after dawn, but the unloading went quickly and by 8am Bangor was back to its normal peaceful self.[19]

Although there was plenty of intelligence indicating that the UVF was bent on a major landing of weapons, the British Government was taken by surprise. Once again the Unionists had shown that they were not prepared to be subjected to Home Rule. Furthermore, the Irish Volunteers, formed the previous November to counter the UVF, saw themselves as the defenders of Home Rule and realised that they would have to arm themselves as well, if they were to be taken seriously. The third reading of the Home Rule bill took place and was passed on 25 May 1914, with the intention of putting it into effect that September. At the same time the Government introduced an Amending Bill, allowing those counties in the north of Ireland, which chose to do so, to opt out for six years. These, however, were exactly the same terms which the Unionists had rejected in March. Consequently, tension increased once more.

Frank continued to lick his men into shape. At Whitsun he had them in camp in the neighbourhood of Belfast. 'The chief object during that period was to knock the stout out of those who possessed a superabundance of that beverage in their systems.'[20] That he was successful is reflected by a piece in *The Times* on the UVF:

It [Special Service Force] consists of 3,000 men in Belfast and of detachments in the counties. The men are in the prime of life. They undergo a medical examination and agree to serve anywhere at a moment's notice. The Belfast contingent of this force is completely clothed, armed and equipped. It is very difficult to distinguish them from Regular troops. They all wear khaki uniform and have putties, belts, the infantry cap or something very like it, and ammunition boots. Though the writer has not seen this Force in the field, he formed a very high opinion of it from its appearance on ceremonial parades. It is armed with the Mauser and has a full supply of Maxim guns ...'[21]

As far as Frank was concerned, it was the security of the weapons that concerned him most. 'By July, 1914, I had an armoury under my care, containing over a thousand stands of arms, which was guarded nightly by a small guard of UVF men.' Doubting that this was capable of resisting a raid by the police or Nationalists he took to sleeping in the armoury on a camp-bed each night, with a loaded revolver by his side. Another task for his men was collecting ammunition which had been smuggled into Belfast docks in butter casks. A sympathetic Customs official made certain that the casks were not opened for inspection and would then inform Frank by telephone once they had cleared Customs and were ready for collection.[22]

As July wore on the tension continued to rise in Ireland. So worried was King George V that he called a conference at Buckingham Palace from 21–24 July. It was attended by two MPs from each of the British political parties, together with two Nationalists and two Unionists. Little progress was made and two days after the conference broke out Erskine Childers, the well-known novelist and author of the best-selling *Riddle of the Sands*, landed some 900 rifles and ammunition purchased in Germany for the Irish Volunteers at Howth, nine miles north-east of Dublin. The police were unable to prevent this because of the large number of volunteers present, but British troops did fire on a jeering crowd, killing three and wounding thirty-eight others, which exacerbated the overall situation still further. Another batch of arms was landed south of Dublin on the night of 1–2 August by leading Irish surgeon Sir Thomas Myles. By this time, however, tension in Europe had overshadowed that in Ireland and on 4 August Britain had found itself at war with Germany.

Frank claims that he immediately joined up as a private soldier 'at the instance of the late Captain Truman, of the 2nd Manchesters, with whom I had fought in the same battalion in South Africa, as I could not wait for a commission.'[23] Certainly there was a Captain Charles Fitzgerald Hamilton Trueman in the 2nd Manchesters, who was killed at Le Cateau in August 1914 while serving with the battalion. Also, the 2nd Manchesters were stationed at the Curragh when war was declared, but given the circumstances in which he left the regiment it is somewhat surprising that Frank still had any contact with it. On the other hand, if he had met or corresponded with Trueman the latter would undoubtedly have told him that the Manchesters were most unlikely to want him back and may have warned him that he might find it difficult to obtain a commission. On the other hand, Frank does not tell us what regiment he joined or whether he actually put on a private's uniform. Furthermore, he would have surely had to obtain the agreement of the UVF authorities to do this. As it was, he stated that he spent the first weekend of the war compiling a return of West Belfast UVF men who were prepared to volunteer for active service or home defence, or who were not prepared to volunteer at all.[24] This hardly ties in with his claim to have enlisted in the ranks on the first day of war.

Frank also wrote that 'shortly after the outbreak of war I was recalled to the Army as a captain in the Royal Irish Fusiliers, and was ordered to report to Dublin.' This was thanks to the High Commissioner for Canada, 'under whose control I came as an ex-Canadian soldier resident in the British Isles.'[25] It is certainly true that he was granted a temporary captaincy dated 8 September 1914 as an ex-officer in the Canadian Forces in Kitchener's New Armies, together with two other members of the Canadian Forces.[26] He was appointed to the 5th Royal Irish Fusiliers, a New Army battalion formed in Armagh, but which moved to Dublin almost immediately to become part of the 10th (Irish) Division. Since two other Canadian officers received captaincies on the same day, it is quite possible that his application did go through the High Commissioner, but Frank never did join the 5th Royal Irish Fusiliers.

On 7 August 1914 Kitchener had informed Colonel T.E. Hickman MP, president of the British League for the Defence of Ulster and the Union, that he was very keen to incorporate the UVF in his New Army. Hickman replied that Kitchener should consult with Carson. He in turn insisted that the UVF form a distinct entity, wearing the Red Hand of Ulster as its emblem and retaining its UVF titles. Furthermore, he wanted the Government to postpone any decision on Home Rule until after the war. The Government had to balance this against Nationalist demands that unless a measure of Home Rule was guaranteed, they would not support the war effort. It was also aware that recruiting for the 10th Division, the first Irish Kitchener division, was not going well, especially in the north of Ireland. The dilemma was overcome after the BEF's opening battles of Mons and Le Cateau and its subsequent retreat. This produced not only a surge in recruits coming forward for the New Armies, but also a change of heart on Carson's part. He was now prepared to place the UVF at the service of the War Office with no strings attached. The Ulster Unionist Council met in Belfast on 3 September to give its formal approval and recruiting began immediately. The Belfast UVF regiments became battalions of the Royal Irish Rifles, with the West Belfast Regiment being transformed into the 9th Royal Irish Rifles. As for Home Rule, Asquith did now postpone it until the end of the war. For Frank it meant that he became an officer in the 9th Royal Irish Rifles. Fresh challenges were beckoning.

Chapter Six

Irish Rifleman: 1914–1916

The original intention had been to make Frank the adjutant of the 9th Royal Irish Rifles, which is what the UVF's West Belfast Battalion became.[1] He was actually appointed second-in-command, with the rank of temporary major, with effect from 4 September.[2] This was undoubtedly because the main job of the battalion second-in-command was training, and Frank had demonstrated his abilities in this field with his Special Service unit. He also had considerable campaign experience. His first task was to travel to London to select some ex-regular NCOs as instructors. This was important, since the majority of former soldiers serving with the UVF were reservists who were recalled to their regiments once war was declared. The reason for Frank's trip was that from 7 September, and during the next few days, the chief recruiting officer in London organised for ex-NCOs to parade in the late afternoon on Horse Guards. It was here that that Frank made his selections, which included a man who had served with him in West Africa.[3] Thereafter he travelled to Glasgow to collect a group of Orangemen who were keen to cross the water to join the Ulster Division.

This reflects the fact that those who enlisted in the Division were by no means all UVF men. Indeed, the original idea had been that the Belfast UVF should form two out of the three brigades, but it was only able to form one. Apart from the recall of Army reservists, many UVF men had already enlisted in the 10th Irish Division. Others, too, hesitated to join the Army, which would entail service overseas and thus prevent them from defending Ulster. Nevertheless, the four battalions of the Royal Irish Rifles which recruited in Belfast were all up to war establishment by early October, with the 9th Battalion having nineteen officers and 1,102 other ranks.[4] Appointed to command it was Lt Col George Ormerod, who had been commissioned into the Royal Munster Fusiliers in 1878 and had retired as a major in early 1908 after active service in Burma in the late 1880s and briefly in South Africa towards the end of the conflict there. In other words, he was a typical 'dug-out' brought back into harness to help with the training of the rapidly expanding New Armies. Frank clearly liked him, even though there was an age gap of twenty-five years between them: 'He was a sahib in the best and truest sense of the word, and we had unlimited trust in one another.'[5] Reading between the lines, however, indicates that Ormerod allowed Frank, with his wider and more recent experience of active service, a virtual free hand. That George Couchman had been appointed to command 107 Brigade, which contained the Belfast battalions of the Royal Irish Rifles, was also clearly to Frank's advantage.

Another who would come close to Frank and remain so for the rest of his life was his batman David Starrett. The latter apparently enlisted at the age of sixteen, but stated that he was nineteen years old. He recalled: 'I was coming up the hill one day when I saw a heavily built small gent. Someone of importance he looked in tweed riding breeches and sports coat.' Frank told Starrett to collect a horse for him from the railway station. He initially employed him as a temporary groom, but he quickly became his batman. This was not least because Starrett was a fellow teetotaller.[6]

The 9th Royal Irish Rifles first established itself at Donard Lodge, Newcastle, on the coast of County Down. It shared its camping ground with the 10th Royal Irish Rifles under Colonel H.C. Bernard, another Burma veteran. His second-in-command was Brevet Lt Col John Bernard, who had taught Frank much when he had been with the Middlesex volunteers. Like many other Kitchener battalions, it took time to equip the 9th. Uniform was slow in coming and initially they had to make do with obsolete rifles and accoutrements. Frank had a great deal of assistance from the adjutant, Lt Arthur Membry, a former regular colour sergeant of the Somerset Light Infantry. Although he had no active service experience, he proved himself an excellent disciplinarian, especially when it came to bringing the subalterns, whom Frank described as 'wild', under control.[7] It would seem that many of the officers arrived at Donard before they had even applied for commissions and this was only done towards the end of September, with Couchman officially vouching for each individual.[8]

As it was, Frank and his colonel concentrated on 'knocking the beer and politics out of all ranks and building up *esprit-de-corps* in its place on the one hand, while on the other we foster, inculcate, teach and build up the blood lust for the discomfiture of the enemy.'[9] The drink problem was one that would take considerable time to bring under control. With the advent of autumn proper came heavy rain, which collapsed some of the tents. Some members of the battalion took matters into their own hands and set off for home. Frank and the camp commandant rode after them and persuaded them to return to camp with the promise that they would get improved accommodation.[10] This was soon forthcoming.

The other two battalions of 107 Brigade, the 8th and 15th Royal Irish Regiment, were based at Ballykinlar, also in County Down. Here a hutted camp was constructed to accommodate the complete brigade and well before Christmas the 9th and 10th Battalions left their tents at Donard Lodge and moved to join the other two battalions. Ballykinlar proved to be a let-down, however. David Starrett described it as 'a dismal hole, nothing but sandhills hemmed in by Dundrum Bay, a treacherous stretch of water about a mile away.'[11] What had become the 36th (Ulster) Division at the end of October began to come together, including its supporting arms and services, which were all found from Ireland except for the artillery, since the British Government did not want the UVF to possess heavy weapons after the war.* Indeed, the division's artillery was not raised until late spring 1915, and then in London. The divisional commander, Major General C.H. Powell CB of the Indian Army, and former commander of the UVF's North Down Regiment, was especially keen on route marching as a means of developing fitness and each brigade carried out one twenty-five-mile march each week, with the individual battalions carrying out

---

* The same applied to the 16th (Irish) Division, which drew to a significant extent from the Irish Volunteers.

shorter ones. General Powell also arranged for rucksacks to be manufactured in Belfast until regulation knapsacks could be issued and these were worn fully loaded on the march, with ammunition pouches filled with bolts from the shipyards instead of ammunition.[12]

Within the 9th Royal Irish Rifles Frank, at Colonel Ormerod's behest, delivered lectures to the officers, most of whom had no military experience, every weekday evening after dinner in the mess. His first lecture apparently dealt with various topics. He exhorted the officers not to question orders. They must never abandon a position unless ordered to do so. Here he compared Spion Kop in an unfavourable light with Le Cateau. By inference he condemned his stepfather for giving up the hill and stated that the excuses for doing so were 'futile and ill-advised'. Le Cateau, on the other hand, showed that however tired men were they could still fight. He then went on to declare that the officers had to master their fear: 'You must lose your gentle selves. You must steel your hearts and minds to be callous of life or death. That is war.'[13] The training routine otherwise was as Frank described in a letter to Captain Basil Liddell Hart in 1932:

> When we were raising a btn in '14, composed entirely of civilians, officers and men, with a sprinkling of old S.R. [Special Reserve] men and ex-regular Tommies (in Ireland) and the only regulars (officers) being my dear old CO (age 60), the Adjt (a pensioner Colour Sgt) and myself (a Bashi-bazook) when platoon drill had been mastered our routine was (1) Adjt's pde before breakfast(with the CO and myself 'observing' (2) CO's parade (steady drill 1½ hrs 10 to10.30 am after which we wander into the blue not knowing what was going to be done (I never knew myself till I invented the scheme, shouted out the general and special ideas, made the Adjt write the orders and the Coy cdrs give theirs and platoon cdrs explain to their men) and then got going – falling out half the officers as legitimate casualties in the first half hour to repeat the dose with the other half, putting the original half back instead and then – sounding the officers call – changing the whole scheme from A to Z – dinners in cookers and home at 4pm. After mess, discussion of the day's work – followed by a dance until 11pm, bed, sleep, up again.[14]

There was a change in Frank's personal life at this time. On 30 November 1914 Ethel gave birth to another daughter. Hester was born at an address on the Upper Richmond Road, Putney, but according to Mary she was soon handed over to the care of the Thorneycrofts, probably because Ethel could not cope with her. On the other hand, and given the fact that Hester was conceived when Frank was in Belfast, it is possible that he rejected her as being not his. Certainly, Hester is never mentioned in any of his writings. If Mary is to be believed, she and Ethel then immediately went to Scarborough on the Yorkshire coast, where they stayed in a house just below the ruined castle on a headland and next to a Dr Barnado's home for boys. In later life Mary recalled vividly the German Navy's bombardment of Scarborough on 16 December 1914, during which eighteen people were killed.* She remembered

---

* Hartlepool and Whitby were also attacked.

looking not at the German warships, but up into the sky, since she thought that her mother might have been blown up and was floating up above.[15] Frank, however, stated that he took ten days' leave in London after Christmas.[16] Presumably he was with Ethel and Mary, and so their stay at Scarborough was brief. Probably in the New Year Ethel and Mary came out to Ireland on a visit. They stayed with Philip Woods, a brother officer in the battalion and one who had fought in South Africa, and his wife. Starrett met them for the first time in a Belfast hotel and later commented that Ethel 'became my friend, my best friend during those dread war years. A woman who was only happy when she could be doing something for others was Mrs Crozier.'[17] He also recalled returning via London from leave in Belfast. Ethel and Mary took him round the city in a car and then lunched him in a 'flash restaurant'.[18]

In April 1915 the War Office became aware that Frank was wearing two hats. While he was a major in the Royal Irish Rifles, his captaincy in the 5th Royal Irish Fusiliers had not been cancelled. The Military Secretary's branch was not so bothered by this as it was by the fact that Frank had been allowed back in the Army at all. Indeed, it attempted to get Frank removed, but to no avail. All that happened was that his appointment with the 5th Royal Irish Fusiliers was formally cancelled.[19] The muddle was a reflection of the intense pressure that the War Office found itself under as a result of the raising of Kitchener's New Army.

Frank noted that a major problem was that the 36th Division was training in close proximity to where the men's families lived, which provided a major distraction and did little for discipline.[20] He was therefore probably delighted when in July 1915 the division was ordered to England. This move had been expected over the past two months and, indeed, on 8 May it had marched through Belfast in what many thought was its 'farewell to Ulster' parade. It came to rest at Seaford on the Sussex coast. 'It was a healthy place, and the splendid downs behind the town were ideal for tactical exercises.'[21] Many of the officers' wives stayed in the area to be near their husbands, including Ethel, according to Starrett.[22] The 9th Royal Irish Rifles continued to be dogged by discipline problems. Indeed, during its time training in both Ireland and England, no fewer than forty-seven of its members were court-martialled, one of the highest battalion totals in the division.[23] Frank became very concerned about the sexual morals of both officers and men, especially since they were now away from the influence of their families. With the cooperation of the battalion doctor, he was able to ensure that everyone took the necessary precautions against venereal disease after sexual intercourse. Apparently, some of the girls involved also took advantage of this, especially since it was free to them.[24]

At the end of July the 36th (Ulster) Division was inspected by Kitchener. He was very impressed by what he saw and considered the division ready for active service. But, as the Deputy Chief of the General Staff, Sir Archibald Murray, pointed out, musketry and machine-gun courses had not been completed. Furthermore, the training of the artillery was lagging behind. As a result the division moved to Bordon and Bramshott in Hampshire to complete its range firing. Its artillery was replaced by the 1st/1st London Territorial Artillery Brigade, which was handed over by 56th London Division. Some senior officers were sent out to France to carry out brief attachments to the 5th and 18th Divisions. While they were away the division received a new commander. Although Powell had done well in forming and training the Ulster Division, he was considered too old for active service and his place was taken on 14 September by Oliver Nugent, who came from four months of arduous brigade command in the Ypres Salient. He had been very involved with organising the UVF in Cavan while on half pay, but was not prepared to allow Ulster politics to infiltrate his division.

Just two weeks after Nugent took over the division was inspected by the King. It was the sign that it was now finally set for France and, indeed, within a couple of days it was on the move. Frank said that both Ethel and his mother were there to see him off, while Starrett recalled that Ethel and Mary gave him a watch as a leaving present.[25]

The 9th Royal Irish Rifles went by train from Bramshott to Folkestone and then crossed the Channel to Boulogne, arriving there late at night. After a march up a steep hill out of the port they arrived at a rest camp. Next morning it was discovered that a member of the battalion had succeeded in breaking into the bar of the ship that had brought them over to France to purloin some bottles. Frank recompensed the ship and imposed stoppages on those who had been on the part of the deck nearest to the bar in order to obtain reimbursement.[26] Not surprisingly the men were confined to camp throughout that day, 4 October, before boarding a train at midnight. This took them to Flesselles, from where they marched to Vignacourt, which lies some ten miles north-west of Amiens. They spent a couple of days here training and being inspected. Frank claimed that the daughter of the house in which he was billeted attempted to seduce him.[27] It was thus just as well that on 9 October the battalion set out for the trenches. It was to be given its induction in trench warfare by the regulars of 4th Division. First to go into the trenches were C and D Companies, the former with the 1st Hampshires and the latter with 1st Rifle Brigade. D Company had an uneventful time, apart from experiencing a few *Minenwerfer* bombs. C Company, on the other hand, had five wounded from a bombardment and then had a man captured and one wounded when a patrol with the Hampshires was surprised by a German patrol. On 14 October, after three days in the trenches, they were relieved by A and B Companies. They had a relatively uneventful time and suffered a total of three casualties, of which one was accidental. The battalion then marched back to Vignacourt, which was reached on 19 October.[28]

Meanwhile, General Nugent now had time to gauge the quality of his division. He found many of the senior officers wanting. In particular, he was unimpressed by the commander of 107 Brigade and six days after the division arrived in France, and while the brigade was undergoing its trench warfare tutelage, he informed Couchman that he was sending him home. In his place came Brigadier General William Withycombe, who had commanded the 2nd King's Own Yorkshire Light Infantry in 1914 and would prove himself a competent and popular commander. Withycombe could not, however, wave a magic wand over his new brigade and it would take time to lick it into shape. During October alone, the brigade had no fewer than ten of its members up before Field General courts-martial, while the other two brigades had just one man each. No fewer than five of 107 Brigade's miscreants came from the 9th Royal Irish Rifles, and what was especially worrying was that three of them were senior ranks – two sergeants and a CSM. The others were a corporal and a rifleman. In all cases drink had been the problem.[29] Frank recalled that the cause was bad brandy, which the culprits had drunk 'as if they were drinking Guinness in their native land'.[30] He was, according to his batman, understandably furious with them: 'My! How he rated them, and how they wilted as he told them their character and destination.'[31] All officers in the brigade were summoned to a dressing down by General Nugent, who was appalled. As he wrote to his wife:

> The Belfast Brigade is awful. They have absolutely no discipline and their officers are awful. I am very much disturbed about them.
>
> I don't think they are fit for service and I should be very sorry to have to trust them. It is all due to putting a weak man in command of the brigade to start with and giving commissions to men of the wrong class.[32]

All this did, however, solve one problem for Nugent. In the aftermath of Loos it had been decided that the New Army divisions needed stiffening and hence they were each to exchange one of their brigades for a regular Army one on a temporary basis. The Ulster Division was to carry this out with its trench warfare mentor, 4th Division, and Nugent had no hesitation in selecting 107 Brigade to leave the Division. He announced this when he addressed the brigade's officers on 1 November, which, in Frank's words, was 'the complete example of what can be said by the powerful to the powerless in the shortest space of time possible, consistent with the regulations of words and space for breathing, in the most offensive, sarcastic, and uncompromising manner possible.'[33] Four days later the brigade came under the command of 4th Division. According to Wilfrid Spender, formerly on the UVF staff and now Nugent's GSO2, 107 Brigade was 'furious' at Nugent and went to their new division 'swearing that they don't want to come back and will do their best not to if he commands.'[34]

Initially, the 8th and 15th Royal Irish Rifles were sent to 10 and 11 Brigades respectively, while 107 Brigade received the regular 1st Royal Irish Fusiliers and 1st Rifle Brigade, and the Territorial 2nd Monmouths. This situation remained until just before Christmas, when the brigade reverted to its original battalions. The trench sector the brigade occupied was in the Auchonvillers area between Hébuterne and Albert. The 9th Royal Irish Rifles soon got into the rhythm of five or six days in the trenches, alternating with time in support. Lt Col Ormerod was not well and Frank did his best to take as much of his work on his shoulders as he could, but on 10 December he was finally evacuated sick with pneumonia and Frank took over as Acting CO. Philip Woods, with whom Ethel had stayed in Ireland and who had served with the South African Constabulary during 1901–02 and then been a Belfast textile designer before being commissioned as a lieutenant in the 9th Royal Irish Rifles in early September 1914, became second-in-command. Others of the older fraternity were also finding the trenches detrimental to their health. Arthur Membry, who had done so much to help Frank instil the necessary discipline among the junior officers, had fallen sick with lumbago at the beginning of November. He was succeeded as adjutant by a regular, Lt Ernest Hine, who had been commissioned into the East Lancashires in May 1915 from being a lance sergeant in the Grenadier Guards. He would remain in post until the end of September 1917.*

---

* Curiously, at some stage during 1917 he changed his initials from E.E (Ebenezer) to W.H.

Drink continued to be a problem. On the night of 5 December, very shortly before he assumed command, Frank was carrying out a tour of the battalion's trenches. He reached the sector manned by George Gaffikin's B Company, where there was much excitement. What had happened was that the Germans had surprised one of Gaffikin's patrols and captured three men. Gaffikin had therefore decided to send over two platoons to get them back. Recognising the craziness of this, Frank stood the men down and told them to get on with their normal work. He then went to Gaffikin's dug-out and found him fast asleep in a drunken stupor. His second-in-command pleaded on his behalf and so Frank returned to Battalion HQ. Next morning he went back to B Company and got Gaffikin to pledge that he would go on the wagon for as long as he was with the battalion, a pledge that he maintained.[35] A subaltern whom Frank calls Felucan in *Brass Hat* was sent home with his nerves in shreds. 'Wrongly based on whisky in civilian life, he has resorted to it again in order to keep going. He is not drunk. He can never get drunk! A bottle of whisky is found in his valise. His nerves are awful. He is quite unsafe and a bad example. We are well rid of him, though I am sorry for him, as I like him.' In truth, he was probably Ernest Feneran, a thirty-seven-year-old whose only previous military experience had been commanding a UVF half company. Drink, however, continued to get the better of him and during the first half of 1917 he was twice court-martialled while serving with a Home Service garrison battalion of the Royal Irish Regiment. The second resulted in him being dismissed from the Army.[36] Drink, too, continued to be a problem with the men. Willie Montgomery, another of Frank's company commanders, wrote home on 13 December 1915 that he had refused to pay his men because of their drunkenness. The result was that ' they are now blacklisting all the doubtful boys with a view to taking care of them when within a mile of drink.'[37]

Yet 107 Brigade thrived under the tutelage of 4th Division. Writing to his wife in January 1916, Wilfrid Spender recounted:

> Yesterday I had a long listen to a gunner who was holding forth on the infantry and how well they did. He described how one brigade had last week surprised the Germans by advancing out of their trenches at night, crossing their wire in force, and building a new line of entrenchments 100 yards closer to the Germans. None but wild Irishmen would have dreamt of doing such a thing, he said, and I pricked up my ears, and beamed when he added (without knowing who I was) 'I think the Brigade – the 107th – is about the best out here.'[38]

Looking, however, at the relevant 4th Division war diaries, it does not seem that the brigade did anything particular, except on one occasion. This was on the night of 18–19 January, when the 8th and 10th Royal Irish Rifles successfully dug and wired a new forward trench without the Germans detecting it.[39] Frank, however, certainly respected Major General the Hon. William Lambton and the staff of 4th Division: He was 'a Guardsman with the "Guards touch". I believe I am right in saying from the beginning to the end 4th Divisional Headquarters were streets ahead of any other formation in France, save the Guards, and accordingly got more than most out of their men.'[40]

Frank himself was confirmed in command on 1 January 1916 and promoted to lieutenant colonel. According to a letter written by Wilfrid Spender to Sir James

Edmonds, the Official Historian of the war on the Western Front, there was some hesitation on General Nugent's part. He was concerned about Frank's 'roughness and the ruthless way in which he handled his men.' He apparently spoke to Spender, who believed that Frank's 'courage and leadership would counterbalance his other disabilities.'[41] John Stewart-Moore of the 15th Royal Irish Rifles, which alternated with the 9th in the trenches, was also highly critical of Frank in the context of officer's patrols, for which he saw no good purpose: 'Colonel Crozier who commanded the 9th Rifles was particularly keen on sending out patrols all to no purpose. He had the reputation of being a callous and overbearing martinet.'[42]* Yet Willie Montgomery enclosed to his parents a note that Frank had written to him on 23 December while he was in the trenches, but expecting to be relieved. It was concerning work that still needed to be done on the trenches. Frank wanted Willie to stay behind after his company had been relieved and supervise this work. He did not put it as an order, but was asking a favour. 'I know you have already had a hell of a time, but I am sure that if you direct the crowd a bit of energy would be saved; and at the same time you can by delegating jobs to others get some sleep in C [Company] dugout.'[43] This is hardly the 'callous and overbearing martinet.' On the other hand, he was often clearly not willing to let his subordinates get on with it. David Starrett wrote:

> You could not keep my man out of the front lines. Holding a long staff to grope for holes he'd wade waist deep anywhere and everywhere, his trench coat bulging out over the tide, and picking up things on the way like a ship collects barnacles. Comical, he looked, his short sturdiness almost hidden, and only his angry face being plainly seen. But twas in his mind that where the boys went he should go. They were then wearing skin coats, and many a joke we had about the shepherd seeking his sheep. You see, he trusted his officers and men but he left nothing to chance.[44]

Starrett also recalled that Frank 'was always wanting baccy, and sometimes it had to be scrounged with the skill that burglars are supposed to use in other pursuits. I've never seen a man in my life smoke so much – the pipe seemed never out of his mouth.' Frank did not like cigarettes, however. His other passion was tea: 'Tea and tobacco at hand, he was happy.'[45]

Terry Duffin, the staff captain of 107 Brigade, writing to his father at the end of January 1916, recalled:

> … we still remain with our present Divn but go back for a rest somewhere … Naturally we are all glad that we are staying with our present Division, but rather surprised, as we were only told 3 days ago that we were to go back to the original one, which would have been a very unpopular move for all ranks.[46]

---

* It should be borne in mind that Stewart-Moore did not record these memories until January 1976, many years after the events. Also, long before then Frank's name had become much vilified in Ulster for reasons which will become apparent.

In fact, on 7 February 36th Division relieved 4th Division, which was withdrawn for a rest, and 107 Brigade returned to its parent formation. The Ulster Division now occupied the sector from the Mailly-Maillet–Serre road in the north down to the River Ancre, with 107 Brigade initially responsible for the northern half.

Frank, however, had other concerns on his mind. On 1 February 1916, one of his subalterns, Arthur Annandale, was found guilty by a Field General court-martial of conduct to the prejudice of good order and military discipline 'in that he, in the fire trenches, when his commanding officer was discussing certain military matters with him, left the dug-out in which the discussion was taking place without permission and did not return.' Frank had, some time previously, organised for this officer, whom he called Rochdale in *Brass Hat*, to go to Amiens for ten days in order to get cured of gonorrhoea. He had visited Annandale and his company commander in their dug-out and they were discussing a new type of German rifle grenade, an example of which they had just obtained. At that moment a German trench mortar bombardment began and Annandale bolted and was eventually discovered, come daylight, in a disused French dug-out. The court had sentenced Annandale to be dismissed from His Majesty's service, but did recommend mercy to be shown on account of Annandale's health, noting that he had been hospitalised four times since he had been in France. In one instance a mortar bomb had exploded near him, which affected his nervous system. As a result the sentence was not confirmed and, according to Frank, an attempt was made to return him to the battalion, which Frank successfully resisted. Annandale was therefore sent back to England and in August 1916 relinquished his commission on the grounds of ill-health, specifically neurasthenia and myopia.[47]

Twelve days after Annandale's court-martial, Rifleman James Crozier of the 9th Royal Irish Rifles was up in front of another court-martial and charged with desertion. The battalion had gone into the trenches near Serre on 31 January. Crozier had been ordered to remain in a dug-out until it was his turn to do sentry duty, but he had then vanished. Four days later he was apprehended some twenty-five miles behind the front without cap, badge or equipment. At his trial Crozier said that he had not been feeling well and could not remember what happened, although he did recall rifle grenades exploding near him. The court found him guilty and, after looking at his conduct sheet, which revealed that he had been twice found guilty of absence without leave, sentenced him to death. In Rifleman Crozier's case there would be no leniency. This was partly because of his bad conduct sheet, but also because two other riflemen in the 9th Royal Irish Rifles had been found guilty of desertion the previous month, but had had their sentences commuted to two years' hard labour. Indeed, Frank was conscious of this when he forwarded his comments on the sentence, although he mentioned only one rifleman. He observed that his namesake was fully aware of what had befallen this man when he decided to leave the trenches. He also considered Crozier of 'no value' as a fighting soldier and 'a shirker'. General Withycombe pointed out that it was impossible to obtain medical evidence of Crozier's state when he absconded, and that the sentence should be carried out as a deterrent. He did, however, observe that the battalion's discipline was 'good for a service battalion'. Oliver Nugent pointed out that there had been a number of cases of desertion in 107 Brigade. The sentence was upheld and duly carried out on 27 February 1916.[48]

According to Frank, he ensured that Crozier was drunk when he faced the firing squad. He was also very upset by the fact that Annandale had got off without a blemish to his name, even though his crime was the same as Rifleman Crozier's. Indeed, he later claimed that the Adjutant General's branch at GHQ tried to 'break' him for objecting to Annandale being let off and that he would not have survived without the support of Nugent and Withycombe. He was also very remorseful over Crozier's death, although at the time he was unequivocal in demanding the death sentence. There was, however, a footnote. Some time after the end of the war Frank apparently ran across Annandale in a night club. The latter had been drinking and was offensive to him. Frank asked the commissionaire, an ex-Guardsman, what he would do to a soldier who had run away from the line. He replied that he would knock his head off, which is what he did.[49]

At the beginning of March the division extended its front to take in the Thiepval sector south of the Ancre, with 109 Brigade taking over the new sector. The 9th Royal Irish Rifles continued to occupy the northernmost part of the divisional front, alternating with the 15th Royal Irish Rifles. When out of the line they were billeted in the village of Beaussart. One day, the house which battalion HQ used was burnt, David Starrett being the culprit. A court of inquiry into the cause was convened. John Stewart-Moore recorded:

> President of the court was my friend Captain Patton. He had a strong sense of humour of his own peculiar brand with a strong infusion of wrong. Colonel Crozier, the tyrannical commander of the 9th Rifles, was of course officially responsible for the fire but it was not really his fault. Patton knowing and disliking Crozier's reputation seized the opportunity to put him on the spot by a close cross-examination.[50]

There is no evidence that Frank received any form of admonishment and on 29 March the battalion was relieved and began what was to be a lengthy period out of the trenches. It was based in the village of Puchevillers, some twelve miles north-north-east of Amiens, until 20 April, working on a railway, as well as carrying out company training. It then moved eastwards to Forceville, which lies seven miles north-west of Albert. It continued to provide working parties there, but also practised attacks against dummy trenches. Then, on 8 May, the 9th Royal Irish Rifles moved to Martinsart, even closer to the front line, and began to provide working parties for the trenches in Thiepval Wood. During this time Frank organised a battalion mess for the officers and allowed one officer per company leave in the nearest town from after lunch until midnight. Married officers could take leave in Paris to meet their wives and the men were given as good a time as possible, with sport every afternoon and the laying on of concert parties. Frank was, as ever, concerned about venereal disease and got the battalion doctor to lecture each company and make arrangements for its prevention among both officers and men.[51] Finally, on 30 May the battalion relieved the 15th Royal Irish Rifles in these very trenches. The situation now was that 107 Brigade held the division's sector, with 108 Brigade in support and 109 Brigade training. But, so as to enable both these brigades to train together, at the beginning of June a brigade of 49th Division relieved 108 Brigade.

All this was, of course, in preparation for the great Anglo-French offensive which was soon to be mounted astride the River Somme. Even the most newly-joined rifleman could not have failed to sense what was in the offing. The establishment of ammunition dumps, fresh camps, water points and the like were clear indicators that a major attack was soon to take place. In the trenches themselves life was relatively quiet, apart from occasional German trench mortar bombardments. As noted in the war diary, the battalion was also mentioned by Sir Douglas Haig for its good work in his despatch dated 19 May, the first he had submitted since becoming commander-in-chief the previous December. It was the only unit in 36th Division so honoured and this reflected well on Frank's performance as commanding officer.

The 9th Rifles did two tours in the Thiepval Wood trenches, providing working parties in the wood when they were out of the line. Then, on 23 June, they marched to Léalvillers, three miles west of Forceville, where they spent a day cleaning up before carrying out two days of practice attacks. On the 27th they marched back to Forceville. In the meantime, the preparatory bombardment had begun on the 24th, with the intention of launching the attack on 29 June. The previous day the battalion was to have moved up to assembly trenches in Aveluy Wood. This was cancelled after it was decided to prolong the bombardment for a further forty-eight hours and so Frank and his men marched back to Léalvillers, where they rested for a day.

The 36th Division was part of Sir Thomas Morland's* X Corps and was its left-hand division, with 32nd Division on its right. Morland's task was to secure the high ground above the village of Thiepval. This represented the north-western part of the Pozières Ridge, the main initial British objective. The 32nd Division was to capture the village of Thiepval and then secure the spur beyond it. The Ulster Division, on the other hand, had two tasks. It had to cooperate with the VIII Corps attack on Beaumont Hamel on the other side of the Ancre, which meant that two battalions would have to attack there. On the east bank the initial assault would be made by 109 Brigade on the right with the object of reaching the Grandcourt-Thiepval road to the north of Thiepval. On the left, since 108 Brigade had to commit two of its battalions to the attack on the west bank of the river, it was given the 15th Rifles from 107 Brigade. The mission of 108 Brigade was to secure the north-west corner of Schwaben Redoubt, a strongpoint consisting of a number of machine-gun emplacements and trenches and lying north of Thiepval itself The remainder of this position was 109 Brigade's responsibility. A further task for 108 Brigade was to clear the remaining ground up to the Ancre of Germans. In support was 107 Brigade with its remaining three battalions. Once the other two brigades had achieved their objectives it was to pass through and seize the high ground beyond the Schwaben Redoubt.

On 30 June Frank and his men moved to the trenches in Aveluy Wood. He recalled:

I spend much of the night with Colonel Bernard [CO 10 R Irish Rifles] resting against a tree trunk, eating sandwiches and drinking tea. He is dubious about the success of the assault on Thiepval village by the division on our right. 'If

---

* Morland was known to Frank, since he had been a senior officer in the WAFF during Frank's tout in West Africa.

that fails,' he says, 'where are we on the flank?' We agree, if we see, on marching through Thiepval Wood, that Thiepval village is still in enemy hands, we shall meet in no man's land, to alter our plans, if necessary. If only one of us arrives there, then it will be up to him to carry on for both battalions. If neither of us gets as far, then the senior officers present will carry on.

He then attempted to get some sleep, but without success and wandered around talking to some of his men. At dawn the company cookers began to prepare breakfast for the men and Frank cadged a mess tin of tea from one of them.[52] The battalion then fell in and moved across the Ancre to the western fringes of Thiepval Wood. Reaching these at 6.30am, one hour before Zero Hour, the 9th Rifles waited on a track called Speyside.

At 7.30am 108 and 109 Brigades began their assault. Their leading battalions had moved out into no man's land just before Zero Hour and this gave them a head start. They were through the German front line within minutes, catching the defenders as they were coming up out of their deep dug-outs. They pressed on and, as they did so, the 9th and 10th Rifles moved out of Thiepval Wood, their COs with them, which was in direct contravention of General Nugent's order that no commanding officer was to go further forward than Thiepval Wood.[53] They took up position in a sunken road which ran in front of the foremost British trenches. To Rifleman Malcolm McKee, Frank looked like a tiger and McKee had a 'feeling of glee that we were in the battle together.'[54] Frank looked out for Herbert Bernard, who was going to give the signal to advance, but could not see him (he had been killed). Therefore, at 8.05am he gave the order for both battalions to advance. Having seen them on their way Frank made for his battle HQ, accompanied by Ernest Hine. It immediately became clear, however, that 32nd Division had failed to capture Thiepval village and 107 Brigade now began to suffer casualties from fire from there.[55] Meanwhile 109 Brigade had been fighting for the Schwaben Redoubt. The German resistance was still stiff and it was inevitable that 107 Brigade was drawn in.

In the meantime, although Nugent had established himself in a tall tree with a view of the German lines, battlefield obscuration meant that it was difficult for him to see what was happening and information from his forward troops was sparse. He had therefore contacted Morland at 8.30am asking him whether he should commit 107 Brigade or not. He received answer forty minutes later telling him to hold it where it was. Morland was aware that the corps on his left and right had met with little success and did not want to find himself out on a limb. By then it was, of course, all too late, since Frank had jumped the gun. As it was, the Schwaben Redoubt had been captured, but 109 Brigade's casualties were by now very heavy, and two of the battalions were each left with just one junior officer standing. The Belfast Brigade was keen to push on to its objective, the German second line on the ridge. The laid down Zero Hour for this attack was 10am, but the Rifles got themselves into no man's land too early and were hit by the British barrage. Corporal Lloyd of the 9th Rifles recalled: 'We were pinned down in the open just outside the German wire which was covering their second line. It was just Hell; the British artillery were at us, the German artillery were at us, and rifle and machine-gun fire as well.'[56] Furthermore, only company commanders were available, as a result of Nugent's order, and the

9th Rifles had lost two of theirs, leaving just Major George Gaffikin and Captain Willie Montgomery on their feet. The former took charge. Some forty men managed to get into the German trenches, but were driven out by grenades. Frank was kept abreast of what was happening by runners and he was able to gather that Gaffikin was now digging in, with his forward positions between the German first and second lines. He also met demands for more ammunition, especially Lewis Gun pans and grenades. By now, Morland was beginning to deploy his reserve formation, 49th Division, and its 146 Brigade was moving in behind 36th Division. This was as well, because the Germans were now counterattacking from both flanks. Frank sent his intelligence officer up to find out what was happening. He saw both Gaffikin and Montgomery, who said that they could hold out provided that the supply of grenades was maintained, but they were much troubled by machine-gun fire from Thiepval village. Frank sent him back to Brigade HQ to report. He also sent messages to Gaffikin stating that help from 146 Brigade would shortly be on its way.

As it happened, two battalions from 146 Brigade were committed to yet another fruitless attack on Thiepval village and just two companies were made available to reinforce the remnants of 107 and 109 Brigades. Frank learned of this when his intelligence officer, 2nd Lt Christopher Harding, returned from Brigade HQ at 6.30pm. Frank now sent him to intercept the two 146 Brigade companies, which were part of the 1st/4th West Yorkshires, and direct them to the 'best place'. Harding returned at 9.40pm. He had positioned the West Yorkshires, although they never linked up with the 9th Rifles, and reported that there was heavy grenade fighting in progress. Ammunition and water were, however, needed urgently and Frank arranged for a carrying party to take these up. Sadly, though, Harding said that George Gaffikin had been seriously wounded (he died later that night) and that Montgomery was now in command.[57] The truth was that the Germans had deployed additional reinforcements and the pressure was becoming too great for the now-exhausted Ulstermen to bear. Montgomery and Major Peacocke, second-in-command of the 9th Inniskillings, attempted to rally them, but they began to drift back towards the British lines. At one point Montgomery apparently shot at a group of men who were moving back, but it did not have much effect.[58] Realising that nothing more could be done, he himself came back and reported to Frank at 10.30pm. According to Frank, he was in a state of collapse and had also been wounded in the head. Frank therefore sent him down to Brigade HQ, expecting not to see him for some time, but Montgomery rejoined on the night of 3 July.[59]

During the night 107 Brigade received orders to attack the Schwaben Redoubt again and was given three battalions of 148 Brigade. Only one of these turned up and so General Withycombe proposed that such an attack be cancelled on the grounds that it would be difficult to organise during the hours of darkness and come daylight the attackers would be totally exposed to fire from Thiepval village. Nugent supported this view and Morland accepted it. When daylight did come, however, an observation post reported that there were some British troops still in the German lines. As a result Nugent ordered Withycombe to send across reinforcements to strengthen and consolidate the trenches still occupied. At 11am he issued orders to his battalions. He placed Frank in charge of the operation and stated that all available officers and men from all four Rifles battalions were under his command for it. The idea was to block all the German communication trenches and also bring up more grenades and small arms ammunition. Frank was also to appoint an officer to report on the situation as it developed. He intended to lead the party and do this himself, but Withycombe apparently stopped him and Philip Woods, his second-in-command, went instead. Frank managed to gather a total of 360 men, sixty men from the 10th Rifles and 100 each from the other three battalions. The party eventually set off at 2pm and fifteen minutes later a prearranged artillery barrage was laid down to keep the Germans at bay. The 15th Rifles suffered from German shellfire while on their way up, but otherwise the men managed to get across into the original German front-line trench. The Germans now woke up and began to bombard the British trenches and no man's land. Nevertheless, Woods's party managed to hold on to the lodgement. They were helped by two parties from the divisional pioneer battalion, the 16th Rifles, bringing across further supplies of ammunition and grenades under heavy fire. One group which Woods found fighting on the extreme left of the position was a party of some thirty 7th West Yorkshires under Corporal George Sanders, which had been fighting throughout the previous night, had rescued some Ulstermen, and taken some prisoners.* The relief, though, was at hand. The plan was that 36th Division, or what remained of it, would be relieved by 49th Division that night. In particular, 148 Brigade was to relieve 107 Brigade, with Withycombe having already given 109 Brigade permission to withdraw in the early afternoon. He then issued his orders at 7pm, laying down that the relief of his brigade was to be handled by Frank in conjunction with the CO of the 4th York and Lancasters. The most important element was the relief of Woods and his men, which would be carried out by two companies of the York and Lancasters at 11pm. Unfortunately, only one of these companies turned up on time and so Woods was only able to send back half of his men and still had to repulse several bombing attacks during the night. The other company did eventually arrive, but it was not until 10.40am that Frank was able to inform Withycombe that the relief was complete.[60]

The Brigade withdrew to the village of Martinsart to lick its wounds. Frank later said that one of his officers had fled from the trenches and was found asleep in the village. With the Annandale case in mind, coupled with the fact that there were no surviving witnesses, Frank did not seek a court-martial. The officer was returned to Britain and resigned his commission.[61] The division as a whole had suffered some 5,500 killed, wounded and missing. The 9th Rifles had five officers and over 100 other ranks killed.[62] As David Starrett put it, 'we were dazed for a day or so, Bob Martin [Frank's orderly] and I shadowed the colonel, who could not rest sitting or standing.'[63] Others, too, felt the losses. Willie Montgomery wrote in a letter home: 'Mother would have cried and quite possibly you also, when I called the remnant of my coy. to attention … Not a few of the men cried and I cried. A hell of an hysterical exhibition it was. It is a very small coy. Now. I took 115 other ranks and 4 officers (incl myself) into action. I am the only officer and only 34 other ranks are with me

---

* Sanders survived the Somme and was awarded the VC for his work on 1–2 July. He was later commissioned into the West Yorkshires and won an MC during the fighting around Mt Kemmel in April 1918, during which he was wounded and captured.

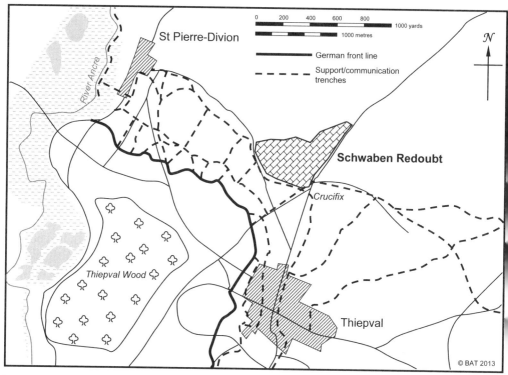

Map 3: The Assault on Thiepval, 1 July 1916.

now out of the 115.'[64] There were, too, the letters of condolence to be written. The company commanders usually did them, but Frank certainly wrote one, which was to the widow of CSM Joseph Martin, whose company commander, Capt J.H. Berry, had been wounded and taken prisoner. While many such letters spoke of the victim's gallantry, Frank's letter took another tack: 'Your husband was killed just as the battalion was about to deploy from the wood for the attack … He had persevered to remain with the battalion all this winter, in spite of being ill, and when he came back from hospital it was only because he knew it was his duty to be in the firing line, come what may.'[65] Some compensation was to be had in the fact that the Ulster Division had done all that was asked of it and more, and it could be justifiably argued that it had been forced to give up much of its initial territorial gain because of the lack of progress by the neighbouring divisions. Acknowledgement of this was reflected in the honours and awards to the division. Among those won by the 9th Rifles was a DSO for Montgomery, but nothing for Woods, whom Frank certainly recommended, or for Frank himself. He explained this as follows: 'I saw the initial recommendation for a DSO for me, made out by Withycombe, scrawled across in red by Nugent (a great friend of mine), "Rank disobedience of orders, should be court-martialled"!!!'[66] This, of course, referred to Frank accompanying his men into no man's land on 1 July. Withycombe did, however, recommend him for command of a brigade, which Nugent clearly did not block.[67]

The immediate priority now was rebuilding the division. This was to be done in Flanders, to where it moved by train during the latter half of the second week in July. The 12th of July was celebrated by 107 Brigade , which had just detrained, marching past General Nugent and his staff, each man wearing a marigold in his cap as an Orange token and the band playing King William's March. The division was given a training area west of St Omer and it was there that fresh drafts began to arrive to replace the losses. Indeed, the Division was to receive nearly 200 officers and over 2,000 men.[68] Some of the replacements lacked something of their predecessors. Willie Montgomery received a draft of 'undesirables from the 3rd Battalion [Royal Irish Rifles] – mostly old soldiers.' They tried some old soldier's tricks on Willie and so he instructed his CSM to administer beatings to those who merited it. This was, of course, illegal, but he was reluctant to make entries on their conduct sheets.[69] One has the suspicion that Frank approved of this course of action.

Before July was out the division was back in the trenches. It was 108 Brigade which entered them first, relieving elements of 20th Division on 23 July. Then 109 Brigade came up on the right, relieving battalions of 41st Division, while 107 Brigade relieved 108 Brigade. The divisional sector ran from the Neuve Eglise-Warneton road to that running from Wulverghem to Messines. Frank liked the new sector: 'The surroundings are distinctly pleasant, and the weather is good. Our headquarters, when in the line, are actually in a farmhouse, free from enemy observation and therefore quiet. I can ride my horse up to the very door, and almost walk up to the line, unobserved, without entering the trenches.'[70] The division was now in Plumer's Second Army and its policy was to keep the Germans opposite tied down to such an extent that they would be dissuaded from sending divisions down to the Somme. This meant active trench warfare in the shape of frequent artillery and trench mortar barrages, although the former were restricted because of a need to ration ammunition, and trench-raiding. This suited Frank perfectly. He saw his mission as preparing his battalion for this next major attack and raiding was an excellent way to do it. First, though, the battalion needed to gain an accurate knowledge of no man's land, especially where gaps in the wire were and German sentries positioned. Frank organised nightly reconnaissance patrols and even went on some himself. On one occasion, one of his young officers, 2nd Lt Adolphe Amy (Frank calls him Army in *Brass Hat*), claimed to have discovered a gap in the wire. Frank did not believe him and ordered Amy to show it to him. The young subaltern was unable to locate any gap, but he and Frank did identify a German sentry. Frank invited Amy to breakfast and then gave him a dressing down. Amy volunteered to go on patrol again the following night so as to prove himself to his colonel. The war diary entry for 18 September tells what happened. '2/Lt Amy went out on patrol tonight. Near the German wire he went on ahead & came unexpected on party of enemy in a shell hole. He was shot & killed. The patrol attempted to rescue his body but were driven off. A strong patrol immediately went out from our lines but enemy had retired.'[71] Indeed, this patrolling was a nerve-wracking business and only three nights later another young officer was badly wounded.

These patrols did, however, enable some successful trench raids to take place. The 9th Rifles mounted their first on the night of 15/16 September. It took place while the battalion was out of the line and was carried out by 2nd Lt E.J.F. Holland, with two other officers and forty-one other ranks. They passed through a previously identified gap in the German wire and reached the front line. Spotting six Germans, 2nd Lt Crawford knocked over two with his revolver and jumped on a third, who was made prisoner. The remaining Germans fled. They came across two sentries. 2nd Lt Kane killed one with his revolver and grabbed his pack. The raiders then dropped grenades into the dug-outs. The Germans now began to react, sending along their own bombers. Rifleman Kidd, who had a reputation as a long-distance grenade thrower, kept them at bay and the raiders then withdrew, cutting two sets of telephone wires as they did so. This highly successful enterprise, which the division's historian judged the best of all those conducted during September–November 1916, was carried out at the cost of just three men wounded.[72] Frank would have certainly been delighted, and was even more satisfied to take temporary command of the brigade a week later while Withycombe took some leave. As Willie Montgomery remarked, 'I think it is a case of "coming events."' He hoped that Frank would take him with him when he got his brigade, but experienced company commanders like himself 'don't get away that easily.' Willie complained that he had not even been sent on a course:

> I asked the CO the other day when I was going on one and he said "Go on a course indeed! Go to hell!" – a nice polite friendly person he is, but soldier [sic] – He did [sic] end up by telling me that any time I really needed a course I could go on any one I liked for just the asking. Mother will know this CO knows men because that 'just for the asking' is a perfect masterpiece. The little ugly devil just plays with the inside of us and that is what has made this Battalion what it is. Those he cannot play on he doesn't keep ...'[73]

Frank did, however, send Philip Woods away to attend the Senior Officers' Course at Aldershot, designed to prepare officers for battalion command. He also welcomed the return of Horace Haslitt, one of the 9th Rifles' original company commanders, who had been badly wounded, losing an eye, at the beginning of the year. However, when Frank went off on five days' leave in mid-October he arranged for Montgomery to be in temporary command of the battalion. Montgomery was then promoted major and second-in-command of the 9th Rifles.

On 19 November, just a few days after Montgomery's promotion, Frank received momentous news from Teddy Duffin, still 107 Brigade's staff captain, that he had been appointed commander of 119 Brigade in 40th Division as a brigadier general and that he was to take up his appointment the following day. Frank himself later claimed that he first had intimation of his promotion from his mother, who had been told by General William Peyton, Haig's Military Secretary and an old friend of Alec Thorneycroft, having served under him in South Africa, that Frank 'had been very well reported on.'

> My officers were genuinely glad and genuinely sorry. And it was with a heart full of both pride and regret that I went up the line immediately to say good-bye to everyone, and to thank them one and all individually for my promotion, for I was not, and am not, so silly as to think that a regimental soldier gains his own promotion, because his men gain it for him.[74]

David Starrett recalled that most men wanted to go with Frank. 'For the Colonel's bark was worse than his bite. He never asked them to do what he himself was afraid to do.'[75]

Early the following morning Frank, accompanied by Starrett, left the 9th Rifles and went to HQ 36th Division to see Nugent, at the latter's behest. He advised Frank to treat his brigade like a large battalion, but not to forget 'the oddments'. Nugent than asked Frank who should command the battalion in his place. He recommended Haslitt, with Montgomery as second-in-command. That he did not recommend Woods was because he was not popular in Orange circles for reasons that have never been clear.[76] As it was, it was Woods who was selected to command, presumably because he had done the Aldershot course and was more experienced than Haslitt. After seeing Nugent, Frank set out back to the Somme to join his new division.

Chapter Seven

The Welsh Bantams: 1917

The 40th Division had had a frustrating infancy. It had originally been formed in September 1915 as the second of the two Bantam divisions (the other being 35th Division), drawing on men below the standard minimum height of five feet three inches for the Army. By this time volunteers were available in ever-decreasing numbers and some of them were physically of low quality, especially the Bantams, whose physiques often did nothing to compensate for their lack of inches. They were only accepted for service because of lax medical examinations. The division found itself with brigades of Scots, English and Welsh Bantams respectively, 119 Brigade being made up of the Welsh and originally intended to be part of Lloyd George's Welsh Army Corps. This never came to fruition because of the lack of sufficient manpower. Many of the division's men were found to be medically unfit and they had to be weeded out and replaced. As a result two of the brigades, 120 and 121, lost much of their Bantam character and only Frank's brigade could consider itself a true Bantam brigade. The problem with the physical quality of its soldiers meant that the 40th Division was the last New Army formation to cross to France, doing so at the end of May 1916.

The 35th Bantam Division suffered badly on the Somme during July and August and was not considered to have performed well. It was perhaps because of this that the 40th Division escaped taking part in the battle. It was deployed to the Loos sector until late October, when it moved to the area north of Doullens. It was during this move, which was done on foot, that Frank joined 119 Brigade, having apparently been warned by the Divisional GSO1 that it was the worst brigade in France.[1] He was therefore going to have his work cut out to make it efficient. Luckily, though, the division was to be out of the line for a time.

Major General Harold Ruggles-Brise had commanded 40th Division from its formation. He was a Guardsman, who had been commandant of the School of Musketry at Hythe when war was declared. He had then commanded in a brigade in 7th Division before being wounded during the First Battle of Ypres. Frank wrote that he was 'a sincere and good friend' who gave him a 'free hand' to run his brigade.[2] The previous commander of 119 Brigade was Brigadier General Charles Cunliffe-Owen, a Gunner who had only been in post since mid-August 1916, and Frank found himself its fourth commander, a clear indication that it was a problem brigade.

Frank's two staff officers were his brigade major and staff captain. The former was Captain Arthur Granville Soames* of the Coldstream Guards, who had gone to war as the staff captain of 4th Brigade in the 2nd Infantry Division in August

---

* He was the grandfather of Nicholas Soames, the Conservative politician of today.

1914. He had remained in this post until October 1916, when he was appointed brigade major of 119 Brigade. He had been in the job less than a month when Frank arrived. In contrast, Percy Hone, the staff captain, was a 1914 volunteer who had been commissioned into the 17th Welsh Regiment and had been in post since just after the 40th Division came into existence. He was in his mid-thirties and had originally worked in the mines department of the British South Africa Company. He had also served as a trooper in the South Rhodesia Volunteers during the Boer War.[3] The latter experience would have certainly endeared him to Frank, but with Soames it was a different matter. Frank stated that he sacked him after a short time.[4] Whether it was merely because the two men fell out is not recorded, although Frank does note 'a staff officer' objecting to his plan to hold a simultaneous kit inspection for all units in his brigade; 'that staff officer changed his job.'[5] Whatever the reason, Soames left 119 Brigade at the beginning of March 1917. He was made a GSO2, but that May was invalided back to England, either from wounds or sickness, and finished the war as brigade major of a Training Reserve brigade. In his place came Guy Goodliffe, a regular Royal Fusilier who had arrived in France with the 1st Battalion of his regiment in September 1914. He was also a keen cricketer. Goodliffe had been awarded the Military Cross in the 1917 New Year's Honours and this was his first staff appointment. He was to serve Frank well during the next year and more.

The four battalions under Frank's command were the 19th Royal Welsh Fusiliers, 12th South Wales Borderers, and 17th and 18th Welsh. There were also the brigade machine-gun company and trench mortar battery. The brigade was on the march when Frank joined it and eventually came to rest in the area of Bellancourt, just east of Abbeville. There it embarked on some intensive training and to this end Frank also set up a brigade training school for junior officers and NCOs. He also established bombing and Lewis Gun schools. On Boxing Day 40th Division's spell out of the line came to an end and it moved to join XV Corps, which was responsible for the southernmost sector of the British front.

On the night of 27–28 December 119 Brigade relieved 98 Brigade (33rd Division) in the Rancourt sector north of Péronne. It remained in the line for a week, a period largely spent in improving the trenches, which had recently been taken over from the French. There was some German shelling, which on one occasion struck a French ammunition dump within Frank's sector, causing a number of casualties. Going back into divisional reserve, Frank received some welcome news. Not only had he been mentioned in despatches, but he had also been awarded the DSO in the New Year's Honours, both in recognition of his time with the 9th Royal Irish Rifles. It was confirmation that Nugent had forgiven him for his disobedience on 1 July 1916. Frank would also have been delighted to learn that Philip Woods's DSO had also finally come through and also that Ernest Hine, his erstwhile adjutant, had been awarded the MC, both also in the New Year's Honours.

By now Frank had a reasonable feel for his brigade. He was impressed by the 12th South Wales Borderers and put this down largely to the CO, Lt Col Alexander Pope (also awarded the DSO in the New Year's Honours 1917) and his adjutant, William Brown, as well as the RSM, who had 'properly grounded' the battalion 'when young.'[6] As for the other battalions, January 1917 saw some major changes. Lt Col Richard Grant Thorold of the 18th Welsh was wounded on the 3rd when visiting isolated posts. He was succeeded by the second-in-command, Hugh Wood. Later in the month, Lt Col Bryan Jones, commanding the 19th Royal Welsh Fusiliers, was also wounded, and succeeded by Major James Downes Powell of the Glamorgan Yeomanry, who had been second-in-command of the battalion since October 1916. In the same month Frank found Lt Col C.B. Hore of the 17th Welsh, a regular officer in the Royal Warwicks, wanting and relieved him after just three months in command. The fact that his battalion recorded 113 cases of trench foot during the first few days of January was the last straw.[7] His place was taken by Lt Col Alan Bryant DSO of the Gloucestershire Regiment. He had been on the staff since the outbreak of war, latterly as a GSO1, but had not arrived in France until October 1916. Frank himself claimed that Bryant did not arrive until April and that he was looking for a recommendation for command of a brigade.[8] Whatever the truth, he had revealed early on that he was determined to have subordinate commanders with whom he was *simpatico* and he would maintain this policy until the end of the war.

The brigade carried out two further trench tours during January 1917. The weather had been very wet during November and December, but in January it turned very cold. One consolation was that there was little German activity, apart from in the air. Indeed, one of the few excitements came when a German aircraft was brought down some 200 yards from Frank's headquarters. Then, on the 27th of the month the division was relieved by 8th Division and withdrew for a further bout of training. Frank reopened his brigade schools, but the emphasis was now on 'fighting platoons.'[9] This reflected a radical change in the organisation of the infantry platoon. The experience of the Somme had caused the authorities to conclude that in the context of trench warfare the platoon needed to have much greater flexibility in its tactics than mere reliance on the rifleman. Hence the new platoon would consist of a bombing section with grenades and a rifle section, supported by rifle grenadier and Lewis Gun sections. This required much more tactical and weapon-handling skills and hence the need for concentrated training. On 11 February, however, 119 Brigade was back in the Rancourt sector. It was the only brigade in the division actually in the trenches, 121 Brigade being in a reserve and 120 Brigade carrying out labouring and other tasks for XV Corps. After ten days relatively quiet the brigade was relieved and took over 120 Brigade's role. It also formed a composite training company to induct new drafts and those soldiers considered backward. It would seem that Frank went on leave at this time, since the brigade war diary for February is signed by Lt Col Bryant.

Before the end of February 1917 rumours were beginning to circulate that the Germans were preparing to withdraw to the so-called Hindenburg Line, which they had been building during the winter. This would enable them to compensate to an extent for the heavy losses they had incurred during 1916 by reducing the length of front. The rumours were confirmed on 26 February, but the Germans remained strong in front of 40th Division. Frank's brigade took over the Clery sector on 9 March and the Brigade war diary recalls him carrying out a personal reconnaissance of the sector the following day. It was not, however, until 119 Brigade had been relieved a week later and had gone into divisional reserve that the Germans did begin to pull back, enabling the division to advance to Péronne. Then, on 21 March, Frank was ordered to form a mobile all-arms column. It consisted of some corps cavalry, a field artillery section, the 17th Welsh and a platoon of the 12th Yorkshires, the division's pioneer battalion. As the divisional history put it: 'When the commander first received his appointment, visions of dashing through a gap at night and exploiting the gain at once floated through his brain. Verbal instructions were forthwith issued to his various subordinates. "But all that was washed out" is his wistful comment.'[10] The column, which had been placed on twelve hours readiness to move, was stood down after two days, its role being taken over by a cavalry brigade. The division itself was then relieved and Frank's men found themselves engaged on road-mending duties so as to improve the somewhat stretched supply lines.

The advance continued during the first three weeks of April. It was, however, a slow business, thanks to the skilfully handled German rearguards. By the 20th the division had reached the Gouzeaucourt area eight miles south-west of Cambrai and was now closing up to the Hindenburg Line. The Germans were now standing and fighting and so a corps set piece attack was organised. While 8th Division on the right was to capture the village of Gonnelieu, 40th Division was to assault the ridge running north-west from the village, and known as Fifteen Ravine, and also advance in touch with 20th Division on the left. The attack took place on 21 April. Within the division, 120 Brigade was on the left and sent forward patrols shortly after midnight. These discovered that the objective was clear of Germans and so it was quickly secured. Frank's brigade on the right had the so-called Fifteen Ravine to tackle and this proved a slightly tougher task. Zero Hour was 4.20am and Frank attacked with two battalions up, the 19th Royal Welsh Fusiliers on the right and the 12th South Wales Borderers on the left. The latter, though, had a new commanding officer. On 17 April 1917 Pope had tripped over some barbed wire, cutting his face badly, and had to be evacuated. Indeed, it partially paralysed his left cheek. His place was taken by Robert Benzie, who had arrived in the battalion just the day before as second-in-command. He shared something in common with Frank in that he had been a civil engineer in Ceylon and had joined the Ceylon Planters Rifle Corps, with whom he had fought in the Dardanelles. In June 1916 he had transferred to the 2nd Scottish Rifles as a captain and served with them until being posted to the 12th South Wales Borderers. He would soon prove himself to be a highly capable commanding officer.

As for the attack itself, the Royal Welsh Fusiliers experienced few problems and secured their objective by 5.15am. In response to a request from 8th Division they carried out a successful raid on a position to the north-west of Gonnelieu and also deployed a company to provide covering fire east of the village. The Borderers initially faced both artillery and machine-gun fire and then snipers. Nevertheless, they got onto the objective at 5.15am and thirty minutes later had consolidated on it. The cost to the brigade was 157 all ranks, but forty Germans were made prisoner and a goodly number killed. Frank could feel justifiably pleased with the first deliberate attack he had conducted as a brigade commander. Indeed, there was immediate praise for the division as a whole from not only the corps and army commanders, but also from Haig himself.[11]

The current phase of operations was not complete, though. The next divisional objectives were the villages of Villers Plouich, to the north-west of Gonnelieu, and Beaucourt, west of Villers Plouich. Again, 119 Brigade was on the right and 120 Brigade on the left. Frank was tasked with seizing the high ground between and beyond Villers Plouich and Gonnelieu. This time the 17th and 18th Welsh would lead, with the 19th Royal Welsh Fusiliers in support and the 12th South Wales Borderers in reserve. On the right the 18th Welsh's task was to establish a company in four strongpoints on the spur north of Gonnelieu to protect the right flank of the brigade. They moved out just before midnight on 23–24 April and in just over two hours accomplished their mission without coming across any opposition. The 17th Welsh set off at 4.15am behind a creeping barrage. They were held up by thick wire for a time, but the artillery was effective in suppressing much of the German fire and they eventually found a gap. They then entered the German trenches and by 7am had secured the objective. On the left 120 Brigade had experienced more difficulty. Although Villers Plouich was entered, heavy German artillery fire brought many down before it was consolidated, forcing a withdrawal to the eastern outskirts of the village for a time. Efforts to capture Beaucamp were frustrated by heavy German fire, especially from the village of Bilhem. For a time 119 Brigade was stood by ready to restore the situation, but eventually it was decided that 20th Division should attack Bilhem the following night. Once this was achieved, 120 Brigade could renew its efforts against Beaucourt. This duly happened and Beaucamp was captured. Frank, however, could again feel well pleased. His attack had gone like clockwork. As the Divisional History put it: 'It had been a smart and well-managed attack. The artillery barrage was well timed and accurate. Brigade headquarters were throughout in constant communication by telegraph with battalion headquarters, and although telephone communication was constantly being interrupted, it was always promptly restored.'[12] It was certainly for these two successful brigade attacks that Frank was, on 15 May 1917, mentioned in despatches for a second time.

There was now a pause while the division consolidated, but there was still one German–held village in front of the Hindenburg Line: La Vacquerie, north of Gonnelieu. The original plan was to capture the village, but there was then a change of heart. This was probably because it would create a small and unnecessary salient in the British line. Hence, it was to be subjected to a large-scale raid. This was to be carried out by 119 Brigade on the night of 5–6 May in conjunction with a raid by 8th Division against Sonnet Farm, just to the south of La Vacquerie. Frank selected the 12th South Wales Borderers and 17th Welsh to carry out the raid, and their aims were to inflict casualties, gain unit identifications and do damage to the defences. On 18 April the 17th Welsh had received a new second-in-command in the form of Major Richard Andrews. He was a man very much after Frank's own heart. He had fought in the South African War, rising to be a Sergeant in the 28th Imperial Yeomanry, and had subsequently been in South America. He had returned home in July 1915, enlisted in the ranks of the London Scottish and then, in February 1916, gained a commission in the Devonshire Regiment. He won a very good MC for occupying the near lip of a crater of a mine which the Germans had just blown, driving the attackers off, while a platoon commander with the 2nd Devons. He was given a company and then sent home to the Senior Officers' School at Aldershot to learn how to be a battalion commander.[13] Very soon after Andrews arrived it would seem that Alan Bryant asked to go on leave, primarily, according to Frank, so that he could see his son into boarding school for the first time. Believing that Andrews was perfectly capable of commanding the battalion, Frank granted him leave and

Andrews led the 17th Welsh during the two April attacks. Frank also recommended Andrews for the DSO, which he did not receive.[14] Bryant arrived back on 5 May, but Frank had already appointed Andrews to coordinate the raid and oversee the withdrawal, so the CO was a mere observer.

The plan itself called for each of the two assault battalions to deploy two companies forward, with a company in support and the fourth in reserve. The other two battalions were to be the brigade support and reserve. Supporting the raid would be all sixteen Vickers machine-guns of the brigade machine-gun company, the four Stokes mortars of the brigade trench mortar battery, and 224 Field Company Royal Engineers, which was to be responsible for destroying the defences. The idea was that the leading companies would pass through the village and the German trenches to its south-west and then establish cover for the follow-up troops, who would cause as much damage, to both humans and the defences, as they could. Zero Hour was to be 11pm and the withdrawal would begin two hours later. The support companies would now provide cover for the raiders as they made it back to their own lines. On the left 121 Brigade would mount a similar operation.

At 11pm on the night of 5 May the guns opened fire and the raiders set forth. They encountered wire, but managed to get through it, although they met more once they got into La Vacquerie. While the Germans did put down effective artillery and mortar fire, there were comparatively few of their troops actually in the village. The lead companies duly took up position while the 'moppers up' and sappers got to work. Richard Andrews wrote in his report:

> A few prisoners were sent to the rear, a number of the enemy were also reported to have been killed and a number of German wounded were left out including one officer who was dealt with by the S.W. Borderers.
>
> I reached the spot allotted to me punctually at 11.30pm where I received and transmitted reports from the companies, R.E's and T.M's [trench mortars]. Assaulting companies withdrew through support lines. Reports were received all correct and as far as known all casualties evacuated.

The support companies then withdrew and Andrews and his small party returned, bringing in their telephone lines with them. He himself had been slightly wounded in the foot by a shell splinter.[15] The other brigade had similar experience, although the withdrawal did not go so well, with a number of men lost. Even so, the operation had been a great success, earning Andrews a DSO 'for conspicuous gallantry and resource when in command of a brigade.'[16] This reflected the fact that he had been effectively controlling the whole brigade during the withdrawal phase. Frank's men won several other awards. Indeed, during May 1917 alone they received no fewer than thirty-two immediate awards, compared to eleven for 120 Brigade and just four for 121 Brigade, a clear indicator of Frank's growing success as a brigade commander.[17]

After the La Vacquerie operation the sector quietened down. Indeed, it was decided that a mainly defensive posture should be adopted, as the emphasis on the British front now switched to preparing for a major offensive in the Ypres area. This did not mean, however, that the 40th Division was prepared to adopted a 'live and let live' policy. Far from it. When Frank's brigade was in the line there were nightly 'officer's patrols' of no man's land. During the second half of May the 17th Welsh also carried out two successful raids. Then, at the beginning of June 40th Division came under command of General Sir William Pulteney's III Corps, HQ XV Corps being redeployed to Flanders. Otherwise June was uneventful.

The 18th Welsh got a new commanding officer in late May 1917. This was Lt Col J.R. Heelis MC, who came from being a brigade major in 61st Division and had been three times mentioned in despatches. What might have discomfited Frank was the fact that he was a Manchester, having been commissioned into the regiment just a year after Frank. Heelis had also served in the West African Frontier Force, although after Frank's time. It is likely, therefore, that Heelis knew of some of Frank's pre-war misdemeanours. As it was, he remained in command for a bare six weeks, part of which time he was on leave. Frank later wrote that he had known Heelis in Aldershot and had considered him 'a very smart young officer in every way.' He stated that Heelis had served in England since being wounded in 1914, while adjutant of the 1st Manchesters, and was unable to adjust to the changed conditions of 1917. This was why he was removed.[18] Yet Heelis had remained adjutant of his battalion until April 1915 before returning to England. He had then gone back to France with 61st Division in May 1916 and so was hardly out of touch with the nature of warfare as it now was. It is therefore difficult not to conclude that Frank felt personally uncomfortable about having Heelis in his brigade. On the other hand, Frank's report on him is likely to have been damning, since Heelis never obtained another battalion command. The battalion also got a new second-in-command while Heelis was on leave. Hugh Wood, who had reverted to this position on Heelis's arrival, was wounded on 11 June.* His place was taken by thirty-one-year-old William Kennedy, a lecturer at the London School of Economics, who had joined the Inns of Court Officer Training Corps in December 1914 and been commissioned into the Highland Light infantry the following March. Although he did not go to France until the beginning of 1916, Kennedy proved himself a natural soldier, quickly gaining command of a company and then winning a good MC on the Somme. Kennedy clearly impressed Frank from the outset and, as a result, was given command of the 18th Welsh in Heelis's place.

As for what others in the brigade thought of Frank at this time, Fred Turner was serving in the ranks of the 19th Royal Welsh Fusiliers:

> I must admit that I never saw the Brigadier in No Man's Land [a reference to *A Brass Hat in No Man's Land*] but quite frequently in the front line. On one occasion he caught three or four of us sitting down on the firing step and said 'You (pointing to one of us) go and get your Company Commander.' When the CO arrived, he got a wigging for allowing his men to be idle when there was plenty of work to be done. He made himself so unpopular with the officers that a number of them transferred to the Air Force.[19]

---

* Wood's contribution had been recognised by a mention in despatches in April 1917 and the DSO in the 1917 Birthday Honours. He was wounded in the right eye, which unfortunately could not be saved. (TNA WO 339/28853)

Harold Jones, a junior subaltern in the 12th South Wales Borders, had a similar experience:

> Early one morning, soon after we had our trenches in fair order again, I was looking over no-man's-land with my eyes glued to my glasses, when I heard a voice alongside. 'What are you doing, sir?' Thinking it was my sergeant or corporal I did not trouble to turn but mumbled something about watching Jerry. Again the voice and again the same answer. Then the voice: 'Are you asleep, sir?' I replied rather shirtily, 'Damned near it.' Then the voice, now like thunder: 'Come here, sir!' I turned and to my horror found myself facing General Crozier and his staff in all their glory. Phew! How he ticked me off, threatened to place me under arrest and made me follow on his heels for a distance, finally dismissing me with more awful threats. A general in the front line was a very rare event and one I had never expected.

In contrast to Turner, though, Jones claimed that this was the only occasion that he saw Frank in the trenches.[20] Captain Eric Whitworth, another South Wales Borderer, was scathing about Frank:

> … [He] was different in every respect to his predecessors. He lacked the presence, charm and the dignity of them both. He was essentially a hustler, who probably overestimated the results obtained by energy alone, and his authority was not strengthened by the issue of impossible orders, which could not be carried out owing to conditions he never saw. No doubt he hustled his own battalion with great success, but his reputed boast on arrival, that he had never obtained discipline in his own battalion until a man had been shot, was indicative of his own characteristics rather than of strength or greatness as a commander of men. Not that the efficiency of the brigade suffered much under his command; in many details it was more efficient than it had ever been before, but this was from fear rather than as a response to any real leadership.[21]

While Frank's manner clearly did not go down well with many, the accusation that he did not visit the trenches, or very seldom did so, is not fair, although it was probably much less frequent than when he was a battalion commander.

June and July 1917 were generally quiet months for 40th Division. Frank's men attempted a number of raids, but none were successful. On the night of 4–5 July 119 Brigade mounted no fewer than three of these. One was foiled by problems with Bangalore torpedoes, which were used to blow gaps in the German wire. The second had the same problem, but the raiders managed to cut holes in the wire, discovering that the German front line trench was empty, but when they moved on to the support trench they were met with heavy fire and forced to withdraw. The third was challenged and fired on before the German trenches were reached. Indeed, it was noticeable that the Germans were considerably more alert than they had been in May.

As for Frank, he stated that he took leave every three months, although this cannot be confirmed by the divisional and brigade war diaries. One assumes that he saw Ethel and Mary, and sometimes Hester. But while Hester remained with her grandparents,

Ethel and Mary appear to have led a somewhat nomadic existence. They spent some time with an aunt of Ethel's in Ilfracombe on the North Devon coast, but also at various addresses in London, and in Kent. According to Mary, her mother became a VAD for a time and a photograph does exist of her in nurse's uniform, with Adelaide Hospital embroidered on the breast. The only Adelaide Hospital in existence at the time in Britain was in Dublin and so it is possible that she worked there, but the British Red Cross Society Archive, which holds records of 80–90 per cent of the VADs who served during 1914–18, does not have her name on its books. It is quite possible therefore that Ethel wore it in a tableau for a fundraising event. Mary also claimed that Ethel was a munitions worker at another point during the war, but this too cannot be verified. She was certain, though, that at no time was she separated from her mother.[22]

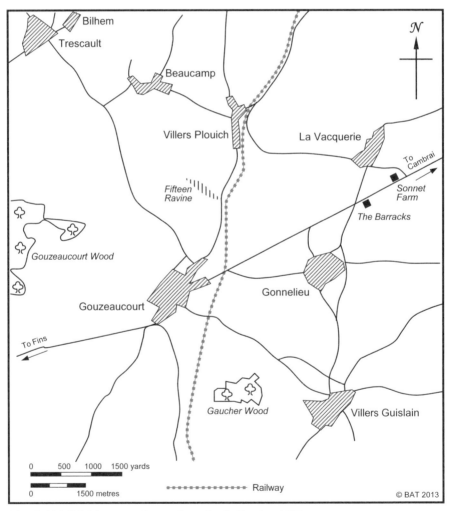

Map 4: 40th Division area of operations. April–October 1917.

During the summer there were further changes at the battalion command level. This largely concerned the 19th Royal Welsh Fusiliers. Downes-Powell, who had taken over from Bryan Jones after he was wounded in January 1917, fell sick in May with trench fever and general debility. He was succeeded by Major Arthur White DSO of the King's Own Yorkshire Light Infantry, but he, too, succumbed to what turned out to be tuberculosis after a few weeks in command. Consequently, in July Bryan Jones himself returned to his old battalion and reassumed command. Within a month, though, he had been replaced by Major James Frederick Plunkett. He had risen through the ranks of the Royal Irish Regiment to RSM during a career of some twenty-four years. He had been awarded the DCM in December 1914 for 'conspicuous good work and repeatedly distinguishing himself under fire'.[23] He had also appeared in the 1915 New Year Honours list in the first list of recipients of the newly created Military Cross. Commissioned in May 1915, he had been sent home in poor health, but early in 1916 became a company commander in the 22nd Middlesex, which was in 40th Division. This, however, was disbanded in April 1916 and so Plunkett joined the 12th Suffolks, also in 40th Division, and went to France with them. In the weeks before joining 119 Brigade he had been filling in for other COs in the division while they were on leave. Plunkett observed, of Jones being sent home, that this appeared 'to be quite a common occurrence in this brigade as a few more were sent home later.'[24] Under Frank's command Plunkett would add considerably to his laurels. As for Jones, he was killed in action in October 1918 when commanding the 15th Royal Irish Rifles and subsequently received a bar to his DSO. It would thus seem that it was personal differences with Frank rather than his qualities as a battalion commander which caused him to be removed.

In September, Richard Andrews took over command of the 17th Welsh from Alan Bryant. The reason cannot be established. Frank claimed that Bryant was only in command for a month and had then allowed some Germans to get into his trenches without speedily evicting them. Frank went up early in the morning to see what was happening and apparently discovered Bryant asleep. He therefore placed Andrews in command of the battalion, woke Bryant, and told him that he was relieved of command and that he would try to get him another staff job. The battalion war diary for September 1917 makes no mention of such an incident, and neither does that of 119 Brigade. The former merely notes that on the 15th Bryant reported to Divisional HQ for duty. However, the Divisional AQ war diary states that Bryant was posted to command of a battalion in 34th Division.[25] This was the 9th Northumberland Fusiliers and he was killed at its head at Ypres barely a month after he had left 40th Division. It would therefore seem that it was, as with Jones, a personal falling-out rather than any professional deficiencies on Bryant's part. Whatever the circumstances, Frank now had four commanding officers in whom he had total trust. Only Plunkett was a professional soldier, but one who had seen long service in the ranks.

August also saw the arrival of a new divisional commander. Ruggles-Brise returned to England to take up a command. In his place came John Ponsonby, another Guardsman. Before the war he had made his name as Commandant of the School of Musketry and had been commanding 2nd Guards Brigade since March 1917. Frank's opinion of his new commander reveals as much about Frank as it does his superior:

I think there were times when Sir John Ponsonby may not have approved of me, or at least my methods. We were so different. He was always amusing. I was not. A good soldier, and a firm friend, a man once said to me, 'He has only one fault, if fault it is, he suffers fools too gladly.' I, on the contrary, was always, during the four great years, so engrossed in war that I could not tolerate anything or anybody I thought might clog the wheels of victory. Thus we were opposites, but, as his was to command and mine to obey, I shall ever be grateful for the entirely free hand he gave me.[26]

The two men would go through some grim times together.

The 40th Division continued to man its sector during August. There were a number of patrol clashes in no man's land. Malfunctioning Bangalore torpedoes scuppered more raids, but the 19th Royal Welsh Fusiliers did mount a successful one on the night of the 28th–29th, killing fourteen Germans and capturing one at a cost of two officers wounded, one other rank missing and eight wounded. September had much the same pattern and by the end of the month the division had been in the line for virtually six months, with little break. True, it had escaped the growing misery of the Third Battle of Ypres, which had been raging since the end of July, but it was still in need of a rest. On 1 October the Division issued orders for its relief by 20th Division, which was scheduled for the second week in October. Frank's brigade had been cooking up another raid, however. It was to be carried out by the 18th Welsh. On 1 October the Division confirmed that ammunition would be available and the date was fixed for the night of 5–6 October. On the same day the raiding party itself was sent to the brigade school at Nurlu to train for the raid and the following day the artillery cut gaps in the wire. This continued for the next two days. Frank himself inspected the raiders at Nurlu on the 4th. During this day and the next the German artillery was active, causing some damage to the brigade's trenches. The raid itself was mounted with artillery support at 8.40pm on the 5th. It was accompanied by a Chinese or feint attack at another point in the line. The raiders had little problem in getting through the German wire, but found that the occupants of the front-line trench had mostly fled, although two were bayoneted. Two dug-outs were destroyed before the raiders returned to their own lines, having suffered seven wounded. It was therefore reasonably successful and an appropriate farewell to the Gouzeaucourt sector. Forty-eight hours later the brigade was relieved by 59 Brigade, a relief that was completed in a very short time, thanks to a lack of German activity.

Initially, Frank's brigade moved to Péronne, where it was inspected by the corps commander, who also presented ribands to those recently awarded medals. On the following day, 10 October, the brigade was moved by train to Beaumetz-Rivière, a railhead south-west of Arras. It then moved to three villages, with Brigade HQ, 12th South Wales Borderers, 18th Welsh, a field company RE and field ambulance in one, the machine-gun company and trench mortar battery in the second, and the other two battalions in the third. For the next two weeks the brigade trained in the morning and did sport in the afternoon. The culmination was two brigade attack exercises. On 29 October the brigade moved by foot to another collection of villages a little further west and then continued training as before, with the emphasis very much on offensive operations. On 16 November it returned to its previous villages and the following day marched to Gomiecourt, further to the east.

The training that 40th Division had undergone was for a specific purpose. It had been earmarked as a reserve formation for an operation which was shortly to take place in the sector in which it had served throughout the spring, summer and much of the autumn. Codenamed Operation GY, the aim was to launch a surprise attack on the Germans with the object of breaking through the Hindenburg Line and securing crossings over the St Quentin Canal at Masnières and Marcoing. Thereafter Bourlon Wood and the ridge on which it stood were to be seized, as well as cavalry passed through to capture crossings over the Sensés river. Finally, Cambrai was to be liberated and the German forces cut off by this double envelopment eradicated. The initial assault was to be carried out by IV Corps (6th, 36th, 51st, 62nd Divisions) and, on its right, 40th Division's former master III Corps (6th, 12th, 20th, 29th Divisions). They would be supported by nine tank battalions and the whole of the Cavalry Corps. Besides 40th Division, the Guards and 59th Divisions were also in reserve. Apart from using the tanks en masse to spearhead the attack, surprise was to be achieved by not having a preliminary barrage or even preregistration of targets. This reflected the fact that developments in the science of artillery during the past two years meant that it was now possible to fire accurately 'off the map'. The attack was to be launched at dawn on 20 November.

As the attacking troops made their final preparations, which included getting the tanks in position, 40th Division started to move closer. Once Frank's brigade was established in Gomiecourt, he gathered his COs, second-in-commands and adjutants to discuss the Cambrai attack. The next move, on 19 November, was to Barastre, south-east of Bapaume, but it was late at night before everyone had arrived. At 6.20am on the following morning the British artillery opened up and the tanks began to move forward amid fog. Surprise was initially complete, with the tanks crushing the wire and then breaking through the German first line of defences. On the left some tanks did actually manage to get into Bourlon Wood, but withdrew before dark. In the centre Flesquières Ridge proved a problem, with German artillery proving very effective against the tanks. On the right things went better, with bridgeheads established across the St Quentin Canal, but, unsure of the situation, the cavalry was slow to react and only one squadron of Canadian cavalry actually made it over the canal. It did reach the German gun lines but, unsupported, was forced to withdraw. As for 40th Division, it stayed where it was, although sappers and divisional pioneers were sent to repair a bridge over the Canal du Nord. Frank, however, was given a warning order to be prepared to move his brigade at one hour's notice to Doignies, which lay north of Havrincourt Wood and just south of the Bapaume-Cambrai road. Accordingly, that afternoon he sent forward large advance parties from each battalion to construct trench shelters for his men. No order to move to Doignies came, however.

On 21 November the attack was resumed, but the Germans had been bringing in reinforcements, some from the Eastern Front thanks to the revolution in Russia. The attacks were not coordinated and generally started late because of the problems of getting sufficient tanks ready in time, not least because their crews were generally exhausted after the previous day. The Germans had evacuated Flesquières Ridge during the night, which was a bonus, but an attempt to capture Bourlon village failed,

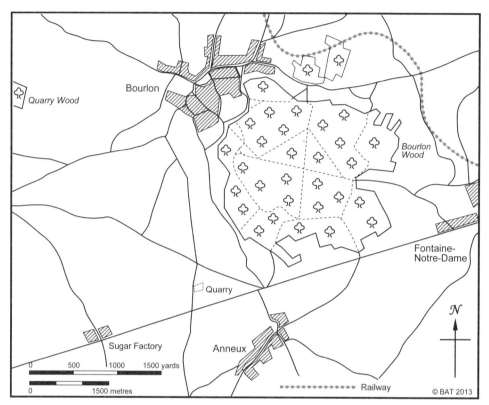

Map 5: Bourlon Wood, November 1917.

although there were some territorial gains. Frank received orders at 10.30am to move to Doignies. He himself, together with his staff captain Percy Hone, COs, second-in-commands and adjutants went forward to check the routes across the Canal du Nord to Graincourt, which lay south of the Bapaume-Cambrai road midway between Boursies and Fontaine. That night Ponsonby was informed that his division was to come under IV Corps and its likely task would be the capture of Bourlon Wood. The following morning, when Ponsonby and his GSO1, Lt Col Charles, attended a conference at HQ IV Corps, his task was confirmed. He was to capture Bourlon Wood and village. Frank's old division, the 36th, would attack on the left and 51st Highland Division on the right. Ponsonby decided that Frank's brigade was to capture the wood, with 121 Brigade attacking on his left and keeping in touch with the Ulster Division, as well as trying to get round Bourlon village from the west. Fifty tanks would be made available to support 40th Division's attack.[27]

That afternoon Ponsonby held a conference at his headquarters during which he gave out his orders for the attack, which was to take place the following day, and for the relief of 62nd Division that night. Frank also carried out a hurried mounted reconnaissance of Bourlon Wood with the same group as the previous day, which amounted to some sixty horsemen:

We rode along the supporting line of the Ulster Division from the left flank in order to get to our place of deployment and passed though some of my battalion, who turned out and cheered for all they were worth as we galloped past, going hell for leather in extended order, like M.I. [Mounted Infantry] of old. A hostile aeroplane spotting us, followed, flying low, spitting fire from machine-guns, no damage being done.[28]

Lt Col Plunkett also remembered this ride, especially since he was 'by no means a first class horseman':

We stumbled over shell holes, went up and down embankments of sunken roads which I would no more face today for fear of the fall that never came, we jumped wide trenches, our artillery was popping off from concealed positions and I felt sure they enjoyed our discomfiture, the Boche shells were bursting everywhere and to add to our discomfiture a Boche plane met us near Graincourt ... I can safely swear that my old horse Tommy kept me on his back that day because I could never have managed it.

As for Bourlon Wood:

The wood was of oak, about a mile in width and about the same in depth. The trees were very close, and the wire on the southern end appeared thick, but by means of glasses I could see that there were diagonal lanes through the wire which decided me to advance in line of platoons in the attack and not in extended line.[29]

The two assault brigades set out at 4pm and had relieved the 62nd Division brigade manning the trenches by 1.30am. Frank's headquarters were in cellars in the village of Graincourt, which the 62nd Division had seized on the 20th. Remarkably, as David Starrett recalled, it had electric light:

Going down to where that light came from I found two German prisoners at the dynamo, quite happy to be working for us rather than their own kith and kin. They had been working as electricians in a shipyard in Hamburg.

Later it was discovered that the Germans had mined the cellar and the prisoners were used to cut the detonation wires.[30]

The attack itself was originally laid on for 6.30am on 23 November, but was put off until 10.30am. Part of the reason was that the tanks were delayed by congested routes during their move up. The boundary between 121 and 119 Brigades was the western edge of Bourlon Wood. The idea was that the tanks, numbers of which had been reduced to twenty for the former brigade and twelve for the latter, would advance behind a creeping barrage at Zero Hour, with the infantry following behind. The tanks were also to be covered by smoke, but for some reason artillery smoke shells could not be made available. Frank planned to attack with the 12th South Wales Borderers under Benzie on the left and Plunkett's 19th Royal Welsh Fusiliers on the right. The 17th Welsh (Andrews) were in support and the 18th Welsh (Kennedy) in reserve. Frank stated that he said to his men just before the attack: 'Remember Spion Kop. If I want you to come back, come back. I decide your fate. You hold on or die.'[31] As it was the tanks passed through on time and ten minutes later the assault battalions stepped into no man's land.

The Fusiliers and Borderers quickly got into the wood itself and, with the tanks, advanced to a sunken lane which ran east-west through the centre of it. Apart from shellfire, there was little opposition; machine-guns were captured and prisoners made once the advance reached the sunken lane. Continuing north from the lane the German resistance stiffened. Plunkett's men managed, however, to establish posts on the northern edge of the wood at around midday, while Andrews did the same, albeit more slowly on the left, with one of his companies actually reaching the outskirts of Bourlon village. Frank had put Plunkett in charge on the ground. With little idea of what was happening on his right, but sensing he had an exposed flank, Plunkett called up the 17th Welsh. While two companies were used to reinforce his line, the other two were deployed to cover this vulnerable right flank. He was also aware that Bourlon village had not been taken and neither had Fontaine-Notre-Dame on the right. He sensed a German counter-attack brewing and so asked for the brigade reserve, the 18th Welsh, to be deployed. This was timely, since at just after 3pm the Germans did launch such an attack. The 18th Welsh under Kennedy stabilised the situation. One of his officers recalled:

> One of the finest commanders a battalion could wish for rode right up to us on horseback, jumped off when he got up to us, and rushing in front of us rallied us and waving his cane urged us on; he had only gone about half a dozen yards when he fell dead, shot by the Bosch.[32]

The second-in-command was then severely wounded and command of the 18th Welsh devolved on the adjutant, even though he, too, was wounded. The German pressure remained intense. Frank threw in his works company and salvage section. Then the 14th Argyll & Sutherland Highlanders from 120 Brigade arrived, and finally 200 dismounted 19th Hussars, whose CO caused a 'real disaster' at Brigade HQ, according to Frank, when he upset a bottle of port and glasses[33] – Frank certainly did not insist on his brigade HQ being 'dry'. By the time darkness at fallen, 119 Brigade still held much of the wood, but its right flank was exposed because 51st Highland Division had been unable to capture Fontaine. On the left, too, 121 Brigade had suffered heavily in its attempts to seize Bourlon village and this meant that Frank's brigade was now holding a salient.

The night of 23–24 November was cold and wet. Frank's men repulsed another counter-attack. Ponsonby's main concern was to capture Bourlon village and he gave orders overnight for 121 Brigade to carry this out. It would be reinforced by a battalion from 120 Brigade and a dismounted cavalry battalion. Twelve tanks would be made available to support the attack and Zero Hour was to be 3pm. However, at 8.30am Plunkett reported the Germans to be massing for another attack. Fifteen minutes later it was launched against both flanks of 119 Brigade, but was repulsed. A second attack followed at 11am, this time against 119 Brigade's right flank. The

17th Welsh suffered in particular. Two companies were cut off and the other two lost all their officers as the defenders of the wood were forced to give ground. Richard Andrews himself was severely wounded in the right buttock. Plunkett then organised a counter-attack, which involved men from all units under Frank's command. This did regain some ground. Meanwhile, the corps commander had visited Ponsonby's HQ. The two agreed that twelve tanks were insufficient for the attack on Bourlon village. Since no more could be made available they agreed to cancel the attack. Orders went out to 121 Brigade to this effect, but they were not received and the attack went ahead as originally planned. It reached the village, but was unable to clear it. The situation of 119 Brigade thus remained parlous. Frank had no clear idea of what was happening to 121 Brigade and there was still German pressure to his front and on his right flank. After two days of constant fighting his men were becoming exhausted. Apart from the continual conventional shelling, the wood was also reeking with gas and communications both forward to the battalions and back to division were at best intermittent. At about 5.30pm Frank's HQ received pleas of help from the wood. His intelligence officer, whom he had sent forward to gauge the situation, returned at much the same time, reporting that lack of numbers and fatigue meant that the men were no longer capable of holding a determined German attack. The problem was that reserves were now thin on the ground, since 120 Brigade had had to deploy much of its remaining strength to support 121 Brigade in the battle for Bourlon village. Frank was given two companies of the 11th King's Own Royal Lancasters. Shortly afterwards, Ponsonby was informed that three battalions from the Guards Division were being placed under command. Accordingly, he immediately sent the 2nd Scots Guards to help Frank. He sent them forward with instructions to Benzie, whom he had now placed in command of the forward area, that they were not to be used piecemeal.

The capture of Bourlon village remained the priority. Consequently, at 2am on 25 November Ponsonby issued orders for 121 Brigade to have another attempt at it, twelve tanks being promised. Zero Hour was 6.15am and the tanks were due to turn up fifteen minutes before this, but they failed to appear. The brigade did not have sufficient strength to secure the village and a German attack drove its men back to the southern outskirts. Frank's men also faced a counter-attack, early in the morning and against their right flank. Two companies of the Scots Guards were sent to reinforce the flank, followed by the other two. The 4th Grenadier Guards also arrived and became Frank's reserve. There were, however, no further German attacks and in the very early hours of the following morning 40th Division was relieved by the 62nd Division. David Starrett was part of the Brigade HQ advance party sent to find somewhere to spend the rest of the night. It turned out to be the family vault of the Havrincourt family. He left a red light on one of the tombstones to indicate to Frank where they were. Frank recalled:

> By the dim light of a torch I could see the feet of the members of some of my staff, who were asleep on stretchers, sticking out of the niches which had once contained coffins. I had been given a very special bed on a stone slab which had, no doubt, at one time supported the mortal remains of some famous member

of the family, as I had a little slightly elevated recess all to myself ... the musty smell was dreadful.

Not surprisingly, after all he had been through Frank's sleep was very broken.[34]

Recognition of what 40th Division had achieved was quick in coming. On 26 November Haig personally visited Ponsonby to congratulate him. Julian Byng, commanding Third Army, wrote to him as follows:

> Whatever may be the final result of the operations as a whole, I cannot let this particular period pass without sending you a line to convey my most sincere congratulations on your feat of arms.
>
> The capture of Bourlon Wood to my mind stands out amongst all the other splendid actions of our infantry since the attack started on the 20th and in years to come I shall remember with unqualified satisfaction that it was performed by the splendid Division with which I have now been associated for some time.[35]

It showed that higher command recognised the hard work which had been put in during the last year to make 40th Division a true fighting formation. Frank himself, in a special order of the day, stated: 'The valour and endurance displayed was beyond all praise.'[36] Bearing in mind Lloyd George's interest in the Welsh troops, Frank wrote him an account of Bourlon Wood and eventually received a reply dated 20 December. The prime minster wrote: 'I would like to compliment you on the gallant way in which your brave men seem to have carried out what was a very difficult piece of work.'[37] The cost, though, had been high. The 40th Division had suffered 467 killed, 2,034 wounded, and 795 missing. Plunkett estimated that seventy-five per cent of 119 Brigade were casualties by the end of 25 November.[38] Typical of the losses were those of the 12th South Wales Borderers, whose total casualties were twenty-two officers and 304 other ranks.[39] Sadly, the sacrifices made proved to be worth little. On 30 November the Germans launched a major counter-attack, which eradicated the gains made during the Cambrai assault. It meant, among other losses, that Bourlon Wood was once more in German hands.

Having had a little sleep, Frank's men marched back to Léchelle, south-east of Bapaume, on 26 November. Next day they entrained at Ytres, passing the night in their trains at Bapaume, before moving northwards to the Beaumetz area, south-west of Arras and close by where the brigade had been in October 1916 when Frank first took it over. There the battalions were given a few days to reorganise themselves prior to relieving a brigade of 16th Division in the Bullecourt sector. Such was the shortage of junior officers that the brigade had to borrow from elsewhere in the division and even within the brigade. Thus, during December, the 17th Welsh, which had lost nineteen officers at Bourlon Wood, received an attachment of eight officers from elsewhere in the division, five from outside the division, and six from the 18th Welsh. Receiving no fewer than seventeen subalterns from England at the end of the month enabled it to return these loans. The battalion also received a new commanding officer. Major Harry Gough MC, the second-in-command, had assumed command when Andrews was wounded and briefly wore the badge of a Lt Col, but on 24 December he was superseded by Major F.E. Bradshaw DSO, a fifty-two-year-old retired Indian Army officer. Gough reverted to second-in-command, but did have some consolation in being awarded a bar to his MC for his part in the Bourlon Wood battle. The 18th Welsh also had a new CO, Basil Coulson of the King's Own Scottish Borderers. He was a former regular officer, who had been badly wounded in the Boer War and then been forced to resign his commission because of being made bankrupt (shades of Frank!). He had been allowed to rejoin in autumn 1914 and had at various times commanded a service battalion of his own regiment, but had suffered bouts of sickness. Then in August 1916 he had been wounded in a mine explosion while attached to the 24th Northumberland Fusiliers.[40] There were also large drafts of men to make good the losses. James Plunkett noted that his battalion reached a strength of 500, but that many of the new officers were Territorials with no active service experience. Nevertheless, on 15 December the 19th Royal Welsh Fusiliers carried out a highly successful attack designed to capture portion of trench held by the Germans. A delighted Frank sent him a message: 'Just a line to congratulate you and yr bttn on yr very fine [sic] effort of this afternoon. World cannot express in any reality what I and the rest of the Bde think of yr performance.'[41]

Frank also gained satisfaction in the award of two DSOs to Benzie, one in the New Year Honours for general good work and the second specifically for Bourlon Wood. Plunkett also gained a bar to his DSO, but Frank was not so pleased about this, since he had recommended him for the VC.[42] He himself was made a Companion of the Order of St Michael and St George and also mentioned once more in despatches. There was, however, a new award announced at this time, the 1914 Star. This was to be granted to all those who had served in France and Flanders up until midnight 22–23 November 1914. Guy Goodliffe, Frank's brigade major, was entitled to the Star and so Frank thought that he would apply, claiming that he had crossed to France on 5 September 1914 and was attached to the 2nd Manchesters.[43] This, of course, was totally untrue and his application was rejected. What disappointment Frank might have experienced at this was soon to be superseded, however, by a series of events that would cause 119 Brigade to be radically reorganised, and not just once.

Chapter Eight

A Turbulent Year: 1918

As 1918 opened the Bullecourt sector remained cold, although there was a thaw in the middle of January, which resulted in trenches collapsing and flooding. There was daily artillery activity on both sides, but little of particular significance, except for a major German raid against 121 Brigade on 5 January, which was repulsed. This was followed by repeated minor attacks during the next few days. The Divisional History noted that Frank did organise the occasional raid by his brigade, but otherwise the situation remained relatively quiet.[1]

What was on everyone's minds at this time, especially with a major German offensive becoming ever more likely, thanks to the new Bolshevik regime in Russia suing for peace, was the manpower situation. By the end of 1917 each British battalion in the BEF was on average a company's worth of men under strength. Consequently, after some debate, the decision was made to reduce every infantry division by three battalions. The general rules were that no regular battalion would be disbanded and that priority would lie with later formed Territorial and service battalions. A number of pairs of 1st and 2nd Line Territorial battalions amalgamated, but otherwise it was disbandment, with just the very occasional amalgamation of service battalions. As far as 40th Division was concerned, the decision on which battalions should go to the wall was based on those recruited in areas where manpower was drying up. Wales was identified as being a problem and, as a result, Frank found that he was to lose both the 12th South Wales Borderers and the 19th Royal Welsh Fusiliers. One of his Welsh Regiment battalions also had to go and Frank decided that it should be the 17th Welsh, since this had suffered slightly more at Cambrai than the 18th Welsh.[2] In their place Frank received the 13th East Surreys from 120 Brigade and the 21st Middlesex from 121 Brigade. His two new commanding officers were a contrast to one another. Hubert Metcalfe of the Middlesex was aged fifty-three, old to be a CO at this stage in the war, and had retired from the regular Army in 1902. He had little active service experience. Herbert Warden, on the other hand, had already proved himself as a commanding officer, having just been awarded the DSO for his performance at Cambrai. Frank himself was not impressed by either battalion. He felt that Metcalfe was too old and did not consider Warden a good leader.[3]

As for Frank's other commanding officers, Robert Benzie was given command of the 14th Argylls in 120 Brigade. James Plunkett, on the other hand, succumbed to his exertions of the past few months, suffering a heart attack as he led his battalion back from its very last tour in the trenches. As for the CO of the 18th Welsh, he proved to be of little value. Having assumed command on 9 December, Basil Coulson went off on a week's leave to Paris on 30 December. Ten days after his return he fell sick, but managed to wangle another couple of days in Paris before rejoining on 5 February. Three weeks later he was once more in hospital and that was the end of his time in command, since he was evacuated back to England.[4]* One suspects that Frank was delighted to get rid of him, especially since he was able to arrange for his place to be taken by William Brown, whom Frank had so admired as adjutant of the 12th South Wales Borderers and who had then become its second-in-command.

Frank spent the first two weeks of February on leave in England. Aware that the German offensive was imminent he had decided to grab the opportunity while he could:

> For the first time in the war I feel this leave will be my last. I put in a theatre a night and a matinee when possible. I say nothing about my forebodings to my wife, but she knows intuitively, as does even the child [Mary] aged seven. The time comes for parting. They come to the station to see me off by the staff train from platform three at Charing Cross. I give the child a pound note to buy a book or two, and to keep her quiet. We are just on time. There is no hanging about on the platform. A fond farewell, a last embrace … I vow to myself that I shall never come on leave again, even if I do get through.[5]

This shows that Ethel and Frank were still close, but there is no mention of Frank's younger daughter Hester, who was still with his mother and stepfather.

The 40th Division carried out its reorganisation south of Arras, beginning in mid-February. Those officers and men of disbanded battalions who could not be accommodated in other battalions of their regiments were sent off to join newly created entrenching battalions. These were to be used to improve defences and to act as a reservoir for reinforcements. A further adjustment was that the brigade machine companies were formed into the 40th Machine Gun Battalion. There was also considerable training carried out, including cooperation with tanks and aircraft. In addition, there were a number of divisional conferences on the impending German attack. Frank, too, had to get to know his two new battalions and their officers.

At the end of February the division was placed in GHQ reserve. This meant a move and on 1 March 119 Brigade marched to Gouy and then to Blaireville six miles south-west of Arras. They were now in the sector of Sir Alymer Haldane's VI Corps and on 4 March, the day after arriving at Blaireville, Frank took all his commanders down to company commander level on a reconnaissance of the corps front. There

---

* Coulson was apparently suffering from bronchitis and laryngitis, which he claimed at a later medical board had been caused by gas in January 1918. The board, which sat in September 1918, also found that he had syphilis, which he claimed to have originally contracted some fifteen years earlier. In spite of this, in February 1919 he was appointed head of the British Military Mission to the former principality of Teschen in Silesia, which was claimed by both Poland and Czechoslovakia. Three months later he was appointed Military Attaché to Prague and was made a CBE for his work in Teschen. During 1920, however, he took to the bottle and ran up sizeable gambling debts, many to local dignitaries and tradesmen. He had also used public monies and had further debts in Paris. All this came to light when he was handing over to his successor at the end of the year. He left Prague in January 1921 and vanished. His CBE was revoked. (TNA WO 374/15760)

was also further training involving offensive operations in cooperation with tanks and contact aircraft and with gas being notionally present. Initially, it was believed that the Germans would attack on 13 March. In consequence, all three brigades in the division were moved to the Boisieux area, some four miles to the east of Blaireville. The 13th passed without a German move. On the 17th a Polish deserter stated that they would attack using gas the following day. On the 19th another prisoner said that the Germans were expecting a British attack. Both 19 and 20 March were dull and

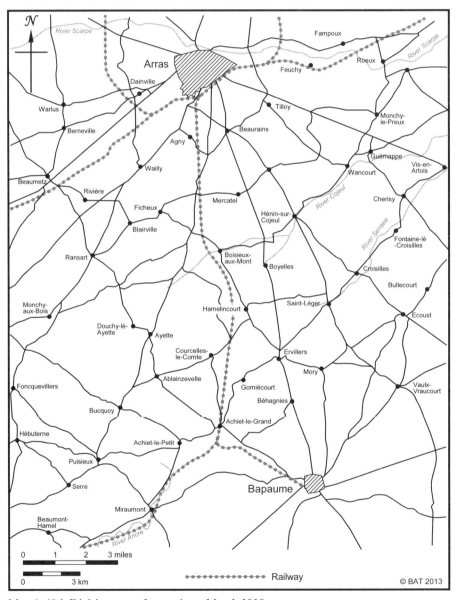

Map 6: 40th Division area of operations, March 1918.

misty. During the latter Frank and his brigade major attended a tank demonstration and then Goodliffe and Hone carried out a reconnaissance of 76 Brigade's (3rd Division) sector.[6] The brigade also moved to Mercatel, just to the north of Boisieux.

On the night of 20–21 March thirteen Germans were captured by troops of XVIII Corps in the St Quentin area. What was significant was that these were not from the *Landsturm* (Territorial) division which had been holding this sector, but from a known first-line division. Further questioning revealed that the long-awaited offensive would be launched at 4.45am the following morning. There was time enough to send out a warning. At 3am the British guns opened up with a mixture of high explosive and gas designed to catch the German reserves as they moved up. Then, precisely at 4.43am, the German bombardment began, initially concentrating on the British artillery, command posts and road junctions. It finished with fire, including gas shells, on the British forward trenches. At 9.40am, and covered by fog, the German assault troops launched their attack along a front of over forty miles. The blow fell on Gough's Fifth Army in the south and Byng's Third Army, of which 40th Division was again part.

Haldane's VI Corps had three divisions in line, from Guemappe, five miles south-east of Arras, to Noreuil, two miles south of Bullecourt. It was against 59th Division in the southern part of the sector that the main blow fell. Soon the Germans had torn a hole in the line and it was now that 40th Division began to move. Ponsonby was ordered to deploy 120 and 121 brigades, but Frank remained at Mercatel. The only change was that his notice to move had been reduced from three hours by day and ninety minutes at night to just thirty minutes. Even so, the morning passed quietly and the brigade was able to complete football competitions. In the afternoon Frank inspected his battalions in full battle order. At 5.30pm he received orders to move to Hamelincourt. Fifteen minutes later, just as his men were marching out, the order was rescinded and they returned from whence they came. It may have been this obvious frustration which later caused Frank to comment to the Official Historian that Lt Col Claud Black DSO of the 12th Lancers, Ponsonby's newly appointed GSO1, was 'the worst GSO1 in France in March 1918.'[7] As it was, proper orders were not long in coming. At 6.45pm 119 Brigade was ordered to move to Henin and defend it at all costs. It lay two miles east of Mercatel and so it was not too long before the battalions were in position, with the 21st Middlesex defending the hill from positions in front of it, the 13th East Surreys in close support and the 18th Welsh in reserve. The brigade was now under the operational control of 34th Division and shortly after midnight orders came to abandon Henin Hill and withdraw west of St Léger, some three miles south of Henin.

What in fact had happened was that Ponsonby had been ordered to take up a new line of defence south of 40th Division's current positions. Consequently, Frank's brigade had to be recalled, but to carry out a withdrawal by night and in contact with the enemy is never easy. As an officer of the 13th East Surreys recalled:

On Henin Hill the most extraordinary row was going on – the transport of two battalions [Middlesex, East Surreys] seemed to have got thoroughly mixed, our companies were streaming into the road, the Lewis Gun sections were shouting for their respective limbers, and, when they had found their limbers, lost their companies and so started to find them; to add to the confusion, a couple of six-inch guns came through with eight horses apiece … Eventually the battalion was concentrated and moved off at about 200 yards interval between companies, but as it was very dark it was rather difficult to keep in touch.[8]

The brigade managed to get in by dawn, a reflection of Frank's training, and took up positions astride the Sensée river and covering Ervillers, which lies some four miles north of Bapaume. This was behind the other two brigades in the division. Frank conferred with Ponsonby at Divisional HQ at 9am and then he and Goodliffe spent the rest of the morning visiting the battalion HQs. During the afternoon 119 Brigade was subjected to heavy shelling and two companies had to be sent out towards Croisilles, west of Bullecourt, to support 34th Division, which was under severe pressure. It was then noticed that troops were withdrawing from St Léger. Ponsonby now ordered Frank to attack the village so as to assist the withdrawal of 120 Brigade. Frank detailed the East Surreys for this task and two tanks were made available to help them. The Germans now attacked Brown's 18th Welsh. He was equal to the task and well justified Frank's faith in him. Not only did he repulse the attack, but grabbing the two tanks earmarked for the East Surreys counter-attacked, knocking the Germans off balance and making the East Surreys' attack unnecessary. The other crisis concerned the VI Corps Club, although Frank calls it an Expeditionary Force Canteen. It had been evacuated, but held large stocks of liquor. Frank ordered them to be destroyed, but when asked about the large number of cigars it held, he apparently replied 'Oh anyone can have them. No man has ever yet, that I know of, been put in the guardroom for over-smoking!' Subsequently, he noted that 'going up to the line I found the little Welshmen doing rapid fire, each with a big cigar in his mouth.'[9]

By dusk on 22 March, 40th Division had succeeded in stabilising the situation to an extent, but was inevitably suffering from a degree of disorganisation. As far as 119 Brigade was concerned, the pressure eased a little overnight thanks to 4 Guards Brigade. This took over the so-called Sensée switch line from the 18th Welsh, who withdrew into brigade reserve. The 13th East Surreys were now west of St Léger and covering Ervillers, with the 21st Middlesex echeloned back on their right. Reports now came in that Mory, 1.5 miles to the east-south-east, had fallen to the Germans. If this was so it meant that 119 Brigade's right flank was now open. Frank told Colonel Warden to fall back, but to check the situation in Mory and Ervillers, also rumoured to be in German hands, as he did so. Warden sent two companies to see what was happening. They found Ervillers still in British hands, but Mory was not. Frank therefore gave orders that it should be recaptured. Meanwhile, the 21st Middlesex had attempted to regain the high ground between Mory and St Léger. They suffered heavy casualties, but managed to secure a line some eighty yards below the crest. The East Surreys' attack on Mory took place in the afternoon of the 23rd and was highly successful. They ended up occupying the old depth defences beyond it. Warden now took command of the three 119 Brigade battalions on the ground, as previously directed by Frank, and established contact with 4 Guards Brigade on his left. His right flank remained rather in the air, though, since he could not make contact with the left flank of 41st Division, which happened to be held by the 12th East Surreys.

At dawn on 24 March the Germans came on again. Advancing from the south in an effort to retake Mory and capture Ervillers, both the Guards and 119 Brigade were forced to turn south to deal with the threat. However, advancing up the Mory valley after their scouts were allowed through, the German main body found itself caught in a crossfire from 4 Guards and 119 Brigade and suffered accordingly. The Germans were not to be denied, however, and launched another attack, this time up the St Léger valley. The danger was that both brigades might now be attacked in the rear. They were therefore forced to withdraw in accordance with previous orders. Frank's HQ was in a farmhouse with a round tower. Frank spent a lot of time at the top of the tower and spotted a mass of German troops advancing. David Starrett recalled:

'Germans, Starrett,' he said putting away his glasses, 'Here is where we cut and run!'
    We did. Through thick gas. Across a road, through a hedge, the General running like a two year-old. Then a succession of flat drops, lying still, up and another sprint. The din flew the words out of our mouths, but Crozier kept sprinting ahead and behind, then waving the direction, and leading the way there. My! But I was lost altogether. But he was not. He'd a sense of direction that must have stood him in good stead when he was out in those West African stunts years before. Perhaps he learned the art then.[10]

Brigade HQ retired to Gomiécourt, to the south-west of Ervillers and, with the Germans now pushing into the latter, the battalions established a new line west of the village. News now came though that the division would be relieved by the 42nd (East Lancashire) Division that night. Indeed, in the afternoon the commander of 127 Brigade met Frank to discuss the details. But at dusk the relief was postponed because 42nd Division was called upon to deal with a German attack elsewhere. The night was reasonably quiet, but at dawn on the following day, 25 March and the divisional commander's birthday, the Germans launched a further series of heavy attacks, which continued for most of the day. It was now that Frank experienced his Spion Kop moment. He had continually impressed on his subordinates the vital importance of not withdrawing unless ordered to do so. Darkness fell and Frank then learned that the brigades on either side of him had received orders to withdraw. Worried that all might be lost, Frank therefore sent his groom back to Divisional HQ with a personal letter explaining the situation. Eventually the hoped-for order came and he was able to pull back his brigade.[11]
    Frank's men initially withdrew to Bucquoy, five miles west-south-west of Ervillers, where they had breakfast. Thereafter they marched to Bienvillers, a further five miles to the west. Reports were then received that the Germans had broken through at Hebuterne, just to the south, and were using armoured cars. At the time just the 21st Middlesex had arrived at Bienvillers; the other two battalions had been retained by Divisional HQ to cover the left flank in the Monchy-au-Bois area. Luckily the German breakthrough quickly proved to be a false alarm. That night the division was finally pulled out of the line and 119 Brigade marched back to Sombrin. There the brigade spent a couple of days sorting itself out. This also enabled Frank to replace his kit, which had been destroyed by shell fire. Casualties had been heavy. While

only one officer and sixty-one ranks were actually reported killed, twenty-two and 437 were wounded, and a further three officers and 201 other ranks were posted as missing. Frank, however, could be well pleased by the way his men had performed and was especially impressed by the leadership displayed by Hubert Metcalfe, about whom he had had such doubts and who grabbed the first opportunity when his men came out of the line to go trout fishing in a nearby river.[12] William Brown had also been outstanding, but Frank did not, at least in later days, think much of Herbert Warden, and considered that his battalion had 'deceived me, as I thought that they were better than they really were.' While he admitted that they had recaptured Mory without artillery support, they only launched the attack after 'great "pressure" on the telephone from Brigade Headquarters.'[13] Yet all three commanding officers were later awarded DSOs, while Frank was mentioned in despatches for a fourth time. Frank would also have been saddened to hear that Robert Benzie was severely wounded in the right shoulder while commanding the 14th Argylls, a wound that would mark the end of his active soldiering.

There were changes at Brigade Headquarters. On 31 March Goodliffe was appointed GSO2 HQ IV Corps, but no successor was immediately posted in and so Frank made Percy Hone his acting brigade major. He had apparently earlier told Frank that he was confident that he could do the job and was keen to be a brigade major, but Frank felt that he had had too little time at regimental duty, although he had a high opinion of him. Hone was a man 'who got things done and was a cheery soul'. Frank had also seen to it that Hone's services were recognised, with the award of the MC in the 1918 New Year Honours, followed very shortly by a bar for Cambrai. Frank also later claimed that he arranged for Goodliffe to be sent on the six months' staff course at Cambridge University so that Hone could fill in during his absence, but that was not the way it happened.[14] As for the staff captaincy, Reggie May, the brigade intelligence officer who had also been awarded an MC for Cambrai, stood in.

The 40th Division was now moved to Flanders, where it was intended that it should be allowed to recover in a quiet area. On 31 March it took over the sector bounded by Bois Grenier in the north and Laverntie in the south from 57th Division. Initially, 119 Brigade was in reserve, with Frank's HQ in the village of Nouveau Monde, which lay just east of Estaires. This gave a little more time to absorb the new drafts, many of whom were under nineteen years of age, the so-called 'A4 Boys', those who were medically fit, but too young to be sent to a theatre of war. To meet the losses incurred during the German March offensive there had been a change in policy and a large number of young soldiers aged eighteen and a half to nineteen were being rushed out to France. Colonel William Brown commented to Frank that they were 'Babies',[15] but they were probably better trained than any previous drafts, most having had some six months' of instruction and more. Some, though, only arrived with the battalions after 119 Brigade had relieved 120 Brigade in the Fleurbaix sector on the night of 6–7 April. This placed Frank with 121 Brigade on his left. On his right, however, was the 2nd Portuguese Division.

Germany had declared war on Portugal in March 1916 and, after much persuasion by the Allies, it had begun to send troops to Flanders just over a year later and built up its strength to two divisions, together with some heavy artillery. It was allotted its own sector in July 1917 and that November came under command of the British First

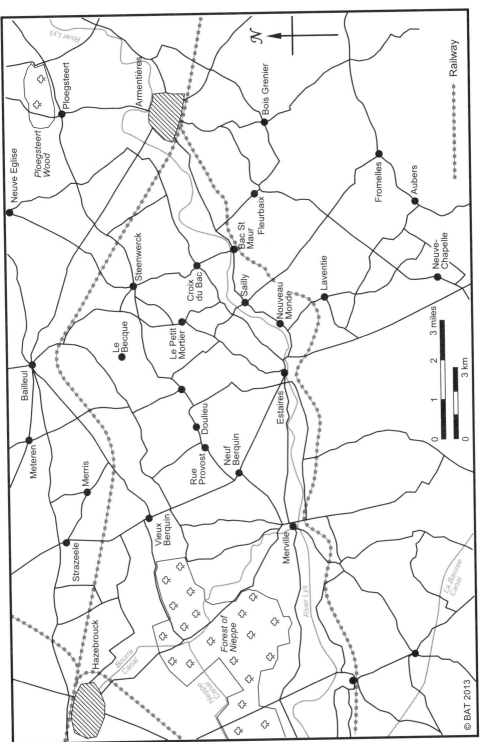

Map 7: 40th division area of operations. April–November 1918.

Army. All, however, was not well with the Portuguese. The officers were generally of poor quality. While they were allowed home leave, the other ranks were not, which did little for morale. The war, too, was not popular at home and this was aggravated by a successful right-wing revolution led by the former Portuguese ambassador to Berlin in December 1917. Furthermore, many officers on leave from Flanders did not return. Rations were poor, and there were insufficient reinforcements to compensate for the steady stream of casualties. No wonder Frank was aghast when he inspected their trenches:

> We walk seven hundred yards and scarcely see a sentry. We examine rifles and ammunition lying about. All are rusty and useless. The bombs are the same. 'Where are the men?' I ask my companion. A snore gives me the answer. Practically all the front line sleeps heavily and bootless in cubby holes covered with waterproof sheets while their equipment hangs carelessly about.[16]

Frank was right to be very concerned. The German Michael offensive against the British Third and Fifth Armies, which had been designed to split the BEF from its ally, had by now run out of steam. Another offensive, codenamed Georgette, was in preparation, however. This time the aim was to disrupt the BEF in Flanders by seizing the key communications centre of Hazebrouck. The Germans massed twenty-six divisions on a twelve-mile front between Armentières and La Bassée. Facing them were six British divisions, all, apart from 55th Division, weakened by the March offensive, and the Portuguese. It was on the latter that the initial main blow would fall.

Frank's brigade was deployed with two battalions forward, the 13th East Surreys on the left and the 18th Welsh on the right, with the 21st Middlesex in reserve. His headquarters was in a farm some 800 yards north-west of Fleurbaix church. The night of 8–9 April was suspiciously quiet. The 18th Welsh sent out patrols. One entered the forward German trenches, but found no Germans. Then, at 4.15am a heavy bombardment opened with a mixture of high explosives and gas. As on 21 March, this initially concentrated on battery positions, road junctions, and likely positions of headquarters. The Portuguese Division was soon reporting that it had lost all communication with its forward units. Worse, at around 7am, an hour and three-quarters before the German Zero Hour, infantry were already infiltrating the Portuguese trenches. It proved too much and the Portuguese troops who could began to flee to the rear. This, of course, exposed the right flank of 119 Brigade. The 18th Welsh fought as best they could, but the Germans soon got round behind them. The Portuguese uniforms were similar to the German ones and in the fog it was difficult to tell one from the other. Consequently, a number of fleeing Portuguese were killed by the Welsh. The Germans also penetrated between the Welsh and East Surreys. Frank was in contact with the Welsh and ordered Lt Col Brown to fight his way back. When he did manage to get through to the East Surreys it was a German voice which answered the field telephone. They, too, had been surrounded and while a few fought their way back, the majority of the twenty-one officers and 464 other ranks left felt forced to surrender. The others were killed. Unfortunately, Lt Col Warden had been admitted to hospital on 6 April and would not be discharged until the 14th, so it may have been lack of strong leadership that contributed to this disaster. Frank certainly thought so.[17] With his reserve, the 21st Middlesex, now also engaged, there was no option but to move back to the other side of the River Lys. He sent Reggie May back to establish a new HQ at Bac St Maur. He then organised a covering force from elements at his HQ. David Starrett recalled:

> Back came General Crozier, swearing dreadfully, to lead us or drive us once more in hurried retreat to Bac-St-Maur the other side of the Lys. Our reserve battalion did its best to put some guts into the Portuguese defence, and how the general managed to be with them and with us at the same time passes my understanding to this day. But there he was whipping us into some sort of order and there he was steadying the reserve, with every bit of ground he trod torn to pieces by heavy stuff. My! His charmed life was being proved just then.[18]

In spite of growing congestion, especially by the one crossing over the Lys in this area, a temporary trestle bridge built over the ruins of the original, destroyed earlier in the war, Frank got back across the river and established his HQ. By this time the few remnants of the Welsh and East Surreys were fighting their way back towards the Lys, where the 21st Middlesex, still on the south bank, were heavily engaged. Then came Frank and his headquarters, their attention now on guarding the bridge at Bac St Maur to prevent the Germans rushing it. Finally came 121 Brigade, which still held Fleurbaix, but with its right flank echeloned back because of the destruction of the East Surreys.

By midday 40th Division's situation was that 120 Brigade was on the right, holding from Nouveau Monde to Sailly along the line of the main road. Then came the remnants of Frank's three battalions, the 18th Welsh reduced to only the commanding officer and seven other ranks. What remained of the East Surreys had placed themselves under Lt Col Brown. Metcalfe and his men were in only slightly better shape. True, a brigade from 34th Division was arriving and hence thickening up the line, but Frank's brigade was still woefully thin on the ground. By 1pm the pressure was building up again and Frank's men were forced to withdraw north of the river. The bridge at Bac St Maur was defended by Brigade HQ elements, including two Vickers machine-guns under twenty-one-year-old Major Douglas Amery Parkes MC, commander of the supporting machine-gun company and another Old Wellingtonian. He was gravely wounded, dying of his wounds some three weeks later. The brigade signals officer was also seriously wounded, but the defenders held on to the bridge until it was blown by a sapper officer, on Frank's instructions, at about 2.30pm. Three floating bridges were also on the river. William Brown managed to destroy two of them, but persistent heavy machine-gun fire prevented his men from dealing with the third. His command had been strengthened by a reinforcement draft of a junior subaltern and 150 men bound for the East Surreys. With Bac St Maur under intense fire, Frank and his HQ withdrew to La Croix du Bac, where Divisional HQ was. The latter, however, was now moving back to Doulieu.

Brown and Metcalfe, each with their collection of oddments, continued to fight on. At one point Metcalfe's men reported a broken-down mail lorry. He at once set a party out to collect the mail bags. Every parcel likely to contain food or tobacco was opened and the contents distributed to his men, which did much to help them stick it out. Even so, with the Germans now across at Bac St Maur, in spite of the blown bridge, and the last of 119 Brigade crossing over the Lys shortly after 4pm, the situation was still perilous. Help, though, was at hand in the shape of 74 Brigade, recently arrived from the Somme and placed under command of 34th Division. Even so, the Germans forced Frank's men out of La Croix du Bac. By now he himself had little idea what was happening. The commanding officer of the 11th Lancashire Fusiliers, part of 74 Brigade, recalled:

> We could get no definite information as to the exact whereabouts of the enemy. The retiring brigade [119] had apparently melted away and it was only later that I met its Brigadier in a car when he had just got clear of Croix du Bac and was looking for his men.[19]

Joined by a company's worth of Royal Engineers, whom Frank had hastily made into infantry, 74 Brigade advanced and brought the German attack temporarily to a halt. Meanwhile Frank was ordered to concentrate the remnants of his brigade at Le Petit Mortier, together with 120 Brigade. Each brigade now formed a composite battalion from its survivors, with that from 119 Brigade commanded by William Brown. The defensive line as far as the 40th Division was concerned was still not cohesive, with the remnants of two brigades on the right and 121 Brigade, which was now under the command of 34th Division, having become very entangled with it, on the left. In the middle was a mass of Germans.

In the early hours of 10 April Frank was told by General Ponsonby that he was to defend a position known as the Steenwerck Switch, which lay two miles north of Croix du Bac and was a long communication trench with little wire. He passed the order to Colonel Brown, who occupied the line, with the 21st Middlesex, still under Metcalfe, on his left, and the divisional pioneer battalion, the 12th Yorkshires, on his right. Shortly after they had deployed they came under heavy artillery fire, but, as Brown later reported: '... the men stuck to their posts with really admirable fortitude.'[20] Then, at 9am, Ponsonby received orders from HQ XV Corps for a counter-attack. This was designed to drive the Germans occupying the loop in the Lys south of Croix du Bac back across the river. It was to be carried out by the remains of 119, 120 and 74 brigades. However, concerned by the constant artillery fire to which his men were being subjected, the commander of 74 Brigade jumped the gun. Communications with 120 and 121 Brigades were virtually non-existent because of damage to cables and so the first that 120 Brigade knew about the attack was when survivors came back through their lines, the German machine-gun fire having proved too much. A yawning gap also opened up between 74 and 119 Brigade. Germans were pushing hard against the Steenwerck Switch and had got behind 120 Brigade. They had also set up machine-gun nests in the small copses which characterised the local terrain and artillery fire continued to rain down on the hapless defenders. At about 4pm, and probably at Frank's bidding, William Brown's composite battalion got out of their trench and, with bayonets fixed, advanced some 450 yards and occupied some shallow depressions. Besides regaining some ground, it also provided a respite from the German artillery, which took some four hours to realise what had happened.

The night of 10–11 April was marked mainly by German reconnaissance probes, but morale in 40th Division increased when news came through that the 29th Division, a regular formation which had earned its spurs on Gallipoli, was on its way. Indeed, one of its brigades was now about a mile north of Steenwerck. As for 40th Division, 74 Brigade, which was still under command, was just south of Steenwerck, 120 Brigade was covering the village from south and west, 119 Brigade was based on Le Petit Mortier and below them was a battalion from 120 Brigade which had been holding the bridge at Sailly. Finally, 121 Brigade was to the west of Le Petit Mortier. General Ponsonby visited his brigades, or what was left of them, during the morning of 11 April. Arriving at a small farm north of Doulieu, 'I found both Crozier and Hobkirk [GOC 120 Brigade]; they both seemed tired out. All I could tell them was that divisions were coming up behind and that we must hang on as long as possible and stop the Bosch.'[21] The Germans had indeed renewed their attacks. In particular, 74 Brigade came under immense pressure and was forced to pull back. Frank's men, too, were up against it, with each man covering twenty yards of front. He requested and received a battalion from 29th Division as reinforcement. He himself moved his HQ back to Vieux Berquin, three miles north-west of Doulieu. There he learnt that he was to be relieved by 31st Division. Luckily, the Germans did not maintain their attacks in this particular area, although the left flank was very much in the air.

The actual withdrawal of 119 and 120 Brigades was to be covered by William Brown and his composite battalion. He was helped by a counter-attack launched by a brigade from 31st Division which retook La Becque, but it took time for him to link up with the relieving brigade. Even so, Brown managed to extricate his men and withdraw them to behind the line by 11pm. There was then a delay in confirming that the relief was complete and it was not until after dawn that 119 Brigade's composite battalion could leave for Strazeele, where the brigade was concentrating.

Frank's brigade had suffered grievously. While eight officers and fifty other ranks were confirmed killed, twenty-four and 350 were wounded, and no fewer than fifty-three officers and 967 other ranks were posted as missing.[22] The Brigade and 40th Division as a whole were no longer a viable fighting force. Frank himself was later bitter:

The dilatory methods employed prior to the opening of the battle was appalling. The advice of those on the spot who were in the best position to judge was not taken.* The guns were not moved back prior to the fight, and so were lost. The unevenness of the worth of battalions, the hopelessness of certain Commanding Officers and even Generals and the want of vision of GHQ brought their own rewards, and for them GHQ alone can be held responsible.[23]

---

* This refers in particular to Frank reporting the total inability of the Portuguese to withstand an attack, which he thought imminent. The intention had been to relieve the 2nd Portuguese Division by the 51st Highland Division on the night 7–8 April, but the Highlanders were exhausted after a battering on the Somme and needed a little time to absorb newly arrived reinforcements. The relief was therefore postponed by 48 hours. (Baker *The Battle for Flanders* p29).

Frank himself believed that the problems on the ground had much to do with battalion COs:

> All these leaders would have been shot if I had anything to do with it, both the battalion colonels and their staff. How can you explain that in one corner of a battlefield one battalion will put up a good show against odds and get away with it while in another, against the same pressure, a whole battalion get taken prisoners? The answer is colonels. An amazing number of objectives are not being taken and three quarters of them could be, given pushful and able leadership.[24]

Yet Brown and Metcalfe had proved themselves to be inspiring leaders. Their performances on the Lys earned Brown the DSO and Metcalfe, who was badly wounded on 11 April, a bar to the DSO he had earned in March. Frank's efforts were also rewarded. He received a further mention in despatches and in the 1918 Birthday Honours was made a Commander of the Order of the Bath.

On 14 April 40th Division moved to the Tilques area, just north-west of St Omer, with Frank's HQ in Tilques itself. Now some reorganisation could take place and fresh reinforcements were absorbed, but there were problems. First, on 17 April the division was ordered to create a composite brigade to form part of Second Army's reserve. At much the same time there were demands to supply drafts from battalions to others in the same regiments in other divisions. Thus, within 119 Brigade the 21st Middlesex had to supply 200 men to the 1st Middlesex in 33rd Division. As for the composite brigade, which was based on 121 Brigade, both the 21st Middlesex and 13th East Surreys each had to supply a company. The remainder of the brigade was engaged on training, but on 21 April the division moved again, this time to the Boisdinghem area, some nine miles west of St Omer. The following day Ponsonby had lunch with the corps commander, Sir Alymer Hunter-Weston, who told him that 40th Division was to be denuded of men, with merely headquarters remaining. The hope was that it would be re-formed after three months. The following day Ponsonby visited GHQ and the division's fate was confirmed to him. Then 119 and 120 Brigades were ordered to each form a composite battalion to help prepare defences on the line Wylder to St Sylvestre. These moved by bus to the Cassel area on 24 April. Then came an order to form a second composite brigade. This was to be established under Frank and his headquarters and was to consist of the 18th Welsh (Brown), 13th East Surreys (Warden) and a composite battalion formed from the 10th/11th and 14th Highland Light Infantry. They were to be known as A, B, and C battalions respectively.

The second half of April brought a significant change to Frank's staff. Percy Hone had stood up well under the stress of this new German assault; indeed, Frank now considered that he had potential as a battalion commander. Matters came to a head when Frank received a new brigade major on 25 April. This was Captain Anthony Muirhead MC. An Old Etonian, he was a 1914 veteran, but was not a regular soldier. He had gone to war with the Queen's Own Oxfordshire Hussars and then, in October 1915, been appointed ADC to Major General Robert Fanshawe, commanding the 48th (South Midland) Division. Thereafter he served as a GSO3 in the same division and joined 119 Brigade from Italy, where 48th Division was deployed. Frank later wrote that Muirhead 'was much more than a good soldier, as he was clever with it all, yet unobtrusive in his cleverness.'[25] The two would forge a close bond.

As for Percy Hone, Frank succeeded in getting him made commanding officer of the 21st Middlesex in mid-May, but by this time the battalion had been reduced to cadre status. Hone managed to obtain another command in October 1918, that of the 13th Durham Light Infantry. He was badly wounded in the right thigh during the first attack he conducted, but earned two DSOs to add to the three MCs he had already won – the third being for his performance as brigade major during the Lys offensive. All this meant that May was confirmed as staff captain. Another who joined 119 Brigade HQ at this time was Herbert Lamb, who took over as signalling officer in late April. He had served in the ranks of the RE Signal Service in both the Dardanelles and Mesopotamia and had returned to Britain to be commissioned. He noted in his diary on joining 119 Brigade that Frank was 'most awfully nice.'[26]

Meanwhile, the German offensive had continued throughout most of the remainder of April. By the 25th they had penetrated nearly fifteen miles. Bailleul had fallen and so had the dominant Kemmel hill. But the Germans were experiencing increasing difficulties in maintaining momentum, largely because their supplies could not keep up. In the light of this, they halted their attacks late on the evening of the 29th and began to make preparations for an assault against the French. As far as the British were concerned, the fact that the Germans retained large forces in Flanders made it appear likely that they would renew their attacks there. It was in this context that 40th Division was now to be used.

On 1 May the Division was given instructions that all available infantry and machine-gunners within the division were to be drafted to other units. First to go were the gunners from the 40th Machine Gun Battalion. Then, the remnants of the 18th Welsh, 21st Middlesex and 13th East Surreys entrained for the base, but not before General Ponsonby had presented Military Medal ribands for the German March offensive to those who were still with their units. This left 119 Brigade's battalions at merely cadre strength, but it was given two new roles. The first of these was the construction of a new defence line in the rear area. Known as the Winnizeele Line, it essentially covered Cassel. This meant not only reconnoitring the line, in conjunction with Royal Engineer officers, but drawing up plans for its defence and supervising its construction, which was to be carried out by field companies RE, Labour Corps, and Chinese Labour Corps units. This kept Frank and his staff busy for the remainder of May. Indeed, he was out virtually every day on reconnaissance. Yet there was still time for some relaxation. Herbert Lamb recalled taking his signal section by lorry to play a football match and Frank sitting on the grass beside him to watch it. On another occasion: 'General and everyone played rounders in the evening.'[27]

The other expected role was the training of Americans, now arriving in ever-increasing numbers in France. At the beginning of June, however, it was decided that 40th Division would not take on this role, although six of its battalion cadres, including the 13th East Surreys and 21st Middlesex, were transferred to 34th Division for this purpose. Both were destined to have a turbulent time. It was decided to reconstitute 34th Division as a fighting formation in mid-June and so the East Surreys were passed on to 39th Division, which did retain a training role for the remainder of the war. But this formation had too many battalion cadres and so the East Surreys were passed on to 25th Division, which was about to move back to Britain to re-form. The battalion did regain its strength in manpower, absorbing the 15th East Surreys, but never returned to France. The same experience befell the 21st Middlesex.

The work on the Winnzeele Line and another defence system, the Balemberg Line, continued during the first half of June, but further changes were afoot. On 10 June six so-called garrison guard battalions were allotted to the division. These had been formed from the medically fitter members of the Labour Corps in France for just holding the line, although as medical Category B men, they were, at least in theory, unfit for front-line service. They were placed under HQ 120 Brigade. On the following day these units were recategorised as infantry garrison battalions and rebadged as infantry. Thus No. 6 Garrison Guard Battalion became the 11th Garrison Battalion Cameron Highlanders. Then the division was told that it would be designated a 'Garrison division' for 'holding quiet parts of the line'. It was now to withdraw from all work on the defence lines and train with this in mind.[28] Each brigade was allocated a training area and four additional garrison battalions were posted in from 59th Division, which had also suffered heavily during the German offensives. This meant that the brigades could become properly established once more, with Frank's brigade now consisting of the 12th Garrison Bn Royal Inniskilling Fusiliers, 13th Garrison Battalion East Lancashire Regiment, and 12th Garrison Battalion North Staffordshire Regiment. All had been garrison guard battalions. Frank and the other brigade commanders were ordered to form light trench mortar batteries from within their own resources. As for the one original 119 Brigade battalion, the 18th Welsh, its cadre was transferred to what had been the 16th (Irish) Division. This also went back to Britain to re-form, but returned to France at the end of July and included a refurbished 18th Welsh.

Frank himself claims that he took some leave in early June, although this is not recorded in either the divisional or brigade war diaries. Sticking to the vow he made when he returned from leave in February 1918, he did not cross the Channel, but went instead to Paris Plage on the Channel coast near Le Touquet. He hoped that this would revive his spirits, since he was 'ever so tired'. He 'certainly saw fun' and enjoyed dancing and was even propositioned by a young French girl. At this moment he was told that there was an urgent letter for him in the Town Major's office. It told him of the re-formation of the division and said that he could have four more days' leave, but he decided to return to his HQ the following day.[29] Back at his HQ in the village of Nieurlet, north of St Omer, he was delighted when who should appear but none other than that old war horse Lt Col James Plunkett DSO & bar MC DCM, who had been appointed to command the Royal Inniskillings battalion in his brigade after managing to get himself back to France after his heart problems earlier in the year. Frank's reaction was to think that at least one of his battalions would be good with Plunkett in charge.[30] Plunkett, though, was aghast when he saw his new command: 'When they marched in my heart sank to the lowest as they straggled badly, looked old and weary, with not the slightest sign of discipline in them. These remarks apply to both officers and men.' He noted that only his signals officer had any previous experience in the job. His adjutant had not worked in an orderly room and his quartermaster was also unversed in his role and later had to be replaced. He noted, too, that initially every man had some medical problem that he complained about. [31] Frank's solution:

> We 'electrified' our 'B' men into activity by a simple process, perhaps akin to psycho-analysis. We got them all to play games, take part in sports, take a pride in their new regiments, march, shoot and forget about their ills – real or imaginary – with the result that, during the last three and half months of the war, they behaved like and carried out the duties of [category] 'A' men …'[32]

This approach soon reaped dividends. On 24 June Sir Douglas Haig came to see one battalion from each brigade in 40th Division at work, with Plunkett's battalion representing 119 Brigade:

> I saw some at drill, others musketry, one whole battalion was on parade in open order. The latter presented arms and handled their rifles well. I was greatly surprised and pleased with the class of men in the ranks. They can shoot and will hold a position, but cannot march very far, say, 5 miles slowly is the normal.[33]

The marching limitation was soon removed, however, through sound training. This was recognised in mid-July when 'garrison' was removed from the titles of all battalions in the division, meaning that they were now to be regarded as any other front-line infantry battalion.

What always concerned Frank, as we have seen, was the quality of his battalion commanders. He knew that the Inniskilling Fusiliers were in good hands and the commanding officer of the 13th East Lancashires seemed acceptable. He was forty-three-year-old Robert Johnson, who had retired as a captain in the Royal Welsh Fusiliers in 1913, but had rejoined in 1914 and won a DSO in Mesopotamia in 1917. The problem child was the North Staffords. Its first CO was also a retired regular officer and DSO holder, but he had only nine days in command before Frank sacked him. His successor, a 1914 veteran, also with the DSO, lasted less than a week. The third had been a major in the 1st East Surreys at the outbreak of war and had gone to France with them and subsequently been wounded. He had briefly commanded a brigade in 1916, had been made a CMG, and been mentioned four times in despatches during 1914–16. He, too, does not seem to have lasted for very long and it is probable that Frank considered him past it as far as being a fighting CO was concerned. Indeed, the 12th North Staffords never seemed to have a commanding officer who stayed for very long until almost the end of the war. As James Plunkett observed, Frank was 'a thorough fighter', but 'had no sentiment' when it came to his battalion commanders.[34] Frank himself put the blame on the CO's Pool at Base, which was full of '"dud" colonels' and 'into which some good people occasionally fell, by mistake, and clambered out as soon as they could, while others revelled in the waters of stagnation like tadpoles in a cesspool.'[35]

The beginning of July also saw a change in divisional commander. John Ponsonby was appointed to command the regular 5th Division. In his place came Sir William Peyton, a cavalryman. Failing to pass the Sandhurst exam, he served in the ranks of the 7th Dragoon Guards, which had been commanded by his father, for two years prior to being commissioned into the regiment. Nine years later he transferred to the 15th Hussars. He campaigned in the Sudan in the late 1890s and was badly wounded. Significantly, he served with Thorneycroft's Mounted Infantry in South Africa, but just after Frank's time, and had been invalided home sick. He was certainly an admirer of Alec Thorneycroft and this helped in developing a good relationship with Frank. His service in the current war had been varied. Returning from India, where he had been Military Secretary, on the outbreak he was given command of a Territorial Force mounted division. He then served at Gallipoli in command of a mounted division, albeit dismounted, before commanding the Western Desert Force in a successful campaign against the Senussi in early 1916. He subsequently became Douglas Haig's military secretary for almost two years before caretaking HQ Fifth Army after Hubert Gough was sacked at the end of March 1918.

Throughout this time the Germans had switched their attention to the French. In late May they attacked in the Chemin des Dames sector, driving the French and four tired British divisions, sent to recuperate, back across the Aisne. The French mustered their reserves along the line of the next major river, the Vesle, and when the Germans came up against them they had run out of momentum. They were then counter-attacked. The Germans tried again in mid-June, attacking between Noyon and Montdidier. Once again they gained some territory, but could not achieve a decisive breakthrough. Finally, in mid-July, they attacked on both sides of Reims. The French were expecting the attack and allowed the Germans to come on before counter-attacking in the flanks and forcing them to withdraw.

Yet the Germans still had sizeable forces in Flanders and Haig was well aware of this. He feared another attack there, which, in fact, was the German intention, and it was in this context that, as part of its training, 40th Division occupied the Hazebrouck reserve line so as to give the troops experience of the trenches and trench routine without the threat of hostile fire. Patrolling was carried out, but the realism was somewhat reduced by the presence, some 500 yards forward of the trenches, of a battalion canteen from 31st Division.[36] This practising was as well, since in the middle of July Peyton was informed that his division would now take its place in the line. First to do so was Frank's brigade, which on 18 July relieved 87 Brigade (29th Division) and became attached to the 1st Australian Division in the Meteren. The reason for having a British brigade under the Australians was to enable them to remain in the line, by having one brigade in the trenches and two in the rear, as opposed to the usual two brigades forward. The background was that the 1st Australian Division, in conjunction with the British 9th and 31st divisions, was enjoying some success in nibbling at the German lines, what the Australians called 'peaceful penetration'. There was some tension during the relief since the Germans were expected to renew their Flanders offensive on 18 July, but nothing happened. Instead, the 9th (Scottish) Division secured Meteren on the following day. Plunkett noted how active the Australians were at patrolling and decided to test his men by sending out a fighting patrol to capture Germans. It was highly successful, with two prisoners being made, and Plunkett considered that his men had now become 'a fighting force'. Furthermore, Frank had offered £5 for the first prisoner captured and £1 for each subsequent one: not inconsiderable sums given the fact that a private soldier's pay was one shilling and sixpence per day.[37] The 13th East Lancashires also captured prisoners and benefitted greatly from having an Australian officer and four NCOs attached to each company.[38]

Just before 119 Brigade was relieved, the Australians carried out some further peaceful penetration. This was to capture the village of Merris, which lay just to the left of 119 Brigade's sector. The operation took place in the early morning of 29 July. Plunkett's Inniskilling Fusiliers were on the Australian flank and their role was to connect up with them if the attack was successful, which it was. Being a canny old soldier, Plunkett moved his men up during the night, assuming that the Australians would be successful. They were, 'but were rather surprised to find us in position as, knowing we were a B1 division, they had not much faith in us.'[39] Frank could therefore feel very satisfied when his men came out of the line on the night 31 July–1 August after being relieved by 121 Brigade. The latter would not, however, have the experience of working with the Australians, since they now left Flanders to take part in the impending attack in front of Amiens.

Frank's brigade continued with its training, although he spent the first half of August as acting divisional commander, since Peyton went on leave. In the meantime, the first of the Allied blows which would mark the final 100 days on the Western Front had taken place at Amiens on 8 August. There was a sense that the Germans might begin to withdraw in Flanders and it was with some anticipation that 40th Division relieved 31st Division in the sector Merris south to Neuf Berquin during the night 22–23 August. Probing patrols revealed that the Germans were still very much in place, however.

The first significant 40th Division action came on 27 August and was very much a 119 Brigade affair, with Plunkett playing the lead part. Indeed, the plan was his. His battalion was the southernmost of the division. On 24 August the brigade on his right had attempted to capture a hamlet called Rue Provost and the ground immediately north of it without success. Presumably recalling his part in the Australian capture of Merris, Plunkett believed that he could do it by moving his left flank round during the night and attacking southwards. It would also pinch out an unwelcome salient jutting into the British line. Frank liked the idea and Plunkett presented the plan personally to Peyton, who approved it and arranged for no fewer than fifty-four 18pdr guns and some heavy artillery to support the attack. Plunkett was also given an additional company from the North Staffords and a battalion from 120 Brigade. On the night 26–27 August he deployed his two left-hand companies and they waited in position until H-hour, which was 10am.* Covered by a creeping barrage the assault companies initially met little resistance. Then they began to come up against machine-gun nests, but good minor tactics overcame them and a number of rifle posts. Within an hour they had advanced south some 1,000 yards, but were held up by machine-guns from Rue Provost. Then, at 11.30am 121 Brigade, in conjunction with 61st Division on their right, assaulted towards Rue Prevost, but were also held

---

* In *My War* Plunkett states that Zero Hour was 5am, but the accounts given in the divisional war diary (TNA WO 95/2594) and that by 13th Royal Inniskilling Fusiliers (TNA WO 95/2606) both say 10am.

up by machine-guns. Continued pressure by 119 Brigade enabled a link-up between the two 40th Division brigades to be made that evening. It was a generally successful operation, with fifty Germans counted dead on the ground and thirty-two captured, together with two heavy and seven light machine-guns, and three Lewis guns. There was a cost, however. Plunkett's battalion alone suffered seventeen killed, including two officers, and nine officers and sixty other ranks wounded. It earned Plunkett a third DSO, his officers four MCs, and eleven MMs for his men. The last vestiges of the belief that 40th Division was only good for line-holding had vanished. Rue Prevost remained in German hands, though, but they were driven out of it forty-eight hours later.

The Division's nibbling away at the German defences continued, as the ground lost during the April offensive was gradually regained. By 7 September it was closing up to the Lys north of Armentières. The Germans were not prepared to surrender the river without a fight and there was now a pause while the British Second Army, of which 40th Division was a part, and the Belgians prepared for a major attack. The first phase of this took place during the first week of October and saw the division isolate Armentières and cross the Lys to its north and south. On 7 October Frank welcomed an old friend, Richard Andrews, who had arrived back in France after recovering from the wound he had received at Cambrai. According to Frank, he had asked for Paris leave, but, having found out where Frank's brigade was, took a train to Bailleul instead.[40] As it happened, Lt Col Robert Johnson had gone on leave to England on 28 September and so Andrews took over command of the 13th East Lancashires.* Frank therefore now had two of his old 'war dogs' commanding battalions in his brigade and it was only the North Staffords which remained a concern.

By 12 October the Germans had evacuated Armentières and it soon became clear that they were intending to begin a withdrawal. This resulted in a period of very active patrolling in an attempt to detect a withdrawal at the earliest possible moment. It was on the night of 16–17 October that this began, with 121 Brigade following up. Roubaix was occupied on the 18th, but the following day the division was pulled out of the line for a couple of days of rest. It then began to relieve 31st Division on the west bank of the River Escaut on 26 October. In the meantime, the problem of a suitable CO for the North Staffords was finally solved when Frank apparently found Acting Major Ernest O'Connor MC, who had been serving under Plunkett in the 13th Royal Inniskilling Fusiliers, but whom Frank had placed temporarily in command of the 13th East Lancashires between when Johnson went on leave and Andrews arrived. Frank himself states that he had been an NCO in the Irish Guards in 1914. In fact he had been a CSM in the 2nd Grenadier Guards and had been commissioned into the Manchester Regiment in January 1915, thereafter serving with the Royal Munster Fusiliers for almost two years prior to joining 119 Brigade in August 1918, although

---

* There is a slight mystery here. The 13th East Lancashires' war diary (TNA WO 95/2606) records Johnson going on leave and Andrews assuming command. Yet the *London Gazette* (12 December 1918, 15 January 1919) states that Johnson remained in command of the battalion until 26 November. It is possible that Johnson fell sick while on leave or maybe Frank had fallen out with him and unofficially suggested that he extend his leave.

Frank states that he had just arrived when he 'fingered' him, having no wish to try the CO's Pool again. As it was, O'Connor '"electrified" that battalion [North Staffords] and really transformed it within ten days.'[41]

The Germans resisted stubbornly for a time on the Escaut, but on 2 November posts were established on the far bank. Frank's brigade did not, however, do much until it relieved 121 Brigade on 4 November in the area of Pecq and Warcoing on the west bank of the Schelde, to the north of Bailleul. Should the German defence of the river appear to weaken, Frank was under orders to deploy strong patrols across the river and secure the ridge overlooking it. His reserve battalion was then to pass through to seize the next ridge to the east. He immediately pushed patrols across the river, but the Germans were still in strength. Not until the 8th were there indications that they might be beginning to thin out. Accordingly, that night Frank pushed his two forward battalions across and quickly seized the ridge overlooking the river. Plunkett was convinced that he wanted his brigade to be the first across the river. Assisted by one company from the corps cyclist battalion, the advance continued without pause. Frank was clearly urging his men on. In the end, on 10 November the brigade found itself pinched out by 29th Division on the left and 59th Division on the right and withdrew, having, in the words of the East Lancashires' chronicler, 'advanced seventeen kilometres in thirty-two hours.'[42] It was a spectacular end to Frank's war. For, on the following day, the Armistice came into effect.

Chapter Nine

Lithuanian Inspector General: 1919–20

In the immediate aftermath of the Armistice coming into effect, 40th Division issued orders that the existing outpost line was to be held and that the priority for those formations, including 119 Brigade, not engaged in this was finding comfortable accommodation for the troops. No one was to be allowed forward of the outpost line and fraternisation with the Germans was strictly forbidden. All units were to be in the same state of preparedness as they had been before the Armistice. Next came a redeployment of the division to the Roubaix area, with 119 Brigade placed around Croix. While there would be some military training, the emphasis was on education so as to prepare men for their re-entry into civilian life. Keeping the troops entertained through sport and variety shows was another priority. Demobilisation itself began at the beginning of December and by mid-January well over 4,000 men had departed the division.

While all this was taking place, Frank was thinking about his future. He might have assumed that his fine record during the past four years of fighting would enable him to continue in the Army. Indeed, he submitted an application to this effect before November 1918 was out. He attached a handwritten record of service, which included some of his former fallacious claims of having taken part the 1900 Ashanti expedition and 1906 Zulu uprising in Natal. In addition, he asserted that he took part in operations in Liberia during 1906–08 and had been employed with the Canadian reserve forces 1908–12. Nevertheless, his request was strongly supported by Sir William Peyton. He wrote:

> General Crozier's services during the present campaign have been such as to bring him continuously to notice as a leader of marked ability with great capacity for the administration and training of his troops, and his name has accordingly, with every confidence in his capacity, been submitted for command of a division … I am strongly of the opinion that it is in the best interests of the public service that he should be re-employed in the Army and accordingly recommend that he be reinstated with the substantive rank of Lieut.-colonel.

This letter went up through the channels, but the Military Secretary's branch was adamant that Frank's pre-war misdemeanours precluded him from being granted another regular commission in the post-war Army despite his proven fighting record.[1] With a wife and family to support, and realising that he had not enough service as a regular to have earned an army pension, he did some hurried rethinking and decided that the newly-created League of Nations might well have posts that would suit his qualities. Accordingly, while in London on leave in December he knocked at the doors of the Colonial Office, the Foreign Office and the Treasury, those government departments concerned with the League, only to be told that he would have to make

Map 8: The Baltic States, November 1919.

his application through the correct military channels. He also wrote to his former divisional commander, General Ruggles-Brise, who was now the Military Secretary at GHQ, asking whether there might be a post for him with the occupation forces in Germany. Ruggles-Brise replied that he would certainly think of Frank if something came up, adding 'but what will the 119th Brigade do without you?' and inserting a postscript: 'I hear that you and your men did wonders.'[2]

Once back in France, Frank therefore penned another application, this time in quadruplicate. He stressed that 'at the outbreak of hostilities I immediately threw in a permanent and lucrative appointment to serve with the Armies in the field.' What this position was is not clear; it certainly does not seem to tally with Frank's work with the Ulster Volunteer Force. One therefore suspects that he was once more gilding the lily. Peyton again provided a strong recommendation, while Frank's corps commander, Beauvoir de Lisle, added merely that he recommended Frank for employment. Fifth Army forwarded the application to GHQ without comment, where Haig's assistant military secretary, Lt Col G.E. Vesey, asked in his covering letter that the War Office look on the application favourably in view of Frank's 'valuable services' during the war. The reactions of the Colonial Office and Treasury are no longer recorded, but it is fair to assume that they were negative. As for the Foreign Office, which replied to the War Office on 19 March 1919, it regretted that Frank was too old, at the age of forty, for the diplomatic or consular services, but that his name had been added to a list of possible candidates to help administer former Turkish territories.[3]

Meanwhile, Frank's efforts during the final Hundred Days had been recognised by another mention in despatches. He also had his own Christmas card made. It featured the Royal Irish Rifles' crest on the front and the badges of all the regiments which had been represented in 119 Brigade on the back. The inscription inside read: 'Wishing you lots of Good Luck in 1919 from Brig Gen F.P. Crozier.' One recipient was Herbert Lamb, Frank's erstwhile signals officer. He had been gassed and evacuated in early October and Frank tried to obtain an immediate MC for him, but without success. Nevertheless, Lamb must have been cheered that Frank took the trouble to stay in touch.[4] One problem that Frank did have at this time concerned Richard Andrews. Sir William Peyton had told Frank to impress on his commanding officers the importance of the education scheme then being introduced to prepare the troops for their return to civilian life. Frank did this, but was informed by one of Andrews's company commanders that he had rubbished the scheme and been insulting about Peyton on a battalion parade. Frank summoned Andrews's adjutant and the battalion doctor to his HQ and put them in one room while he interviewed Andrews in another. He then placed Andrews under arrest, but the latter went back to his own mess while Frank was talking to his adjutant and the MO. There he lined up all his officers and asked them who had told Frank about his behaviour. He was in the process of drawing his revolver when Frank's staff captain, Reggie May, stalked him from behind and disarmed him. Frank then had tea with Peyton and obtained his authority to release Andrews from arrest on medical grounds. He then arranged for Andrews to be medically evacuated. In this way he was able to preserve discipline and the name of Andrews, who had become a close friend.[5] It would, however, not be the last time that the paths of the two men crossed.

As demobilisation took an ever firmer hold, Frank departed in late February for a few days in Brussels and Cologne. He was horrified by what he saw: 'Brussels is an orgy of vice in which many British soldiers join.' Cologne was little better, with girls trading their bodies for food. It caused him to tighten up discipline on his return. Indeed, he had already been concerned over the rise in the incidence of venereal disease among his men and had told his commanding officers to provide lectures and 'every convenient and reliable means of protection and sterilisation.'[6] Soon after he returned, 40th Division was reduced to virtually cadre strength. Indeed, on 24 March Sir William Peyton relinquished command of the division and it was retitled 40th Division Cadres, with Frank appointed to command them. But this new appointment lasted a mere three weeks and on 14 April he apparently flew, rather than going by sea, back to England.* He had previously turned down the offer of command of a battalion on the Rhine on the grounds that he hoped to obtain a post in Palestine, but stated that he would be happy with a battalion command at home. As it happened, the commanding officer of the 3rd (Reserve) Battalion the Welsh Regiment had died suddenly. This was Alexander Pope, who had commanded the 12th South Wales Borderers during the first few months of Frank's time in command of 119 Brigade. He had had an attack of septic bronchitis in November 1917 and then suffered another attack, which killed him.[7] The Military Secretary's branch therefore proposed that Frank succeed him, especially since he had had command of Welsh troops and was used to them. The Adjutant-General's branch agreed and so, nine days after leaving 40th Division, Frank took over the battalion.[8] It had spent the second half of the war as part of the Tees Garrison in north-east England, but had now moved down to Chatham and was under Thames & Medway Garrison. Frank clearly did not enjoy his time there, since it was largely taken up with dealing with the unrest triggered by the poorly-conceived demobilisation policy. The one bright spot was a visit to Buckingham Palace to be invested with the three orders that he had been awarded during the war. His final task was to take the battalion back to Cardiff, where it was dismantled.

It was now late July and Frank was out of a job, although he had been granted the honorary rank of brigadier general. True, while still at Chatham he had applied for a post in the police force being created to take care of the newly-created League of Nations mandate of Palestine, writing that 'it is a country possessing opportunities suitable to my temperament.' The Colonial Office was sufficiently interested to ask the War Office for further details on him, but that was as far as it went.[9] He also proposed himself for command of a Territorial Brigade, but that, too, was turned down. Clearly he was getting short of money, since he asked the War Office for an advance on his war gratuity, but again he met with a rebuff.[10] Matters then took a more promising turn.

In June 1919 it was announced that the French had conferred the *Croix de Guerre*** on him and an invitation arrived to go to Paris to receive it in person from General

---

* This is what he stated on his disembarkation form (TNA WO 374/16997), but in *Brasshat* p240 he says that he took the leave boat from Boulogne and implies the same in *Impressions and Recollections*, p240. He therefore may have been being flippant on the form.

**He was mentioned in despatches yet again in Haig's final despatch (*London Gazette* 5 July 1919). Crozier himself claimed that his Croix de Guerre was avec Palme, but this is not reflected in the *London Gazette* (19 June 1919).

Jean Degoutte, who had commanded the French Sixth Army during 1918.[11] Frank travelled to a France basking in the fact that the peace treaty with Germany had finally been signed, with its terms, especially with respect to the swingeing financial reparations that Germany was forced to pay, very much to French liking. Yet while the Versailles Treaty may have formally brought the war with Germany to an end, a number of loose ends needed to be tidied up, especially in the Baltic states.

These had been part of the Russian empire until 1915, when they had been overrun by the Germans. The October 1917 revolution had caused Russia to sue for peace and the resultant March 1918 Treaty of Brest-Litovsk formally ceded the Baltic states to Germany. The Allied reaction to Lenin's determination to end the war against Germany was a desire to lend support to the anti-Bolshevik elements which were now taking up arms against the new regime. There was, too, a belief that Lenin was a German pawn. It was, however, the deployment of 50,000 German troops under General Rudiger von der Goltz to aid the White Finns in overthrowing the Bolshevik regime which had been established in Finland which triggered a deployment of forces. This was because the German move was seen as a threat to the munitions stocks built up at Archangel to support Russia prior to it leaving the war and fears that the Germans might establish a U-boat base at Murmansk. Consequently, British troops began to be sent to the port in early 1918. In June the Allies agreed to substantial reinforcement and further troops were landed at Murmansk (codenamed Syren Force) and Archangel (Elope Force). There was hope that these might combine with other anti-Bolshevik forces, apart, of course, from the Germans, in order to overthrow Lenin.

The Baltic States had, at the end of the war, declared their independence. Indeed, thanks to its large diaspora in North America, Lithuania had attempted to do this in 1914. As a result, and unlike Latvia and Estonia, there were no purely Lithuanian formations in the Imperial Russian Army. Be that as it may, the turmoil that afflicted Germany in the immediate aftermath of the Armistice caused the Russian Bolsheviks to believe that the country was ripe for revolution and they launched an invasion of the Baltic states with the aim of passing through them and then helping the Spartacists in Germany to seize power. In November 1918 they invaded Estonia and had overrun much of the country by the end of the year. Help came in the form of 2,000 Finnish volunteers and German *Freikorps* under the overall command of von der Goltz, and British-supplied weapons and support from a naval squadron in the Baltic. This was sufficient to halt the Red Army advance and to remove the Bolshevik presence in the country. Lithuania and Latvia also suffered, losing their respective capital cities to the invader. It was primarily von der Goltz's men who eventually brought the Red Army to a halt, however. Matters were further complicated for Lithuania in March 1919, when the Poles joined in the fray. They expelled the Russians from Vilnius, the capital, but held on to it. Meanwhile, the Germans attempted to secure both Latvia and Estonia, but without success. They did, however, seize part of north-western Lithuania.

The Allied reaction to all this was to send a number of missions to the region. A British diplomat, Sir Horace Rumbold, was sent to Poland, accompanied by a military mission led by Brigadier-General Adrian Carton de Wiart VC. The French also sent a sizeable mission to Poland. The Foreign Office sent a mission to the Baltic

States under Lt Col Stephen Tallents, who had been badly wounded in 1915 while serving with the Irish Guards and had been seconded to the Ministry of Munitions and then Food. A further mission was headed by General Sir Hubert Gough, the sometime commander of the Fifth Army. His task was to represent the Allies in both Finland and the Baltic States, advising on how best these countries could withstand the Germans on one hand and the Bolsheviks on the other. While he did have some success in getting von der Goltz to withdraw his forces, the White Russians in the area saw this as removing a valuable weapon in their war against the Bolsheviks. Indeed, this enmity eventually led to the withdrawal of Gough's mission in October 1919 and its replacement by an Allied mission led by the Frenchman General Henri-Albert Niessel, with Brigadier General A.J. Turner as the senior British officer, and tasked with removing the German presence from the Baltic states.

It was the Lithuanians who found themselves in the worst position. The Poles had taken their capital Vilnius and the surrounding territory, there was the threat from von der Goltz, although the Germans had paid them some much-needed money as reparations, and that from the Bolsheviks. They also enjoyed an uneasy relationship with Latvia and Estonia. They had raised an army and a small air arm (equipped mainly with German aircraft), but were desperately short of equipment. Like the other Baltic states, they sent a delegation to Versailles early in 1919, but were frustrated by the fact that the Allies would not give full recognition to the state. They also distrusted the French, whom they suspected, quite rightly, of being pro-Polish, and looked to the British for material help. The British, though, were unwilling to do this, given their other post-war commitments. The only brightness lay in the United States, where Lithuanian expatriates began to organise a legion to go to Lithuania to fight for its secure independence. They received no backing from the US government, however, and so a plan was hatched for these volunteers to go to Canada, masquerading as labourers, and from there to sail to Riga in Latvia.[12] The Lithuanians needed experienced officers to help train and organise their infant army, however. Given their suspicion of the French, they decided to recruit British officers.

While in France, Frank probably heard that the Lithuanians were looking for British officers to help them organise their armed forces and wrote to their delegation to the Peace Conference, but it was the Foreign Office which officially informed him of the fact. Thereafter events moved very rapidly. On 11 September, and back in London, he wrote to Kazys Bizauskis of the Lithuanian delegation to London. 'I desire to join the English speaking Legion, now being formed for service in Lithuania, in any capacity.' He gave a brief resume of his Great War service, adding a short record of his military service on a separate sheet. This stated that he had served throughout the South African War and repeated the myth that he had taken part in crushing the 1900 Ashanti revolt, although he said that this was in 1901. He also claimed not to have left the British Army until 1912 and to have served in northern Nigeria until 1907. He included Peyton's very favourable January 1919 report on him and ended his letter: 'I can bring many good officers and men with me, with whom I am in close touch, and who have served under me.' He added a PS: 'I have raised troops all over the world for 20 years.'[13] His offer seems to have been taken up immediately and on 19 September Frank was back in Paris to be enrolled as a brigadier general on the Lithuanian General Staff. He also had to swear an oath of allegiance to 'support and defend the Constitution of the Republic of Lithuania against all enemies, foreign and domestic, that I will bear true faith and allegiance to the same, that I take this obligation freely, without any mental reservation or purpose of evasion, and that I will well and faithfully discharge the duties of the office upon which I am about to enter: So Help Me God.'[14] Once signed up, Frank got the Lithuanians to agree that his team would be paid at British Army rates, although they would adopt Lithuanian ranks. He also successfully argued that he should be a major general, on the grounds that the Lithuanians were more likely to listen to him. In addition, he was allowed to select his own team. They would have to swear the same oath as he had. The initial contract was to be for one year and would allow expenses for visits back to Britain.[15] With everything agreed, Count Vincent Czepinski, who headed the Lithuanian delegation to the United Kingdom, wrote to the Foreign Office on 22 September, stating that Frank had been attached to the Lithuanian delegation at Versailles. Probably on Frank's prompting, he also reminded the Foreign Office that Frank's name was on a list for possible appointments in the Middle East.[16]

Frank established a good rapport with Colonel Gedgaudas, head of the Lithuanian Military Mission in Paris. Indeed, the latter became very enthused:

We are very glad to hear that several officers of the General Staff are willing to go to Lithuania – it is a mighty good piece of news – and I may assure you that they will be cordially welcomed in Lithuania. I shall appreciate greatly if you will be kind to send them to Paris as soon as they are ready to proceed. They will be sent to Lithuania at the earliest opportunity. The fares of officers and interpreters will be paid in Paris.

The interpreters, whom Frank understandably considered essential, were also to be enlisted in the Lithuanian Army. Of major concern was the procurement of arms and munitions. Frank had obviously intimated that he could obtain them from Britain: 'We are very anxious about arms and munitions; your information seems to be promising, and I shall be very obliged for further news on this subject.'[17] What Frank did or did not tell the Lithuanians is not known. Suffice to say, their delegation to the Peace Conference wrote to the British Foreign Secretary on 1 October pleading for equipment so that Lithuania could continue the fight against the Bolsheviks and the Germans in the Baltic states. A detailed list of requirements was attached to the letter and it is significant that it was largely US equipment and for a force of 7,000 men. This was precisely the number that the American Lithuanians intended to despatch.[18] The Foreign Office turned down the request.

As for the officers that Frank chose to take with him, he needed a chief of staff and looked no further than Anthony Muirhead, his erstwhile brigade major in France. He was, according to Frank, playing in a cricket match when he received the message, but agreed with alacrity to join his former brigade commander.[19] Another old comrade-in-arms was Jim Newton, who had been quartermaster of the 9th Royal Irish Rifles and had been awarded the MC. He had, however, been invalided in unfortunate circumstances. He had been going through a recently killed officer's kit during the Battle of Cambrai in November 1917 when he accidently discharged the man's revolver into his knee. Newton would clearly not be of much use in Lithuania and Frank planned to employ him to run the London end of the operation. Accordingly, he set up an office in the Lithuanian delegation's premises at 14 Cornwall Gardens, London SW7.[20] Frank also enlisted other former members of his battalion. Among them were Stephen Lynch, who had spent the last part of the war as a prisoner of war,[21] and Philip Woods, Frank's second-in-command in the 9th Royal Irish Rifles. On Frank's elevation to brigade command, Woods had been promoted to command the battalion, but fell foul of General Oliver Nugent during the Third Battle of Ypres in summer 1917 and had then commanded a reserve battalion of his regiment at home. He volunteered for service in Russia and found himself commanding a battalion of Karelians involved in driving a mixed force of Germans and Finns out of part of Karelia. Indeed, he found himself in Lithuania a bare two weeks after returning home.* Others, too, joined Frank after seeing service in Russia. One was Charles Dowding, who had originally been commissioned as a Kitchener volunteer into the Somerset Light Infantry in September 1914 and rose to command a battalion of the North Staffords, earning two DSOs and an MC along the way.[22] Another was C.E.G. Nye MC, who had served in the Special Brigade RE for much of the war. Although demobilised in January 1919, he was recalled to the colours that June and sent to Russia as a gas warfare expert. He would perform the same role in Lithuania.[23] The Russia veterans were probably attractive to Frank for two reasons. First, they had hopefully developed some understanding of that part of the world, and secondly they had picked up a smattering of the Russian language, which many Lithuanians spoke.

Frank's team would eventually consist of sixteen officers, but he would also take an additional five individuals partially under his wing. They were under a separate contract to create a fully operational Lithuanian air force. Their leader was New Zealander Roderick Carr. He had originally been in the Royal Naval Air Service and had commanded No. 2 Slavo-British Squadron, which had a mix of Russian and British pilots. He would be gazetted with a DFC for his work in Russia while in Lithuania. Joining him was a Welshman, Parcell Rees Bowen, who had served with the 5th Welsh Regiment on Gallipoli and Palestine. He had then transferred to the machine-gun corps before joining the Royal Flying Corps as an observer. He continued to serve in Palestine, winning an MC and DFC, before returning home in January 1919 suffering from venereal disease. After his recovery he flew with No. 3 Slavo-British Squadron, earning a bar to his DFC.[24] Another observer, also with service in Russia, was Joseph Esebius Pereira, who was domiciled in British Guiana and had served in the ranks of the ASC (MT) in Mesopotamia before being commissioned and then serving in Egypt and Aden with the RAF.[25] Carr also had another British pilot, Alfred Saunders, who had achieved twelve victories flying with No. 60 Squadron on the Western Front in 1918, winning a well-deserved DFC, and this in spite of having smashed his face the previous summer in a plane crash in England.[26] He had not served in Russia, but the final member of Carr's team had, although he was not an aviator.

---

* A good account of Woods's life, including his own reminiscences of Russia, is Nick Baron's *The King of Karelia: Colonel P.J. Woods and the British Intervention in North Russia 1918–1919*, Francis Boutle, London, 2007.

Thomas Girdwood Macfie had a chequered background. Born in London in 1892, he became a 'rolling stone'. As a teenager he made to visits to the United States and then went to Australia, where he claimed to have been a journalist. By 1911 he was back in Britain and had enlisted as a private in the RAMC. He then seems to have gone to South Africa, where he served a period of time with the Witwaterstrand Rifles and gave his occupation as surveyor. He came back to England and was married in July 1912 and had a son the following year. Yet by November 1914 he was in Canada and was granted a commission in the Canadian infantry. He was posted to England and attached to the staff of the Canadian Training Division, based at Shorncliffe, Kent. In November 1916, however, he was court-martialled for attempting to divert official money into his own pocket and was dismissed from the service. He then joined the South African forces, rose to the rank of sergeant and was commissioned in January 1918. Thereafter he won an MC on the Western Front and a DSO in Russia for retaking a village from the Bolsheviks. What work he did with Carr is not clear.[27] Macfie, however, would become closely entwined with Frank.

While Frank was gathering his team together, he was also attempting to get government backing for his venture. On 5 October he wrote to the Foreign Office stating that among his tasks on arrival in Lithuania would be advising on the policing of the country. He continued: 'Personally I am of opinion that a constabulary based on the lines of the Royal Irish Constabulary, of which I have had considerable opportunity to observe in Ireland, would be suitable for the country as a whole.' If the Lithuanian government agreed with him, Frank asked whether a 'small commission' could be sent across by the Irish Office. The Foreign Office's view was that his mission was purely a private one and that the British government was not prepared to become involved.[28] As for the Lithuanian Army being supplied with British weaponry, Frank saw the processing of this as one of Jim Newton's main roles, but again the Foreign Office wanted nothing to do with it, much to Lithuanian disappointment. The War Office distanced itself as well. One of Frank's team, Lt Col R.H. Monck-Mason DSO, with whom Frank had served in Nigeria, had commanded the 1st Royal Munster Fusiliers during the middle part of the war. He had been removed from command in December 1917 for lack of drive brought on by ill-health, but had then gone to Russia in Elope Force in June 1918.[29] He was now on half pay. After taking the oath of allegiance to Lithuania, he was prompted to formally ask permission to go to Lithuania. Lord Hardinge, the Permanent Under-Secretary of State for Foreign Affairs, replied that there was no objection to retired officers participating, 'provided that it is clearly understood that they would be doing so on their own responsibility.' Half pay, however, was another matter since the officer was still 'nominally under the orders of the War Office' and 'might be required, as a servant of a Baltic government, to take part in a policy disapproved by His Majesty's Government.' By the time Monck-Mason received this guidance he was already in Lithuania, but he took heed and on 3 January 1920 informed the Foreign Office that he had severed his connection with the Lithuanian government.[30]

Frank was undeterred by the lukewarm official policy towards him. On 12 October his advance party left Britain, going by train from Paris to Kovno via Berlin. It consisted of Anthony Muirhead, now promoted to colonel in the Lithuanian Army, and two others. One was Major Edward Mills MC, who had enlisted in the ranks

Hopetoun Dormitory, Wellington College, 1894. Frank is cross-legged on the ground in the centre. (*Wellington College Archive*)

Manchester Regiment mounted infantryman, South Africa, 1900. (*Tameside Local Studies and Archive*)

Lieutenant Frank Crozier of the Northern Nigeria Regiment, 1902. He is wearing the Queen's Diamond Jubilee medal riband.

Ethel Cobb before she married Frank. She was called Babbie by her family and close friends. (*Carol Germa via Mike Taylor*)

2nd Northern Nigeria Regiment detachment on the march, 1905. (*National Army Museum*)

The 'siege' of Craigavon House, March 1914. Frank, wearing his UVF brassard, using a field telephone. (*Somme Association and Heritage Centre*)

H The UVF's Belfast Brigade parading in Belfast shortly before the outbreak of war in 1914. (*Imperial m War Museum Q081771*)

Some of the members of Frank's training mission to Lithuania. Muirhead and Philip Woods are on either side of Frank. In the rear row Tom Macfie is on the extreme right with Roderick Carr next to him.

Frank and Tom Macfie inspect new Auxiliary recruits, Dublin 1920. (*Pathé*)

Typical Auxiliaries, probably from F Company, which was based in Dublin.

Grace and Frank, with, from left to right on the bench, Hester, Mary and an unknown boy, September 1921. Probably taken at Alec Thorneycroft's house near Reading. (*Carol Germa via Mike Taylor*)

Dick Sheppard advertising a Peace Pledge Union rally in Hyde Park on 28 February 1937. Frank is featured among the sponsors. (*Peace Pledge Union*)

Frank, shortly before his death, with Grace and Barri the Great Dane. (*Carol Germa via Mike Taylor*)

Frank's miniature medals. From left to right: CB, CMG, DSO, Queen's South Africa, Ashanti Medal (X), King's South African General Service, Zulu Uprising Natal (X), 1914–15 Star, British War Medal, Victory Medal, Queen's Diamond Jubilee (?), Edward VII Coronation (?), Croix de Guerre with palm (?), Africa (X). (X) = not entitled, (?) = doubtful entitlement.

of the Middlesex Regiment in 1898 and served throughout the South African War. He landed with the 1st Middlesex in France in August 1914 and rose to the rank of company sergeant major before being commissioned into his own regiment in November 1916. Thereafter he had been attached to the 19th Royal Welsh Fusiliers, which, of course, had been in Frank's brigade in France.[31] The other was Ronald Vanstone Millard (wrongly called Rowan Stone Millard by the Lithuanians), who is something of a mystery. Educated in Canada and the USA, he claimed to have served in the French and US armies from March 1916 until October 1917, and then with the American Red Cross. He joined the 2nd Artists Rifles in July 1918 for officer training and then transferred to the Household Brigade Officer Cadet Battalion, but was hospitalised with neurasthenia. On discharge in January 1919 he was attached to No. 11 Officer Cadet Battalion, but then, in the company of several others in the Artists Rifles, was commissioned second lieutenant on the General List that March. Demobilised three months later, although not before being acquitted by court-martial of a charge of gross indecency, he returned to the United States, but then appears to have come back to England. He was appointed lieutenant in the Lithuanian Army, but what his function was is not clear, although the suspicion is that it was possibly as an interpreter.[32] The original plan had been for them to go by sea from the French Atlantic port of La Pallice to Libau (present-day Liepaja) in Latvia, the only port of entry to then virtually landlocked Lithuania.[33] The uncertain situation in the Baltic caused a change of plan, however, and the journey would now be made by train. On 13 October, the day after the advance party left, Frank wrote to Oliver Harvey of the Russia department at the Foreign Office from the Pavilion Hotel, Folkestone, from where he was also preparing to leave for Lithuania. He informed Harvey of the departure of Muirhead and the others and also said that he had passed on the Government's decision not to provide arms to Lithuania to the delegation in Paris – '[I] do not know where they prepare to try to buy'. Frank went on to mention Jim Newton's role in London and concluded: 'My one idea now is to get the Lithuanian Army fit before Master Von der G thinks of counter marching to Kovno [Lithuania's temporary capital]!!' What the letter did show was that while the Foreign Office was happy to brief Frank on official policy towards Lithuania, it was not prepared to give him any material backing, even though Harvey in his reply did state that 'within the limits of our policy … you may be sure that we will assist you all we can.'[34]

In *Impressions and Recollections* Frank recounts that he took Ethel and Mary with him to Lithuania. He describes it as a tedious journey, with a stopover in Berlin for a number of days. News that he was bringing his family with him was already known and the junior Lithuanian officers prepared themselves to pay court to Mary, not realising that she was only nine years old.[35] In another account Frank states that he had to change trains on the East Prussia-Lithuanian border in the middle of the night. William Marshman, formerly of the Royal Berkshires and now Frank's ADC, managed to obtain a handcart for the baggage and manpower to push it and the party crossed on foot into Lithuania. As they did so, a dozy Lithuanian sentry fired at them, knocking Frank's stick out of his hand. The sentry then called up reinforcements, who deposited much of the baggage in a stream.[36] Eventually order was restored and Frank proceeded to Kovno, arriving there on 22 October and establishing himself and his family in the Hotel Metropole. *The Times* published a telegram from its

Warsaw correspondent that same day stating that 'demobilised officers' had arrived to train the Lithuanian Army, presumably referring to the advance party, and on the following Saturday it noted Frank's arrival, reporting that 'other officers of high rank are leaving London shortly for Lithuania to help General Crozier.' Yet neither the Foreign Office nor the War Office saw fit to warn Tallents and Turner. Indeed, on 31 October General Turner telegrammed the War Office stating that Colonel Henry Rowan-Robinson, his man in Kovno, had reported Frank's arrival and asked: 'Is this officer part of a British mission, and have I any authority over him? If not, what are our respective roles?'[37] Not, however, until 11 November did Tallents's representative in Lithuania, Lt Col Richard Ward AFC, report Frank's arrival.[38] There was, however, no immediate guidance from London as to how Frank and his officers were to be treated.

The next group of Frank's officers arrived in mid-November. They were led by another redoubtable warrior, Lt Col H.S.J.L. Hemming DSO. Originally commissioned into the East Lancashire Regiment in 1900 he had served in the South African War and then Somaliland prior to resigning his commission in 1906 and settling in South Africa. At the outbreak of war in 1914 he joined the South African Forces, taking part in the crushing of the initial rebellion by the Boers and then in the German South-West Africa campaign. At the end of 1915 he went with the South African Brigade to Egypt, where he lost an arm during the February 1916 Battle of Aqaqir against the Senussi. Undeterred, Hemming went with the brigade to France and was again wounded during the Somme fighting. He also took part in the Third Battle of Ypres and was gassed. He finished the war commanding the South African Reserve Battalion.[39]

Frank, in the meantime, had already set to work. Colonel Tallents set out to visit Kovno from Riga on the night of 31 October. He had an adventurous journey, first suffering a broken axle to his car and then nearly losing his life when attempting to cross a bridge, the central section of which had been blown by the Bolsheviks, at 30mph. Luckily the supporting beams of the bridge were still intact and it was on these that the car came to rest. He eventually reached Kovno on the evening of 2 November. He met Ward and Rowan-Robinson and came into contact with Frank for the first time. The two clearly hit it off and, with Rowan-Robinson, agreed a plan of action. The first essential was that Lithuania and Courland be cleared of German and Russian troops. If the worst came to the worst the Poles would be allowed to intervene, but only if Memel was occupied and the Lithuanians provided with equipment, either through Poland or purchased from General Bermondt's so-called Western Russian Army. This had originally been raised to fight the Bolsheviks, but in autumn 1919 combined with von der Goltz and attacked Latvia, but was repulsed. Tallents telegrammed these views to London while he was still in Kovno, but in his report written after his trip he also stated: 'I also arranged with General Crozier that I would try to bring about a military conference between the Lettish and Lithuanian commands. General Crozier obtained agreement of the Lithuanian Prime Minister to this conference.'[40] The Foreign Office sent a copy of this report to the War Office, which expressed concern over Frank's involvement in setting up the Latvian–Lithuanian conference. In a letter to the Foreign Office dated 18 December 1919 Bertram Cubitt, the Under-Secretary of State for War, wrote:

In view of the fact that General Crozier proceeded to Lithuania in a purely private capacity, and has severed his connection with His Majesty's Forces, I am to suggest that His Majesty's Commissioner for the Baltic States and His Majesty's Minister in Warsaw might be instructed that in dealing with General Crozier, care should be taken to avoid giving the impression that he is one of the British Military Representatives or in British Service. It seems important that in any official dealings with him he should be regarded and treated simply as an officer in the Lithuanian Army.[41]

In other words, Tallents* and Sir Horace Rumbold, the minister in Warsaw, were being told to keep Frank at arm's length.

However, Frank would have been cheered by a report in *The Times* of 9 December. It stated that progress was being made in training the Lithuanian Army and that the cooperation between the Latvians and Lithuanians, which was now being achieved, was 'a triumph for the British Diplomatic Mission and for General Crozier and his staff, who have pressed the cooperation point of view on the Governments of both countries.' He was also working hard to reform and equip the Lithuanians, but it was an uphill struggle. As he himself wrote in *Impressions and Recollections*: 'The Lithuanian private soldier was, and is, "a first-class fighting man," but he was atrociously led. His generals and colonels knew nothing about tactics, and cared nothing for their men.'[42] Much of the problem apparently lay in the fact that in the old imperial Russian Army few Roman Catholics were allowed into the higher echelons. Lithuania was, and is, a staunchly Roman Catholic country, and hence Lithuanians in the Russian Army had been restricted to the lower ranks. Consequently, according to Frank, 'the higher posts [in the Lithuanian Army] were filled by patriotic Lithuanians who lacked military training for those posts.'[43] It was not helped by the fact that the commander-in-chief, General Pranas Liatukas, 'let the discipline of the army steadily deteriorate and had no personal touch with the army,' according to Colonel Ward.[44] Frank, too, later claimed that Liatukas resented his presence and schemed against him.[45] Nevertheless, both Frank and Rowan Robinson made several visits to the Lithuanian Military School, which had been established early in 1919 to provide officer training.[46]

By Christmas 1919 another problem had arisen for Frank and his officers, and a much more serious one. Colonel Ward again:

The Lithuanian Government realised very soon after engaging these officers it would be very hard to find the money to pay them, and as the mark steadily

---

* Interestingly, Tallents makes no mention of Frank or his officers in his autobiography *Man and Boy* (Faber, London, 1943), although he devotes several chapters to his time in the Baltic States. In his autobiography *Happy Odyssey* (Cape, London, 1950) Carton de Wiart does mention Muirhead. When a prisoner of war in Italy in the middle of World War Two one of his fellow inmates was General Dick O'Connor, who had been captured in April 1941 during Rommel's first offensive in Libya. The two men had not met before but discovered that they had a mutual acquaintance in Anthony Muirhead. O'Connor had known him in Italy during the Great War and Carton de Wiart had come across him when in Warsaw.

declined in value and these officers were to be paid in sterling at British rates of pay, the situation of course became continuously worse. No pay was forthcoming and from Christmas onwards General Crozier refused to send his officers out to the outlying districts of Lithuania to continue their work. That meant, of course, that all the officers had been in Kovno doing little or nothing, which apparent idleness naturally the Lithuanian Government was not likely to explain away to its own disadvantage.

To illustrate the point, Ward stated that Frank was earning 50,000 marks monthly, while his Lithuanian major general counterpart received a mere 1,800 marks. He put the blame on both sides: the Lithuanians for failing to take the cost into account when engaging the team, and Frank for not being more conciliatory once he realised that they could not afford such a large team on the agreed rates of pay. General Turner, in another report written at the same time, felt that Frank had been reasonable in refusing to negotiate until the Lithuanian government had paid his people up to date, which it eventually did in early February. It was thereafter agreed that all British officers, apart from Frank and two others, were to be withdrawn, and four new officers recruited in England, but at reduced rates of pay, which would also apply to the three remaining in Lithuania. Thus Frank's monthly pay would be reduced from £135 to just under £42. Those whose services were no longer required would receive an additional month's pay in lieu. This agreement did not, however, initially apply to Major Carr and his team. Colonel Ward also noted that Colonel Reboul of the French military mission had offered to replace the British team in its entirety at no expense to the Lithuanians, but that they had declined the offer.[47]

But if Frank was having difficulties with the Lithuanian government, so were the American Lithuanians. An advance party arrived in Kaunas on the last day of 1919. They found that the Lithuanians were insistent that the US Lithuanian Legion be broken up and its men distributed among Lithuanian Army units. The fact that the vast majority of them had been brought up in the USA and did not speak Lithuanian was of no account in breaking up the Legion. Eventually only some 700 US volunteers actually travelled to the country, many of the others clearly put off by the Lithuanian refusal to allow them to fight as one body.

Money may have been the main reason why Frank's mission was failing. But the behaviour of some of his officers was also ruffling Lithuanian feathers. He himself admitted that some sent out were 'of the wrong type'.[48] This is supported by a handwritten Foreign Office minute dated 7 September 1920. The author, whose signature cannot be deciphered, was reporting on a meeting he had had with Count Tyszkiewicz, who had taken over as the Lithuanian representative in London. The latter complained about British personnel who had been in Lithuania during the past two years. In particular he mentioned 'the 40 [sic] officers with General Crozier', a commercial agent, and Colonel Ward, who at the time was still in Lithuania. According to the Foreign Office official, the Count had said 'the behaviour of nearly all of these had been "deplorable". The officers had been dishonest – cheques disallowed and so on.' As for Ward, 'he is constantly drunk and given up to debauchery to such an extent that the Lithuanians are now completely scandalised.' Only Ward was of Foreign Office concern, since he was on an official mission sponsored by them, but a subsequent investigation of his behaviour found nothing to support the Lithuanian accusations.[49] Yet Major General R.B. Pargiter, who at the time was serving as a captain under Rowan-Robinson, supported the Lithuanian view. Apart from the problem of Frank's mission being paid at British rates, 'the officers had been hastily recruited and were not of high standard.' As for Ward:

> … [He] had gained the nickname Rasputin because of his insatiable sexual appetite. He certainly was an extraordinary type. I remember on one occasion in the middle of one of his own dinner parties, he suddenly rose and took the lady of his choice upstairs, reappearing in due course as if nothing had happened, although the lady looked a trifle embarrassed. And the rest of his staff took their cue from him.[50]

Frank himself later wrote that his officers were 'a queer collection' and that only two were 'absolutely reliable', Muirhead and Mills.[51]

Frank was also continuing to have problems with scheming by the Lithuanian hierarchy. He recounted that on 5 January 1920 he arrived in Riga for a conference with representatives of the Great Powers. On arrival he heard that Dvinsk had been captured by the Poles and Letts. This took him by surprise, since the Lithuanians should have been involved in the attack. The reason they were not was because there was evidence that they were trading with the Bolsheviks. What had actually happened was that a Lithuanian regimental commander, acting on the authority of General Liatukas, the commander-in-chief, had given safe passage through the lines to a Jewish convoy laden with boots, medicines, and a considerable quantity of roubles. Certain individuals were clearly feathering their own nests, but Frank's efforts to have them purged were in vain.[52]

In terms of slimming down the team, Jim Newton had already been stood down on 1 January. Dowding, too, had left Kovno on 12 January. The mysterious Millard left at the beginning of February and on the 9th of the month a further nine officers departed. They were followed on 19 February by Major John Hibbert MC. He had been taken on as the ordnance expert, having served much of the war in the Army Ordnance Department, and while visiting a Lithuanian ammunition depot on 8 January 1920 had been injured in an explosion which necessitated the amputation of his right foot. Rowan-Robinson had presided over a subsequent court of enquiry that established that Hibbert was in no way to blame and the Lithuanians subsequently awarded him £500 as compensation.* This left just Frank, Muirhead and Woods. Major Carr and his team were also still at work, although Saunders had left since he had to attend a medical board back in Britain. An indication of how Frank was thinking at the time is revealed in a letter he sent to Brigadier General Thomas Hickman, who had been inspector general of the UVF and then commander of 109 Brigade until May 1916. He was now Unionist MP for Wolverhampton South and Frank was clearly looking to his future. Dated 13 February, Frank wrote:

---

* On returning to England, Hibbert asked HQ London District if he could go to a military hospital for further treatment. The reply was that he could, but that he would be charged six shillings a day for his bed.

I am taking the liberty of writing you a line to ask you to be good enough to put in a word for me to the under Secretary of State for Foreign Affairs, for my future [sic], which at present is pretty vague.

My position here as Inspector General of the Army is satisfactory and fairly secure, in so far as nothing in the Baltic is secure, in the strict sense of the word.

With the elections coming off in April, the whole attitude of the Lithuanians towards the world in general (and me in particular!) may then be changed.

The present Government and House of Assembly is a self constituted one, a coalition of moderates. The elections, on April 4th, may bring in, and probably will, advanced socialists and a sprinkling of Bolos [Bolsheviks]. In the meantime I am learning the languages and conditions. I have travelled all over the Baltic Provinces on duty, Estonia, Latvia, East Prussia etc., and have been in conference with the Commanders-in-Chief of Estonia and Latvia and the politicians of those countries, so I am gaining experience.

I hit it off very well with both the Military and Foreign Office Missions throughout the Baltic.

When the veil is lifted, as appears probable in the near future, and we have contact with Russia I should be sorry to have the experience I have gained lost for all time.

My view is that if I was given the opportunity I could put in many years of useful work in Russia, if I live.

Frank went on to state that he believed that the Allies must adopt a new approach to Russia, especially since he believed that the Bolsheviks were becoming more moderate. If 'a moderate Government and Democratic Constitution is found' he saw no reason why Russia should not be recognised, since this would be the best way to halt its expansionism. Hickman duly sent the letter to Cecil Harmsworth, the Under Secretary of State, who in turn showed it to Curzon. In his reply to Hickman, Harmsworth stated that Curzon appreciated Frank's work and would bear him in mind ' in the event of any opening occurring in the future in that part of the world.'[53]

Events now moved quickly in Lithuania. On the evening of 22 February soldiers, disaffected by poor pay and food and the fact that they were barred from voting in the forthcoming election, revolted in the artillery barracks in Kovno. This spread to one of the reserve battalions and part of the cavalry. Frank was dining in his hotel at the time and recalled shells flying overhead. The government called out loyal troops, but General Liatukas was captured by the rebels when he went to parley with them. At 7am next day, loyal troops launched an attack across the River Niemen against the artillery barracks and by lunchtime the rebels there had surrendered. Further fighting also took place on the airfield, where the rebels had tried to capture the aircraft, but all was over by mid-afternoon. As for Frank's part in this, he and Muirhead found an armoured car, with engine running, and used this to rescue General Liatukas. He was immediately replaced by General Silvestras Zukauskas, who, according to Colonel Ward, immediately set to, 'working indefatigably to improve the discipline of the army.'[54] The only foreign fatal casualty during the brief revolt was an American officer with the Lithuanian Legion, but the Lithuanian government did pay his mother a pension.[55]

Frank had apparently been working hard since he arrived in Lithuania to get Zukauskas made commander-in-chief.[56] Yet now that he was finally in post, hopes that Frank might be able to provide worthwhile assistance to the Lithuanian Army were quickly dashed. The government was not prepared to grant him the powers that he wanted and Zukauskas, not being a member of the Lithuanian cabinet, could do nothing.[57] Consequently, Frank and his remaining officers felt that they had no option but to resign, which they did on 1 March. Major Carr and his team resigned at the same time. Frank's view was that, in spite of Carr – 'an excellent fellow'* – there had been problems with the Lithuanian air arm from the outset. He blamed much of this on Tom Macfie, 'who I believed exercised a baneful influence over the whole Corps and some of my other officers. Through the machinations of Macfie the British connection with the Flying Corps was broken up.'[58] Frank and Tom Macfie would, however, work together, and even more closely, in the near future. Frank departed Lithuania immediately, but he left Anthony Muirhead in Kovno for a few more weeks 'to report progress'. Apparently, Muirhead told him that the Lithuanians were convinced that they had been conned over the mission's pay.[59]

Once back in London, Frank was not afraid to voice his views on the situation in the Baltic States. He saw Cecil Harmsworth at the Foreign Office and also addressed the House of Commons Services Committee, stating that the Allies had to settle the question of Poland's frontiers and see that Memel and 'Little Lithuania' were incorporated with Lithuania.[60] He also thought that the Lithuanians might want him back. On 21 April he wrote from Bootle, near Liverpool, where he was staying, to Mr J.D. Gregory at the Foreign Office:

> As I have been out of Town for some time I am rather out of touch with the Lithuanian Legation & cannot get any definite policy out of them regarding their ideas regarding myself. Tyszkiewicz keeps saying that they want me back but I do not trust them. I do not want to lose touch with that fascinating part of the world, if I can help it. Can you help me, either by probing the Lithuanians for information or getting me out under the F.O. to some part of Russia?

He finished by pointing out that his kit was still in Libau, as was Ethel, who had apparently gone there 'on the advice of the Lithn [sic] War Minister.' This was Antanas Merkys, who had taken over the post in mid-March. Frank had apparently sent her and Mary there when the abortive revolution took place in Lithuania. Be that as it may, Gregory was in no hurry to deal with Frank's request and did not contact Count Tyszkiewicz until 19 May. In his reply, the Count expressed 'astonishment at General Crozier's request' since he had already written to Frank stating that he had been in touch with his government. On 26 May he saw Gregory in person and

---

* Carr would go on to have a distinguished career in the RAF. After taking part in Sir Ernest Shackleton's final 1921 Antarctic expedition, he rejoined the RAF and helped to set up a new non-stop flying distance record in May 1927, when attempting to fly from England to India direct. He commanded No. 4 Group Bomber Command for much of World War Two and became AOCinC India in April 1946.

told him that he thought Frank's request 'odd' and remarked that, in any event, 'the General was now more concerned in political & commercial matters than military.' He also did not expect an early reply from the Lithuanian government.[61] There matters rested, although a report in *The Times* of 9 July did state that Frank had received an invitation to return to Lithuania, but had declined it.

That Frank became interested in commercial matters is supported by a letter he wrote to Oliver Harvey at the Foreign Office in early July. He asked that the British government intercede on behalf of a syndicate which was interested in buying up large timber estates in Estonia and Latvia, since their respective governments were blocking the deal. A question was also asked in the House of Commons of the Secretary for Overseas Trade. In both cases the answer was that it was purely a matter for the Estonians and Latvians and the British government declined to be involved.[62] Meanwhile, Ethel and Mary had remained stranded in Libau. According to Mary's later recollections, Ethel had refused to return to Britain by train because she had been put off by the incidents on the Lithuanian border on their journey out. They eventually ran out of money and ended up on the beach, where a local baroness took pity on them and provided them with black bread and milk to subsist on. With the help of some British sailors and the local consul they managed to get on board a refugee ship and eventually reached London. Here they were given shoes and food by the Salvation Army and ended up staying in a vicarage, maintained by funds supplied by the family solicitor.[63] Frank makes no mention of this in his writings and nothing else exists in the Foreign Office files on the dilemma that Ethel and Mary found themselves in. Thus, if Mary's memory is correct, it would seem that Frank did little to extract them and the indication is that he had finally broken with Ethel, perhaps on account of her behaviour in Lithuania.

While Frank's connection with Lithuania was now finally severed, there was still one loose end to be tidied up. During their time in Lithuania, Anthony Muirhead had kept an official diary and, on his return to Britain in April, Frank asked him to send the diary and some other papers to Cecil Harmsworth. Muirhead duly did this and nothing more was heard until Frank wrote to Gregory in late May asking for the diary to be returned to him. Gregory denied that the diary had ever reached the Foreign Office. Frank persisted and eventually got Muirhead to write to the Foreign Office, enclosing a copy of an acknowledgement of receipt of the diary from Harmsworth. Finally, in November 1920, the Foreign Office was forced to admit that it had lost it.[64] By this time Frank was deeply involved in another challenge.

Chapter Ten

Trouble in Ireland: 1920–1921

Frank's attention had now been drawn to Ireland, where since the Armistice a grave situation had arisen. The truce between the British government and those who wanted Home Rule that had come about as a result of the war in Europe had been interrupted by the Easter Rising of 1916. At the time the majority view in Ireland was that it had been carried out by extremists and had done nothing for the Home Rule cause. But the executions of the leading rebels in the immediate aftermath caused a wave of revulsion, which swelled the ranks of the Republicans. This was reflected in increasing Sinn Fein success in by-elections for the Westminster parliament. Matters were aggravated by the British Government's intention, brought about by the manpower crisis, to introduce conscription in Ireland. In the face of a Nationalist outcry the Government backed down, but Sinn Fein increased its strength. This was borne out by the December 1918 General Election, when Sinn Fein won seventy-five per cent of the Irish seats. Instead of taking up their seats at Westminster, the Sinn Fein members set up their own parliament in Dublin, the Dail. With no positive reaction from the British government, more extreme elements of the Nationalist cause decided to take matters into their own hands. On 21 January 1919, on the very day that the Dail met for the first time, Irish Volunteers killed two members of the Royal Irish Constabulary (RIC) as they escorted a consignment of gelignite to a quarry in Co. Tipperary.

Throughout the remainder of 1919 the Irish Republican Army (IRA), as the Irish Volunteers renamed themselves, continued to target the RIC. By the end of the year fourteen RIC men had been murdered and twenty wounded. Furthermore, on 19 December the IRA unsuccessfully ambushed the Lord-Lieutenant of Ireland, Field Marshal Viscount French. It was this last act which prompted the Westminster government to involve the British Army. At the time there were in Ireland two complete infantry divisions, each of three brigades, based on Cork and the Curragh, two brigades covering Dublin, six additional battalions of young soldiers, a cavalry brigade, and various other ancillary units, including an armoured car battalion. Loathe to introduce martial law, the Government laid down that the Army could now apprehend individuals whose arrest warrants had been issued by the Chief Secretary for Ireland. It could also search individuals and premises for arms, explosives and seditious literature. This, however, was not enough to stem the increasing number of attacks against the RIC, especially in the rural areas of the southern part of the country. Members of the RIC soon felt beleaguered in their barracks. Threats to their families forced some to resign. Recruiting declined.

To stiffen the RIC, in May 1920 the Government appointed a police adviser to the British administration in Dublin Castle. This was Major General Henry Tudor, a gunner, who had had a good war, rising from captain to command the 9th (Scottish)

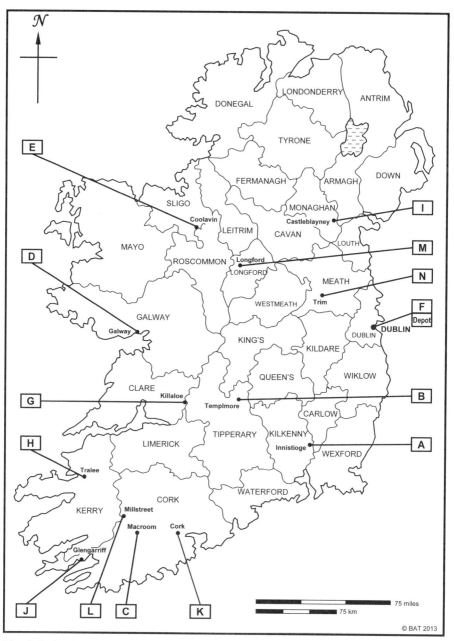

Map 9: Ireland, showing the deployment of ADRIC companies in January 1921.

Division in Flanders, where Frank had known him. He also knew Winston Churchill, then Home Secretary, personally and this probably influenced his appointment. Clearly Tudor's first task was to improve police morale and he believed that this was best done by strengthening its numbers. One solution to this had already been found as early as May 1919, when the First Lord of the Admiralty, Walter Long, suggested that ex-servicemen could be used to swell the ranks of the RIC. Viscount French was in favour, but Joseph Byrne, the inspector general of the RIC, was against. In December 1919 French replaced Byrne with his deputy, who gave the green light for this source of recruits. At the very beginning of the new year the first mainland recruits came forward and thereafter they averaged about 100 per month. There appears to have been a shortage of the RIC's bottle-green uniforms and so the ex-service recruits were clothed in khaki with an RIC cap and belt.[1] This motley dress earned them the nickname of the Black and Tans, after a famous pack of Tipperary foxhounds.

The Black and Tans might have bolstered the RIC, but Tudor wanted to take the war to the IRA, who had now begun to organise themselves into mobile 'flying columns'. He wanted to use the same concept, employing men with dash and initiative. This he believed was a job for ex-officers, rather than the ex-rank-and-file who were making up the Black and Tans. Again, the concept of employing ex-officers was not new. Sir John Taylor, the Assistant Under-Secretary for Ireland, revealed in a letter dated 18 February 1920 to the Treasury that Viscount French, after consultation with the RIC's hierarchy, had come to the conclusion that 300 demobilised officers could usefully be employed in organising RIC barracks defence. They would be given a year's contract and be paid one pound per diem. The Treasury did not think much of the idea and instead proposed that a few such individuals be used to inspect barracks defences and advise on how they should be improved. It stated that it would be prepared to support up to fifty ex-officers in this capacity.[2] This does appear to have been put into effect. Now Tudor wanted to provide the RIC with a proactive mobile force and revisited the idea of employing ex-officers. On 6 July he addressed a memo to the Under-Secretary at Dublin Castle. He recommended extending the employment of ex-officers to assist in the defence of barracks by recruiting a further 500, who would be known as Temporary Cadets, but who would rank as RIC sergeants for disciplinary purposes. They would wear khaki uniform, with RIC badges and buttons, with the letters 'T.C.' worn on the shoulders, or the uniform of a RIC sergeant. Pay would again be seven pounds per week and the contract for one year.[3] This appears to have been approved very quickly, since at a Cabinet meeting held on 23 July 1920 General Tudor stated that it was important to 'develop the idea of temporary cadet officers, 500 of whom he had obtained'. Their role was to reinforce the RIC 'in certain parts of the country.' He also claimed that they had had 'a great effect', which was an odd statement to make since the first recruits for what was soon to become known as the Auxiliary Division of the RIC (ADRIC) did not come forward until the same day as this Cabinet meeting and did not report to the RIC training centre at the Curragh until 27 July.[4]

As for Frank's own part in this, his interest in Ireland appears to have been renewed soon after he returned from Lithuania. He recalled going to see the Ulster politician Sir James Craig (later Viscount Craigavon), then Parliamentary Secretary to the

Admiralty, soon after the murder of Tomas MacCurtain, the Lord Mayor of Cork, in March 1920. Sir James told him that the government was looking to resolve the situation through the partition of Ireland. Lord Londonderry, the Under-Secretary of State for Air and another Ulsterman, said much the same thing. Frank then went over to Dublin and saw the RIC's Inspector-General, T.J. Smith, who spoke of the chaotic state of the police in Ireland. He also heard that the UVF was being reformed under the now Lt Col Wilfred Spender and in July 1920 applied to rejoin, but Spender turned him down for reasons unknown.[5] He then heard that Tudor was about to be appointed police adviser and so, on the pretext that they had served together in France, Frank buttonholed him in the Army & Navy Club and asked for a job. Tudor offered him command of a company, but said that he would be initially ranked as a temporary cadet.[6] This implies that this meeting probably took place when Tudor was in London for the 23 July Cabinet meeting on Ireland, a good two months after he had been appointed police adviser, and not before he left for Ireland for the first time, since in May 1920 ADRIC had not been conceived. As it was, Frank was enrolled in Tudor's new police force on 3 August 1920 and given ADRIC number 65. This, of course, was after the first recruits had already come forward and belies Frank's later claim that he raised ADRIC.[7]

Before Frank left for Ireland, however, there was a change to his personal life. The delay in Ethel's return from Lithuania and the fact that Frank appears to have done little or nothing to help her get back are further indications that the two had, to all intents and purposes, separated, probably because of Ethel's continued drinking. A new woman now came into Frank's life. Her name was Grace Roberts. She was the seventh of nine children born to Richard Croker Roberts and his wife Elizabeth. Her father was a land agent to the Earl of Leitrim and steward at Lough Rynn for twenty-eight years, although Grace always claimed that he was a physician. She was born in 1893, but both her parents died when she was seven and it is probable that she was then looked after by her eldest sister. According to the 1911 Irish Census she had by then found employment as a nursemaid to the three small children of Thomas Henry Kimmis, a landowner with an estate some fifty miles south-west of Dublin. He died in 1915 and it is not known what Grace did thereafter, but in summer 1921 she was in London. Frank left no record of how he and Grace met, but she did write an account, albeit somewhat garbled, which appeared in *Reynold's News* after Frank's death.

Grace recalled that Frank was 'just back from Russia', when he invited one of his old colonels to dine with him. She meant, of course, Lithuania. As for the colonel, it is probable, for reasons which will become apparent, that this was Richard Andrews, who had so distinguished himself when second-in-command and then CO of the 17th Welsh Regiment in the Cambrai sector in 1917 and then subsequently in command of the 13th East Lancashires during the final offensive in 1918. Thereafter he had gone to North Russia, where he became the chief liaison officer with the Onega River Force, which was part of Elope Force and made up of White Russian units. On 20 July 1919 the 5th North Russian Rifles, which was based at the headquarters of the Force, mutinied and arrested all the British officers and NCOs, including Andrews, present at the time. The party was taken to Moscow, where they were incarcerated until being repatriated in April 1920, with Andrews eventually reaching England on 22 May.[8] Grace was therefore likely referring to Andrews's return from Russia.

In any event, Andrews had already arranged a dinner party, to which Grace had been invited, and he asked Frank to come as well. They apparently had little to say to one another, but established that they were both Irish and, according to Grace, that their families knew one another. Frank was asked to see Grace home, which he did and then went to his club to write her a letter of proposal. He called her next morning to find out if the letter had arrived, but it had not and so Frank explained that it asked whether she would be prepared to visit his mother if asked. That afternoon Grace had tea with Frank at his club. He took her back to her house and saw the letter lying in the hall. At this he fled. For Grace 'the letter was a shock to me. But I realised that this was a man I could really love.' An invitation duly arrived from Frank's mother and they went to visit the Thorneycrofts at their house near Reading. Grace also told Frank that she was related to Lord Roberts of Kandahar,* and he was worried that his stepfather might learn of this and take against Grace on account of the rebuke he had received from Roberts after Spion Kop, but all clearly went well. How much Frank told Grace about Ethel, to whom, of course, he was still married, is not known, but he certainly looked to her to take care of his elder daughter, as is evidenced by the fact that he brought her and Mary over to Dublin.

When Frank arrived at the Curragh he was aghast at what he found. Little thought had been given to the organisation and administration of the Temporary Cadets when recruiting began. Writing in March 1921, when events were still fresh in his mind, Frank noted that the first cadets arrived in Ireland on 27 July and thereafter there was a steady stream, but:

> … misery, inconvenience, and hard drinking could have been avoided had arrangements been made for the reception of these men, for their ordinary comfort – quartering, messing, and discipline, – but instead the men were running about the Curragh as they liked. The original members of the division, which then had no name, had to arrange their own messing and canteens, and there was nobody in command. Conditions were appalling.

Matters improved 'on or about the 10th of August', when the existing cadets were formed into A and B companies.[8] The latter was commanded by Frank and the former by Major J.H.M. Kirkwood DSO.[9]** Kirkwood would have been someone with whom Frank got on well and was typical of some of the adventurous types who joined ADRIC. He was well known in North Devon, where he lived the life of a country gentleman. A keen yeoman, he joined an irregular unit in South Africa, was badly wounded in the right hip and then joined the 7th Dragoon Guards, being mentioned in despatches for saving two wounded men under heavy fire. During 1910–12 he was the Unionist MP for South-East Essex. When war broke out in 1914, John Kirkwood was on a German vessel bound for East Africa, where he intended to go big-game hunting. He disembarked at Naples and made his way to Paris, where he succeeded

---

*   No evidence can be found that Grace was related to Lord Roberts and it is probable that this was another myth, like her claim that her father was a doctor.

**   Frank states that Kirkwood was a Lt Col.

in gaining a commission in the 4th Dragoon Guards, but was badly wounded in the same right hip, as in South Africa, at Messines on the last day of October 1914. Once recovered from his wound, instead of rejoining his regiment, he apparently took himself off to Russia, obtained a commission and served with a Cossack regiment on the Eastern Front. He then left for East Africa, but later returned to France, joining the newly-created Household Battalion in autumn 1916. He rose to second-in-command and earned a mention in despatches and a DSO, before being appointed to command the 1st Royal Irish Rifles in September 1917. Unfortunately, it would seem that his health broke down after six weeks and in February 1918 he was forced to resign his commission and was granted the honorary rank of major.[10] Clearly he had not lost his sense of adventure when he joined ADRIC, but, as we shall see, it is probable that Kirkwood was still not fully fit.

As far as organisation was concerned, Tudor had written a minute to Sir John Anderson, the Chief Secretary at Dublin Castle, on 28 July recommending that the cadets be formed into companies, each made up of eight platoons of twenty-five men each and that company and platoon commanders receive additional command pay of 15 shillings and seven shillings and sixpence per diem respectively. The Castle appears to have considered these amounts to be too high. On 11 August Tudor wrote again. He had now looked into the company organisation more deeply and had decided that it should now consist of four platoons. Company commanders should receive ten shillings per day command pay, their seconds-in-command five shillings, platoon commanders four shillings and section commanders two shillings. Furthermore, he recognised that a 'small depot staff' was needed for what he was now calling 'this Temporary Cadet Corps' and that this should consist of a quartermaster and a mess caterer. Throughout this time one suspects that Frank was pressuring Tudor to establish the force on a properly organised footing. Seven days later, and with the 'Temporary Cadet Battalion' now grown to ten companies, at least on paper, Tudor addressed another memorandum to the Castle proposing that a 'head' of the sub-depot at the Curragh be established so that each company would receive its fair share of leaders at each command level and recommended 'Brig-General T. Cadet Crozier' for the job, with command pay of one pound per diem.[11]

Frank's appointment was duly confirmed and at much the same time his command was designated the Auxiliary Division, Royal Irish Constabulary. By this time A Company had been deployed to Kilkenny and B to Limerick and during the first week of September the depot was moved from the Curragh to Beggar's Bush Barracks in Dublin itself. Frank also took on an adjutant, selecting Edward Mills, who had been with him in Lithuania and had enrolled in ADRIC on 24 August, probably persuaded to do so by Frank.

Enlistments into ADRIC were growing steadily. By 4 September it could boast a strength of 405 men and a month later this had increased to 605. By Christmas 1920 its strength was over 1,150.[12] Volunteers were initially interviewed by Major Cyril Fleming, the RIC recruiting officer at the Army Recruiting Office, Great Scotland Yard in London (recruiting for the new force was quickly extended to Liverpool and Glasgow). If found acceptable, they made their way to Dublin, where they were attested. Initially, they did not begin to be paid until they reached Ireland, but at the beginning of October it was agreed that they should receive up to three days' pay to cover the period between acceptance and attestation.[13] As for the cadets themselves, the vast majority had been officers, although many had seen service in the ranks. Interestingly, the largest contingent had been in the Royal Air Force. A good number had also been decorated for bravery and they included three VCs.* Significantly, only a small proportion had an Irish background. As for their motivation for joining the auxiliaries, it would appear to have been a mixture of difficulty in obtaining civil employment and an inability to settle down in civilian life after the stress and excitement of the war years.[14] Given this and the failure to establish a proper structure for ADRIC, including selecting proven leaders prior to recruitment getting under way, it is not surprising that discipline was likely to prove a problem. Frank explained how it operated:

> It was found that the RIC code was not suitable, in so far as punishment was concerned, and a scale of fines was drawn up by me and approved by the Police Adviser [Tudor]; this scale has since been increased and was in operation before I left the division. A company commander could fine a man five days' pay 'off his own bat' (£5.5s); the commandant could fine a man seven days' pay (£7.7s).
>
> The question of dismissals was carefully dealt with. At one time the commandant had the power of dismissal; in October [1920] the power was, by the Police Adviser's orders, reserved for the PA alone and the following rules became operative:- (a) the commandant could call upon a man to resign; if he refused he could dispense with his services as being 'unsuitable for service with the Auxiliary Division,' the man having the right to appeal to the Police Adviser; (b) the commandant could dispense with services as above; (c) the commandant could recommend dismissal.

In addition, Frank lectured every draft arriving in Ireland on the dangers of drink and treatment of the local population and a qualified RIC officer also addressed each company, as did Tudor before it deployed.[15] Frank's main problem was that once the companies had moved to their operational areas it became difficult for him to exercise strict control over them. Indeed, much depended on the individual company commanders and it soon became clear that some were simply not up to the job.

The reaction by the RIC to the establishment of ADRIC was initially mixed. While they welcomed the reinforcement, there was a suspicion that the auxiliaries might make promotion within the ranks of the permanent RIC more difficult since the competition would be considerably fiercer. There was also resentment that the cadets were paid the same rate as an RIC sergeant. The police authorities were quick to counter this in their in-house publication *The Weekly Summary*. ADRIC had been specifically created to 'combat murder' and 'will not compete with the Force – but co-operate with it.'[16]

---

* They were Capt James Leach late Manchester Regt, 2Lt James Johnson late Northumberland Fusiliers, and 2Lt George Onions late Rifle Brigade, who had won his Cross as a LCpl in the Devons.

The ADRIC companies themselves were highly mobile, each being equipped with seven Crossley tenders, two Ford cars, and, on occasion, one or two Rolls-Royce armoured cars. They were armed with service rifles, revolvers, Winchester repeating rifles and shotguns, Lewis guns, Vickers machine-guns and grenades. They were dispersed throughout the southern part of the country, but no one seems to have had clear-cut operational control over them. Certainly the local police authorities seem to have had little or no influence over the ADRIC companies, apart from to an extent in Dublin, where they were directly under the eyes of both Frank and Tudor. Lt Gen A.E. Percival, who surrendered Singapore in 1942 but was commanding the 1st Essex in Cork during 1920–21, observed:

> They [the Auxiliaries] consisted entirely of ex-officers and worked by companies, each company being allotted a district where the rebels' organisation appeared to be strongest. They entirely came under the Military area commandant for tactical purposes, and were of assistance in taking over responsibilities for parts of the Military areas, but their independent status did not always make for smooth working, and the old difficulty arose of a force being under one commander for tactical purposes and another for administration.[17]

In these circumstances one would have expected Frank to make visits to military commanders to ensure that his companies were doing as the Army wanted, but there is no evidence that he did so. General Sir Nevil Macready, commanding the Army in Ireland, professed to have never met Frank,[18] and General Sir Peter Strickland, who commanded 6th Division, makes no mention in his diaries of Frank visiting him, and he was conscientious over recording the names of visitors.[19] As it was, the main tasks of the ADRIC companies were conducting surprise raids and searches, but as often as not these were as a result of faulty intelligence or simply on the whim of the company commander, which did little for the reputation of the Auxies, as they were popularly known.

One of Frank's early problems concerned Kirkwood's A Company. In early October 1920 Kirkwood sent in his resignation, asking to return to the mainland immediately. Frank told Kirkwood to come and see him, which he did. One look at Kirkwood's haggard appearance and Frank put him on the mail boat forthwith. Kirkwood had had an apparently unnerving experience when lunching with a well-known Kilkenny figure, Major Dermot McCalmont. An IRA gang had broken in and were after the major's weapons. While the gunmen searched for them, Kirkwood, who luckily was not in uniform, and his hostess were held, with their hands up, in the dining room. As it happened, McCalmont had handed over his weapons to the police for safekeeping. The gang departed and only just missed Kirkwood's ADRIC car, which arrived to collect him. At the same time Frank discovered that one of Kirkwood's platoon commanders had been up to mischief. Major Evan Cameron Bruce DSO MC had served in the Tank Corps and in Russia. He had also lost an arm. He claimed to have a personal grudge against Sinn Fein and, indeed, Frank dismissed him from ADRIC for striking an Irishman. Yet a few days later he was still in Kilkenny with his nephew, who was also an Auxie. They hired a car and, with a subaltern and sergeant from the Devonshire Regiment, drove to the creamery at Kells, where they held up the manager and robbed the safe. Bruce himself was arrested in Cheltenham a few days later and was tried by court-martial at Waterford. Found guilty, he was sentenced to a year in gaol. His nephew was tried separately and imprisoned for three months. The two soldiers asserted that they did not get out of the car and served merely as witnesses. All this had also contributed to Kirkwood's stress, which Frank reckoned drove him to an early grave.[20]

During his investigations into A Company Frank renewed the acquaintance of Tom Macfie, whom he had known in Lithuania. It would seem that when he was in that country Macfie hatched a plan to murder Frank because he had taken steps to try to end an undesirable love affair in which Macfie was involved. Warned, Frank had apparently confronted Macfie, dismissed and expelled him from Lithuania.* Now he discovered that Macfie was second-in-command of A Company. According to Frank, the latter came up to him and offered to resign immediately on the grounds that Frank would have it in for him. Frank, however, was prepared to let bygones be bygones. Indeed, he appears to have immediately arranged for Macfie to be posted to HQ ADRIC, probably so that he could keep an eye on him. He was then sent to London on recruiting duties before, as we shall see, Frank made Macfie his adjutant.[21] Another Lithuanian hand who joined ADRIC, probably enlisted by Frank, was the one-armed Lt Col Herbert Hemming. Richard Andrews also joined and Frank gave him command of G Company. Another from Lithuania days was the airman Parcell Bowen. He had become a secret agent, one of a number of British officers employed in this role in Ireland. He was murdered by person or persons unknown in late October 1920. Frank was aware of all this and resented Dublin Castle's propaganda department for attempting to cover up the murder.[22]

October 1920 saw ADRIC suffer its first fatality. On the 10th,, Temporary Cadet William Anderson was accidently shot at Beggar's Bush Barracks. November was, however, to prove to be a grim month, not only for ADRIC but also for Ireland as a whole. The IRA claimed its first two ADRIC victims on 6 November when two cadets, Bertram Agnew and Lionel Mitchell, were abducted and killed. Worse was to come just over two weeks later on what came to be known as Bloody Sunday, 21 November 1920.

Frank recalled that shortly after 9am on that fateful Sunday he was inspecting an auxiliary company which was about to deploy to its operational base. Once he had completed his inspection he planned to go round and see Mary and Grace at the flat they were staying in. Suddenly, a motorcycle dispatch rider and a hospital nurse appeared on the parade ground and told him that there had been murders in Lower Mount Street and that two auxiliaries (Cecil Morris and Frank Garniss) had also been shot by an IRA picquet as they made their way to Beggar's Bush to summon reinforcements. Frank did not hesitate. He mounted a platoon in Crossley tenders and led it in a Ford car to Lower Mount Street. The street was initially quiet, but then they heard screams from an upstairs window at No. 22. Noting that the front door was open, Frank jumped out, revolver in hand, and rushed in, followed by his

---

* There is actually no evidence that Macfie did not leave at the same time as the remainder of Major Carr's team, which had been assisting the Lithuanian Air Force.

men. He fired at a man jumping out of a window, but missed. One of his men also fired and brought the man down in the garden behind the house. The victim turned out to be Frank Teeling (Frank spells him 'Tealing'), an IRA man and one of five who had entered the house. He was carried back into the house, where, according to Frank, an RIC man threatened to kill him on the spot. Frank disarmed the man and arranged for Teeling to be taken to hospital.* Within the house itself he discovered the body of Lt Henry Angliss DCM, an intelligence agent operating under the name of McMahon. Another agent residing at No. 22, Lt C.R. Peel, was also an IRA target, but he had barricaded himself in his room and, although the IRA men fired seventeen shots through the door, they failed to hit him.

Having cleared matters up, Frank drove to Dublin Castle to report what had happened. He then returned to Beggar's Bush and apparently resumed his inspection. This completed, he went to see Mary and Grace. It would seem that they were living in an upstairs flat at 38 Upper Mount Street, since Frank states that two officers living in the flat below had also been attacked by the IRA that morning and that they had been murdered outside a bathroom. This ties in with the deaths of Lieutenants Peter Ames and George Bennett, who were residing at that address. By the time Frank arrived the bodies of the two men had been removed and their flat was in the possession of the police. Not surprisingly, Mary and Grace, and another person whom Frank said was with them, were very shaken. What had taken place was a concerted effort by the IRA to destroy the British intelligence network in Dublin and, in all, it resulted in fourteen dead and five wounded.

Frank himself does not seem to have stayed long at Upper Mount Street to comfort and reassure Grace and Mary. Instead, he went off to lunch at the Shelborne Hotel.** It was there that he states that he received orders to despatch an Auxiliary company to Croke Park, where there was to be a Gaelic football match, and it was suspected that some of the spectators might be armed.[23] In fact, the operation was to be a combined army-police operation. The 2nd Duke of Wellington's Regiment (part of the Dublin Brigade) had been ordered to provide picquets of no fewer than one officer and fifteen men at each entrance to the ground. The commanding officer was told that the game was scheduled to start at 2.45pm and that fifteen minutes before this a 'Special Intelligence Officer' would address the crowd through a megaphone, telling everyone to leave by the proper exits at the end of the game and warning that anyone attempting to leave the ground by any other way would be shot. In his written orders Lt Col Robert Bray was also told that two armoured cars would arrive at 3.15pm to support him. Once the spectators began to leave, all males were to be searched

---

*   Once he had sufficiently recovered from his wounds, Teeling was court-martialled and sentenced to be hanged. On the night of 21 February 1921 he escaped, with two others, from Kilmainham Jail and lived until 1976.

** In *Ireland For Ever* p103 Frank makes no mention of seeing Mary. He states that after completing the inspection of the auxiliary company, he had breakfast, went through his mail in the orderly room, and then played squash prior to lunching at the hotel. In *Impressions and Recollections* opposite p258 he does reproduce his diary for 20–22 November, but there is nothing on his movements in the entry for the 21st.

for weapons and 'Special Party C' was to be deployed to assist in this.[24] This group consisted of a detachment of Black and Tans and regular RIC police from Phoenix Park barracks and one from the ADRIC Depot Company, with Mills, still the ADRIC adjutant, in overall charge of the group. In his written statement, made shortly after the event, Mills said his mission was to search the Croke Park spectators as they came out of the ground through the four gates surrounding it. He was instructed to leave the barracks and arrive at the Russell Street gate at about 3.35pm:

> I was travelling in a car in rear of the RIC leading the Auxiliaries. As we approached the railway bridge in Russell Street near SW corner of the ground I saw the men in the tender in front of me trying to get out of their car and heard some of them shouting about an ambush. Seeing they were getting excited I stopped my car, jumped out and went to see what was the matter. At this moment I heard a considerable amount of rifle fire, as no shots were coming from the football field and all the RIC Constables seemed excited and out of hand. I rushed along and stopped the firing with the assistance of Major Fillery who was in the car with me. There was still firing going on in the football ground. I ran down and into the ground and shouted to all the armed men to stop firing at once and eventually the firing ceased.

Mills noted that the crowd was in a panic, but he managed to get them into some order and they were searched as they filed out. In the ground itself he noted a number of dead and injured, some of whom had been trampled on. He declared that his auxiliaries did not fire and concluded: 'I did not see any need for firing at all and the indiscriminate firing absolutely spoilt any chance of getting hold of any people with weapons.'[25] As it was, twelve people were killed and eleven seriously injured. The cause was probably the RIC element, which was commanded by an ADRIC officer, Major G.V. Dudley DSO MC, and which arrived at the ground before the military picquets. The police claimed to have been fired on, but there is no firm evidence of this, and it would seem that trigger-happy Black and Tans were to blame.* Frank forwarded Mills's report to Dublin Castle, and he claimed they 'blacklisted' Mills as a result.[26] Significantly, it was Tom Macfie who countersigned the report on Frank's behalf, which indicated that he was in fact taking over from Mills as adjutant of ADRIC.

Frank also had other matters on his mind at this time. On 22 November, the day after Bloody Sunday, he left for Galway, where D Company was stationed. His mission was two-fold. First, he wanted to replace the company commander, who had a drink problem. This he did, appointing Lt Col F.H.W. Guard CMG DSO in his place.

---

* George Dudley himself had served in the British South Africa Police and the Canadian Royal North-West Mounted Police prior to 1914 and served in the Royal Garrison Artillery during the Great War. According to McCall *Tudor's Toughs* p269, he deserted the RIC in early January 1921. He eventually landed up in Fiji and in 1924 was appointed Commissioner of Police for the Australian Northern Territory. Three years later his appointment was terminated on account of his drinking and indebtedness.

More serious was the death of a local priest, Father Michael Griffin. D Company had already established a reputation for itself during the month or so it had been in Galway for coming down hard on those suspected of having IRA connections. Griffin had been lured from his presbytery on the night of 14 November and then vanished. Six days later, his body was found in a shallow grave in a bog. There were grave suspicions that ADRIC had been involved and this is what Frank went to investigate. His work completed, Frank set off for home, going via Killaloe in County Clare, where he inspected Andrews's G Company, which was based in the picturesque Lakeside Hotel. While there he learned that there was a plot to do away with Bishop Michael Fogarty of Killaloe because of his Sinn Fein sympathies. Frank therefore arranged for him to be warned and the bishop then apparently went 'on the run'. Whether Frank told Andrews to leave Dr Fogarty alone is not known, but his men raided the bishop's house on 3 December. Certainly, though, he was not absent for very long, since Mark Sturgis, one of the senior civil servants at the Castle, records Archbishop Cluny visiting Bishop Fogarty in his diary entry of 14 December.[27] Frank then continued his journey, intending to inform General Tudor of what he knew,* but on reaching Naas, the Crossley tender in which he was travelling took a corner too fast and crashed. He and his escort were thrown out and he was rendered unconscious, as well as breaking an arm.

There is something of a mystery about what happened next. Frank's ADRIC escort appears to have vanished, as does his pistol and his briefcase. He himself ended up in the Curragh Military Hospital, where he spent a month before moving to a rest home in Dublin. The ADRIC deputy commandant, Brigadier General Edward Wood CMG DSO now took over as acting commandant. He was another colourful character, who had originally served in the ranks of the 2nd Dragoon Guards and 17th Lancers. He then became an officer with various East African police forces and took part in the famous 1895 Jameson Raid, in which he was captured. He saw service in the South African War with the British South Africa Police, which he left in 1906. In 1914 he volunteered for service in the Army, joining the 6th King's Shropshire Light Infantry as a company commander and later becoming the CO. During the last year of the war he commanded 55 Brigade. Wood was decorated with the DSO no fewer than four times, but, like Frank, was unable to obtain a permanent commission after the war, and so joined ADRIC.

Wood was to have his work cut out from the start. On the evening of 28 November 1920 ADRIC suffered its worst disaster of the Troubles. Two Crossley tenders full of men from C Company, which was based at Macroom Castle, Co. Cork, were travelling from their base to the village of Dunmanway. One and a half miles south of Kilmichael a flying column from the IRA's 3rd (West) Cork Brigade was lying in wait. That they were able to do this, in the expectation that the Auxies would oblige them, was because the Auxies did not vary the routes they took when on patrol. The result was an ambush in which sixteen members of C Company were killed and only two escaped – one lay shot in the head in the road until found by security forces the

---

* This is what he stated in *Impressions and Recollections* p257, but in *Ireland for Ever* p108 he says that he planned to go to London to inform Lords Carson and Craigavon.

following day and was paralysed for the remainder of his life, while the other got away in one piece only to be shot by the IRA two days later. Three IRA men also lost their lives, but this could not disguise the fact that the IRA had scored a significant success. It was the trigger for the institution of martial law in the counties of Cork, Kerry, Limerick and Tipperary on 10 December.*

The following day a grenade was thrown into a Crossley tender belonging to K Company of ADRIC, which had recently arrived in Cork. Cadet Chapman died of his wounds and ten others were also wounded, albeit less seriously. Shortly after curfew that night a number of auxiliaries went into the centre of Cork. Soon afterwards a fire was seen and this was joined by others. The army officer in charge of enforcing the curfew called for reinforcements, but took no action to apprehend those responsible for starting the fires on the grounds that he feared that this would result in a fight with the police. St Patrick's Street had several buildings suffer from fire damage, as did City Hall and the Carnegie Library across the river. The Nationalist press was quick to accuse the security forces and an inquiry conducted by General Strickland, in whose area of responsibility Cork lay, concluded that K Company was to blame, but also criticised the deployment of 'a unit so raw a state to an area where active operations might be expected.'[28] Tudor was clearly angered by Strickland's insinuation that he should not have sent K Company to Cork and organised his own inquiry. In his conclusions, dated 10 January 1921, he stated that he had been unable to identify any culprits. He thought that possibly anti-Sinn Fein 'wild spirits' had been involved. On the other hand, it could have been Nationalists themselves who had caused the fires, seeing the propaganda value in them. Tudor also asserted that Lt Col Latimer, commanding K Company, had informed an RIC chief inspector that he had no intention of starting any fires. The following day Tudor did, however, add a handwritten postscript: 'I have not been able to disprove [sic] that some members of "K" Co. were implicated, but found such evidence as I could get.'[29] What the affair did show was how little control the Army and Dublin had over the ADRIC companies once they were deployed.

Matters were made even worse on 15 December, when an auxiliary cadet named Harte, also of K Company, sought to seek revenge for the death of the cadet in the grenade attack that precipitated the 'burning of Cork'. He was in charge of the second of two Crossleys on their way to Cadet Chapman's funeral in Cork. They came across an elderly priest and a farmer's son trying help a resident magistrate whose car had broken down. Harte dismounted and began abusing the two men before shooting them dead, to the horror of the resident magistrate and the other auxiliaries. For General Strickland it was the last straw and he had K Company moved out of Cork. Shortly afterwards it was disbanded. Harte was immediately put on trial for murder and found guilty, but was declared insane. Mark Sturgis's view of Harte was 'I am sorry for him, as I have already said, as these men have undoubtedly been influenced by what they have taken to be the passive approval of their officers from Tudor downwards to believe that they will never be punished for anything.'[30]

---

* It was extended to Clare, Kilkenny, Waterford and Wexford on 5 January 1921.

Given the growing condemnation of ADRIC from all sides, it is perhaps not surprising that in mid-January Tudor should ask Frank, now convalescing in Dublin, to reassume his role as commandant. Frank said that the doctors had recommended that he take two months' sick leave in the south of France, but he was prepared to sacrifice this to return to his post.[31] Wood therefore reverted to being the assistant commandant and Macfie remained as adjutant. Problems with ADRIC continued to surface, however. One who defended the auxiliaries was Sir Hamar Greenwood, the Chief Secretary for Ireland. Inspecting ADRIC's N Company at Beggar's Bush Barracks on 22 January, with Frank present, he declared that the Government was determined to crush the 'conspiracy'. 'In this matter we feel we are the custodians of civilised government that depends not on argument, but upon the revolver, the rifle, and the bomb.' The cadets were up against 'dirty fighters', but they were ex-officers turned policemen, who primary job was to maintain law and order.[32] Words like this were not enough to prevent the auxiliaries from continuing to take the law into their own hands.

On 9 February, a search party from N Company was hunting for IRA ammunition in the village of Balbraddagh, near Trim, in Co. Meath. In particular, they turned their attention to a grocer's shop, even though it was owned by a couple who were Unionists. The shop was looted and the Chandlers, who owned it, claimed damages of £325. It was an incident from which the IRA drew maximum propaganda value, calling it 'the notorious looting of Trim'. On the same day, in Dublin itself, there was a more serious crime. It concerned two IRA men, James Murphy and Patrick Kennedy, who were arrested by members of F Company on the evening of 9 February. Two hours later, they were discovered in Clonturk Park, Drumcondra, a Dublin suburb, by constables of the Dublin police. Kennedy was dead, having been shot. Murphy had also been shot, but was still alive and lived long enough to tell his brother what happened and how the 'soldiers' had put old tin cans over the heads of both men before shooting them.[33] According to Frank, and as a result of an inquiry, General Macready ordered the arrest of Major William Lorraine King, the commander of ADRIC's F Company, who had been in the South African forces during the war and had won two MCs and a DCM, and two of his men.[34] Mark Sturgis believed that sinister forces were now at work. He noted in his diary on 13 February 1921 that he had been told that the representative of Basil Thomson, the London-based head of intelligence on Ireland, was putting pressure on Crown witnesses not to testify.[35]*

As for Frank, he took it upon himself to investigate the Trim incident, travelling up there on Sunday 13 February. During the course of three and a half hours he apparently gathered sufficient evidence to have five members, all platoon or section commanders, charged with looting and for the services of a further twenty-one to be

---

* This individual was Capt J.L. Hardy DSO MC, a regular officer in the Connaught Rangers, who had been captured during the retreat from Mons in August 1914. He succeeded in getting back to England in early March 1918 after his twelfth attempt at escaping from a German POW camp. He returned to France, this time serving with the 2nd Inniskilling Fusiliers, but was gravely wounded in early October, with a bullet wound in the stomach and his leg so badly mutilated that it had to be amputated.

dispensed with. On returning to Dublin that same day, he handed over the evidence on those he had arrested to the 'military authorities' for safekeeping. He claimed that his actions were supported by Tudor, even though Frank no longer had the power to dismiss ADRIC members. He then related that one of the dismissed cadets, who had been moved to Beggar's Bush prior to being returned to the mainland, climbed over the barracks wall and managed to gain entry to the Castle, where he warned that he would reveal the dark side of the British policy and operations in Ireland unless he and his fellows were reinstated. Frank was then telephoned from the Castle and asked to reconsider.[36] No firm evidence can be found to support this version of events, but what is certainly true is that Tudor, who was now titled Chief of Police and was in London to brief prime minister Lloyd George on the burning of Cork, sent Frank a letter dated 14 February, which read as follows:

Dear Crozier

I think it will be best for you to keep these twenty-one T/C [temporary cadets] till I come back. I want to discuss it with the Chief Secretary. He gets all the bother. My main point is that it is an unfortunate time to do anything that looks panicky. I think also these T/Cs will have a distinct grievance if the platoon commanders and section leaders are acquitted. Tell these twenty-one they are suspended pending my return, or if you prefer it, keep them on by not completing their accounts till I come back.

Yours sincerely

H. H. Tudor[37]

Frank says that he did not receive this letter until after he had sent the cadets back to England on 15 February. On arrival in London, they immediately went to the Irish Office to complain about their treatment. Tudor was still in London at that time, but he was back in Dublin on the 17th, attending a meeting with Frank and seventeen company commanders. The Chief of Police informed all present that he considered the dismissal of the cadets 'politically inadvisable' and that he had sent a telegram to the ADRIC recruiting officer in London. It read: 'Send over the 26 N Company cadets now in London for investigation by the Chief of Police.' That evening Frank received a telegram back from Major Fleming: '26 T/Cs report N Coy. Meet. Order of Police Adviser [Tudor's old title]. Chief Recruiting Officer ADRIC.'[38]

Frank has a somewhat different version of events. He claims that Tudor was still in London when the meeting of company commanders took place and that in the middle of it he received a telegram from the Chief of Police instructing him to suspend Lt Col Latimer, the commander of K Company, who was present at the conference. He later stated that it was the administration in Dublin Castle that was behind this, notably Alfred Cope, the Under-Secretary.[39] It was certainly true that the British government wanted a scapegoat for the burning of Cork, especially since Lloyd George did not want to publish the Strickland Report for fear that it would raise serious questions about British conduct in Ireland, and Latimer seemed to be the obvious victim. Frank apparently duly suspended him, but considered this an illegal act, since the matter had been taken out of the hands of the police. As it happened, K Company was broken up and Latimer demoted, but not dismissed. Indeed, by March 1921 he had become second-in-command of Q Company. In the end, no one was properly called to account for what had gone on in Cork.* Tudor now returned to Dublin and briefed Frank on what had occurred in London. Frank then warned him that if the Trim cadets being sent back from London were allowed back he would resign. Tudor then saw all the senior ADRIC officers who had been at Frank's conference and they all apparently stated that they were against the cadets being reinstated. This took place on Thursday 17 February. Frank stated that Tudor telephoned him that evening and offered all sorts of inducements to stay on in command. When Frank stood his ground, Tudor threatened to sack him.

As it happened, Frank was off to the mainland on ten days' leave the following day. It would seem that Grace and Mary remained in Dublin, but Frank was accompanied by Tom Macfie. The reason for this was that he was due to unveil a memorial to the 17th Welsh Regiment at Newport, Monmouthshire on Saturday 19 February, but because he was still having problems with his left arm after his road accident the previous November, he needed Macfie's help to get dressed in uniform. Saturday thus saw Frank staying with Sir Leonard Llewellyn, a well-known Monmouthshire figure and coal magnate, at his home, Malpas Court. Just before Frank unveiled the memorial he received a telegram from a friend, whom he does not name, informing him that the Trim cadets were back in barracks, in spite of an instruction that Frank had given before he left Dublin that this must not happen. On that same day he penned a letter to General Tudor:

> The more I think over the matter, the more I am of the opinion that your attitude in the 'Trim incident' has made my position quite impossible in the Division, as I am all out to have the discipline unquestionable [sic]. I therefore propose to resign at the end of my leave. I still consider that theft on the part of the policemen in the course of their duties is impossible, and I cannot honestly associate myself with a force in which such acts are condoned.[40]

Before Frank knew what had happened he was thrust into the public limelight.

---

* Owen Latimer himself was an interesting character. He had originally enlisted in the Somerset Light Infantry as a private soldier in 1905 and transferred to the Royal Flying Corps, on its formation, in 1912. He was commissioned in the RFC in autumn 1916 and in less than two years had risen to the rank of Lt Col and head of the Clothing and Rations Department at the Air Ministry.

Chapter Eleven

Mired in Controversy: 1921–23

On 22 February 1921 *The Times* published a letter written by someone signing himself 'Patria'. It was in response to a letter published in the edition of 12 February, which called for the dissolution of ADRIC. Patria accused the writer of sweeping statements and claimed that the division should not suffer for the sake of a few rotten apples. He went on:

> 'Britannicus' is wrong when he says that the Auxiliary Cadets are an armed force without discipline, but he is right when he asserts that it [ADRIC] has been put in an impossible position by the Government. The force was hastily conceived and brought into being before any organisation whatever had been provided for it. It still, six months after its foundation, has no disciplinary code on which to work. The responsibility for any lack of discipline in the Division lies not with the Division itself, but with the politicians who cannot or will not realise that a state of discipline can only be maintained by the officers of the Division, wholeheartedly supported by and not interfered with in the discharge of their duties by their political superiors.

By way of example, 'Patria' cited the Trim case, stating that Frank had 'carefully investigated' it before remanding the five ringleaders for court-martial and dismissing the rest. The cadets then obtained an interview with Tudor in London. The result was that Frank was 'arbitrarily overruled by someone who had never investigated the case. The commanding officer and adjutant of the Division have, as a natural consequence, resigned, and, in exchange for them, the Division is richer by so many convicted thieves.' What is significant is that this letter is dated 19 February, the very day that Frank wrote his letter of resignation to Tudor. Frank therefore deduced that 'Patria' must be Tom Macfie, since he was probably the only person privy to Frank's letter on that day. Certainly Macfie did resign on the same day, but what his personal motives were is not altogether clear, as we shall see. On the other hand, it is perfectly possible that Frank himself wrote the letter, especially since there was a greater need for him personally to defend his actions.

The letter acted like a lit fuse. On that very same day, 22 February, Captain Willie Redmond, a moderate Nationalist MP, asked a question of Sir Hamar Greenwood in the House of Commons, as did the Conservative Lord Henry Bentinck, about what steps the Government was taking regarding the situation. Sir Hamar replied that he had that day been in touch with Tudor, who had furnished him with a statement. He declared that as soon as he heard about the Trim looting he ordered Frank to investigate. While he had no problem with the five men that Frank had remanded for court-martial, dismissals from ADRIC were not in his remit. Unfortunately, his order to Frank to suspend action on what he now stated were twenty-six cadets until he, Tudor, returned to Dublin, took twenty-four hours to arrive, by which time the cadets were en route to London. Consequently, he ordered that 'the dismissed cadets be recalled without prejudice to any future disciplinary action if found guilty.' A court of inquiry had been set up and there was no question of the cadets returning to their unit until this had completed its deliberations. Members then pressed Sir Hamar on why Tudor had accepted Frank's and Tom's resignations, but he could give no answer. Other members tried to establish that the authorities in Ireland were condoning ill-discipline.[1]

The story now broke in the Press. The *Irish Times* had carried a piece on Patria's letter in its edition of 22 February, but it merely reported what the letter had said. The following day, however, the papers were full of the story of Frank's resignation. The *Daily News* called it a 'shocking scandal' and reported the Archbishop of Canterbury as being horrified by the policy of 'calling in the aid of devils to cast out devils'. *The Times* reported that Frank had been at the House of Commons the previous evening to brief Willie Redmond and Labour MPs, who were supporting Redmond's motion for an adjournment debate on the matter. Frank's version, apparently, was that he had ordered the raid and that it was on a farm owned by a man named Charles at Robinstown, near Trim. Five members of N Company then informed Frank that the farm had been looted, hence the investigation. The report, however, stated that five men had been remanded for court-martial and twenty-six dismissed, subject to Tudor's approval, which was given. *The Times* also referred to the discomfort felt by Government supporters for Sir Hamar Greenwood's ignorance of what had gone on and condemned the Executive's failure to support Frank in his actions. The Irish nationalist newspapers were about to have a field day. *Freeman's Journal* cited the political correspondent of the *Evening News* in his comment that the affair illustrated the lack of coordination between Dublin Castle, which controlled the civil side, General Macready (in charge of the Military), Tudor (police), and Frank (Auxiliaries). The *Irish Independent* thought the revelations 'ironic' in the context of previous utterances by Greenwood and the Lord Chancellor that any member of the forces of the Crown who transgressed would be punished.

That evening Captain Redmond pressed Sir Hamar Greenwood once more in the House of Commons, although he was told that he would have to wait for his adjournment debate. He asked the minister whether Frank had tried the twenty-six cadets of N Company and if Tudor had approved his actions, and whether the cadets had been returned to duty against Frank's advice. Sir Hamar replied that Frank had, as a result of a preliminary investigation, decided that the twenty-six cadets should be 'discharged'. Tudor had initially approved this, provided that the cadets understood the reason for their being discharged. Tudor then appears to have had second thoughts and sent Frank the letter ordering him to put matters on hold until he returned from London. It arrived too late and the cadets complained to Tudor that they had been 'summarily dismissed without trial'. Dismissal, of course, was a more severe punishment than mere discharge. The cadets had not been returned to their company and were the subject of an inquiry being conducted by two RIC Assistant Inspectors-General. Redmond was not satisfied with this answer. He now asked if it was correct that Frank had consulted with Tudor both before and after his investigation and that Tudor had approved Frank's actions, both intended and actual, as he did for a third time when Frank took action without consulting him. If this was so, why did Frank resign? The Chief Secretary merely replied that 'everything will be done to bring to justice these men who are accused of a very serious crime, and no one would be more pleased than I would be to see them most summarily punished [HON MEMBERS: "If guilty."] Of course, if guilty.' Other members tried to press Sir Hamar over Frank's resignation, but he stated that Tudor had never discussed the matter with him. One even proposed that ADRIC be disbanded.[2]

Again, the newspapers of 24 February were full of the story. *Freeman's Journal* claimed that 'a few weeks ago we received several anonymous letters saying that the authors understood that General Crozier's life was in danger, and threatening dire vengeance upon all and sundry if a hair of the General's head were touched. To-day General Crozier has resigned.' Again, the report spoke of the Robinstown farm, instead of the Balbraddagh grocer's shop, although Robinstown did and still does embrace the latter. Papers also published the letters that Tudor and Frank had written to one another, presumably passed to them by Frank. The *Manchester Guardian* considered that Sir Hamar Greenwood's declared ignorance of what had transpired as an example of 'departmental incompetence'. The next day saw further Press coverage. The *Daily Express* quoted a telegram that Frank had sent to Willie Redmond on 24 February: 'He [Tudor] admitted condonation to me in presence of second in command, adjutant, seventeen company commanders, and ordered reinstatement in original company. I apologised to N Company commander, who is now suspended. He was not responsible owing to absence on duty.' In other words, Frank was alleging that Tudor condoned the looting. The paper now likened the case to the Dreyfus affair that had so rocked France in the 1890s. Major General Sir Frederick Maurice, writing in the *Daily News*, argued that: 'the creation of these soldier police has been a criminal blunder, wrong in method and wrong in principle.' What was clear was that the media were generally supportive of Frank.

As for the reactions among those in authority in Ireland, General Macready, writing to Sir John Anderson, the joint Under-Secretary at Dublin Castle, on 25 February, opined:

> By the way, what a horrid mess C.S. [Chief Secretary – Greenwood] and Tudor are making of that Crozier affair. I should have thought the C.S. might have taken the line to refuse to answer any questions until he had the whole case before him from Tudor. Whatever happens, I do hope that you will not allow Crozier ever to come back again. I never personally could understand how Tudor could have taken him on, as although I have not seen him, I have very good reason to believe that his record in the War Office is one which is hardly a recommendation as an administrator of discipline in any capacity whatever.

In his reply, Sir John felt that the General was being too hard on Greenwood and Tudor in that it would have been impossible to merely stonewall the questions being asked in Parliament. He concluded: 'Anyway there won't be any more Crozier and a good thing too.'[3] Mark Sturgis commented in his diary:

L'affaire Crozier monopolises attention. This beauty who is, I am sure, more truly responsible for indiscipline in the Auxiliaries whom he commanded than anyone else has seized a golden opportunity to resign posing as the upholder of order who was not supported from above; a glorious martyr! Poor simple Tudor has been carted again. He often half made up his mind to sack him – pity he didn't quite. There is no doubt he is a perfectly worthless fellow.[4]

Basil Clarke, the head of publicity in the Castle, wrote a jingle, of which the initial verses were:

> Brigadier General C
> Was Head of the Auxiliaries
> When Skies were serene
> You couldn't have seen
> A bucko more lordly than he.

> Brigadier General C
> Was right at the top of the tree
> Everything that they did
> They did as *he* bid –
> A towzer for discipline he![5]

The general view was that Frank was no better than the men he commanded. As for Tudor, there is no record of what he thought of Frank.*

Redmond's adjournment debate took place in the House of Commons on 1 March. He wanted to highlight the 'lack of control of the Irish Administration.' He went on to state that he knew nothing of Tudor's background and wanted to establish precisely what his position and responsibilities were. He now proceeded to read out a long statement, which Frank had submitted to him, on precisely what had happened. It now transpired that it was two members of N Company who came to Dublin on 12 February to report on the Trim looting. They happened to meet Tudor first at a hospital, where they were visiting a wounded comrade, and told him. Frank then met Tudor at the Castle and, on learning what had transpired, hurried back to his HQ. There he interviewed the two men in Macfie's presence and went to Trim the following day, after informing Tudor's private secretary and obtaining his approval. He arrived at N Company, with Macfie, unannounced, and fell in all the available cadets and told them why he was there. He then went to the orderly room and interviewed every cadet in the presence of the company commander and second-in-command. Five cadets gave information on the looting, the remainder stoutly denied that it had taken place. Frank concluded that Major Daniel, the company commander, was not guilty of any crime, since he had been away on duty at the time of the incident, which Frank

---

* Interestingly, Tudor's unpublished biography, Joy Cave's *A Gallant Gunner General: The Life and Times of Sir H.H. Tudor KCB CMG* (held in the Imperial War Museum, London under Misc 175 Item 2658) contains no mention of Frank whatsoever.

said took place at 'Robertstown'. This is a little curious, since Daniel is recorded as being relieved of command on 12 February.[6] Frank apparently needed to get back to Dublin before nightfall. He had, however, identified some of the looted property and was satisfied that there was a case to answer. He invited the cadets to own up, but they did not. He arrived back in Dublin and saw Tudor over a cup of tea and told him that everyone who had been on the raid was implicated and that he proposed that the ringleaders, together with one cadet who was found with looted items in his possession, should be remanded for field general court-martial. The others should be dispensed with as unsuitable. Tudor apparently approved of all this and Daniel sent all those involved to Beggar's Bush on the following day. Frank placed those who were to be remanded in close arrest, while the others were to be under open arrest. They included a few whom Frank had not interviewed the previous day and so he saw them in Macfie's presence. He then dispensed with the services of the ordinary cadets and informed the Castle at noon that he had done so. At 6.30pm Tudor phoned him to check what was happening and Frank told him that those who had been discharged were crossing to the mainland that night. Tudor apparently accepted this and then himself also departed for London, but clearly had a change of heart once aboard the vessel taking him to England, hence his letter of 14 February, quoted previously. Frank, however, said that it took twenty-four hours to reach him because it had been sent care of Tudor's private secretary. When Tudor returned to Dublin, he indicated to Frank that the plan was to divide ADRIC into two, giving Frank one half, with the N Company cadets going to the other. Frank was then adamant that Tudor, when he arrived at Frank's company commanders' conference, stated that the discharged cadets were to be returned to their own company. Redmond claimed that the cadets had been the subject of a 'properly constituted trial'. This, however, is difficult to swallow, since Frank, on his own admission, spent a mere three and a half hours interviewing the cadets, and interviews are hardly the same as a trial. Redmond then went on to claim that Tudor's change of heart, if that is what it was, was solely for political reasons. He also referred to the burning of Cork and asked whether there had been a proper inquiry. Finally, he called upon Sir Hamar Greenwood and General Tudor to resign on the grounds that their actions had been such as to condone criminal activity.

Alfred Newbould, the Liberal member for Leyton West, seconded the motion and claimed that Tudor, in having initially approved of Frank's actions, was warned by 'some highly placed official in Dublin' of the political consequences of sacking the men, hence his change of heart. He concluded: 'Then what is the use of the Government prating in this House about the maintenance of law and order, when they propose to condone larceny in the very force which is there to maintain order?' Sir Hamar Greenwood now rose to his feet. He defended both Tudor and ADRIC. Not until 22 February had he been aware of any form of disagreement between Frank and Tudor. He could not understand 'how an ex-general officer, instead of asking for an interview with the Chief Secretary, should use the medium of the public Press or the friendship of Members of this House' to complain. Redmond now interjected to deny that he was a friend of Frank's. Greenwood then went through the sequence of events, stressing that it was Tudor who sent Frank to Trim. When Frank reported back to him, Tudor agreed that the two platoon and two section commanders, together with one cadet, should be remanded for court-martial, but he expressed disquiet over Frank's intention to dismiss the other cadets without a proper investigation, which, of course, Frank had stated that he had carried out. Sir Hamar, however, could not see 'how it was possible to hold an adequate trial of 26 cadets in the 3½ hours which General Crozier occupied.' He then went on to deal with what Tudor had said about the N Company cadets at Frank's company commanders' conference. He had been informed by Frank's deputy, Brigadier General Wood, who had also been present, that Tudor had actually said that the cadets were to be brought back from London to face trial and not, at Frank had claimed, to return to N Company. He reiterated the fact that an inquiry was already underway, not only into the behaviour of the suspended cadets, but also that of anyone else in N Company who might have been implicated in the events of 9 February. Those charged would be the subject of a court-martial arranged by General Macready. He stated that Tudor did not receive Frank's resignation letter of 19 February until the 22nd, and actually saw reports of his resignation in the Press prior to receiving the letter. Since Frank was accusing him of condoning larceny, he telegraphed Frank straightaway accepting his resignation, not from the end of his leave, but from the date Tudor received the letter. Sir Hamar then emphasised that Frank had not conducted a trial and Tudor had never said that the men should be reinstated. He also made the point that no one officially knew anything about Macfie's resignation and he was considered to be on leave. Finally, he announced that, on Tudor's recommendation, Wood had been appointed in Frank's place, with Colonel Guard as his deputy. He stressed that he always received reports from the War Office before appointing officers, although he did not say whether this had applied in Frank's case.

It was former prime minister Herbert Asquith who replied. He claimed that it was one of very few cases where misconduct by part of the 'Auxiliary forces' in Ireland had been investigated by its commander and dealt with, with the approval of his superior, only to be overturned by the Chief Secretary. He then repeated Frank's version of events and went on to ask what had been said at the London meeting between Tudor and the cadets, and whether the latter returned to Dublin 'under the impression they were going to be put on trial.' Furthermore, what offences were they going to be charged with and what did Tudor say about the matter when he met Frank and his senior commanders back in Dublin? The stories were conflicting and the only way to resolve the situation would be through an independent board of inquiry. The Leader of the House of Commons, Bonar Law, responded to this by accusing Asquith of being 'taken up with one side of the case.' He also stated that Wood had asked all twenty-six cadets to say what Tudor had told them in London and also enquired whether they wished to go back to N Company. They replied in the affirmative, but Tudor warned them that if the evidence warranted it they would stand trial. The cadets had signed a statement giving this version of the meeting. He then went on to defend the Government's record. Lord Henry Cecil said that he would not be voting against the Government, but did stress that the security forces must be properly controlled if the rule of law was to be restored in Ireland. The House then divided and the motion was defeated by 253 votes to 60.[7]

There is no doubt that Frank's case had been damaged by Wood's revelation of what Tudor had actually said to the ADRIC commanders and what he told the cadets in London. He also realised that he had given up a £1,200 per year job and the allowances that went with it. As far as can be gathered, Grace and Mary were still in Dublin. In any event, Frank now immediately returned there to continue his medical treatment and because he believed Sir Hamar had implied that his presence was required to give evidence to the Trim inquiry. For some strange reason he took with him a veritable armoury comprising a .45-inch service revolver, a 0.38-inch service revolver, and a German automatic pistol with 900 rounds of ammunition. Since carrying arms as a civilian, which Frank now was, without a permit could make him liable to a year's imprisonment, he arranged for an officer to come and collect them from him. He later claimed that they were 'stolen' from him, although he did receive back a case containing a revolver and ammunition early in 1922. He then claimed that the authorities tried to plant a revolver and ammunition on him, but he circumvented this by changing rooms in his lodgings.[8] While there, he contributed a long piece to the *Manchester Guardian* entitled 'The RIC and the Auxiliaries: Their Organisation and Discipline'. This related the history of the formation of ADRIC and the Black and Tans and stressed that initially the Commandant of ADRIC had total sovereignty over his men, but in October 1920 this had been diluted and he could no longer dismiss or discharge a cadet without the approval of the Police Adviser. He then complained that he had received no external help when it came to enlisting suitable company commanders. He implied that Tudor had not given him the necessary backing when it came to discipline and asserted that 'lengthy and long drawn-out courts of inquiry are not suitable for the discipline of the division.' Finally, he argued that ADRIC should be placed under military law on the grounds that it comprised 'irregular policemen on a temporary contract' and hence was not amenable to the RIC's discipline.[9] He also had clearly undergone a radical change of heart over what should happen in Ireland. In a letter to *The Times* he declared that the only way to end the violence was to grant Ireland self-government within the Empire.[10]

While in Dublin Frank was summoned to the office of the Judge Advocate General's office in order to make a statement on the Trim affair. He claimed that a 'senior officer' in the department told him that the five men that Frank had originally remanded for court-martial would be tried on the evidence that he had provided. The remainder would also face trial, but the majority would be found innocent.[11] But all was not well with the administration of ADRIC. It concerned the accounting for the expenditure of public money.

On 1 April 1921, one of the RIC's Deputy Inspectors General, Charles Walsh, submitted a memorandum to Tudor and Sir John Anderson. Each RIC sub-accountant was required to submit monthly accounts, showing income and expenditure, within the first seven days of the following month. Walsh's duty, as the RIC accounting officer, was to consolidate these accounts and furnish them to the comptroller and auditor general within two months following the month in question. In truth, no such consolidated account had been submitted since September 1920. This was because ADRIC had failed to furnish any accounts from October onwards, in spite of Walsh's best efforts to obtain them. The reason was that this responsibility had been passed to the company commanders, who generally had no experience of accounting.[12] Yet J.G. Smyth, the then Inspector General of the RIC, had issued very clear instructions to Frank and his company commanders in a document dated 30

September 1920. These made very plain that Frank was to keep a close eye on the company imprest accounts, which covered pay, allowances (and these were detailed), and other justifiable expenses against the public purse.[13] Frank had obviously done little to ensure the proper accounting for the expenditure of public monies.

During the next few months it became apparent how bad the situation was. The worst culprit was G Company, which was commanded up until the end of January 1921 by Richard Andrews and thereafter by Lamond Hemming. Almost £2,000 could not be justifiably accounted for. Among the items that Andrews had spent public money on was a grandfather clock, purchased at sale in Killaloe, and £18.8.3 on food and drinks for himself and some of his cadets when they were supposedly away from their base and on duty one night. Indeed, the RIC officer who inspected the accounts noted that some £230 could not be accounted for and that monies had been spent on items without prior approval. Indeed, when Hemming took over the Company at the beginning of February he refused to sign for the accounts.[14] Andrews himself had resigned. According to Frank it was on account of a double murder by police at Killaloe, for which he felt responsible, but it is quite possible that he did so because his company accounts were in such a mess.[15] Indeed, Colonel Umfreville, the RIC's director of personal services, commented in a minute dated 20 April 1921 to Alfred Cope, the Assistant Under-Secretary at the Castle: 'Colonel Andrews I should very much like to find myself, but I believe that he heard something was in the air and immediately vanished into the blue, and you and I will see him no more. It is a pity in one way, yet I cannot but consider him a good riddance.'[16] There was also controversy over a vessel called the *Shannon*, which Andrews had commandeered, supposedly with Frank's approval, from the Board of Public Works. Hemming thought the boat 'too slow, old, and expensive' and tried to return it to the owners. Unfortunately, before this happened it ran aground and Hemming had to place it in a dry dock at Limerick. He claimed £56 from HQ for repairs and then handed the boat back, but the Board of Public Works asserted that she was in a dreadful state and claimed over £2,200 to restore her, as well as £574 for missing stores.[17] The business over ADRIC's accounts dragged on into 1922, and well after it had been disbanded, with nearly £10,000 having to be written off.

A court of investigation, which sat on 7 May 1921 on Tudor's orders, to look into financial irregularities in ADRIC, revealed further incidents concerning the handling of monies at Frank's headquarters. It appeared that Tom Macfie kept no proper accounts and it was difficult to establish precisely what incomings and outgoings were. The court also noted that the practice of company commanders of submitting monies produced from fining their men, their main means of maintaining discipline, direct to the ADRIC adjutant, was open to abuse. An audit carried out in March 1921 had revealed a discrepancy of £359.8.3 in accounting for the fines money and the auditor observed that Macfie had, on 20 December 1920, paid a cheque for £341.10.0 into his own bank account in Dublin, inferring that this was more than just coincidence. The court also questioned Brigadier General Wood, who stated that when he was acting commandant of ADRIC after Frank's road accident he still had to refer all decisions and questions to him. He had no knowledge of any instructions on accounting for public monies being issued to the companies. He did raise the matter of fines being paid direct to Macfie by the companies and asked whether his handling of them should be checked, but Frank turned this down, expressing every confidence in his adjutant. When he took over command after Frank's resignation, Wood said that he was not happy about the state of the accounts and obtained the services of Detective Inspector Conlin to audit the company accounts. However, once he had obtained the keys to Macfie's safe and discovered that he had been keeping an unofficial account, he summoned Conlin back to headquarters and it was then that the irregularities were found.[18]

It may well be that Macfie saw Frank's resignation as removing the protection from prying eyes that he had enjoyed and that it was this that brought about his resignation. As it was, Frank later admitted that he was aware of the embezzlement of the fines money, but claimed that it was done at the time of his resignation, which was, of course, not so. Frank said that he knew Macfie's address in London and informed the Irish Office of it, but nothing was done.[19] What actually happened was that Sir Hamar Greenwood wired Sir John Anderson and instructed him to obtain a summary of evidence from Frank for the Trim court-martial and also to find out Macfie's address from him. Anderson wired back on 17 March that Macfie's address as at the 4th of the month was 22 Jermyn Street in London's West End.[20] Thus, there was an intention to at least interview him. Tom appears to have stayed no longer in London than the time it took to divorce his wife on the grounds of her infidelity with a Belgian citizen.[21] He then left the country and by the late summer of 1921 he was in Egypt and, it would seem, up to his old tricks. In August of the following year he persuaded a Miss Maude Dale of Alexandria to allow him to invest £200 of her money, guaranteeing to return it and an additional twelve per cent in three months. The due date of 24 November arrived, but Tom, who had remarried that September, did not appear with the money. Miss Dale then heard that he was intending to leave Egypt and so resorted to the law. Macfie was subpoenaed to appear at the British provincial court in Alexandria on 1 December and when he did not show up a warrant was issued for his arrest. It was too late. He and his new wife had taken passage in a ship bound for Marseilles on 27 November.[22] He then appears to have become something of a rolling stone, marrying for a third time, this time a French girl. According to Frank, Macfie was sentenced to a long spell of imprisonment by a French court for embezzling monies belonging to a fashionable club on the Riviera, but was pardoned because he held the Croix de Guerre.[23] It has not been possible to substantiate this, but it is certain that he and his wife settled in Morocco for a time. In 1934 he successfully sued the author and publisher of a book entitled *Filibusters of Barbary*, which had implied that he was involved in subversive activities in Morocco, including the smuggling of arms. Returning to Britain in October 1936, he was again successful in suing the *News Chronicle* for asserting that he had been active against General Franco in Spanish Morocco, when he had never been there. Thereafter he engaged in business before dying at Windsor in 1941.[24]

If the authorities wanted to interview Macfie over ADRIC's financial irregularities, one would have expected that they would do the same with Frank. There is no evidence that they did so, even though he stayed on in Dublin at 92 Lower Leeson Street until 24 April.[25] In the meantime Ethel, still Frank's lawful wife, died on 9 April in Charing Cross Hospital, London. The causes of death were given as a lumbar abscess and streptococcal septicaemia, and only her mother was present. We do not know how Mary and Hester reacted to her death, although Mary had not seen much of her since Lithuania and Hester had never had much to do with her. As for Frank, he married Grace in London three days after he left Dublin and just two and a half weeks after Ethel's death.* The couple then spent their honeymoon in Kent.

Meanwhile, the Trim business rumbled on. During April a number of questions were asked in the House of Commons. In answer to one of these, Denis Henry, the Attorney-General for Ireland, replied that seven of the cadets were to be brought to trial and the other nineteen remained under investigation. He then mistakenly claimed that this was in line with Frank's original recommendations and that he had concluded that there was no evidence against the nineteen.[26] Six days later Denis Henry announced that eighteen of the cadets were to be court-martialled on charges of 'robbery, larceny and receiving.'[27] On 20 May Sir Hamar Greenwood told Sir John Anderson that it was essential that Frank appear as a witness and that he would only nurse another grievance if he was not called. His last known address was that of his mother and stepfather at Blandford Lodge, but a check with the local police revealed that he was not there. Frank now launched into print once more, this time in the anti-Government *Daily News*. In an article published on 24 May he claimed that ADRIC had been responsible for numerous atrocities. He cited, among others, Croke Park on Bloody Sunday, the unexplained murder of the Mayor and ex-Mayor of Limerick on 7 March 1921, which was, of course, after his time, and the murders of James Murphy and Patrick Kennedy at Drumcondra on 9 February, the same day as the Trim incident. Frank accused the Government of suborning witnesses, perhaps with the Drumcondra court-martial in mind, since Captain King, commander of F Company, and the two Auxiliaries charged with him were acquitted on the testimony of two other members of F Company who declared that the men were elsewhere at the time.[28] Frank also claimed that he had been forced to resign because of his attempts to enforce discipline. That evening the Nationalist MP T.P. O'Connor and the Liberal Lt Cdr Joseph Kenworthy (later Lord Strabolgi) asked Sir Hamar Greenwood about Frank's allegations, with the former demanding a public inquiry. Sir Hamar said that if Frank had evidence of wrongdoing he should produce it. He also declared that his resignation had not been forced because of his efforts to enforce discipline. 'On the contrary, the discipline and efficiency of the Auxiliary Police have greatly improved since his resignation.' Lt Col Walter Guinness, a Conservative, proposed that Frank's credibility be tested by publishing the confidential reports on him held by the War Office, which indicated that he might have known something of Frank's pre-war misdemeanours. T.P. O'Connor now pressed for an adjournment debate. The Speaker said that he would look into it, but could not promise one.[29]

Frank's *Daily News* article prompted the Irish authorities to try to contact him through the newspaper. They were successful to the extent that they had a response from Grace that Frank was sick and a medical certificate would be forthcoming. This did not specify any illness and merely stated that he was unfit to travel to Dublin.[30] Commenting on the demands for an inquiry into the allegations that Frank had

---

* On the marriage certificate Grace once more claimed that her father was a doctor of medicine.

made, the centre-left *New Statesman*, in its issue of 28 May 1921, did agree with Frank that the witnesses in the Drumcondra trial had been got at: 'The parrot-like evidence which was given by the police witnesses, including the *alibi* upon which the accused [King] was acquitted, was quite obviously false from beginning to end and it is impossible to believe that any civil judge or jury in England would have paid the slightest attention to it.' It attacked Colonel Guinness's veiled insinuations that Frank had a 'past' and 'we believe, indeed, that he is an honourable and truthful man.' An impartial inquiry was, however, a waste of time. What was needed was settlement of the Irish question. Frank himself echoed this in an article entitled 'The Future of Ireland' in the *Manchester Guardian* of 31 May. A new Viceroy and the first Roman Catholic to hold this office since James II's reign, Lord Edmund Talbot had been appointed in April in the hope of appeasing Nationalist opinion, but Frank argued that this was having no effect on the Irish. Furthermore, 'you cannot expect to out-murder the murderers when you are operating in *their* country with the sympathy of the population against you, with your enemy invisible, whilst you yourself are too well known and marked down.' An impartial colonial statesman should be appointed to reach a settlement within the context of the relationship of dominions to the Mother Country 'as best he could within certain reasonable limits.' He recommended Lord Derby, who had been the Secretary for War during the second half of the Great War and then ambassador to Paris, for the task. This was significant, since that April Lloyd George had deployed Derby to take part in secret talks with Eamon de Valera, indicating that Frank had some current inside knowledge. He declared that in the meantime the RIC should be withdrawn and the Army sent back to its barracks, leaving the Irish themselves to sort out their hotheads. If he was fit enough to write this article, one wonders what really made Frank unwilling to return to Dublin.

Colonel Guinness did manage to get Sir Laming Worthington-Evans, the Secretary of State for War, to read out Frank's record, but it was merely a factual record of service with no reasons given for why he resigned his commission twice before 1914. He denied recommending Frank for the post of commandant of ADRIC, which seems to have been Tudor's decision alone.[31] The question of Frank's *Daily News* allegations was raised again in the House of Commons on 2 June. Sir Hamar denied that Frank had made any report to him, even though he had seen him at the parade of an ADRIC company at Beggar's Bush. He also stated that the summary of evidence taken from Frank for the Trim inquiry contained nothing that would aid the prosecution and if the defence wanted to call him as a witness, they could ask for an adjournment of the trial in order to do this. As it was, Frank had furnished two medical certificates to support his unwillingness to travel to Dublin, the second explaining that he was suffering from neurasthenia and the effects of his November 1920 motor accident, at which point Lt Cdr Kenworthy claimed that Frank had been ambushed on this occasion.[32] The Trim trials went on into July. Eight cadets were eventually found guilty of looting and larceny and sentenced to terms of hard labour ranging from six months to one year. Ten other cadets were brought to trial and acquitted. Sir Hamar pointed out:

I may here mention that only 4 of the cadets convicted were among those placed under close arrest by General Crozier and that 18 of the cadets whose services

General Crozier proposed to dispense with were exonerated as a result of the preliminary official enquiry, there being no *prima facie* case against them to warrant them being brought to trial.[33]

Frank himself did not comment on the Trim trial, but he did later say that the two cadets who had originally reported the Trim looting had to be protected from their fellows, while he himself was the victim of the Propaganda Department in Dublin Castle.[34]

Towards the end of 1920 the British parliament had passed the fourth Home Rule Bill, which granted both Dublin and Belfast their own parliaments, thus recognising that the Government considered the partition of Ireland between the Protestant north and Roman Catholic south the only answer. In the context of the bill elections were held for both parliaments in May 1921. In Belfast the Unionists gained forty out of the fifty-two seats, while in the South Sinn Fein enjoyed a landslide, failing to win only four of the 128 seats. They then declared a provisional Republican government of all Ireland, which ran counter to the Home Rule Bill, since this granted independence only in domestic affairs. Just after the election the IRA mounted its biggest operation to date. Some 120 of its men occupied the Customs House in Dublin and set it alight. They were then trapped in the building by the security forces and forced to surrender. This blow and the fact that Irish of all hues were becoming tired of the violence, prompted Eamon de Valera and other Sinn Fein members to meet General Macready and representatives from the Castle on 9 July. Two days later a truce was signed.

On the day before the signing of the truce, Frank apparently received a cryptic telegram from James Meredith, a prominent Irish barrister and president of the Dail Supreme Court, to come over to Dublin. He took the Irish mail train that night, accompanied by Grace and her sister. Also on the train were Generals Macready and Tudor. They were accompanied by men whose attitude to Frank and his womenfolk was so hostile that the girls thought that they were IRA gunmen. Once in Dublin, Meredith introduced Frank to de Valera and Erskine Childers, who had successfully run guns for the Nationalist movement in 1914 and then served in the Royal Naval Air Service during the war, but was still Nationalist. Frank said that he emphasised to de Valera that there was no point in reviling the Black and Tans during the settlement negotiations, since Sinn Fein had begun what had turned into a vicious circle of murder. Furthermore, geography meant that an independent Ireland could never be outside the British Empire. Frank also spent much time that day with Childers and his American wife Molly. They had struck him as 'both absolutely sincere', but he noted that Childers was never one to compromise.[35]

In autumn 1921 Frank went to stay once more with Jessie Platt on Lewis. While there he enjoyed a correspondence with Erskine Childers. It would seem that, when in Dublin, Frank had asked Childers for advice on a book that he hoped would be published. Childers wrote to him, but the letter took time to reach Frank at Eishken Lodge and when Frank replied on 13 October Childers was in London as part of the Irish delegation negotiating Ireland's future. Frank hoped that Childers would 'afford me the opportunity of keeping up with detail of an administrative nature, where my knowledge of the present official Régime [sic] should be of benefit to Ireland.' It would seem that Childers doubted Frank's sincerity, since Frank wrote to him again on 18 October explaining his position on Ireland. It was his discovery of 'the iniquity of the Régime of the Govt of England' which brought about his resignation from ADRIC. When he returned to Dublin in March 1921 he 'was more convinced than ever that a truce was necessary.' He had worked towards this during the rest of his time in Ireland and during May and June in England. 'The Exposures were part of the plan', he wrote, presumably referring to his utterances in the *Daily News* in May. He assured Erskine Childers that he had never advocated the partition of Ireland. He now believed that Sinn Fein represented the Irish majority and was certain that the religious minorities would be safe. In conclusion, Frank wrote: 'I am with your party thick & thin, as Ireland must be consolidated' and 'anything that I can do, in any small way, I will do, at any time.'[36] Frank was probably still with Jessie Platt when a momentous event took place in France. This was the unveiling of the Ulster Tower as a memorial to the 36th (Ulster) Division by Field Marshal Sir Henry Wilson at the scene of its attack on 1 July 1916. This took place on 19 November 1921, but it is not known whether Frank received an invitation to attend or, given his feelings about Ireland, was just not inclined to be present.

The negotiations themselves continued until early December, when both sides reached agreement that Ireland would be allowed Dominion status within the British Empire under the title of the Irish Free State, but that any county could vote to opt out of this, which the six counties in the north promptly did. The Dail approved the treaty in January 1922 by sixty-four votes to fifty-seven. This split Sinn Fein, and among those who opposed the treaty was Erskine Childers, who wanted nothing less than an Irish republic. Many of the active IRA members were also opposed and during the next few months tension rose as the British withdrew their forces. Then, on 22 June 1922, two IRA gunmen shot dead Field Marshal Sir Henry Wilson in London. This moved Frank to write to David Lloyd George. He made the point that 'people in a humble position such as myself, have greater opportunities for rubbing shoulders with the world, than the Prime Minister.' He went on to stress his Orange background and how he had joined the 9th Royal Irish Rifles' Lodge at the request of his men. As a result, he had had to take a modified oath when he joined ADRIC in August 1920 because the official oath included swearing that he was not a member of a secret society other than the Freemasons. As for Sir Henry's murder, Frank was convinced that it was in retaliation for the murder of six male members of the McMahon family in Belfast. This atrocity had taken place three months earlier, in the early hours of 24 March, when, in a reprisal for the murder of two Ulster Special Constables (USC) the previous day, their fellows took their revenge on the Catholic McMahons, even though they were neither members of the IRA nor Sinn Fein. He saw the violence in Ulster, which was brought about by opting out of the Free State, as a 'vicious circle' and declared that the British Army should be sent in to deal with internal security, leaving the police to concern themselves with police affairs *per se*. Frank went on to remind the prime minister that he had been an assassination target in Ireland and claimed that he had had police protection in London during May–July 1921 because of the threat from disgruntled Auxiliaries. He believed that Lloyd George was not in possession of all the facts and matters were being hidden from him by the 'Die Hards'. The Prime Minister does not appear to have replied to this letter.[37]

As for Ireland itself, the split between the Free Staters and those who opposed the Treaty degenerated into open war after Wilson's assassination, which Michael Collins, the IRA's foremost leader but now a Free Stater, was convinced had been carried out by anti-Treaty elements. This, combined with the kidnapping of one of his lieutenants, caused Collins to move against the anti-Treaty elements in Dublin. It was the beginning of the Irish Civil War, which would continue until late May 1923. Among the many victims was Erskine Childers, who was actively against the Treaty and was executed in November 1922 after being captured with a pistol in his possession.

Meanwhile, by early 1922 Frank had embarked on a new venture, this time with Richard Andrews. They set up the Ex-Officers' Automobile Service, which not only bought and sold cars, but also carried out repairs, bodywork, and even sold insurance. It had two outlets, the head office and works near Euston Station and a garage in Leyton, where Andrews lived, in east London. Andrews appointed himself principal and general manager, while Frank was chairman and director. How they found the money to establish themselves is not known, although they may have used their war gratuities. It is also strange that two men with such little financial acumen could have succeeded in getting the company up and running.

However, the controversy surrounding Frank's resignation from ADRIC continued to haunt him, even after the Irish Treaty had been signed. On 1 March 1922 he wrote to the Secretary at the War Office, enclosing various documents concerning his resignation from ADRIC which he wished to be 'placed on record'. They included his exchange of letters with Tudor. His real reason for taking this action concerned Captain King's acquittal in the Drumcondra court-martial and the apparent arrest on 14 January of 'an ex-officer called Hardy, for using language threatening to interfere with justice, in the King-Drumcondra case, coupled with the voluntary evidence of Lieut. Commander Fry, in the same case, and on the same day, caused a panic in Police circles at the Castle.'* Frank followed this up with a further letter on 11 March. He complained that Tudor had made false statements concerning his resignation and revealing that it was Macfie who arranged for the publication of what Frank called Tudor's 'panicky' letter ordering Frank to do nothing about the Trim cadets until Tudor had returned from London. He seems to have received a noncommittal reply from the War Office, since he wrote again on 19 March, this time on his business writing paper, but with the address amended to read care of his stepfather, acknowledging such a letter. He now stated he had taken legal advice on the matter. He believed that joint action was required by the War Office, the Irish Office and the Law Officers of the Crown to resolve the matter of 'a false & misleading statement [which] is alleged to have been made, to the High Court of Parliament assembled.'[38]

---

* Presumably prefers to Captain Jocelyn Hardy, whom Mark Sturgis had noted in his diary as applying pressure on witnesses (see page 140). Frank does not specify whether Hardy's arrest was in 1921 or 1922 and I have been unable to find any record of it. Robert Fry was a Royal Navy Reserve officer who had some form of clerical job under Tudor.

After what appears to have been a lengthy delay, Frank began to bombard Prime Minister Bonar Law, who had been appointed after Lloyd George's resignation in October 1922. What became clear was that the statement that Frank was objecting to was the one made by Bonar Law, then Leader of the House, during the House of Commons debate of 1 March 1921, namely that the twenty-six Trim cadets were liable to be tried on their return to Dublin. It was drawn from a written statement by General Wood, who had personally asked the cadets what Tudor had said to them in London. Arthur Hemming, who had been Sir Hamar Greenwood's private secretary, recalled Wood's statement, but did not think that any copies had been made of it and he could not find the original. However, he was certain that the document was genuine and not false, as Frank claimed. A letter was sent back to the prime minister's office on 2 December 1922, stating that there was no merit to Frank's case. He had also apparently asserted in a letter to the prime minister that the RIC 'chiefs' had plotted to murder him and 'do harm ' to Lady Bonham-Carter, Herbert Asquith's daughter, which showed Frank 'is not in his right mind.'[39] Thus, he got nowhere and worse was to happen.

On 16 January 1923 disaster struck the Ex-Officers' Automobile Service. The man who lived next door to the works in Hampstead Road discovered Richard Andrews lying dead, with a chisel in his hand and a still-running electric motor. It would seem that he had been sharpening the chisel when a fragment from it struck him. One of Andrews's employees, a Thomas Roberts, stated at the inquest that there was a flaw in the sharpening wheel, in that the protective flange was not fitted, and that it was therefore unsafe to operate the machine without it. Tellingly, he also asserted that Andrews did not have much practical knowledge of machinery, which makes one wonder even more about the viability of the company. Roberts's evidence was supported by the Home Office's engineering inspector, who concluded that the wheel was unsafe to use.[40] Frank claimed that he was present when Andrews had his fatal accident, but the inquest does not seem to bear this out.[41] It does appear, however, that it was Frank who penned a glowing tribute to Andrews in the London *Times*.[42] What happened to the business is not clear, but it was probably wound up, since Frank was probably not confident of running it on his own. Indeed, he apparently attempted to obtain a post with the League of Nations, but this fell through.[43]

Ireland, though, continued to concern Frank. In March 1923 the British police arrested up to 100 suspected Irish Nationalists on mainland Britain and sent them to the Irish Free State. These deportations caused an outcry in Liberal circles and Frank appears to have offered an article to the *Manchester Guardian*. T.P. Scott, the Editor, rejected it, writing rather cuttingly: 'You made a great stand against injustice in Ireland, but I think the recent deportations must be discussed on their merits, or demerits, and not by reference to past iniquities such as you justly detail.'[44] The mismanagement of Ireland during 1920–21 still rankled, however. In August 1923 Frank wrote a paper entitled *Imperial Lessons from the Irish Settlement*. He argued that valuable lessons could be learnt, especially in the event 'that in England, in years to come, some form of anti-government or even anti-monarchical movement might spring up.' The Government had failed because of its refusal to declare martial law throughout Ireland and should have withdrawn the RIC, leaving responsibility for restoring law and order to the troops. As for ADRIC, Frank described its members as 'shock troops' and asserted that it was 'military in all but name and pay'. The legislation that was introduced – the Act for the Restoration of Law and Order in Ireland and that for the Better Government of Ireland – was ineffectual. The former act was useless, apart from granting the power to arrest and search premises without a warrant, while the latter was very unpopular in southern Ireland and hence unworkable. In summary, he wrote:

> Facts were not faced. The will of the majority was ignored. Impossible legislation was carried through. The Military were badly employed. An 'Ad hoc' political machine was introduced to bolster up the Government of the day. The Courts were deliberately perjured. Powers were given to individuals to arrest and search, which led to murder and theft. Numbers of irregular quasi police-soldiers were let loose, under no disciplinary code, to do as they liked in isolated places. In the end the whole country, rich and poor, high and low, revolted against injustice.

In all, it was a rather muddled piece of work, but Frank sent it to the Labour Publishing Company in the hope that it might be produced as a pamphlet, but was told that it was too short. Nothing ventured, nothing gained, so he then sent it to George Bernard Shaw, who was staying in Ireland at the time. He in turn sent it to G.W. Russell, a well-known Irish Nationalist politician, poet, artist, and mystic, who was editor of a new publication, the *Irish Statesman*, but he too was not interested. Frank now tried the *Daily Herald,* a Labour-supporting newspaper, but was told that it was too long for publication. Finally, he passed it to a prominent local Labour politician in Reading, Arthur Lockwood, whom he had presumably come to know when staying with his mother and stepfather. Lockwood appears to have done nothing with the article and in the early 1950s gave it, together with the relevant correspondence, to the Reading Museum.[45]

The reason that Frank had offered this paper to the Labour Publishing Company was that he was by now totally disillusioned with the Establishment, especially the Conservative Party. He thus decided to stand for parliament on the Labour platform 'with the notion of calling attention to the defects of British Bureaucracy'. He felt that 'unless the drawing-room, boudoir and smoking-room electors of the "All's well" class were taught that their heads were in the sand, the mess that had been occasioned in Ireland might be extended to this country.' Frank also wanted to improve the lives of men like those whom he had commanded during the war.[46] This was a common aspiration, especially since a severe economic downturn in Britain during the second half of 1920 had meant that the country was no longer the 'Land fit for heroes', and a number of ex-officers were doing as Frank was. He was given the seat of Portsmouth Central to fight in the December 1923 General Election. At the time it was held by the Unionists, and the Liberals were the main threat, rather than Labour. In the end it was the Liberal candidate who came out on top, winning from the Unionist by some 1,200 votes. Frank came third in the three-horse race, but did succeed in increasing the Labour vote by some 1,800. It was, however, not enough to motivate him to remain in mainstream politics. Besides which, an event was about to take place which would cause him considerable angst and provoke another drawn-out campaign against the Government.

Chapter Twelve

Defending his Reputation: 1924–26

In 1924 the publisher Herbert Jenkins brought out a book entitled *As Others See Us*. The author published it under the *nom de plume* of 'A Woman of No Importance', although she was actually Mrs Stuart Menzies, a widow who wrote thrillers and books of gossip. She was also what was known as a 'political hostess', and very much in the Conservative camp. *As Others See Us* was a collection of pen portraits of well-known figures of the day. They ranged from leading politicians, including Lloyd George, Bonar Law and Winston Churchill, to those who had been involved in the recent events in Ireland. Among the latter was General Tudor, with whom the author clearly had much sympathy. Inevitably, Frank's resignation from ADRIC was covered and used as a vehicle to lambast him. For a start, Mrs Stuart Menzies thought that Tudor's choice of Frank to command ADRIC was 'most unfortunate' and 'probably if General Tudor had had time to make more enquiries General Crozier would not have been employed.' She also referred to Frank's 'secret record', which Tudor had clearly not seen. Frank 'did not set a very good example in the matter of discipline' and, rather than come down hard on his men over the subject of reprisals, he actively encouraged them. Indeed, the author claimed that 'a relation of mine and some of my friends' were present when Frank first addressed his men after he had been placed in charge of ADRIC. He apparently stated:

> You are here to replace the fine old RIC, who have many of them been murdered. I look to you to take an eye for an eye, a tooth for a tooth. Aye! Even more than that; for every eye take four eyes, and for every tooth take four teeth.

She saw Frank as a 'soldier of fortune', but not of the right type. 'He has been false to his salt, and faithless to his comrades in arms.' She claimed that opponents of the government had used Frank as a stick 'to beat it to death', but he had proved 'a broken reed'. 'His charges against the authorities and the police were charges against himself.' Now, 'he is scorned by his one-time friends and seeks solace in certain sections of the Press. It is a sad end for a man with a good fighting record in the past, and we must leave him to his self-sought fate.'[1] Elsewhere in the book, in a chapter on Brigadier General Wood, Mrs Menzies wrote that his appointment to the post of commandant of ADRIC was 'greeted with sighs of relief from every responsible individual in the Division' and praised him for his efforts in sorting out the mess Frank had left behind.[2]

When Frank saw the book and what Mrs Menzies had written about him, he took the matter up with his solicitors and they initiated a libel action against the author, the publisher and printer. As part of his preparation for the case, Frank wrote to T.P. Scott, the Editor of the *Manchester Guardian*, asking for copies of the articles he had written on Ireland for the paper in March and May 1921. He also proposed that the *Manchester Guardian* republish a letter from Frank, which had appeared in the *Daily News* on 17 May 1921.[3] In a further letter to Scott Frank wrote:

> The case is truly one (v) [versus] Dublin Castle [sic] ad hoc officials. I do not know if they intend going the whole hog with it but if they do some important people must give evidence – L.G. [Lloyd George], Asquith, Lt Col Archer-Shee, etc. Tudor has been subpoenaed by me.[4]

But if Frank hoped that the case would come quickly to court, it would not be so. Instead, and especially upsetting for him, documents were revealed by the defence.

Frank had had his suspicions all along that Mrs Menzies had been privy to confidential information and believed that this was through her son Hugh. He had originally been in ADRIC and, according to Frank, the intelligence officer of A Company.[5]* He had then gone on to work for the propaganda department in Dublin Castle. At the beginning of 1925 Frank's solicitors managed to obtain copies of documents in Mrs Menzies's possession. What especially concerned him was one headed 'Synopsis of the Plaintiff's Record at the War Office' and another titled 'Notes on General Crozier'. It was clear that they drew on information contained in Frank's personal file at the War Office. Other documents in Mrs Menzies's hands pertained to ADRIC and included a signed statement by a number of cadets that he had, indeed, uttered the words quoted by Mrs Menzies, when he made his first address to them. Frank immediately wrote to his old boss in 40th Division, General Sir William Peyton, who was now the Military Secretary. He said that he was about to write to the War Office concerning these documents and that Mrs Menzies's use of them in her book 'has done its best to make my life not livable.' He went on to say:

> Some of these items go to prove that any 'fake' must have been 'faked' in the War Office, or by inmates of that office charged with responsibility and they have been flirting with politicians. The 'Motive' of the book appears to me to uphold those politicians and political policemen ... Apart from the case itself I can only see at present that some sort of judicial Enquiry will have to be held by the Government to clear up the matter. That might come by the Government's own decision or be forced on the Government, in default of they themselves taking action.[6]

---

* According to the ADRIC register (TNA HO 184/20) he joined ADRIC on 20 August 1920 and was posted to the Depot Coy on 28 February 1921, prior to becoming the IO of F Coy on 14 March. He re-engaged in August 1921 and was seconded to the propaganda department. A Home Office file (HO 45/24819) has him joining the publicity branch of the Chief Secretary's office on 7 March 1921. Earlier, he had enlisted in the Grenadier Guards in August 1914 and then been commissioned in the Gordon Highlanders. In summer 1915 he was gassed while serving in France with the 1st Gordons and was diagnosed with pulmonary tuberculosis. This forced him to be placed on the Retired List at the end of 1915. (TNA WO 339/23150)

Two days later, on 14 January 1925, Frank duly wrote to the War Office referring to the synopsis and requesting an 'impartial synopsis of my record as an Officer'. He also made the point that his request had 'nothing to do with the very much larger question which will be brought forward later and which has arisen owing to the circumstances under which the book "As Others See Us" has been written.' The War Office replied on 3 February, but clearly not in a satisfactory manner as far as Frank was concerned. Three days later he wrote again, asking for a copy of the synopsis itself.

Frank now bombarded Peyton with a series of letters. He wrote twice to him on 10 February. In the first he made it clear that he had resigned from ADRIC as a result of his condemnation of crime and made the point that his resignation had been so speedily accepted because of the court-martial of Captain Lorraine King. Frank claimed that he had warned Tudor that King had a perjured alibi, but that he had replied that he himself would resign if King were hanged. In the second letter Frank claimed that his enemies were accusing him of stealing public money in collusion with Macfie. He also stressed that he had resigned on his own, and not with Macfie, whom he believed had disappeared. Indeed, he stated that he had read in the newspapers that Macfie was now languishing in an Italian jail after stealing £10,000 belonging to the Winter Club at San Remo. He now turned to the synopsis, which he claimed his enemies had shown to reporters in 1921. One of the names mentioned in it was a Miss Latta, with whom the document accused Frank of immorality. She had written to the War Office asking for Frank's address, but Frank pointed out: 'She is probably well over 60 years of age.' He said that she had been a friend of Ethel's, but that he had never set eyes on her.

As it happens, there is a two-page typed document headed 'COPY' in Frank's personal file. This relates by date Frank's pre-war financial misdemeanours, his efforts to remain in the Army after the war, as well as various personal enquiries as to his whereabouts. Thus, Miss Latter, as spelt in the document, asked for his address in September 1919, stating that all letters sent to him had been returned to her. Likewise, in his letter to Peyton, Frank stated that another woman, to whom Ethel owed 'a large amount of money', accused him of letting her down by ceasing payments to her. According to the War Office document this was a Miss Hilliard, who in January 1921 stated that Frank owed her £50–£60, which he had promised to pay back at £10 per month, but she had received just one payment, and that was two years earlier. Frank's answer to this was that this should have been paid through his bank at £20 per month from Ethel's allowance of £40 per month. The War Office document also mentioned a gentleman, who wrote in June 1920 that Frank had left Bognor Regis suddenly, leaving some items behind, and asking for his address. A solicitors' firm had made the same request in December 1919. Also, in December 1920, Ethel had called personally at the War Office stating that she was destitute and would have to take herself to the workhouse. She also asked for Frank's whereabouts as she wanted to institute civil proceedings against him. Frank made no comment on these statements in his letter to General Peyton, but did tell him that 'Notes on General Crozier' accused him of immoral relations with Grace in Dublin while Ethel was back in England.

On 13 February Crozier wrote to Peyton again, stating that his solicitors had sent a copy of the synopsis to the War Office. 'It is a very disgraceful document and one which should run the Dreyfus scandal close.' He also added a postscript: 'It has taken 4 years & a stupid woman to bring it to light.' The following day he wrote to the War Office again demanding an official enquiry or compensation for the personal damage he had suffered from 1921 onwards. The day after this letter, 15 February, he wrote again to the War Office, this time in a much more legible script than his usual scrawl. He made the point that the business with Mrs Menzies 'is far removed from the greater question, ie the circumstances surrounding events in 1921, regarding Ireland, and the conspiracy as revealed in evidence now produced.' He believed that it was either collusion of military and political 'chiefs' or 'intrigue' among their subordinates. Either way, 'the intrigue of partisan-political serving soldiers must be put an end to and the supremacy of the people over the Army must remain unquestioned.' He went on to request not only both an enquiry and compensation for himself, but also that the matter be placed before the Cabinet. He followed this missive with yet another letter to Peyton, dated 22 February but obviously written in a hurry. He emphasised how important it was 'to get compensation & redress fixed up with the Govt as soon as possible'. He had spent 'hundreds of pounds' on the Menzies case and now wanted to go into business with his brother-in-law (presumably Bill Allan, who had retired from the Army as a Lt Col) and needed £1,000 urgently, which he hoped would come from the expected compensation.

On 25 February Frank wrote once more to the War Office. This time he also took up cudgels on behalf of Major Wake, who had been ADRIC's court-martial and court of enquiry officer. Frank had apparently sent him to Trim to collect evidence from the residents for possible use in a court-martial of the cadets who had looted the shop at Balbraddagh in February 1921. Tudor, according to Frank, became aware that Wake had this evidence and ordered him to resign. When he refused to do so, Tudor sacked him. Wake then attempted to claim the balance of his pay for his year's contract on the grounds of wrongful dismissal, but without success. Frank now wanted the case reopened. He also said that he had claimed £1,250 for his injuries resulting from the accident in November 1920, but had only received sufficient to cover his medical costs, and wanted this resolved. The problem was that neither Peyton nor the War Office as a whole could deal with the matter, apart from the aspect of confidential matter being extracted from Frank's personal file. The rest was a matter for the Home Office, under whose jurisdiction Ireland had been prior to independence. As it was, the War Office merely stonewalled, stating that they unable to enter into correspondence with Frank's solicitors on the documents, since these were confidential.[7]

There now appears to have been a lull in the proceedings. Frank, by now probably very short of cash, withdrew to his step-father's house outside Reading. Before he did so, he spoke at a dinner of the Association of Ex-Service Civil Servants at the Hotel Cecil, which lay between the Embankment and the Strand in London. Besides stating that the future welfare of ex-servicemen was one of his greatest concerns, he also addressed the matter of disarmament. Britain could do nothing to further disarm until the other nations of the world had ceased arming. But perhaps ex-servicemen around the world could call on their governments and say 'enough of this tomfoolery;

we have seen and suffered enough, and we won't let it happen to our children and our children's children.'[8] It was the first glimpse of the path that Frank was later to take.

In June 1925 there was some good news. Unable to prove her allegations, Mrs Menzies settled out of court. All copies of her book still in the hands of the publisher would not be disseminated and any future editions of it would contain no reference to Frank.[9] Since the book had been in the shops for a year, it was almost like shutting the stable door after the horse had bolted. In addition, Mrs Menzies was to pay Frank £50 in damages, but again this was not a very significant amount.

On 17 June Frank resumed his battle with the War Office. After informing them of the outcome of the Menzies case, he reopened the subject of the synopsis, complaining that it contained no mention of his war service and the decorations he had been awarded. He also claimed that he knew who had concocted the document and that there were copies of it in both the Home and Colonial offices. He wanted the War Office to get them back and destroy them. He then softened his tone: 'It is not for me to suggest that recompense should be granted in order that I may be re-established in the public mind, and I leave that to the sense of fair play always displayed by the Army.' He hoped that the redress would be public, since his character had first been attacked in the House of Commons, a public place, on 24 May 1921 in the context of the synopsis.

There was no immediate response from the War Office, and so Frank now attacked from another quarter. He persuaded his mother and step-father to write to General Sir Philip Chetwode, an old friend of General Thorneycroft's and now GOCinC Aldershot Command. Rebecca's letter was a plea to help find Frank work, pointing out that he had a wife and two daughters, although she admitted that Hester had always lived with the Thorneycrofts. 'If he could be made governor of St Helena or some far off place he would be happy!!' In a postscript she said that her husband was an invalid, suffering from neurasthenia.* However, this was not enough to prevent Alec Thorneycroft writing to Sir Philip on that same day, 14 July, a typewritten letter, which may well have been drafted by Frank. He reminded Sir Philip that he had been Adjutant General at the War Office in 1921 when Frank's records 'were tempered with mostly for the purpose of supplying pro Black and Tan propaganda to Dublin Castle Propaganda Dept. Many of the men in that Dept were very common people with no idea of tradition or deportment, Menzies being probably the only gentleman among them.' He said that Frank had had an interview with the incumbent Adjutant General, General Sir Robert Whigham, who had told him that the matter was being dealt with by the department of the Permanent Chief Secretary at the War Office. Frank's other commander of 40th Division, Sir John Ponsonby, had also apparently told Frank that the War Office was blaming the Colonial Office, which had taken over Irish affairs. He concluded:

The fact remains, however, that my son was put in an impossible position in Ireland by the very people who concocted the evidence for Mrs Menzies' book, and then of course let her down. These people intended to destroy my son

---

* For some reason she had now taken to spelling her name 'Rebekah'.

socially, morally, physically and financially. The 'Notes on General Crozier' are too filthy for repetition. I think it an awful thing that a man who has done so well for his country should be so treated ... Surely this is a case when the Sovereign could intervene should other means fail?

There is no record of Sir Philip's response to these letters, but he passed them to the War Office, where they apparently landed on Peyton's desk. Frank was made aware of this, probably by Chetwode, and wrote again to Peyton on 21 July, stating that he had heard that Chetwode had passed him his mother's letter and that he was coming up to London the following day. He commented: 'I have come to the conclusion that by a process of marking time I am being hoodwinked in this matter of the faked stolen & concocted documents. If this is not so the fault is with the WO for creating such an impression... I consider it unreasonable to keep me waiting so long in this simple case.' Frank therefore asked Peyton to get whoever was dealing with the matter to telephone him at the British Empire Club in St James's Square.

The War Office now took stock of the situation. An internal memorandum dated 23 July stated that, as far as the synopsis was concerned, it had undoubtedly been compiled with information supplied by someone who had access to Frank's personal file. The War Office had tried to recall copies of it from other government departments, but none could be traced. It would seem that the leakage had occurred in Ireland, but the War Office had no knowledge of how it might have come about. As for the conspiracy theory: 'This appears to be pure imagination on the part of General Crozier, who, however, seems to be convinced that he is a victim of organised persecution.' With regard to the other documents, the writer stated that neither the War Office, Home Office, nor Colonial Office had any knowledge of ever having had an original copy of them. The remainder, including Frank's letter of resignation to Tudor, had belonged to the Irish Office. The memorandum also stated that Frank had had an interview with the director of public prosecutions to see if a charge could be made of contravention of the Official Secrets Act in terms of the disclosure of these documents.

Frank continued to pester the War Office. On 8 August he wrote to say that he was being persecuted once more and had received information that same day from 'a certain quarter' which confirmed his fears. He was, as a result, incurring 'financial loss'. Five days later, and from an address in Hove, Sussex, he wrote the following to Peyton:

In confidence I may say that Winter is the chief villain and that he has a WO accomplice. Winter, Tudor & Menzies were hand in glove in Dublin. Both these men [sic] attended a lunch she (Mrs Menzies) gave at the Savoy Hotel to 'Conservative Members of Parliament before my case was settled, to decide the question of funds & line of defence for her. The lunch was reported in *The Times*.* How I know is that my solicitor arranged for a waiter to keep his ears open and report.

---

* There was such a report in *The Times* of 7 April 1925, with Mrs Menzies hosting a lunch for 'some members of the new Conservative Parliament'. Those attending did include her son, Tudor, and Winter.

The fact that Mrs Menzies had official documents in her hands meant that:

> I can only hold the Govt responsible for the total breakdown of my wife's health, the health of my mother, my financial losses and my position, as, after all, I was only doing my work, for which I was paid, in the proper manner.
>
> I do not know the name of the man with whom W [Winter] is in touch but all I know is that W has always known every name on the board.[10]

Frank had now put his cards on the table and disclosed those whom he thought were the villains of the piece. The principal culprit, in his eyes, seems to have been Brigadier General Sir Ormonde Winter, a gunner officer, who had been the deputy Chief of Police and director of intelligence at Dublin Castle. Clean shaven, slight, and sporting a monocle, Mark Sturgis described him in his diary as:

> … like a little white snake and can do everything! … He is clever as paint, probably entirely non-moral, a first-class horseman, a card genius, knows several languages, is a super sleuth, and a most amazing original. When a soldier who knew him in India heard he was coming to Ireland he said 'God help Sinn Fein, they don't know what they are up against.'[11]

Whether Winter was involved in the affair cannot be established, but it is clear from a brief passage in his autobiography that he liked his fellow gunner Tudor but had little time for Frank. Indeed, he claimed that it was he who was instrumental in getting Frank removed from command of ADRIC. It concerned a book of Herbert Asquith's letters, which were edited by Desmond MacCarthy, a well-known literary and dramatic critic of the day. Asquith, in a letter dated 2 March 1921, had referred to the 'unsatisfactory debate last night on the Tudor-Crozier business' in the House of Commons. While 'Hamar had got Tudor to deny the truth in fact of the two main points', Asquith had been 'careful not to pin myself to Crozier.' MacCarthy had inserted a footnote that Tudor had reinstated the twenty-six Trim cadets and that 'the refusal of the highest authority to enforce discipline on the ground that it would "appear panicky" seriously undermined confidence in the Government's Irish policy.'[12] This information apparently came from Frank, whom Winter termed 'loquacious'. MacCarthy was threatened with a libel action, presumably by Tudor, but, having checked that there were no grounds for the insinuations, issued a public apology, undertaking to delete the offending passages.

> This, in more ways than one, added to Crozier's complete discomfiture, and henceforth MacCarthy became a staunch friend of Tudor and one of his ardent admirers. In a letter to him he wrote: 'I constantly think of my escape with amazed relief and gratitude. Think of it! If you had taken action, I should have been fighting shoulder to shoulder with Crozier.'[13]

Winter otherwise makes no mention of Frank in his book.

Frank had still not had a reply from the War Office to his letter of 17 June and so, on 24 August, he got his mother to write once more, this time to the War Office rather than an individual. She pointed out that she had had sympathetic letters from both Chetwode and Peyton, the latter writing that Frank was 'the victim of a great misfortune.' She demanded justice, warning that she would 'leave no stone unturned' to achieve it. The War Office did finally reply to Frank on 25 August, but it did not mention redress. He therefore proposed that he place the matter in person before the King, accompanied by a member of the Army Council, or the Military Secretary, as well as Chetwode, on the grounds that he had been Military Secretary in 1921. Frank also informed Peyton of his proposal and told him that he was considering standing for Parliament again, but this was dependent on when an election was called. He did need 'some finality' before he did so.

There was now a period of inactivity, but Frank's parlous financial situation was coming to a head. On 14 October a certain Miss G. Gifford wrote to the War Office stating that Frank had been a tenant in a flat she owned in Hove, but had left on 19 September owing some £30 in rent and gas charges. He had given Miss Gifford three worthless cheques in July and had then apparently told her to get in touch with his mother for settlement, but Rebecca had denied all responsibility and told her that Frank had no business to involve her. Two days before this letter was written, a petition was filed for Frank's bankruptcy.[14] Unlike with his earlier bankruptcy, the papers no longer appear to exist and so it is impossible to establish who initiated the petition and who the other creditors were. Suffice to say, it would seem that Frank had now also fallen out with his mother.

Yet his financial situation did not deter Frank from continuing his fight for justice. He now targeted the prime minister, Stanley Baldwin, writing to him on 28 October to request an interview. He stressed that the matter was 'most serious' and 'of great public importance as the principle involved is a great one while the methods employed would be unbelievable if they were not unfortunately true.' The War Office was, however, finally taking steps. On 30 October Bertram Cubitt, the Under Secretary of State, wrote to his opposite numbers at the Home and Dominions offices. He stated that the synopsis was 'practically identical' to a note compiled in the War Office, probably at the time of Frank's resignation from ADRIC. He went on:

> The [Army] Council are seriously embarrassed by such a document having come into possession of unauthorised persons. But quite apart from this they think that in fairness to General Crozier steps should be taken to destroy any copies of the document which may exist in the records of any Government Department or in the personal keeping of any of its officers. Though the matter in the document may be strictly true, it is a partial and one-sided statement, and unjustifiable inferences might be drawn from it. The Council consider that there is a possibility of Brigadier-General Crozier being unfairly prejudiced by its continued existence.

Cubitt went on to ask for any copies of the document found to be returned to the War Office.

Frank, though, was continuing his bombardment. On 30 October Grace sent a letter to Stanley Baldwin, although it was Frank who actually wrote it in his most legible hand, she merely appending her signature. She referred to 'Notes on General

Crozier', claiming that it libelled her in a 'scandalous manner', presumably referring to the accusation of immoral relations with Frank. She stated that she was Irish, and well known over there, and that her father 'Doctor Croker-Roberts was in his time a leading Unionist.' Grace herself had never been involved in Irish politics and failed to see why she had been made a target for government propaganda. She accused a Capt Darling* and others of blackening her name, noting that the former's signature was on a number of documents. They were 'cads' in her eyes. She was therefore also requesting an interview with the prime minister. On 11 November, Armistice Day, Frank wrote to the Secretary of State for War, Sir Laming Worthington-Evans. He stated that he had had an interview with H.G. Williams, who was the Member of Parliament for Reading, Alec Thorneycroft's constituency. He had given him 'the facilities for examining the 8 faked documents used against me & my wife between 1921 & 1925 by Government servants or agents about which I have written to Mr Baldwin.' He claimed that Brigadier General Wood had 'admitted the whole ramp' and went on to say:

> The point is that through it my wife & I are ruined. The King requests ex-officers to wear orders etc today & mine (a fine collection of 14)** are in pawn to defray costs!!!

Frank had also had to sell 'my Waterloo silver handed down by an ancestor who fought there.' He wrote to Stanley Baldwin again to tell him of the meeting with the MP for Reading. He followed this up with a further letter stating that he was still pursuing the £1,250 claim for his November 1920 injuries and his claim for travel and other expenses while he was in Dublin for the Trim enquiry during March and April 1921. A further letter arrived at Downing Street demanding a response to Grace's letter. Frank also wrote to the Home Secretary, Sir William Joynson-Hicks, demanding action. The Home Office view, given in a minute dated 21 November, was that Frank had not made it clear 'precisely what his demand is in regard to the propaganda documents.' The War Office was deliberating over whether to give Frank any compensation and had asked the Home Office not to give any reply on this until they had made up their minds.[15] Frank now seemed to be concentrating on the claim for expenses for the Trim enquiry. He wrote to the prime minister on 12 December and to the War Office the following day asking for action to be taken. Receiving unsatisfactory replies, he wrote again to Baldwin. Also, angered by a statement

---

* This must have been Capt (later Sir) William Young Darling MC & bar, who served in Ireland during 1920–22, working in the RIC's Information Section and helping to produce the Weekly Summary. According to Gen Tudor (unpublished account of his 1914–18 experiences entitled *The Fog of War*, p127 (copy held by the Centre of Newfoundland Studies, but available online) Darling had served on his staff when he was commanding 9th Division and, at Winston Churchill's suggestion, Darling became Tudor's secretary in Ireland. He was made a CBE in 1923, presumably for his work in Ireland. He was later Lord Provost of Edinburgh 1940–44, and Unionist MP for South Edinburgh from 1945.

** These, of course, included those to which he was not entitled.

made by Worthington-Evans to H.G. Williams that the Irish Office had 'eventually dispensed with his services' in 1921, Frank wrote on 29 December to the War Office requesting an audience with the King.[16]

Meanwhile, Rebecca, Frank's mother, died on 30 November. We don't know how Frank took this, especially since the business over the Hove flat had clearly caused a rift between the two, but it was obviously another blow to him. She had little money of her own – just under £400 – but probate was not granted until June 1932, with Evelyn and Bill Allan acting as executors, after Alec Thorneycroft's death in November 1931. Hester, who had remained with the Thorneycrofts throughout, went to live for a time with Rebecca's sister Maria Besant and her husband.

On 13 February 1926 Frank was officially declared bankrupt for the second time. On the previous day he had met his creditors in court and declared liabilities of £600 and nil assets. He blamed his predicament on the vendetta that had been waged against him.[17] In the meantime he had written to the Home Office pressing for his claim over the Trim enquiry to be settled. The problem lay mainly over the question of on what authority he had travelled to Dublin as early as 2 March 1921, and why he had stayed so long into April, not leaving Dublin until the 24th. A further fly in the ointment was that the Treasury was gunning for him for £72 in connection with the installation, without authority, of a house telephone system at Beggar's Bush. This virtually cancelled out the £77 or so that Frank was claiming. The Home Office wrote to him along these lines and he replied on 18 February:

> I am not surprised that the Secretary of State should find difficulty in understanding the matter covered in the above [Home Office letter to Frank], as the administration in Ireland was such as to be abnormal and understood by a very few people, including myself and excluding the Government of the day – the temporary officials had in fact superseded the permanent officials in all but name.

This was why it had taken so long to organise the Trim court-martial and during this time the evidence was being spirited away. It was for this reason that Frank had remained in Dublin for fifty-four days.

> The subsequent position was almost Gilbertian as on one hand the Chief Secretary [Greenwood] stated in the House of Commons that he [sic] had ordered a subpoena to be issued for me to give evidence (in order to suit the requirements of the Political moment) which meant going back to Ireland, while on the other hand the Attorney General for Ireland stated in the same place that I had no evidence to give!!! So far as accuracy was concerned both statements are wide of the mark. Of course, at one time I had important evidence to give, as had Major G. St. A. Wake who collected evidence in the shape of a sack full of loot which resulted in his services being instantly dispensed with.
> In short the investigation was purposely delayed and I with it.

The Home Office was not satisfied with this reply. In their response of 17 March they pointed out that between 2 and 17 March Frank did not appear to have been in touch with anyone at Dublin Castle over the case. They had found a copy of the statement that he had made on the Trim affair on 23 March, but nothing to authorise him remaining in Dublin after that date. Frank's reply stated that he took Sir Hamar Greenwood's statement during the 1 March 1921 House of Commons debate to mean that he intended to call Frank back to Dublin to give evidence as a signal for him to go, which was what the Home Office suspected. He said that he had sent Greenwood a note there and then to say that he was prepared to travel to Dublin. He also asked the Chief Secretary to phone him at his hotel on the following morning if his services were needed. The call duly came and Frank was told that his expenses would be covered. He stated that he was met by a police car at Kingstown (now Dun Laoghaire) and, on arrival in Ireland, reported to 'the 'ad hoc' officials' at the Castle by telephone, giving the address of where he was staying. He also asked for an officer 'to take charge of my arms and ammunition, as I was a civilian' and this was duly done. He then went to the King George V hospital for treatment of his November 1920 injuries. The Judge Adjutant General's (JAG) department appeared to know nothing about Frank until Sir John Anderson told him by telephone to report there, which he did and provided a statement on the Trim affair. He was informed by the JAG's department that he would have to wait for the trial. Later he was told that he could leave, but might be recalled to Dublin. This, of course, did not really answer the question as to why he had stayed on until 24 April.

In the meantime Frank had continued his bombardment of Downing Street, but on a more massive scale. On 27 February he sent a letter to the prime minister which came to thirty-one pages of double-space typescript. He began by pointing a pistol at Stanley Baldwin's head. Unless he received 'satisfactory settlement' on his wrongs within a week Frank would

> … present myself at Buckingham Palace, to the Private Secretary to the King, and beg to be allowed to hand him the three orders which his Majesty very graciously bestowed upon me, as, manifestly if what has been falsely represented concerning myself was true, I would be unfit to retain those orders, which I prize most highly above all other things. At the same time, and for the same reason, I will hand his Majesty's Private Secretary a request to be permitted to resign my rank as Brigadier General. I shall also enclose a copy of this letter and a full statement of the shameful treatment I have received.

He went on to discuss the synopsis and notes once more and pointed his figure at Winter, whom he noted was a high up in 'the Fascisti,'*, Hugh Stuart Menzies and Darling. He went on to declare that he received the 'medal with seven clasps' during the South African War, which was, in fact, the Queen's South Africa Medal with six clasps, and that during 1914–18 he rose to 'the position of Major General'. Indeed, he had 'in about two years' risen 'from Captain to command of the 40th Division',

---

* Winter was a member of the British Fascisti, which was founded in 1923. Because of internal rifts, it was dissolved by 1930 and Winter does not appear to have been further involved with extreme right-wing organisations.

all of which was somewhat exaggerated. He reminded the prime minister that his stepfather was General Thorneycroft of Spion Kop fame and that Grace was a cousin of Lord Roberts. He mentioned his November 1920 accident, but said that he could remember little about it, but did hint that there might be more to it than met the eye. He then turned to the circumstances of his resignation from ADRIC, claiming that Tudor had offered him another job, with an additional £500 per year, if he did not pursue the case of the Trim cadets. Frank claimed that after his resignation he was encouraged by some to address public meetings, with even an opportunity to rent the Albert Hall, and to write a book on his experience. He had declined these offers and 'have struggled on in extreme poverty.' Grace had 'had to earn a few shillings a week, to assist me and the children.'

Frank now referred to *Hansard* and the debate of 11 May 1921 over the failure to call him and Macfie as witnesses over the Trim affair. He asserted that the conditions in Ireland in 1921 had not improved since 1586 and cited Elizabethan state papers to show that the brutality was the same. He claimed that Lt Col Walter Guinness MP had been set up to attack him after a brief visit to Dublin in spring 1921 and that his claims 'that there was something in my War Office Confidential Reports of a discreditable nature, were an absolute lie.' Guinness had also stated that Frank had been dismissed, rather than resigned, and, in Frank's view, had been rewarded for his efforts by being made Minister for Agriculture. He then returned to his investigation of the murder of Father Griffin and his motor accident. Frank said that he was told who the murderer was and that it was as he was returning to Dublin that the '"accident"' happened. He was replaced by Wood, 'who worked to step into my shoes – and my salary.' Indeed, Wood, and Sir Hamar Greenwood, were added to the list of those whom Frank was accusing of conspiring against him.

Frank moved on to Mrs Stuart Menzies's book and stated that near the time that his libel case was due to be heard in court he and Grace were visited by Hugh Stuart Menzies. He said that his mother was 'an old and unbalanced woman', who had no money, since she had handed over most of her property to her son. She was therefore in no position to pay costs and damages.* Simultaneously, Frank's solicitor also stated that he could not proceed further with the case unless Frank paid him £200, which he was unable to do. This was why the case was settled out of court and with such derisory damages. Frank said that this left him some £400 out of pocket. Because of the propaganda campaign against him he was unable to 'obtain employment suitable to my position'. He therefore 'took a house near South Kensington with the intention of converting it into flats in the hope of letting them off and making a little money.' He made an agreement with a builder to carry out the conversion and to pay him 'in reasonable time'. The work was apparently finished and the builder now demanded his money, which Frank could not pay, since he had been unable to let the flats. Frank told him that he was awaiting settlement of claims against the Government and that if the builder took legal action Frank would be forced into bankruptcy, in which case he would get nothing. The builder then apparently 'blurted out … that he had seen

---

* This is odd, since Mrs Menzies continued to host receptions, etc, which were reported in the Court pages, which she could not have done if she had no money.

some papers connected with me, and that he knew that if I was declared bankrupt he could count upon receiving his claim in full from Captain Stuart Menzies.' Frank said that this conversation had taken place in the presence of a witness, whom he had brought with him. He concluded his epistle with the matters of his unresolved medical claim and the business of the Beggar's Bush telephone. He saw the latter as part of the vendetta against him, and alleged that the officer who had declared that Frank had installed it probably did this himself.

As if this diatribe was not enough for Baldwin to digest, Frank sent him a further letter on 8 March 1926. This time it was concerning a recently published second edition of a book entitled *The Revolution in Ireland, 1906–1923* by Professor W. Alison Phillips. A review in *The Catholic Times* of 5 March had commented that, as a result of criticisms of the first edition, the author had omitted Frank's evidence in connection with the Trim affair. He had, in the preface to the new edition, stated that this evidence could not be published, but gave no reason. The reviewer commented: 'General Crozier certainly was in a position to know much more of the facts connected with the Auxiliaries whom he commanded than anyone else. But Professor Phillips, disliking and distrusting him personally, simply decides to suppress his evidence altogether.'* Frank saw this as further evidence of the continuing vendetta against him. He concluded his letter with an ultimatum: 'Unless I hear by 12 noon tomorrow that you are prepared to right me and thus end this disgraceful vendetta, which originated in high official places, I must, in self defence, write to the King's Private Secretary, at once.'

On 10 March, two days after Frank sent this letter, Grace had an interview with Sir Ronald Waterhouse, Baldwin's Principal Private Secretary, apparently without Frank's knowledge, since he was away. In Sir Ronald's notes of the interview, Grace quoted the exact phrase in notes which had offended her: 'He [Frank] was living with a lady who passed as his children's nurse. Eight days after Mrs Crozier's death this irregular union was terminated when he married the lady in question.' She went through the whole sorry saga, but a couple of new aspects arose. One was that Major General Sir Harold Ruggles-Brise, Secretary of the Officers' Association and Frank's former divisional commander, had checked the slanders in 1921, when dealing with an application for an education grant for Mary and Hester, and found them without foundation. The other interesting point she made was that Brigadier General Wood 'backed out of giving evidence for Mrs Menzies for reasons which he personally gave Mrs Crozier.' Sir Ronald's notes do not say what these reasons were.

The following day, Frank having returned from wherever he had been, the Croziers held a council of war with an elderly retired Indian Army officer, Lt Col Kenneth Foss. Both immediately wrote to Sir Ronald. Frank asked for an interview for himself, Grace, and Colonel Foss, but without a solicitor present, so as to save expense, for

---

* Interestingly, Denis Gywnn, an Irish journalist and editor of the *The Dublin Review*, later asserted that Professor Philips had told him that he did not address Frank's resignation in his book 'because he had got Crozier's complete dossier and that his story was so lurid that one could not discuss it without provoking libel actions of the hottest kind.' (letter to Jonathan Cape dated 22 May 1932, Cape Archive MSS 2446/AA56, University of Reading)

the following afternoon, 12 March. If this was not possible, he would like it to take place at the earliest opportunity. Foss boiled Frank's complaints down to three – his treatment over the Trim affair, his claim for injuries, and his claim for time spent in Dublin during the Trim enquiry. He said that he had known the Croziers for 'over five and twenty years' and commented:

> Both General and Mrs Crozier are wonderfully free from bitterness considering what they have suffered, and because they have seen how persons who were junior to the General but took up the attitude that the Black and Tans could do not [no] wrong were promoted and knighted, and all the while the murders of Roman Catholic clergymen and mayors went unpunished, and were ascribed to 'unknown persons', whereas, if the General is right, the culprits could have been found and convicted.

The Colonel also said that he had persuaded Frank not to hand in his decorations or forfeit his rank until the prime minister had had more time to consider the matter.

Sir Ronald replied to Colonel Foss by return of post. He feared that Foss was under a misapprehension. He wanted just to establish the circumstances surrounding Grace's complaint. Frank's lengthy letter to the prime minister would be answered in due course and there was no question of him holding a further interview with both Croziers. In the meantime, Frank's lengthy epistle of 27 February was passed to the War Office and then sent on to the Home Office. An internal minute by the latter considered the documents in question. One was Frank's alleged addresses to cadets in August 1921. The covering letter does still exist, but the text of the actual addresses, as well as the signatures of the cadets involved, do not. Frank's solicitors had asked for the Home Office to establish who possessed this and other documents acquired by Mrs Menzies. The War Office did possess a copy of the synopsis, but not the Home Office. 'It is not known how this got to Dublin Castle if it ever got there at all.' As for the notes, neither the Home Office nor the War Office had a copy and all that was known of its contents was the sentence accusing Frank of an immoral relationship with Grace. It noted that Frank complained about not being allowed to give evidence at the Trim court-martial, but pointed out that Sir Hamar Greenwood had asked him to do so, but Frank being ill prevented this. As for the financial claims, the Chief Secretary's Office in Dublin had decided that £250 was the maximum that could be granted for Frank's injuries and the case could not be reopened. His subsistence allowance was, however, in the process of settlement, the full detailed claim having only been received 'a few weeks ago'. Sir John Anderson, who was now Permanent Under-Secretary at the Home Office, replied to Lord Onslow, Under-Secretary of State for War, on 1 April. He considered Frank's lengthy letter to Baldwin 'a very ill-balanced document containing many wild charges which can hardly be taken seriously.' The Home Office had no connection with much of it and could only help in so much that on the dissolution of the Irish Office it took over all work connected with the disbandment of the RIC. It could therefore only produce such papers as it had concerning Frank's two financial claims.

The subsistence claim was now being checked out. The Home Office looked at the files they held on the Trim enquiry. While they could not find any summary of evidence taken from Frank, they noted that he did visit GHQ at Dublin Castle on 23 March 1921 and that a Capt Hughes took a statement from him. In a letter to G.M. Martin-Jones at the Home Office, Sir Henry Wynne, who had been the chief crown solicitor for Ireland, stated that at the time he did not think it necessary to call Frank as a prosecution witness at the Trim court-martial, and neither did the officer who was looking after the case at GHQ. Martin-Jones now wrote to Colonel Ivor Price, who, together with a Colonel Barron, had carried out the Trim enquiry, to see if he could shed any light. In his reply, dated 6 April, Price stated that he had never met Frank, but knew that 'he was determined to enforce strict discipline.' He was, however, very busy at the time with other investigations as well. He ended his letter:

> From all I hear of General Crozier, I think it most reasonable that he should stay in Dublin till the matter was fully thrashed out, otherwise he might be called without sufficient notice to give evidence. From all I have ever heard of General Crozier I consider him a most straight & honourable officer.

This letter seems to have helped the Home Office come to a decision. A minute dated 15 April concluded that, although Frank had never explained why had he remained in Dublin after he had given his statement on 23 March, it was perhaps understandable in the expectation that he might be called as a witness. The assumption was that, since he was ill when he was summoned later in May, this must have been why he finally left Dublin when he did. This, however, ignores the fact that he married Grace three days after his departure. The recommendation was that he should be paid some £55, rather than the original £77 which Frank had claimed, and this sum duly found its way to Frank's receivers. As for the Government's claim for the Beggar's Bush telephone, this was dropped.

There remained the question of the documents. To this end, Frank arranged for Labour MP Robert Young to ask a question of the Secretary of State for War in the House of Commons on 20 April 1926. He asked whether anyone had been held accountable for the document referred to in *As Others See Us*. If so, had any disciplinary measures been taken? He also asked whether the passages relating to Frank (Young did not mention him by name) had been published with the approval of a Government department. If this was not so, how could he account for the documents being in the author's possession? Worthington-Evans replied that no department had sanctioned the publication of the book and that, as far as he knew, it did not directly quote from any confidential or secret documents. He went on to say that there had been correspondence with the 'officer concerned', but no copies of any such document had been found. It was regrettable that any such document had found its way into unofficial hands, but the War Office could take no responsibility. In response to further questions, Worthington-Evans stated that he had no knowledge of any such document and that it would be very difficult to institute an inquiry, especially since these events took place 'sometime prior to 1921.'[18]

On 29 April 1926 Frank wrote to the Director of Public Prosecutions, asking him to investigate and take action against those who had leaked the confidential documents that put him in a detrimental light. He claimed that he had first heard about the synopsis when he was in Dublin in April 1921, and that it had been used against him in Parliament on 24 May and 1 June. Then, in early 1923, he had been warned by a Capt Kelly of the Army Education Corps, and then at the War Office, that 'certain people in that office were preparing a further vendetta against me'.* Frank said that he informed the Military Secretary in writing of this, although no such letter exists in his personal file today. He asserted that Mrs Menzies's book was published in autumn 1923, which was inaccurate, and listed the documents in her possession. These included correspondence between Capt Darling, whom he said was Tudor's private secretary, and Capt Martinson, who took over from Macfie as adjutant of ADRIC, on the supposed inflammatory speeches that Frank had made to the cadets. He believed that the motive behind the vendetta was 'pure revenge on me because I chose to uphold the practice of the Crown, as a senior Police Officer.' He told the Director that he had warned the prime minister that he was prepared to seek redress from the King, but had been advised to place the matter before him instead.

Frank, however, was not totally wrapped up in trying to seek redress. On 7 May 1926 he wrote to the Home Office with the request that he be given the facilities to make a broadcast. The General Strike, organised by the Trades Union Congress in defence of the miners' wages and conditions, had broken out three days earlier, bringing much of the country to a standstill. Frank hit upon the idea of getting ex-Servicemen to parade on Sunday 16 May in all towns and cities, as was planned that they should do on 11 November, to demonstrate their loyalty to the Crown. 'Counties & Cities & Towns should select their Committees & work out their own plan – The Salute should be first taken at a prearranged hour throughout the land. For London special arrangements will be made.' Frank clearly saw himself as the overall coordinator and wanted the Home Office to provide him with facilities for 'sending and receiving communications'. How he expected all this to be organised in a mere week is not clear. As it was, the Home Office view was that Frank 'was not the man who should be allowed to organise it.' He was given a polite brush-off on the grounds that the police had too much on their hands already without having to cope with additional demonstrations. In any event, the strike ended on 13 May.

Returning to the question of the documents, on 14 May a conference was held at the War Office to consider the matter, with Sir Archibald Bodkin, the Director of Public Prosecutions, Lord Onslow, and War Office and Home Office representatives being present. Sir Archibald pointed out that his only concern was whether an action under the Official Secrets Act should be brought against Mrs Menzies or 'against some person unknown for having communicated such documents to some unauthorised person.' He pointed out that such a prosecution could only be sanctioned by the Attorney General and that this would only be if he considered it in the public interest. Since there was no public interest involved in this case, the Attorney General would not approve. The only significant document was the synopsis, which Sir Archibald considered perfectly proper for the War Office to prepare and to pass a copy to the Irish Office in Dublin Castle, although there was no evidence that the latter had happened. Even if someone at the Castle had, by malice or through carelessness,

---

* This was probably Capt D.P.J. Kelly MC, formerly of the Connaught Rangers, but his connection with Frank is not known.

passed the document on, there was no evidence remaining and there was clearly no public benefit in investigating possible security lapses in a government department which no longer existed. Sir Archibald proposed that he see Frank and give him the opportunity to state his case. In this way, the Government would be in a stronger position than it would if forced to admit that no investigation of the allegations had taken place. This the meeting agreed.

The Director of Public Prosecutions duly saw Frank and Grace on the morning of 27 May. In his report, written immediately after the interview had taken place, Bodkin stressed that he was not a public prosecutor, but a director of prosecutions of 'general public importance'. Furthermore, 'the criminal law ought, of course, never … be put into force save on reasonably convincing material and with a view to vindicate public justice only and never for the purpose of gratifying feelings, or (save indirectly in certain class of cases) to benefit or improve the position of an individual.' He then went through the synopsis with Frank and asked why he thought it forged. Frank replied that it was War Office practice for an officer to see anything detrimental written about him and to initial it, as well as, where necessary, submitting a written explanation. In this case facts had been 'invented or distorted by some malicious person'. Sir Archibald then said that in that case it could not be considered an official document, in that it had not been properly prepared using 'correct extracts from existing records', to which Frank was forced to agree. Sir Archibald was probably unaware of War Office procedures and Frank was also misleading, since the synopsis was merely a summary of items in Frank's personal file and not a formal report on him, which, he would, of course, be asked to initial (if he were still a serving officer, which he was not at the time it was drawn up). Frank, however, went on to state that a copy of the synopsis had been taken over to Dublin by Colonel Umfreville.* Sir Archibald then said: 'You are now asking me to institute a public prosecution under the Official Secrets Act in respect of a document which you describe as forged or faked, whereas these Acts really relate to the preservation of really genuine official documents affecting the public service in any of the Departments.' The same applied to the other documents, although he had seen none of them himself and could not judge what was true or false in them. Frank assured him that they were all covered in official stamps.

Frank now turned to the document with the signatures of the cadets who had apparently heard his August 1920 addresses. A, C, and D Companies of ADRIC had submitted the return, but B Company had not because its commander, Major B.H.L. Conlan, late Royal Dublin Fusiliers, was a friend of Frank's. He pointed out that Hugh Stuart Menzies had been A Company's intelligence officer and after he went to work in the propaganda department at the Castle he passed all the documents to his mother, who was unofficially engaged in propaganda back in London. She organised a number of meetings on Ireland at Caxton Hall and Frank claimed that Margot Asquith, wife of the former prime minister, had sent him tickets for them, but he could not attend as his November 1920 injuries were playing up. However, he was

---

* Lt Col H.K. Umfreville DSO. He was working in the Ministry of Labour Appointments Department in early 1920, but then became the RIC's Director of Personnel Services.

informed by Major Archer-Shee,* who attended a number of these meetings, that the synopsis was read out from the platform. In which case, Sir Archibald responded, it could hardly be regarded as 'a very secret document, official or otherwise.' As such, it was impossible to apply the Official Secrets Act to a document that had been read out in public five years earlier.

Grace now told Sir Archibald how much she had suffered over 'the imputation conveyed upon her in the book' and was considering her own legal action against Mrs Menzies. While he believed that 'she had been really ill from anxiety and worry' and that she was a 'clever woman', Sir Archibald pointed out that Frank's successful libel action had surely ruined Mrs Menzies's reputation and that therefore no one could possibly still think ill of the Croziers. If Grace wanted to take her to court Frank would not be allowed to appear as a witness and Mrs Menzies would have a 'free hand' to defend herself. She would certainly 'give due prominence to the documents, and so would the newspapers.' This would do little for Frank and Sir Archibald advised her not to proceed, to which they both agreed. Yet Grace emphasised how much she felt for her husband, whom she claimed had been shortlisted for some twenty posts for which he was qualified but had been turned down every time. She could not but help believe that there was a lingering feeling against him at the War Office on account of the documents. Frank then said:

> I want something done to reinstate me in the public mind. I have done a lot for the country and was practically turned out of Ireland, or, as Mr Guinness said 'dismissed'. I have suffered in many ways but nobody seems to do or care to do anything to put me right. The Prime Minister has had nothing to do with Ireland. Why doesn't he, why cannot he, say something for me?

Sir Archibald replied that this was outside his brief and that all he could do was advise on a prosecution under the Official Secrets Act, which he had done. What he did offer to do was to consider whether he was in a position to demand the documents from Mrs Menzies's solicitor. If he did obtain them he assured the Croziers that he would ensure that they did not leave his department. Both Frank and Grace seemed grateful for this and there the interview ended. According to a handwritten Home Office minute dated 22 June, Sir Archibald did write to Mrs Menzies, but she assured him that she had destroyed them. He did not believe her and asked the Home Office if they had any objection to him sending a police officer to interview her. The Home Office did not, but whether Sir Archibald went ahead with his proposal is not known.

Sir Archibald might have felt that he had mollified the Croziers, at least to an extent, but it did not stop them from firing another broadside at the prime minister. On 7 July Frank wrote him another lengthy letter, this time amounting to twenty pages of double-spaced typescript. He reminded Baldwin of his letter of 27 February and of his intention to hand in his three orders to the King and to surrender his rank. He stated that he had been in the Commons in April, when Robert Young had asked his question, and listened to Sir Laming Worthington-Evans's 'poor and lame

---

* Lt Col Martin Archer-Shee MP.

excuses'. He then went on to attack Walter Guinness for his 'deliberate untruth' over Frank's resignation from ADRIC.

> Lt. Colonel Guinness had been to Dublin Castle about Easter 1921, and saw General Tudor, and General Wood, and Captain Walter,* and others. I was in Dublin at the time and I heard, from a senior officer, what they were arranging. At the time the Press had already taken up my case, and it was vitally important to the Prime Minister, Mr David Lloyd George and his Government, that I should be discredited.

Frank then repeated much of what he had written in his earlier letter, likening his case to that of Dreyfus. After a further attack on Worthington-Evans, he then quoted *King's Regulations* on the subject of confidential reports, forgetting, of course, that the synopsis was no such animal. He discussed the atrocities in Ireland, including Croke Park, by the forces of the Crown and then returned to the parliamentary debates, especially Colonel Guinness's statement on 11 May 1921 that Frank had been deprived of his commission. This clearly referred to him being forced to resign his commission in 1908 and not his resignation from ADRIC. He said that he was making enquires through Robert Young as to whether he might be able to appear at the Bar of the House of Commons to protest against Guinness's libel. He returned once more to the Capt King case and his claim for his November 1920 injuries. He was now bankrupt to the tune of £380 and his subsistence claim had only been 'grudgingly' settled. Such was his situation that he was no longer able to pay Mary's school fees and was being forced to withdraw her from the Royal School for Officers' Daughters at Bath. Hester, too, had been removed from his care and was being looked after by relations.** He had received no help from the 'Public Prosecutor' nor from Parliament. He then went on to quote at length from a recently published book, *The Hope of Europe*, by Sir Philip Gibbs, the famous war correspondent. In it he described Macready as 'old and artful in war and civil strife' and Tudor as having 'the soul of a Welsh chieftain in the eleventh century.' He went on: 'The stage was set for the dirtiest kind of warfare that has even happened in modern times … General Tudor gave lectures to his officers about the short way with rebels. The officers passed the word on to the men. There was no sentiment about it.'[19] This strongly echoed Frank's views.

Frank once more raised the question of compensation for his injuries, stating that unless he received it by 15 July he would withdraw 'from all suggestions for a settlement in the honourable and constitutional way I suggested.' He then proposed

---

*   Possibly C.H. Walter MC, late Oxfordshire and Buckinghamshire Light Infantry.

** Mary was admitted to the Royal School in April 1923. She was known there as Betty, a diminutive of her middle name, perhaps partly because it sounded more like Baba, but also because there was another Mary in her class. There is no evidence that Frank withdrew her from the school and she remained there until July 1928. Hester, on the other hand, had, of course, been brought up by the Thorneycrofts from a very early age and after a brief spell with the Besants was being looked after by Frank's sister and her husband.

that £380 be paid immediately to the official receiver to enable him to obtain his discharge from bankruptcy prior to the satisfactory resolution of the compensation issue. He repeated his threat of handing in his orders and resigning his rank should this not come to pass. In addition, he would submit his letter of 27 February and other documents to His Majesty. Grace, too, would represent her case and that of Frank's daughters to the Queen.

The next day Grace followed Frank's missive with another, this time to Baldwin's principal Private Secretary, but again almost certainly drafted by her husband. It was a curious letter. It warned Sir Ronald that 'it would be a great pity if a Prime Minister like Mr Baldwin should be allowed, through absolute unacquaintance with the inner history of my husband's case, to drift into a course in which he [sic] would become responsible for acts done by a former Prime Minister, Mr Lloyd George, and other Ministers who were connected so intimately with him in the past, two of whom have still managed to retain office under the present Government.' One of these was Worthington-Evans, and a reason for his enmity towards Frank may have been to do with something that occurred during the war.

Apparently, in September 1915 Lloyd George, then Minister of Munitions, granted a contract to a Percy José Mitchell and Herbert Shaw, described by Grace as 'one ... a discharged bankrupt and the other a man of straw.' It was to manufacture shells with a newly created company named the Staines Projectile Company. Its capital was a nominal two pounds, but through the good offices of Godfrey Isaacs, the chairman of Marconi, and 'the influence exerted by Mr Lloyd George and his friends,' they obtained £50,000 from the Marconi Company and some of its directors were appointed to the board of the Staines Projectile Company. Lloyd George also gave Mitchell and Shaw a contract to produce aircraft at a premises known as the Goss Printing Works at Hayes, also in Middlesex. In the latter instance Marconi apparently only put up a little money, the main burden of financing it coming from the Government, which also had paid an 'enormously excessive price' for the Hayes works. Friends of Frank's apparently wrote to Lloyd George, now prime minister, on 21 September 1917 to inform him of this and had an acknowledgement from Frances Stephenson, his personal assistant. Frank possessed copies of these letters. Further letters had been sent to Worthington-Evans, then the parliamentary secretary to the Ministry of Munitions, as well as the machine tool department of that ministry. Grace also claimed that Cox's Bank France had advanced £30,000 in debentures to the company on a commission of ten per cent and that it was only thanks to Frank's friends writing three letters to Winston Churchill in his capacity of Minster for Munitions during August–October 1917 that he was prevented from signing an agreement which would have given Mitchell and Shaw the Hayes works and machinery as a gift at the end of the war. She posited that it was the actions of Frank's friends which might have been a reason why Lloyd George, Worthington-Evans and Churchill had turned hostile to Frank. She also made a veiled threat to bring these matters into the open if she and Frank did not receive satisfaction.[20]

That the Staines Projectile Company Ltd was established in September 1915 is fact. Mitchell and Shaw were among its directors, as was a member of Marconi. It also had £50,000 capital and a further £30,000 of debentures was issued in September 1916. The company went into voluntary liquidation in March 1919 and was finally wound up two years later, with a small surplus to be distributed among its nine shareholders, which included Marconi. There is nothing on file to indicate any malpractice and the letters Frank's friends supposedly sent cannot be found.[21]

As far as Baldwin's office was concerned, a Home Office letter was sent to Lord Stamfordham, the King's Private Secretary, to warn him that Frank might make an approach, stressing that 'General Crozier's various grievances have been carefully considered by both the Home Office and the War Office and dealt with so far as it is practicable to deal with them.' Stamfordham replied by return, stating that Frank had already written to the palace and he had informed him that it was not within the Private Secretary's power to 'lay before His Majesty representations relating to the redress of grievances.'[22] Frank seemed to have come up against a brick wall and so began to direct his energy elsewhere.

Chapter Thirteen

The Road to Pacifism: 1927–1937

Still having achieved little to right the perceived wrongs that he had suffered, Frank applied for a job on the staff of the Secretary-General of the League of Nations in Geneva.[1] He was unsuccessful and so joined the League of Nations Union (LNU) as a speaker. This had been formed in Britain in October 1918 to promote the concept of the League of Nations, especially its policy of obtaining lasting global peace through collective security and disarmament. By the mid-1920s the LNU had some 250,000 members and, apart from trying to influence government policy, it also strove to educate the general public through publications, courses, and speakers. That Frank now took an active part in this is indicative that he was beginning to move towards pacifism. Little about his activities is recorded, but the *Scotsman* of 8 October 1928 reported that he spoke at the LNU's autumn 'summer school', which was held at a hotel in Dunblane. He made another speech to the students of Glasgow University that December, when he forecast that the next war would be largely fought in the air.[2] In May 1929 he wrote to T.P. Scott at the *Manchester Guardian* saying that he had been doing a 'great deal of speaking' for the LNU and found that he had often been able to bring the diverse people whom he stayed with round to his way of thinking. His credentials as a former soldier played a large part in this, especially in backing up his argument that military victory had 'disappeared in the flood of scientific methods of destruction.' Even 'Tory squires' listened to him. Therefore, Frank proposed a series of articles 'such as "a soldier favours the League"'. Scott, however, did not think much of the idea and turned down the proposal.[3] At the beginning of 1929 Frank also became involved in a conference entitled 'Modern methods of warfare and the protection of the civil population' held by the Women's International League for Peace and Freedom at Frankfurt-am-Main in Germany. Frank was one of the British members of the conference council, along with such luminaries as Bertrand Russell, Professor Harold Laski and two leading lights of the LNU, Lord Henry Cecil and Professor Gilbert Murray.[4]

He was also involved with the temperance movement. The *Manchester Guardian*, for instance, in its issue of 7 October 1927, reported that Frank spoke at a lunch organised by Messrs Rowntree, the chocolate makers, with the York branch of the National Commercial Temperance League. Frank described drink as 'a soul-destroying piece of mischief making damnation' and asked moderate drinkers to give it up for the sake of others.

It is difficult to establish how Frank and Grace survived financially during the late 1920s. He was still an undischarged bankrupt and his speaking engagements with the LNU brought in little more than his expenses. There is no evidence that Grace had any money of her own and so they must have struggled. They continued to live in a series of flats in London, with breaks at his stepfather's house and with Jessie

Platt on Lewis, but both were getting very old. True, during the latter part of 1928 Frank managed to get eight short articles published in *Chums*, a weekly magazine for boys. One was the memory of an incident during the South African War, while the remainder concerned his time in Lithuania, some of which are referred to in Chapter Nine. He also succeeded in having series of articles published in the *Manchester Evening News*. One was on the futility of war, which indicated that Frank was now firmly in the pacifist camp.[5]

Frank also achieved brief notoriety in autumn 1929 by claiming that an American lobbyist had attempted to bribe him two years previously, during the Geneva Naval Disarmament Conference. This was William B. Shearer, who had supposedly been lobbying on behalf of US shipbuilders to ensure that the US Navy was guaranteed parity with the Royal Navy. He had also spread anti–British propaganda. The aim of the conference was to agree the same proportions in cruisers as had been agreed during the 1920–21 Washington Naval Conference for the major navies' holdings of battleships. The conference ended without agreement. Two years later, in early September 1929, Shearer filed a law suit against three US shipbuilding firms, claiming that they owed him money for his services at Geneva. President Herbert Hoover raised concerns since it was widely believed that people who were against disarmament because it guaranteed British supremacy of the seas were behind the failure of the Geneva conference. Consequently, the Senate Naval Affairs Committee set about an investigation into Shearer and his activities in late September 1929. The hearings were covered by the British Press and this prompted Frank to claim that he recognised Shearer from his photograph as the man who had visited his London flat in 1927 to ask him to stop making pro–disarmament and anti-American speeches in favour of arguing for Britain and the USA to have as large fleets as they wanted. In return, Shearer apparently promised him a lucrative US lecture tour. Frank's response was to kick Shearer down the stairs.[6] It is, however, difficult to believe Frank's claim, since it was only towards the end of 1927 that his views on peace and disarmament began to receive any form of publicity. It is therefore hardly likely that he would have been known to Shearer, or that Shearer would thought him influential enough to be worth bribing.

The year 1930 was, on balance, to prove a good one for Frank. First, he and Grace were able to move out of London and into a house in Westerham, Kent. Still a bankrupt, it was clear that he did not buy The Homestead, as the house was called. He had, however, been in close touch with David Starrett, his batman from the Great War. Starrett had moved to the mainland and become a successful builder, specialising in neo-Tudor and neo-Georgian houses. It seems that he was building a new estate at Westerham and allowed Frank and Grace to live in the show house. Improved quality of life was, however, tempered by daughter Mary. Now aged twenty, she clearly became fed up with life in Britain. Frank could give her little if any financial support and she had never been especially fond of Grace. She therefore decided to take advantage of her Canadian birthright and start a new life in Canada. On 15 August she sailed from Liverpool bound for Montreal. She described herself as a domestic servant, but became a teacher. She initially taught in a mission school at La Longe in northern Saskatchewan, but then moved to a village called Harris in the same state, where she met her husband Charles Harold Anderson. Frank, however, apparently objected to the marriage and severed communications with her. Mary continued, though, to correspond with Hester and her Aunt Evie, as she called Evelyn Allan. The family, which grew to six children, eventually came to rest in Ontario.[7] Hester, meanwhile, remained with Bill and Evelyn Allan.

For Frank, the most momentous event of 1930 was the publication of *A Brass Hat in No Man's Land*, his account of his experiences during 1914–18. Grace claimed that he wrote it in just ten days and in his own hand, as he boasted himself to a Canadian journalist.[8] As it was, he probably wrote it during the last half of 1929 and then submitted the manuscript to Jonathan Cape, who agreed to publish it.[9] Whatever the case, his view of the war was understandably coloured by the pacifist attitude that he was beginning to adopt. He was therefore scathing about much and pulled no punches. His timing could not have been better, since the end of the 1920s marked the beginning of a wave of anti–war literature, with such books as Robert Graves's *Goodbye to All That*, Siegfried Sassoon's *Memoirs of an Infantry Officer*, and Richard Aldington's *Death of a Hero*. It is therefore not surprising that *Brass Hat* received favourable reviews from some quarters. Robert Graves himself declared that 'it is the only account of the fighting on the Western Front that I have been able to read with sustained interest and respect.'[10] The *Daily Mirror* also commented on its 'realism',[11] while the well-known novelist John Galsworthy, writing in the *News Chronicle*, stated: 'I welcome anything which disgusts people with war.'[12]

Among the letters Frank received was one from Sir John Monash, who had commanded the Australian Corps in France with such success. Monash wrote: 'I have recently come into possession of your book "A Brass Hat in No Man's Land" and have enjoyed reading it very much, as it largely presents points of view with which I am thoroughly in accord.' Vice Admiral Sidney Drury-Lowe, a fellow League of Nations Union speaker, also commented: 'I think you have done a great service in putting your experiences down, a genuine and true record and I sincerely hope it will have its effect – or rather that it will show those who don't know what a senseless and absurd way of settling disputes modern war is.'[13]

Yet there was a sensationalist aspect to *Brass Hat*, which Frank and his publisher clearly encouraged. A month before publication, there was a debate in Parliament on the Government's proposal to abolish the death penalty in the Armed Forces, except in cases of treason. Frank wrote to the *Daily Mirror* to protest against abolition: 'To do away with the death penalty is madness. Fear of the consequences is a wonderful weapon in the armoury of society.' He also declared that he knew of 'ten officers who should have been shot.'[14] In an interview with the *Manchester Guardian* he declared: 'I am entirely for abolishing war, but if you put men into war you must leave it to those who have to carry it out as to how it shall be done. War justifies everything men do to secure victory and to bring hostilities to an end.'[15] It may also be that Frank saw shooting one's own men as part of the brutality of war and that he thought this would help to shock people into opposing war.

In an interview with the *Daily Mirror* he defended his passages on sex and the soldier:

I stand by my statement that under the conditions that arose during the war it was almost inevitable that numbers of those taking part in it should indulge in free love.

They were thrown into the middle of difficulties which most of them were quite unfitted to face. Of course, I do not condone free love. I attack the system which made such a thing possible.

He also attacked army chaplains on the grounds that 'during a war a Christian country ceases to be Christian.' Chaplains were therefore 'out of place', although he admitted that 'they served a useful purpose when they gave out cigarettes and that sort of thing. But their usefulness was limited to that.'[16] The *Daily Express* summed up: 'The book deals with "war" in general – its bravery, murders, free love by troops, whisky-soaked colonels, and, not least of all, with the author's provision of liquor to a deserter [Rifleman Crozier] so that the deserter faced the firing party drunk in a state of unconsciousness.'[17]

Inevitably, there were many who did not like *Brass Hat*. General Sir Edward Bethune, who had been Director General of the Territorial Force for much of the war, wrote: 'From the extracts I have read I think it is a horrible book. I cannot understand how a man who has had a career in the army can throw mud at his profession.'[18] General Sir Ian Hamilton proposed a commission to examine the British Army's conduct on the Western Front: 'Then some of these clever writers would be put through the mill of cross-examination.'[19] Sir John Reith, Director General of the British Broadcasting Corporation and Western Front veteran, believed:

Half the truth is sometimes worse than a lie. The inequity and futility of war can be brought home to the younger generation, to whose hands the cause of peace, international understanding and progress are committed, without making them feel that their elders who fought are moral bankrupts.[20]

The book also came to the attention of King George V, and his Private Secretary, now Sir Clive Wigram, wrote to Sir Herbert Creedy, the Permanent Under-Secretary at the War Office, to see what could be done about it. He consulted with the Home Office and they concluded 'naturally with some regret, that there is nothing we could do which would not have the result of advertising the book and so putting more money into the pockets of Crozier and his publisher.' He pointed out that Frank did not have a pension and relied on his writing for money. After giving a brief resumé of his military service, Sir Herbert went on:

We did not feel inclined to retain him in the Army after the war and have been unwilling to give him employment since for your private and confidential information, I may add that his domestic affairs do not rebound on his credit. On the whole, therefore, we feel that the best thing is to let the book sink back into the mud from which it emerged …

Sir Clive showed this letter to the King and agreed with Sir Herbert that, since Frank was 'evidently an undesirable person', back into the mud the book should go.[21]

Notwithstanding the Establishment's disapproval of *Brass Hat*, Cape sold the German language rights to a Viennese publisher, who brought it out as *Im Sturm ums Niemandsland*, and the North American rights to a New York publisher called Harrison Smith Ltd.[22] S.T. Williamson, reviewing the book for the *New York Times*, noted the storm that it had caused in Britain and that it had 'pleased neither the "Up Guards, and at 'em" people nor those who wring their hands and cry "Ain't it awful!".' For this reason 'his evidence becomes increasingly important.'[23] *Time* magazine saw Frank as 'a curious combination of hard, soldierly, efficient officer and humane, sceptical, almost pacifist civilian.'[24] The Canadian newspapers swallowed Frank's claim that he had been a captain in the Canadian forces during 1908–12 and the *Manitoba Free Press* declared: 'Brig.-General Crozier's might be ranked with the best war books written in recent years.'[25] Publication in North America also earned Frank a lecture tour in the USA, although it is not clear whether he was sponsored by his publisher or by some other organisation. It was probably the former, since Frank gave Jonathan Cape's address when embarking on the *Laconia* at Liverpool on 4 October 1930. He entitled his lecture 'War Experiences and Reflections of a Brass Hat in No Man's Land', but it is clear that what he really wanted to speak about was peace. In an address to an audience at the Free Synagogue in Carnegie Hall, New York, he warned, some might say prophetically, that if 'true disarmament' did not come within the decade it would only be achieved after 'the most destructive war the world has ever known.' What was clear was that science had created a situation in which future war would merely result in mutual destruction without victory for either side. In this context it was the 'military experts attached to disarmament conferences' who were to blame because of their unwillingness to scrap their 'outdated military machine.'[26]

The day after Frank had departed for the USA the British airship R101 crashed near Beauvais, France, during its first overseas flight. Among those on board were Lord Thomson, the Minister for Air and Sir Sefton Brancker, director of civil aviation, who had been the driving force behind the R101 and her sister the R100. An official inquiry was held during late October and early November and this prompted Frank to write to T.P. Scott of the *Manchester Guardian* from his New York hotel, the Lexington. He claimed to have known both men before they held their present posts. True, Thomson had been a regular soldier, rising to the rank of brigadier general, but the only time that Frank could have met him would have been in Ireland when Thomson was the military adviser to the Labour Party Commission on Ireland. It may be that Frank resented his comments on ADRIC, which implied that the Auxiliaries were a law unto themselves.[27] As for Brancker, Frank claimed to have turned him down for the post of second-in-command of ADRIC because of his involvement in the sacking of Violet Douglas-Pennant as head of the Women's Royal Air Force in September 1918. All this made Frank conclude that both men 'were so selfish, so wrapped up in their personal [sic] advancement, with their eyes always on the main chance as to be dangerous [sic] to State or individual.' He then went on to promote his new book, of which more later, and finished by lambasting Winston Churchill's son Randolph, who was also on a US lecture tour, for advocating 'big navies' as a means of securing trade.[28] Scott does not appear to have replied to this letter and Frank himself arrived back in Britain on 8 December 1930.

Although the royalty records no longer exist, *Brass Hat* certainly made Frank some much-needed money, although a goodly portion went to his creditors, but not enough to clear his debts. He had, however, been doing further writing before his trip to America. This was an autobiography, for which he signed a contract with the publisher Thomas Werner Laurie at the end of April 1930, with agreement to produce the manuscript of *Impressions and Recollections* by the end of July. Rumours of this book quickly reached the ears of the War Office and Sir Herbert Creedy wrote to Sir John Anderson, the Permanent Under-Secretary at the Home Office, to alert him. He thought that the book would be about the Black and Tans. 'Knowing how reckless Crozier is and what harm he might do by injudicious publication, I thought I ought to let you know what I have heard in case there is any action you would wish to take in the matter.'[29] There was, of course, little that anyone could do. Werner Laurie also took an option on Frank's next book, which was titled *War, Women and Wine*. Frank then went on to sack his literary agent, Erica Beale Ltd, and dealt with contract negotiations and placing of books with publishers himself.[30]

Frank's autobiography was duly published towards the end of 1930. Although it again pulled few punches, it lacked some of the sensationalism of *Brass Hat* and was generally a more accurate account of his life. It therefore did not cause the furore of its predecessor and attracted fewer reviews. The *Manchester Guardian* did carry one, but made no critical comment, noting that Frank was still firmly supportive of the League of Nations as a means of preventing future wars.[31] The *Daily Express* latched on to the chapter on Ireland in what it called 'a lively volume', highlighting some of the ADRIC and Black and Tan atrocities.[32]

The year 1931 seems to have been a relatively inactive time for Frank, although he was writing further books, as we shall see. The one personal event was the death of his stepfather on 4 November. Frank has left no indication of how he reacted to this. Suffice to say that Alec Thorneycroft's estate was worth some £5,400, but whether any of this came Frank's way is not known. The international situation was, however, beginning to worsen in 1931. While the 1927 Naval Conference at Geneva had proved a failure, the signing of the Kellogg-Briand Pact by sixty nations to outlaw war was a promising step on the path to lasting world peace. But the Wall Street Crash of the following year upset the world's economies. On the other hand, the 1930 London Naval Treaty achieved much of what the 1927 conference had failed to do. Britain, Japan and the USA reached agreement on restricting their holdings of cruisers, destroyers and submarines, and also agreed a five-year embargo on capital ship building. September 1931, however, saw a case of naked aggression, when the Japanese seized Mukden in Manchuria and set about overrunning the remainder of the Chinese half of the territory. It was this event which would galvanise Frank into further action.

He had, however, been busy writing a book on his experiences with the West African Frontier Force, which was published by Jonathan Cape as *Five Years Hard* on 8 February 1932. The *Manchester Guardian*'s reviewer was kind: 'General Crozier's rarely objective account of both sides of the life makes easy reading.'[33] But the *Daily Mail*, on publication day, carried a long piece on the book. It 'has much to tell which is interesting, but is all marred by the picture he draws of nightly drunken orgies by British officers, their liaisons with native women, and their treatment of natives generally.' It quoted Sir Charles Orr, who was the Resident in Northern Nigeria at the time and appeared in the book as 'Ash': 'He has put into my mouth the sheerest nonsense.' He went on to say: 'What I regret more than anything is the fact that General Crozier should attempt to besmirch the reputations – and in some cases the memories – of fine men who did a magnificent job for their country.' The *Daily Mail* also sent a copy to Lord Lugard, who had risen to be Governor-General of Nigeria during the Great War and was now British representative on the League of Nations Permanent Mandates Committee, asking for comments. He, too, was horrified, replying to the newspaper that 'I am surprised that any publisher would have accepted it' and that Frank's officers 'are represented as acting as no English officers and gentlemen would act.' He concluded: 'Some of the incidents Crozier relates – mutilating corpses at Sokoto to obtain bangles and other incidents – would not be credible were it not that he relates the facts as having been done by himself.'[34] Major General Charles Foulkes, who had commanded the Special Brigade Royal Engineers, responsible for discharging gas, on the Western Front and another veteran of Frank's time in Nigeria, was equally aghast. Like Lugard, he concluded that the barbarity displayed after the action at Sokoto was 'the act of certain officers of Mounted Infantry', which is as Frank described it in the book, but was the exception rather than the rule. He concluded: 'We can only hope in order to produce a sensational book the author has drawn largely on his own imagination.'[35]

Frank had also been watching events in India. During 1930 Mahatma Gandhi had initiated his civil disobedience campaign beginning with his protest march against the British monopoly on salt. There were a series of conferences in London to address Indian concerns, but the British Government refused to give way to the clamour for self-rule. Frank's thoughts on the matter are revealed in a letter published in *The Times* of 7 January 1932. He noted that Sir John Anderson had been appointed Governor of Bengal, where much of the unrest had been taking place, and assumed that this was because of his experience in Ireland. He compared the arrest of Gandhi in 1930 to that of Eamon de Valera in 1921 and asserted that the measures being taken to control the unrest in India were similar to those used in Ireland. He therefore warned against making the same mistakes, especially '"manufacturing rebels or grievances" owing to misplaced zeal of subordinates.' But Frank had gone further than a mere letter to a newspaper; he had written a book entitled *A Word to Gandhi: The Lesson of Ireland*, a copy of which he sent to Gandhi, who appears to have read it.[36] The book, however, made little impact in Britain.

The growing Japanese aggression in Manchuria and the seeming powerlessness of the League of Nations was also attracting Frank's attention. While Manchuria was quickly overrun and renamed Manchukuo, the Japanese also sought to confront the Chinese elsewhere. They turned their attention to Shanghai, where they and other foreign nations had concessions. On the pretext of taking justifiable action to defend its interests after five Buddhist monks had been attacked and a Japanese factory burnt to the ground, Japan deployed ships and troops to Shanghai and on 28 January 1932 these forces attacked various parts of the city and the surrounding area. Efforts to broker a lasting ceasefire by the other nations which had concessions in Shanghai failed and it looked as though an all-out war between Japan and China might develop. It was at this point that the concept of a 'peace army' was created in Britain. The leading lights were Maude Royden, suffragist, preacher, and tireless campaigner for the ordination of women, and a man who was to have an enormous influence on the lives of Frank and Grace, the Reverend Dick Sheppard. At the time he had just vacated the office of Dean of Canterbury because of ill-health, having previously made his mark as the vicar of St Martin-in-the-Fields in London's Trafalgar Square. In 1914 he had volunteered his services as an Army chaplain and had served in France with the Australian Voluntary (later No. 32 General) Hospital at St Nazaire for two months in autumn 1914 until his health broke down. The suffering of the wounded made a deep impression on him and shortly after the end of the war he became a pacifist. While at St Martin's, Dick Sheppard not only filled the church for his services, but also did all he could to help the homeless, a policy which the church continues to uphold to this day. He had also gained national fame as the BBC's first radio preacher.

Dick Sheppard and Maude Royden believed that the Peace Army could be used to literally place itself between warring armies and thus force them to cease firing on one another. They envisaged people from every member nation of the League of Nations joining the Peace Army. Maude Royden declared: 'I am ready to go now. What does it matter if a few hundred lives are lost by taking up a position between the combatants, compared with millions who may be killed in future wars?'[37] Frank was one of the first to volunteer. He had already voiced his fears that the Shanghai conflict could turn into a world war: 'Only the death of one American sailor at the hands of a Japanese sailor, soldier or airman is needed to cause some American admiral to clear for action in defence of national honour of his country and at the expense of international dishonour and disaster.'[38] Now he declared: 'The only way to stop two men engaged in a fierce argument is to make them laugh. If thousands of civilians interposed themselves between China and Japan the effect would be ludicrous and the war would stop immediately.'[39] But while the Peace Army achieved much publicity, it only attracted some 800 volunteers. In any event, the League of Nations did, on 4 March, pass a resolution demanding a ceasefire and ten days later a deputation arrived in Shanghai to oversee negotiations between the Japanese and Chinese. Sporadic fighting did continue throughout the negotiations, but on 5 May both sides signed the Shanghai Ceasefire Agreement, bringing hostilities to an end, at least for the time being. In the meantime, the Peace Army quietly dissolved.

Frank continued to be busy with his writing. In March 1932 he signed another contract with Jonathan Cape, this time for his account of his time with Thorneycroft's Mounted Infantry during the South African War. *Angels on Horseback* was published in July 1932. The reviews were generally favourable and included one in the *Daily Telegraph* from the eminent military theorist and commentator Captain Basil Liddell Hart, who wrote:

> While General Crozier's unblushing revelations are not to the taste of many soldiers, his reputation as a fighting man is unassailable. Hence there is a special interest in this new book, wherein he turns his devastating candour on South Africa. Even those who doubted some parts of his earlier books may find this one convincing.[40]

At the time Liddell Hart was the *Daily Telegraph*'s military correspondent and Frank had become a fan. In May 1932 he had written to Liddell Hart inviting him to lunch so that they could have a chat. 'I have read much of your work and follow your articles with great interest.'[41] He would have been especially interested in Liddell Hart's reports from the Geneva Disarmament Conference, which had opened on 2 February. Frank had asked Cape to send Liddell Hart a copy of *Angels on Horseback*, which they did, but then had no review copy left to send to the *Daily Telegraph* and so Frank wrote to Liddell Hart asking him to send his copy to the newspaper. There appears therefore to have been a slight crossed wire, in that it would have almost certainly have been Liddell Hart who reviewed the book if a copy had merely been sent to the paper. As it was, Frank was delighted with the review: 'Thank heaven there is one reviewer and critic who recognises the essentials when he sees them and misses them when they are not present.' He also told Liddell Hart that he was thinking of writing 'a light book covering the points never covered (of necessity) in the manuals – "Tips to Subalterns and Field Marshals"!!.'[42]

Earlier in the year Frank had decided to write another book about Ireland and submitted the manuscript to Jonathan Cape. Cape himself was nervous about some of the things that Frank had written and consulted with another of his authors, Denis Gwynn, the Irish journalist and editor of the *Dublin Review*. In his reply, dated 12 May, Gwynn warned that 'the trouble is that there are many people determined to down Crozier because of his attitude during the Black and Tan time; and just now, after his recent book [*A Brass Hat in No Man's Land*] all the old Diehards of the *Morning Post* type will feel it their patriotic duty to discredit him if they have the chance.' He went on to write that there were two versions of Frank's time in Ireland:

A – The general impression (which I suspect he shares himself) is that he was a gentleman with a fine military record in the war, who sacked a lot of Black and Tans under his control for looting, and who resigned at once when Hamar Greenwood would not let them be sacked. Most people at the time believed at once that here at last was an honest man who had strayed in among them, and that his exposure brought the whole system into disgrace.

B – The other version is very different. What I have been told from various sources (and I tell you in confidence without being able to say how much truth there is in the story) is

1 – That Crozier was a typical Black and Tan himself with no object but to find himself a congenial job when demobilised.

2 – That he actually enlisted as a Black and Tan and was discovered among the latest batch of recruits over from England: that he was soon after given command (because of his military rank) of the chief Black and Tan camp at Gormanstown.

3 – That from the time he assumed command looting and other outrages by the Black and Tans became quite shameless and unchecked until

4 – A Batch of his own men looted the house of an important unionist and such a row was imminent that he would have been immediately disgraced.

5 – That he then sacked the looters but found that they were reinstated, whereupon he found the opportunity to resign amid general applause

Now I can't vouch for any of this but it was all told to me by various people who were behind the scenes at the time.

Jonathan Cape duly sent the manuscript to Gwynn. Having read it, Gwynn repeated his warning about the Old Guard wanting revenge on Crozier. As for the story itself:

I can find nothing more discreditable. He accepts a highly paid command and admittedly assists in recruiting for the corps which he writes his book to denounce. He is apparently responsible for the discipline of the whole corps, that was his job. Yet his book is a long catalogue of excesses committed by them and he talks freely of 'my murderers' etc on many pages.

As for the Trim affair, Gwynn thought it 'the weirdest story and leaves me more than ever convinced that there is much more to come out.' He found it especially odd that Frank did not attend the trial of the cadets which would clear his reputation.[43] Even so, in spite of the doubts Jonathan Cape had, an agreement to publish *Ireland For Ever* was signed that July. Curiously, though, the following month Frank passed all rights to the book over to a Mr Noel Rees of Petts Wood, Orpington, Kent.[44] This was Grace's brother-in-law, who had married her sister Annette, and was a builder who was partly responsible for the creation of Petts Wood, in Kent, in the 1920s. It is possible therefore that this was security on a loan or that it was a way of preventing the royalties being passed on to his creditors. The arrangement itself lasted for three years before Frank took back all the rights.

Ireland For Ever was published on 14 November 1932. Frank wrote to Liddell Hart again saying that he had asked Cape to send him an advance copy, but the publisher had failed to do so, for which Frank had to apologise.[45] It was not widely reviewed, but a piece in the *Irish Independent* of 14 November claimed that Frank had been dismissed from ADRIC in November 1920. Frank successfully sued the newspaper, which apologised in public and reached an undisclosed settlement with him.[46]

Although most did not realise it at the time, Hitler's coming to power in Germany in January 1933 presented a threat to peace in Europe, and one that would grow with time. There is little record of what Frank did during the first of part of the year. He was active with what was called the British Anti-War Movement, which enjoyed some limelight, especially after Germany withdrew from the Geneva Disarmament Conference that October, which increased disillusion with the League of Nations. A letter from 'Old Contemptible' in the *Daily Mirror* of 30 August 1933 noted that Frank had contributed an article to the journal of the British Legion in which he declared that everyone should declare war against war. That November Frank made a widely reported speech in which he stated:

A general strike should immediately follow any threat of war. If we must suffer, let us suffer for peace and justice. Armchair and Cenotaph patriotism is all founded on rot and loose talk. Women, instead of encouraging men to become tailors' dummies, might discourage war by pointing at men clad in khaki and exclaiming 'What silly asses you look!'

He went on to declare: 'If we had an understanding with Germany and Italy regarding peace with honour it would be the greatest benefit to Europe.'[47]

Frank was also put up for membership of the Savage Club, one of London's leading clubs for practitioners of the arts and whose members address one another as 'Brother Savage'. C.E. Lawrence, author, playwright and the editor of the literary *Cornhill Magazine*, wrote to Liddell Hart, who was a member, on 3 November 1933: 'Thank you for your kind willingness to support our Brass Hat. He is one of the best and I am glad he wants to join the club.' Liddell Hart then received a notice to attend the Qualification Committee, which was meeting on 29 November, 'to support your candidate.' Two days later Lawrence sent him another note, which stated that 'there is a hitch (only a brief one I hope) over Crozier's candidature.'[48] What the 'hitch' was is not known – perhaps it was to do with Frank's bankruptcy or objections to his membership from other members – but this was the end of his brief flirtation with the Savage Club.

It was at about this time that Frank and Grace moved house. In a letter to Basil Liddell Hart from East Lodge, Walton-on-Thames, Surrey, dated 24 May 1935, Frank wrote: 'We built a small house here about 18 months ago on the site of Ashley Lodge which used to belong to the Sassoons, as, lovely as the surroundings were at Westerham, servants became the devil and wanted a cinema that we couldn't provide.'[49] One suspects that once more Frank was gilding the lily, as he probably could not afford much in the way of servants. Since David Starrett himself was certainly living in Walton-on-Thames by August 1937[50] and developing the Ashley Park estate, it is highly likely that the Croziers moved after he had built East Lodge and that they occupied it under much the same terms as in Westerham.

Frank was continuing to dabble in various organisations. One was the Empire Movement, which dreamed of the creation of a British Empire parliament. Speaking on Empire strategy at a January 1934 meeting, Frank dismissed the 1925 Locarno Treaty, which bound Britain and Italy to act as guarantors of national borders within western Europe, as 'the greatest bit of humbug ever arrived at'. Then, in seeming total contradiction of his numerous pacifist outpourings, he declared that Britain must have an air force five times stronger than at present, as well as a navy which would rule the seas, and a modern army.[51] But Frank and Grace were becoming very firm friends with Dick Sheppard. He was still recovering his health, but later in 1934 would become a canon at St Paul's Cathedral. He had been especially taken by a sermon he had heard in New York on Armistice Sunday 1933. It was preached by a man who had also served as a US Army chaplain in France during the war, Dr Harry Emerson Fosdick. He declared:

I renounce war. I renounce war because of what it does to our own men … I renounce war because of what it compels us to do to our enemies … I renounce war for its consequences, for the lies it lives on and propagates, for the undying hatreds it arouses, for the dictatorships it puts in place of democracy, for the starvation that stalks after it. I renounce war and never again, directly or indirectly, will I sanction or support another.[52]

This got Sheppard thinking seriously on how better to win more people round to the cause of peace. He was also aware, as was Frank, that the League of Nations Union was planning to ballot the country on its attitudes to the League of Nations and the prevention of war. Eventually, after lengthy discussions with Frank, Dick Sheppard hit upon a plan. With the echo of Dr Fosdick's words in his ears, he wrote a letter for publication in the newspapers. *The Times* refused to publish it, but others, including the *Manchester Guardian* and a number of provincial publications, did so on 16 October 1934:

> It seems essential to discover whether or not it be true, as we are told, that the majority of thoughtful men in this country are convinced that war of any kind or for any cause, is not only a denial of Christianity, but a crime against humanity which is not to be permitted by civilised people.

He invited readers to send him a postcard with the following declaration: 'I renounce war and never again, directly or indirectly, will I support or sanction another.' The letter gave Frank's address, since Dick Sheppard was abroad at the time of publication. For two days no postcards arrived and on the third day Frank and Grace began to wonder how they could break the bad news to their friend. The telephone then rang. It was the village postmaster demanding to know why he had not been warned about the deluge of postcards that had arrived. He had, however, managed to obtain a van, and wanted to confirm that someone would be at East Lodge to receive them. During the next few weeks the Croziers received some 100,000 responses, all of which had to be collated and so they converted their summerhouse into an office.[53] All this meant that it was to be some months before Dick Sheppard took action.

During this time Lloyd George was writing and publishing his *War Memoirs*. Volume IV, which dealt with the latter half of 1917, appeared at the end of October 1934. His scathing attacks on Douglas Haig and the conduct of Third Ypres caused a storm and Frank entered the lists by writing to Lloyd George with his views on the campaign. These were clearly supportive of what Lloyd George had written, since Frank received a reply from him saying that Lloyd George had received many letters from men who actually fought at Third Ypres and was thinking of publishing some of them. He wondered whether Frank would allow him to use extracts from his letter.[54] Lloyd George does not appear to have gone ahead with this plan, but there is a sneaking suspicion that Frank might have claimed to have fought at Third Ypres, when, of course, he had not. A hint of what else he might have written in the letter came in one he had published in the *Daily Mirror*. Speaking of 1917 he observed that 'the professional soldier was unable, in the main, to adapt himself to the ever changing conditions, because of his peace training. It is the same today.' He went on: 'By 1917 I had sacked all my "professionals" and put in their places men fit for the job of winning the war, but I became very unpopular in certain high quarters.'[55]

It was not until the early summer of 1935 that Dick Sheppard made his next move. He organised what he called Dr Sheppard's Peace Demonstration at London's

Albert Hall on 14 July 1935. Posters were issued with a drawing by Arthur Wragg. This depicted the Cenotaph encasing a dying soldier dripping with blood. So gory was it that the London Underground refused to display it. The evening was to be a mixture of hymns, readings and addresses. Siegfried Sassoon agreed to read some of his poetry, with fellow trench poet Edmund Blunden giving an address. Maude Royden and Frank were the other two speakers. The programme gave the movement's headquarters as Walton-on-Thames and included a plea for money, since 'we have not one bean behind us.' Curiously, and in line with Dick Sheppard's original letter, only men seem to have attended, some 7,000 in all. They heard Dr Sheppard declare that war was 'a blasphemous betrayal of the future of man' and castigate the leaders of Church and State for their 'lack of moral courage.'[56] Sybil Morrison, later the Peace Pledge Union's first recorder, concluded from quizzing participants that the event was 'unforgettably inspiring, intensely exciting and overwhelmingly successful.'[57]

One other factor which also probably contributed to the success of the launch was the League of Nations Union Peace Ballot. The results of this had been announced at the end of June. Some 11.6 million had taken part and they had been asked five questions. Those concerning Britain's continuing membership of the League of Nations, international disarmament, and the outlawing of military and naval aircraft, as well as the banning of the manufacture of weapons, all received overwhelming votes in support. The fifth question was in two parts and concerned states combining to stop two nations fighting one another. While support for doing this through economic and other non-military measures was again overwhelming, when asked if they should, if necessary, apply military measures, almost seventy-five per cent agreed that they should. This was an anathema to the pacifists and those had who had been supporting the League of Nations began to join Dick Sheppard's organisation. Further disillusion with the League would occur with its failure to prevent Mussolini invading and overrunning Abyssinia.

Dick Sheppard vowed that his movement would have no formal organisation. He did, however, gather together an informal group of advisers, who were known as 'sponsors'. They included the novelist Aldous Huxley, the philosopher Bertrand Russell and George Lansbury, former leader of the Labour Party. Frank and Grace continued to act as unofficial secretaries from their summerhouse.

Later in July 1935 Dick Sheppard took up Frank's case for compensation for his November 1920 motor accident in Ireland. He had an interview with Lord Halifax, then the Secretary of State for War, and arranged for Frank to submit a statement to him. In his covering letter to Halifax Dick Sheppard wrote: 'I asked the little man to make it as short as possible, but you will see he has written a young book.'[58] Indeed, it turned out to be thirty-eight pages of double-spaced typing on A4 paper. Some of what Frank wrote reiterated previous falsehoods and added a few new ones. For instance, he now put his return from Canada as 1913 and said that he had 'come specially back from Service with the Canadian Forces to help Captain James Craig (as he then was) to organise the Ulster Volunteer Force for the defence of Ulster and the Union.'[59] Needless to say, there was no positive response from the War Office. Even so, Frank was still very much in the public eye. In a column headed 'Invalids' *The Times* of 29 November 1935 noted that Admiral of the Fleet Lord Beatty was recovered from his recent chill, Sir John Mart-Harvey, a well-known romantic actor, was on tour again after his recent illness, while Frank had caught a chill at an Armistice Sunday service and was in Walton-on-Thames Cottage Hospital suffering pleurisy and pneumonia, from which he quickly recovered.

Dick Sheppard's plan was now to publicise his movement by holding rallies, similar to that held in the Albert Hall, in other parts of the country. The *Manchester Guardian* headlined one such gathering in Manchester in March 1936 'REMARKABLE PEACE MEETINGS: Three Halls insufficient for Manchester Demonstration.' Frank himself presided and described himself as 'a soldier of 33 years' standing who had fought in 14 wars'. He declared: 'I also say as a soldier that the old methods are gone, and gone for ever, and we must put something else in their place. It is your task and mine to consider, and the sooner we get together and do something the better.' All three gatherings passed a conference urging the Government to pressure the League of Nations intro organising a world peace conference. Among other demands on the Government were to lobby for Germany to rejoin the League* and for a Europe-wide non-aggression pact.[60]

The rallies did raise sufficient money to enable Dick Sheppard to set up an office in Grand Buildings, Trafalgar Square in central London in early summer 1936. He also took on a paid secretary, Margery Rayne. The sponsors also began to meet there and it was decided that the movement should be called the Peace Pledge Union (PPU). Another significant development at this time was the introduction of a weekly newspaper, *Peace News*, the first issue of which appeared on 27 June. While the PPU continued to have no formal structure, local groups were formed and began to organise their own activities. They did not work in isolation, however, and on 20 June 1936 some 12,000 people from various peace groups gathered at Maumbury Rings, near Dorchester in Dorset. Among the speakers were Dick Sheppard, George Lansbury and Vera Brittain, whose account of her 1914–18 experiences, *Testament of Youth*, had recently been published. On the way back to London in the train Dick Sheppard tried to persuade Vera to join the PPU as a sponsor, which she did six months later. This, as he realised, was a contradiction, since the PPU was restricted to men only. It was therefore decided that it must be opened to women, and to encourage them, the novelist Storm Jameson was made a sponsor. Dick explained the changes in a letter to the Press, asking for 100,000 women to join the 100,000 men already enrolled. The women, however, were asked to sign a slightly different pledge: 'I renounce War and never again will I support or sanction another, and I will do all in my power to persuade others to do the same.'[61]

In summer 1936 the PPU held a camp for some 500 people at the Hayes Christian Conference Centre at Swanwick in Derbyshire. The main activities were lectures, but there were also sports and evening entertainments. Dick Sheppard and Frank were present and Ronald Mallone, then a teenage member of the PPU, recalled the two impersonating one another, with Dick Sheppard showing Frank brandishing a sword to make someone sign the Peace Pledge. Indeed, Mallone considered Frank

---

* Germany had left the League in October 1933 after Hitler failed to obtain agreement at Geneva that the German Armed Forces would be permitted to be at the same strength as Germany's neighbours, especially France.

one of the most impressive of the peace leaders and believed that the Government feared him most of all. Frank was a pugnacious speaker and Mallone recalled that when he came to speak at his school, Goldsmith's College, there were some hecklers present from the school's Officer Training Corps, but Frank silenced them in 'about three words'. Mallone also remembered that he invited Frank to speak in a church in south-east London and that he was very reluctant to set foot in the House of God because he had so much blood on his hands.[62] Indeed, he had written to the *Daily Telegraph* at much the same time:

> My attention has been drawn to a misunderstanding which has arisen in regard to my association with the Peace Pledge Union as a sponsor. It is assumed in certain quarters that this union is one entirely founded on the Christian ethic and that to be a member one must be a Christian pacifist.
>
> For me to adopt such an attitude, clothed in the white sheet of purity and pugnastic repentance, would be an impertinence and a piece of hypocrisy which it would be hard to beat, and I beg you therefore to be good enough to contradict this assertion.[63]

Yet Frank's lack of belief did not deter him and Grace from frequently listening to Dick Sheppard's sermons.

Frank's letter to the *Daily Telegraph* also caught the attention of the Metropolitan Police's Special Branch, who filed it. One of its reports, dated 24 June 1936, also noted that Dr Sheppard operated the PPU from The Pavement, Hersham Road, Walton-on-Thames, which, of course, was not Frank's address, and Grand Buildings. It also made mention of the two types of pledge. A further Special Branch report at the end of November 1936 listed the sponsors, with Frank's name at the top, and noted that it had a close alliance with the Society of Friends. It also observed that the PPU was aiming to recruit one million members and was organising groups 'trained in the technique of non-violence.' There is, however, no evidence that Special Branch took any further action.[64]

Frank was still in contact with Liddell Hart and wrote to invite him to join Grace in a box at the Albert Hall for another PPU rally on the evening of 27 November 1936. Liddell Hart accepted and invited the Croziers to dinner before the event, which Frank had to decline as he was one of the speakers.[65] The hall was filled to capacity and heard Lord Ponsonby argue against the policy of collective security, while Frank praised Liddell Hart's articles in *The Times* (for which he had now become military correspondent), in which he feared that a British expeditionary force might find it impossible to get across the English Channel in a future European war – part of his developing doctrine of Limited Liability, which called for no ground forces to be committed to the Continent, only air and naval elements.[66] Frank also wrote a very complimentary review of Liddell Hart's *The War in Outline*, his revisiting of the Great War. The review appeared in *Reynold's Illustrated News*, a radical Sunday paper, for which Frank became defence correspondent and which was 'one of the few papers my rebelliousness permits me to write for.'[67] Frank liked the book because it appeared to echo his own views on the military leadership of 1914–18, namely that its narrow pre-war education had meant that it was unable to adapt to changing conditions and that this was still the case.[68]

The PPU marked the beginning of 1937 with a New Year campaign, which ran from 13 January until 6 February. In a programme that appears to have been organised by Frank, in that his name is at the bottom of it, seventeen separate events took place from Bristol in the south-west to Dundee in Scotland, and Southend-on-Sea in the south-east. Dick Sheppard spoke at all bar two of them, while Frank addressed meetings at Aberdare in Wales, Nottingham, Liverpool and Salisbury.[69] But there appear to have been ructions within the organisation, which are revealed in a letter that Frank wrote to Lord Ponsonby on 7 January, the day after a sponsors' meeting that Ponsonby had chaired, since Dick Sheppard was ill. It seems that Margery Rayne was also ill and had written a letter to the sponsors which hinted at her resignation. She accused the sponsors of being divided. Her grounds appear to be a letter written by the PPU's Edinburgh group, which was headed by Sir Fabian Ware, founder of the Imperial (now Commonwealth) War Graves Commission. The issue was a book written by an American Quaker called Richard B. Gregg and entitled *The Power of Non-Violence*. The Edinburgh group wanted to know where the sponsors stood on campaigns of non-violence. Frank accepted that one or two were in favour, which he was clearly not, since he labelled them as 'cranks', but said that the sponsors were not divided over 'the one thing that matters, the pledge.'[70] As it was, Margery Rayne did resign, it appears, and her place was taken by Max Plowman, who had served as an infantry officer on the Western Front and was author of *A Subaltern on the Somme*. Early in 1918, having, like Siegfried Sassoon, been treated for shell shock, he applied to resign his commission and was court-martialled and dismissed from the Army. He was then excused conscription on the grounds of conscientious objection to the war.

Cape brought out a cheap edition of *Brass Hat*, with Frank providing a new preface. He hoped that younger readers would recognise the futility of war from reading it, and declared that 'the days of the Royal Navy and Army are over', while 'the role of the Royal Air Force is now futile and ineffective and an instrument far too indiscriminate.' As for the supporters of collective security, 'their theory has proved unsound, their method of warfare merely the old method made to look respectable.'[71] That the RAF was indiscriminate, Frank had explained what he meant by this when he addressed a British Commonwealth League luncheon at the beginning of February. Bombers, he said, inevitably struck women and children, who became the first casualties in modern war.[72]

Frank's views were reinforced when, on 26 April 1937, there took place the infamous air attack on the Spanish town of Guernica. Three days later, Viscount Cecil of Chelwood initiated an adjournment debate in the House of Lords by roundly condemning the atrocity and demanding that the government raise the matter at the League of Nations, getting other nations to protest as well. Frank wrote to him the following day, probably along the lines that not only should air warfare be immediately proscribed, but war as a whole. Cecil replied to him on 5 May, reiterating the more pragmatic argument he had used in the Lords, namely that at the outset of hostilities the combatants tended to observe the laws of war and that it was only when they became desperate and feared defeat that they began to resort to more inhumane methods of waging war. The combatant nations also sought the sympathy of the uninvolved world and this acted as a deterrent to employing inhumane weapons. True, there had been the opportunity at Geneva in 1932 to proscribe air warfare and 'the failure to take that chance was a criminal blunder.'[73] As for the Spanish Civil War as a whole, Frank commented rather enigmatically: 'There is only one thing that can save civilisation and that is civilisation. Rating, as I do, Fascism as an anti-social evil I am accordingly opposed thereto. On the other hand, in Communism, I detect the hand of Christ.'[74]

Frank was also engaged in writing yet another book, a diatribe against war based on his own experiences of the Great War. This time Michael Joseph was to be the publisher. He hoped that Harry Wragg, the artist who designed many of the PPU's programmes, would do the jacket for the book. Frank had clear ideas on what he wanted. Writing to Wragg, he explained:

> I would love to have a crushed hatted general in full kit with his hat knocked off, or something, on the front page, plus a pocket bulging profiteer getting away with the swag and an archbishop being led off by merchant of death. Could you arrange it?[75]

In the event, the jacket of *The Men I Killed* was relatively plain, with a picture of Frank in the top right corner, and Wragg was not used.

As the title suggests, Frank was out to shock. He repeated some of the stories that he had told in *Brass Hat* – the execution of Rifleman Crozier, shooting Portuguese troops during the German April 1918 offensive and a British officer in March 1918. He implied that Haig was a murderer in that his famous Back to the Wall message during the height of the Lys offensive condemned some of his men to their death. He claimed to have shot a British soldier during one of the 1918 retreats because he was firing at a Frenchwoman. 'I refused the French Medal of Humanity, which I was subsequently offered for my part in the unhappy incident, as I considered the joke to be rather out of place.'[76] It is, however, not clear which French medal Frank was referring to, and it would have been unlikely that the Frank of 1918 would have turned down another medal, especially after being rebuffed in his attempt to obtain a 1914 Star. Much of the book was, though, a sometimes almost incoherent rant at the Establishment, including the Church. It covered not just 1914–18, but also his experiences in south and west Africa, the Baltic and Ireland. As for contemporary warfare, modern airpower meant that there was no longer such a thing as effective defence.

Given the tone of *The Men I Killed*, it is not surprising that there was an outcry when it was published. James Agate in *The Daily Express* described Frank as 'a fire-eater in the cause of pacifism, and a fire-breather, too', and accused him of hypocrisy.[77] In his defence Frank stated: 'I wrote the book for no other purpose than to expose humbug. It is not my fault that newspapers picked out sensational sentences while omitting three quarters of the book devoted to the constructive argument'. But, as the *Daily Mirror*'s Cassandra pointed out, there could hardly be anything less sensational than the book's title.[78] Frank did, however, have his supporters. The review in *Peace News* accepted that the book was 'repetitive and emotional ... [and] its author lacks logic, tolerance, and objectivity', but 'he is excellent when he writes of the nincompoopery, the humbuggery, the pettifoggery, and the "General Blimpery" of the high Command. These are things of which he can speak with authority and things of which the public should know.'[79] As for Dick Sheppard, he wrote to Frank: 'Delighted to see how your book is being boomed. It ought to go like hot cakes. It will show up war as no other has.'[80] But the biggest upset the book caused was in Portugal, where the government took umbrage at Frank's claim that his men intentionally shot Portuguese soldiers on the first day of the Lys offensive. The British ambassador, Sir Charles Wingfield, had to write a formal letter of apology.[81] The fact that it had proved nigh on impossible at the time to distinguish fleeing Portuguese from advancing Germans in the fog, because of the similarity of their uniforms, was ignored by both Frank and the Government. Frank, however, was probably unaware of this spat with the Portuguese, since he was taken ill very shortly after the book's publication.

Chapter Fourteen

The End

At the beginning of August 1937 Frank was feeling far from well. The cause was problems with his liver and bladder, possibly in part to do with his recurrent malarial attacks. During the second part of the month his condition worsened and he was forced into the local hospital at Walton-on-Thames. Once again, reports of his condition appeared in the Press.[1] David Starrett came to see him and took care of his affairs. Curiously, on 28 August Frank made a formal agreement with Starrett that, in exchange for £150, Frank handed him over the copyright on all his published works, as well as on any future publications.[2] As with the agreement that Frank had with Noel Rees over *Ireland For Ever*, the reason is not clear. Perhaps in this case Frank was aware that he was dying and wanted to ensure that Grace had enough money to cover the funeral expenses. Efforts were made to contact Mary and Hester, but without success. Dick Sheppard could not come immediately since he was caring for one of his children, who was sick, in Cornwall. The end came at 9.50am on 31 August 1937.

Dick Sheppard sent a telegram and followed it up on the same day with a letter to Grace written from the Grand Hotel at Plymouth:

What can I say my dearest Grace? Nothing I fear that is of any use, only that my whole heart aches for you. Just remember what a wonderful wife and loyal companion you have been to your darling. Never, never shall I forget him and his lovely generous goodness towards me.

I am broken at the loss of my beloved friend and I can't bear to think of your loneliness. God comfort you if he can, dearest Grace.[3]

The funeral arrangements were made by Bill Allan, Frank's brother-in-law, and the funeral service was conducted by Dick Sheppard. Frank's ashes were then scattered in his garden.[4]

Once more those who had served under him during the war rallied round. Lt Col W.E. Brown DSO MC, who had risen to command the 18th Welsh in Frank's brigade, wrote to Grace that he had 'the greatest admiration for him as a soldier and a man.' Another member of the Welsh Regiment, George Victor Jones, the holder of three MCs, claimed to have served with Frank from January 1915 until June 1918 and then been given command of A Company of ADRIC by him.* He wrote: 'During the whole of these trying periods I never knew him to do a mean or unjust act. He was

---

* Jones certainly served under Frank in the 18th Welsh and as 119 Brigade's bombing officer. He joined ADRIC on 24 September 1920.

always fearless in action and in speech.' Another of his men, H.E.H. Gill, who served in Frank's brigade signals section, wrote:

> In the retreat from Fleurbaix to Strazale [sic] on the 9th April 1918 he stemmed the advance of the Germans with only the remnants of a Brigade, and with no reinforcements to help him in a desperate situation. I think this country owes much to his bravery and leadership, and those men who served under him, and have survived, will no doubt agree with me.[5]

W.A.C. Morgan MC, also formerly of the Welsh Regiment under Frank, wrote to Grace: 'Altho' General Crozier must have felt very keenly the attacks made on him, one can, I think, safely assume that he found comfort in the knowledge that his message to the world was a challenge too great for immediate acceptance, and that sooner or later the truth of it would be recognised by all serious minded people.'[6]

C.E. Lawrence, Editor of the *Quarterly Review* who had put Frank up for membership of the Savage Club, commented: 'No words, however sincere and sympathetic, can help with your heavy deprivation; but I do hope it will be some comfort to you to realise how much he was honoured by the many he served so disinterestedly and loved by those who really knew him.' Another individual, David A. Peat, who was not known to Grace, wrote:

> In 1929 I was very ill at Tatsfield – a physical and mental breakdown – when he [Frank] came to see me as it was difficult for the people with whom I lived to keep me in the circumstances, he suggested that I might come into his home if I could get a nurse and that you and he could help to look after me. I felt his innate kindness in his voice and manner though I was so ill. He was a complete stranger and yet he came again next day but it proved better for me to go to a nursing home where there was a resident doctor.[7]

More surprising, considering that Frank had not parted from them on the best of terms, was a letter of sympathy from the head of the Lithuanian Delegation to London, B.K. Balutis, who was writing on behalf of the 'Minister of National Defence and many of the officers of the Lithuanian Army, who were privileged to associate with your husband.'[8]

There were obituaries in numerous newspapers. *The Times* noted that Frank 'once described himself as "different to anybody else" and there was some justification for the claim.' It repeated the falsehood that Frank had returned in 1912 because of the Irish crisis and omitted to explain that he was twice forced to resign his commission prior to 1914. Otherwise, it gave a reasonably accurate resumé of Frank's career, commenting enigmatically on his time in command of ADRIC that: 'making no allowance for "political expediency", in a series of trying situations and resigned over a question of discipline in 1921.' Otherwise, the obituary made no comment, except to state that *The Men I Killed* 'is best forgotten. The allegations he made against the conduct of soldiers at the front aroused great indignation among ex-Service men and the relatives of those who lost their lives in the War.'[9] Grace did not like this obituary and *The Times* did publish a resumé of the two main points which she made in response. The first was that Frank resigned from ADRIC because, against instructions, he wanted to punish looting by 'British soldiers' and 'could not condone the murder of Irishmen by Irishmen instigated, as he considered, by Government emissaries to justify what they called the "Black and Tan operations" in Ireland.' Grace asserted that Frank's resignation meant that he forfeited his Army pension, which was totally untrue. She also claimed that Frank was not involved with the League of Nations 'as a professional lecturer and writer.' Rather, he was totally opposed to the League.[10] Another who was not totally happy with *The Times* obituary was its military correspondent, Basil Liddell Hart. It is worth quoting in full what he wrote:

> The controversy created, and the feelings aroused, by General Crozier's fierce propaganda in recent years on behalf of the pacifist movement has tended to obscure, or at least deprive of its due recognition his outstanding performance as a front-line commander in the War. I have had the opportunity of questioning many who served with or under him, both war-time and professional soldiers, and have heard on all sides the most fervent admiration expressed for his qualities as a fighting leader. Some who had wide experience considered that he was the best brigade commander they saw in action, and quote his share in the capture of Bourlon Wood as an epic feat of arms. The revulsion which came to him after the war, if exceptional in degree, was common in nature to many who saw war closest as leaders in the fighting line. His fighting spirit, however, was so fundamental to his nature that it was translated rather than transformed into the sphere where he now sought to communicate his convictions of the futility of war even in self-defence. In throwing himself wholeheartedly and unsparingly into the campaign for pacifism it could hardly be expected that a man of his kind and training should develop a philosophic moderation of argument or scientific exactness of statement. But his honesty of purpose was no more open to doubt than his courage. And such moral courage he showed is so rare, especially in combination with physical courage, that his memory should inspire respect long after the controversies he stirred up have become stilled. There is no sacrifice which comes harder, or calls for more strength of soul, than for a man to sacrifice to his matured convictions the good opinion he has earned and the friendships he has gained in the circle of his profession.[11]

Dick Sheppard also submitted a notice to *The Times*, but it was not published. In it he wrote:

> No man can throw over a career, for conscience's sake in which he is a conspicuous success, to embrace another for which this world had neither rewards nor favour, and escape suffering. This certainly was the abundant lot of Frank Crozier.
> Of his suffering I will not write; it was poignant and very real. Save for the selfless devotion of Mrs Crozier, David Starrett, the happiness of his home and the companionship of his Great Dane dog 'Barri',* there would have been almost no compensations allowed him latterly – not even that of tolerable health.

---

* Dick Sheppard had given Barri to Frank.

But with splendid fortitude he never failed to keep his engagements all over the country, nor write as he felt constrained to about the abomination of war. The last memory many of us have of him was in Swanwick camp some weeks ago, where, with the marks of his grave illness upon him, he compelled himself to take part in our discussions and diversions.

In the latter his impersonation of myself in clerical collar, addressing a meeting while frequently resorting to the use of an asthmatic inhaler, was overwhelmingly amusing.

We from all parts of the land salute the General. We shall not forget his uncompromising witness, his tireless work at Walton-on-Thames, nor the gallantry with which he faced the adversity of ill-health and the criticisms inevitably aroused by the pacifism of an out-spoken solider and General, who knew of what he spoke.

To me, personally, the loss of Frank is the loss of a beloved friend and the most loyal and generous of colleagues.[12]

Frank also had a lengthy obituary in the *New York Times*. It highlighted the shooting of Portuguese troops and Rifleman Crozier and commented that 'he reached a new high in frankness' with *The Men I Killed*.[13] The *Western Australian* described him as 'a stocky little man with an independence of mind which did not make him popular with some of the British regular officers.'[14] Max Plowman in *Peace News*:

The General was a portent and will remain a figure in history when the records of his contemporaries are forgotten, for the English people know honesty and integrity when they see them and in the life of General Crozier they will recognise a man whose moral courage was as great as his personal bravery.[15]

Where, however, the obituaries provided a resumé of Frank's military career, they clearly lifted the details from *Who's Who*, repeating the falsehoods about his pre-1914 service in Frank's entry. Grace herself felt forced to go into print because of the criticisms of *The Men I Killed*. She wrote that it was after just finishing another book* 'that a latent germ from a tropical disease that he had contracted years ago in Nigeria had awakened', but had not thought other than he would recover. She stressed that all he ever wanted was the truth and that it was for this that he was now being attacked. 'But I, and the hundreds of soldiers and their wives who have written to me, know different.'[16]

Grace may have had moral support from those who had known and admired Frank, but he left her financially destitute. Recognising this, Dick Sheppard began to raise money on her behalf. But his efforts were cut short by his own death at the end of October 1937. Meanwhile, Grace went to stay with a friend in Limpsfield, Surrey. George Lansbury, the prominent Labour MP and pacifist, took up her case. It would seem that he contacted Leslie Hore-Belisha, the War Minister. Lansbury showed his response, which was clearly negative, to Grace, who took umbrage. On 14

---

* There is no indication of what this book might have been about.

October she wrote to Hore-Belisha complaining that the minister had stated that he understood that Frank 'left his wife destitute in Russia' and that this was 'most unjust & untrue.' She claimed: 'This can be proved by my step daughter & at least two of my husband's officers who were in Russia at the time. One of these officers now holds an important appointment in the Air Ministry.' It is not clear to which stepdaughter Grace refers, but Mary's memories make it clear that her mother did become penniless after she refused to return from Lithuania by train. Hester, on the other hand, is unlikely to have known what happened, since she did not go to Lithuania, did not see much of her mother and was only six years old at the time. As for the officer in the Air Ministry, this was Anthony Muirhead, who was now the Under-Secretary for Air. However, since going into politics soon after his return from Lithuania he had increasingly distanced himself from Frank.* Even so, Grace did receive a reply from Hore-Belisha's Private Secretary, which said that the evidence for Frank leaving Ethel destitute was provided by herself. In any event, there was no record held at the War Office that Frank had remarried and it was assumed that Frank was living apart from Ethel at the time of his death. Grace was not entitled to any assistance because she did not marry him until after he had left the Army. It might, however, be possible to grant her stepdaughter something from the Relief Fund.[17]

Grace does not seem to have passed this information immediately to Hester, but tried another tack for herself. Another friend of hers, a Mrs Amy Larence of Westerham with whom Grace was now staying, wrote to Viscount Cecil at the end of November 1937. Mrs Larence pointed out that Grace 'has not been trained for any kind of work, and owing to bad illnesses is not strong enough to do very much. She has had to give up her house, and the death of Canon Sheppard put an end to the fund he had begun to raise for her.' She explained that Grace was not entitled to an Army widow's pension or to a civil pension and hoped that Cecil would be able to use his influence to obtain a 'compassionate allowance'. Cecil passed the letter to Hore-Belisha, but again nothing appears to have materialised. Basil Liddell Hart now became involved and attempted to use his influence to obtain a more favourable response from the War Office. He received a letter from General Cecil Liddell, the Adjutant General, once more reiterating that Grace was not entitled to a pension or grant from the Relief Fund, although Hester might be entitled to something.[18] At the beginning of February 1938 he and a group of Peace Pledge Union sponsors sent a letter to various newspapers, including the *Manchester Guardian, Reynold's Illustrated News,* and *Peace News* to plead Grace's cause. They intended to establish a fund for her from donations, with Dick Sheppard's former secretary acting as treasurer.[19] How much money this raised is not known, but in March David Starrett did hand over the rights on all of Frank's books to Grace, together with the sum of £300.[20]

---

* Muirhead later became the Under-Secretary for India. He had continued to serve in the Queen's Own Oxfordshire Hussars, with whom he had gone to war in August 1914. The regiment was amalgamated with the Worcestershire Yeomanry and then became 100th Field Artillery Brigade RA. In 1939 it became 53rd Anti-Tank Regiment RA, with Muirhead in command, but he committed suicide in October 1939 because he was considered not medically fit enough to take the regiment to France.

Liddell Hart now took up cudgels on behalf of Hester. He wrote again to the Adjutant General, stating that he understood that Hester's sole income was one pound per week from a job as a nursemaid. Liddell replied, enclosing a form for Hester to complete. He warned, however, that grants from the Relief Fund were only of the order of £10–£20 and that there was a minimum of three years between grants. Undeterred, Hester completed the form, confirming that her sole income was a mere £52 per annum. She gave an address in Huddersfield, which presumably was her place of work. Her details were authenticated by her uncle Bill Allan, who was now an inspector of constabulary. The result was that that she was granted ten pounds.[21]

Grace remained desperate for money. Apparently, shortly before the outbreak of war in 1939 she managed to obtain a pension of £50 per annum from Sir Henry Wilson's Memorial Fund, thanks to the Duke of Connaught, and then the King was petitioned on her behalf by 'many Peers of the Realm and influential persons.' The Keeper of the Privy Purse responded to her on 29 December 1939 stating that the King had no funds available. She then claimed that she worked for the War Office during the Second World War, but suffered a breakdown in 1946. This was brought about by financial worry. Consequently, in February 1946 she petitioned the King again, claiming that Frank had resigned in 1921 over a point of principle concerning the Trim cadets and hence she was not entitled to a pension. She claimed: 'His action was later justified when the War Office held a Court of Enquiry and as a result of it, the 21 cadets were not only dismissed but sent to prison. Had my husband not been forced to resign and allowed to continue his command, there would be no question of a widow's pension.' Sir Alan Lascelles, King George VI's Private Secretary, responded by merely referring to the Keeper of the Privy Seal's letter of December 1939 that nothing could be done to assist her.[22]

Grace was also keen to publish her own account of Frank's life. It would seem that prior to the outbreak of war in 1939 the publisher Herbert Jenkins had approached her with such a book in mind. Grace then wrote it and delivered the manuscript to the publisher under the title *Guns and God*. By now war had broken out and Herbert Jenkins had second thoughts about publishing it because of Frank's pacifism. Grace's solicitor did, however, manage to obtain a compensation payment from them. She tried several other publishers during the war, but none would have anything to do with it. This Grace explained in a letter to Basil Liddell Hart dated 21 February 1953. She realised that the manuscript needed revision and did not know 'a publisher courageous enough to publish.' Her friends had therefore suggested that she approach him. Liddell Hart agreed to look at the manuscript and wrote back to her on 20 March. He certainly felt that it should be published, but he believed that publishers would no longer be so much objecting to Frank's pacifism as they would take the view that Frank's 'struggles are matters in the past.' Yet his career was 'so intrinsically interesting, and so significant in its message, that the story does not really become out of date.' Nevertheless, it was 'desirable, and probably necessary, to revise and reorientate the book.' Grace accepted his comments, and was most grateful, but she did nothing more with the manuscript.[23] As it was, much of it was lifted from Frank's own books and it added little that was new about him.

Grace herself died in London at Charing Cross Hospital in February 1958, leaving precisely £169. Illfyd Noel Rees, son of Noel Rees and so Grace's nephew, was appointed to administer her estate. Three years later Hester changed her name from Crozier by deed poll. Clearly this is indicative of resentment of her father, probably because of the lack of attention that he had paid her, and maybe she did not wish to upset Grace during her lifetime by taking this step earlier.

Only two of Frank's books were ever republished. *Angels on Horseback* saw the light of day again in 1970, while *Brass Hat* was brought out by Gliddon Books of Norwich in 1989, with an introduction by Philip Orr. Athol Books of Belfast also published *The Men I Killed: A Selection of the Writings of General F.P. Crozier* in 2002. Quotations from his books have appeared in numerous other works. According to Hester, Grace was forced to sell Frank's medals and they have surfaced on occasion. The complete set of his miniature medals, worn with evening dress on formal occasions, came up for auction at Sotheby's in May 1982. Then, in September 2001 his pre-1914 medals, including those to which he was not entitled, were auctioned at Spinks. They had apparently been owned by a collector outside Britain.[24] What happened to his orders and 1914–18 medals is not known.

The physical traces of Frank Crozier remain in his books and some of his medals, wherever these are today. There are, too, some of his letters, scattered in a number of archives. Yet he is still is a very controversial and larger-than-life figure. In many ways he was a child of his times and played a part, as we have seen, in many of the significant events of the first third of the twentieth century. There is no doubt that he was a good fighting soldier, who did especially well as a brigade commander on the Western Front. Peacetime soldiering, on the other hand, was probably not really for him, although a new wife, bouts of malaria and drink more than played their part in the unravelling of his military career prior to 1914. There is no doubt that he was a bit of a martinet, who had little regard for those who did not think his way, and he could be ruthless with them. He was critical of the 1914 regular officers and preferred his subordinate commanders to be from a less narrow background. Yet he clearly had great respect for Withycombe, the commander of 107 Brigade, and for Ruggles-Brise, Ponsonby and Peyton in charge of 40th Division, even though the first two were guardsmen. The likes of Montgomery, Andrews, Plunkett, Muirhead, and Hone clearly had great respect for and loyalty to Frank and there is no doubt that he was very warm towards those he liked. Many others, though, clearly loathed him.

While Frank may have been good at picking men during 1914–18, he was not so subsequently. There is no doubt that a number of the officers in his mission to Lithuania were of doubtful character and the same applies to ADRIC. Indeed, there were some very unsavoury characters among the latter and matters were not helped by the lack of discipline. While Frank may have resigned over his perception that he was not being allowed to discipline the Trim cadets, the fact that ADRIC suffered from ill-discipline at all must be laid at his door. In spite of what he declared, he did not do enough to ensure that the Auxiliaries were properly administered, the failure to account properly for public monies being a prime example. Choosing Tom Macfie to be his adjutant was especially odd, given that Frank knew from Lithuania that he was hardly trustworthy.

One reason why Frank failed to give ADRIC the necessary stiffening may have been the presence of Grace and Mary in Dublin. They would have obviously been a distraction and, as we have seen, provided ammunition for Frank's enemies. His relationship with Ethel was clearly an uneven one, especially after Frank gave up drink and his wife did not. The birth of Hester may not have helped, with the fact that she was taken from her mother very shortly after her birth probably indicating that her father was another man. Furthermore, in all his writings Frank never acknowledged her existence, even though he did see her from time to time. It could also be that when Frank wrote that he vowed that his early 1918 leave would be his last with Ethel and Mary he had had enough of her and Lithuania provided a last chance for a reconciliation, which failed. As it was, his marriage to Grace so soon after Ethel's death indicates that he shut his first wife out of his mind and could not wait to be free of her so that he could make an honest woman of Grace.

Frank was not a very truthful person. His wearing of medals to which he was not entitled was blatant and it is surprising that he was never taken to task for it. He was also prone to lie about his military career. Worse was money. The issuing of dishonoured cheques, and leaving premises while owing rent was not just a pre-1914 youthful peccadillo which could be put down to drink and malaria. He did much the same thing during the 1920s. A few landlords did try to contact him via the War Office, but one suspects that there were many others to whom he owed money, who just put it down to experience and did nothing. Certainly, Frank's letters during this time come from a bewildering array of addresses, usually in London, but not always. Once David Starrett had come to the rescue and provided him with a house this dishonesty ceased. Friendship with Dick Sheppard also undoubtedly helped. Yet he still remained irresponsible with money, giving it away to the needy when he could ill afford to do so. Hence he left Grace and Hester penniless.

The 1920s also saw Frank take on the Establishment. This must have stemmed from the War Office's refusal to retain his services after the war. Consequently, he had not served long enough to secure an Army pension. Lithuania and Ireland were short-lived and he was then left with little means of earning a livelihood. He firmly believed that the Establishment was carrying out a major cover-up operation over Ireland and he relished attacking official policy in the Press. Indeed, it is clear that he enjoyed the publicity and so began to adopt an ever more extreme stance. Standing for the Labour Party in the 1923 General Election was also rebelling against his traditional kind. The League of Nations Union did give him something else to get his teeth into and he also enjoyed public speaking. Yet by the end of the decade the League had become part of the Establishment in his eyes and was also beginning to fail in its mission. Hence Frank adopted full-blown pacifism, although one suspects that this was as much designed to shock as it was, at least initially, genuine belief in the pacifist cause. His books, too, also provided another vehicle for annoying the Establishment. Yet once he came under the influence of Canon Sheppard his pacifism did become genuine and he fought for it with the same intensity with which he had commanded his battalion and brigade in France and Flanders.

In summary, Frank was a character with a mix of good and bad in unusual measure. This made him the controversial figure that he was and still is. One is inclined to regard him partly as a plausible rogue, and partly with a degree of grudging admiration.

Notes

IWM – Imperial War Museum, London
LCVA – Lithuanian Central State Archive, Vilnius
LHCMA – Liddell Hart Centre for Military Archives, London
NAM – National Army Museum, London
PRONI – Public Record Office of Northern Ireland, Belfast
TNA – The National Archives, Kew, London

Full bibliographical details are given only if the work is not listed in the Select Bibliography.

Chapter One

1. TNA WO 16/2810
2. *Impressions and Recollections* pp12–13, *The Times* 15 July 1887
3. Hinchliffe, L.G. *Trust and be Trusted: The Royal Army Pay Corps and its Origins* p36 Corps HQ RAPC, Worthy Down, 1983
4. Details of Burrard Crozier's service with the APD are provided by Ian Bailey, Curator of the Adjutant General's Corps Museum, Winchester.
5. *Daily Express* 29 August 1929
6. *Impressions and Recollections* p16
7. Class lists and the termly *The Roll of Wellington College* in the Wellington College archives
8. TNA BT 226/2653, which contains a copy of Francis Henry Crozier's will, with attached codicils reflecting Burrard's borrowings.
9. *Wellington College Register 1859–1896* Wellington College, 1898
10. Grace Crozier *Guns and God* p14
11. *Angels on Horseback* pp9–16
12. His height measurement is given in TNA WO 76/207 folio 98
13. *The West Australian* 2 September 1937
14. *West London Rifles (4th Middlesex): Detail for Parades, Drills, &c. For the Year 1898–9* London Metropolitan Archives, GB0074 Acc/2569/1, and 1901 Census
15. TNA WO 100/111
16. *Angels on Horseback* p17
17. *West London Rifles* op cit
18. *Ceylon Observer* 20, 27 October & 10 November 1898
19. *Impressions and Recollections* pp18–19
20. *Ceylon Observer* 9 & 29 March 1899
21. Ibid 30 March 1899
22. Grace Crozier op cit p16
23. *Ceylon Observer* 30 March 1899
24. Grace Crozier op cit p17
25. *Angels on Horseback* p235 and research carried out in Sri Lanka by Major Anton Edema late of the Ceylon Light Infantry.

Chapter Two

1. Droogleever, Robin W.E. *Thorneycroft's 'Unbuttoned': The Story of Thorneycroft's Mounted Infantry in the Boer War 1899–1902* p17
2. Ibid pp24–5 and Anglesey, Marquis of *A History of British Cavalry 1816–1919 – Volume 4: 1899–1913* pp70–71, Leo Cooper, London, 1986
3. *Impressions and Recollections* p20
4. Ibid p21
5. Ibid p23
6. Droogleever op cit p60
7. *Angels on Horseback* p46
8. Ibid p83 passim
9. Ibid p63
10. Ibid p86
11. Quoted Droogleever op cit p69
12. Quoted Lock, Ron *Hill of Squandered Valour: The Battle of Spion Kop, 1900* p173 Casemate, Newbury, 2011
13. Quoted Ibid p185
14. *Angels on Horseback* p91
15. TNA WO 105/5
16. Lock op cit pp197–8
17. *Angels on Horseback* p93
18. Droogleever op cit p97
19. Ibid p101
20. TNA WO 105/5
21. *Angels on Horseback* pp106–7
22. *Impressions and Recollections* pp33–34
23. Quoted Droogleever op cit p113
24. *Angels on Horseback* pp149–50
25. Ibid p198
26. *Impressions and Recollections* p43
27. Ibid
28. Ibid p45
29. Ibid p50
30. Information from Alexander Thorneycroft
31. *Impressions and Recollections* p52
32. Letter to Major Abbot-Anderson dated 13 October 1900, Manchester Regiment Archive MR1/16/5/24
33. *Impressions and Recollections* p53
34. Ibid pp58–9 and Scott, Brough *Galloper Jack: A Grandson's Search for a Forgotten Hero* pp84–5 Macmillan, London, 2003& *Impressions and Recollections* pp58–9
35. *Impressions and Recollections* pp57–8
36. Letter home dated 23 December 1900, Thornycroft Papers LHCMA
37. Letter home dated 9 January 1901, Ibid
38. *Impressions and Recollections* pp62–3

Chapter Three

1. TNA CAB 18/15
2. *Conditions of Service for Officers in the 1st and 2nd Niger Battalions of the West African Frontier Force in Northern Nigeria* TNA CO 879/51/2

3. The account of Frank's journey from South Africa is based on *Impressions and Recollections* pp64–71
4. Report dated 17 December 1900 to Joseph Chamberlain, Secretary of State for the Colonies, TNA CAB 18/15
5. *Impressions and Recollections* p72
6. Grace Crozier *Guns and God* p49
7. Ibid p55
8. Ibid p77
9. *Five Years Hard* pp84–5
10. *Impressions and Recollections* p77
11. Letter Gen Tom Cubitt to Lord Lugard, 29 May 1936, Bodleian Library, Oxford, Lugard papers 97/7 127
12. *Five Years Hard* pp93–4
13. Burrard's Army Pay Department record of service, Adjutant General Corps Museum, and *London Gazette* dated 25 June 1901.
14. *Impressions and Recollections* p88
15. *The Times* 3 June 1902
16. TNA WO 100/111
17. *The Times* 2 July 1902
18. TNA WO 100/111
19. TNA WO 374/16997
20. Certificate of Candidate for Election, Royal Geographical Society Archive
21. TNA WO 25/3522
22. *Impressions and Recollections* p98
23. Ibid
24. *Impressions and Recollections* p101 and *London Gazette* 31 July 1903
25. Ibid p103
26. *Five Years Hard* pp149–150
27. *Impressions and Recollections* pp108–110
28. Ibid pp116–7
29. This account is based on Colonel Morland's despatch, *London Gazette* 24 January 1905
30. *Impressions And Recollections* p123
31. Ryan Taylor's incomplete biography of Frank in manuscript, Carol Germa archive
32. TNA WO 25/3524
33. Haywood & Clarke *The History of the Royal West African Frontier Force* p261
34. *Impressions and Recollections* p128

Chapter Four

1. *Impressions and Recollections* p132
2. TNA WO 33/393 (Alderney Defence Scheme as at January 1906) and WO 33/427 (Guernsey Defence Scheme as at April 1907)
3. Information from the Alderney Museum
4. TNA BT 226/2253
5. Letter War Office to Colonial Office, 16 January 1907 and reply TNA CO 445/26
6. Wylie, Col H. C. CB *History of the Manchester Regiment (late the 63rd and 96th Foot) Vol II: 1883–1922* p74 Forster Groom, London
7. The actual reason for him going on half pay is given in WO 374/16997 and his own account is in *Impressions and Recollections* pp132, 134–5
8. Ibid p135

9. This correspondence is contained in TNA WO 374/16997
10. Letter to Lord Lugard, 29 May 1936, Bodleian Library, Lugard 97/7 127
11. See 'The Services' *Manchester Guardian* 15 July 1908
12. Wylie, Col H C CB *The Loyal North Lancashire Regiment Vol I: 1741–1914* p383 RUSI, London, 1932
13. I am very grateful to David Biggins of the Angloboerwar website for checking the medal roll for me.
14. TNA BT 11/26 & BT 226/2253. Full details of Frank's finances are found in his bankruptcy papers, TNA BT 226/2653
15. TNA WO 374/16997
16. *Impressions and Recollections* p136
17. Library and Archives Canada RG 76 Microfilm T-4762
18. *Impressions and Recollections* pp136–7
19. Ibid p136
20. I am very grateful to Col (Retd) Bob Caldwell late Fort Garry Horse for carrying out the search.
21. *Manitoba Free Press* 26 November 1910
22. Letter Mary Anderson to Ryan Taylor dated 25 September 1976 (in possession of Mrs Carol Germa) & Starrett, David *Batman* p30 unpublished manuscript IWM 79/35/1
23. *Impressions and Recollections* pp138–9
24. Ibid p141
25. Letter Cubitt to Lord Lugard op cit
26. *Manitoba Free Press* 28 October 1911
27. TNA BT 226/2253

Chapter Five

1. TNA J 77/1092/3123
2. TNA J 77/1140/4611
3. *Impressions and Recollections* p142 and League letter to *The Times* 27 March 1913
4. *Impressions and Recollections* p143
5. Ibid
6. Bowman *Carson's Army* p98
7. Ibid p155
8. See, for example, TNA WO 141/26
9. *Impressions and Recollections* p143
10. *Ireland for Ever* p37
11. Malone, Edmund & Hawes, George *Elegant Extracts: A Duobiography* p101 Lovat Dickson & Thompson, London, 1935
12. Bowman op cit p90
13. *Impressions and Recollections* pp143–5
14. Letter Gough to HQ Irish Command, 20 March 1014 reproduced in Ian F. W. Beckett ed *The Army and the Curragh Incident, 1914* pp79–80 Bodley Head, London, 1986
15. Ibid p81
16. Farrar-Hockley, Anthony *Goughie: The Life of General Sir Hubert Gough* p111 Hart-Davis, MacGibbon, London, 1975
17. *Ireland for Ever* pp44–46
18. Ibid pp47–48
19. *Impressions and Recollections* pp152–3
20. Ibid p155

21. *The Times* 30 June 1914
22. *Impressions ad Recollections* pp155–6
23. *Impressions and Recollections* p157. There is no mention of this in *Brass Hat.*
24. Ibid p156
25. Ibid pp156, 157
26. Supplement to *London Gazette*, 7 September 1914

Chapter Six

1. PRONI D1498/7
 2. *London Gazette* 27 October 1914
 3. *The Times* 7 & 9 September 1914, *Brass Hat* pp29–33
 4. Bowman, Timothy *The Ulster Volunteer Force and the formation of the 36th (Ulster) Division* Irish Historical Studies Vol XXXII, No. 128 (November 2001) p505
 5. *Impressions and Recollections* p160
 6. Starrett *Batman* p6 Department of Documents 79/35/1 IWM
 7. *Brass Hat* pp36–7
 8. Examination of personal files held at TNA under WO 339.
 9. *Brass Hat* p37
10. Starrett op cit p13
11. Ibid
12. Falls *The History of the 36th (Ulster) Division* pp13–14
13. *Brass Hat* pp39–40
14. Letter dated 29 August 1932, Liddell Hart papers LH 1/207/5 LHCMA
15. Undated letter (late 1970s) to Ryan Taylor, Carol Germa archive
16. *Brass Hat* p40
17. Starrett op cit p23
18. Ibid p53
19. TNA WO 374/16997 and *London Gazette*, 7 May 1915
20. *Impressions and Recollections* p163
21. Falls op cit p17
22. Starrett op cit p31
23. Bowman, Timothy *Irish Regiments in the Great War: Discipline and Morale* p87
24. *Brass Hat* pp48–50
25. Ibid p51–2 and Starrett op cit p34
26. *Brass Hat* pp53–4
27. Ibid p56
28. TNA WO 95/2503
29. TNA WO 213/6
30. *Brass Hat* p60
31. Starrett op cit p39
32. Perry, Nicholas ed *Major General Oliver Nugent and the Ulster Division 1915–1918* p34
33. *Brass Hat* p61
34. Perry op cit p35
35. TNA WO 95/2503 & *Brass Hat* pp68–72
36. *Brass Hat* p79 & TNA WO 339/54123
37. PRONI D2794/1/1/4
38. PRONI D1295/4/2
39. TNA WO 95/1443
40. *Impressions and Reminiscences* p164

41. Letter dated 3 May 1930, TNA CAB 45/191
42. *Random Recollections* Part 2 p26 PRONI T3217/1
43. PRONI D2794/1/1/8
44. Starrett op cit p46
45. Ibid pp 42,43,123
46. PRONI D2109/10/1/A
47. *Brass Hat* pp 64–5, 80–1, TNA WO 339/14160
48. TNA WO 71/450 and WO 213/7
49. *Impressions and Recollections* pp169–70, *Brasshat* pp83–4
50. *Random Recollections* op cit p28 & Starrett op cit p58
51. *Brass Hat* pp89–90
52. Ibid pp97–100
53. Nugent to his wife, 11 July 1916, Perry op cit p89
54. Quoted Orr, Philip *The Road to the Somme* p207
55. *Narrative 9th Royal Irish Rifles, 1st July 1916* by Lt Col F. P. Crozier, TNA WO 95/2503
56. Quoted Middlebrook, Martin *First Day on the Somme* p179 Norton, New York, 1972
57. *Narrative 9th Royal Irish Rifles* op cit
58. Orr op cit p224
59. *Narrative 9th Royal Irish Rifles* op cit
60. This account is based on 9th Royal Irish Rifles War Diary entries for 2–3 July. An identical and more legible document is found in the papers of Col P.J. Woods held in the IWM under 78/24/1. The use of the first person in these entries indicates that this is Withycombe's account of the operations. Possibly the 9th Royal Irish Rifles did not have the necessary records to produce a comprehensive account and so borrowed the Withycombe log.
61. *Brass Hat* p112
62. Grayson, Richard S. *Belfast Boys* p85
63. Starrett op cit p57
64. Quoted Orr op cit p232
65. Quoted Grayson op cit p87
66. Ltr to Sir James Edmonds dated 23 March 1930, TNA CAB 45/132
67. *Impressions and Recollections* p178
68. Falls op cit p64fn
69. Letter home dated 24 July 1916, PRONI D2794/1/1/13
70. *Brass Hat* p119
71. Ibid pp120–5 & TNA WO 95/2503
72. Raid report by 2Lt Holland TNA WO 95/2503 & Falls op cit p74
73. Letter dated 26 September 1916 PRONI D2794/1/1/14
74. *Impressions and Recollections* pp176–7
75. Starrett op cit p74
76. *Impressions and Recollections* pp178–9

Chapter Seven

1. *Impressions and Recollections* pp182–3
2. Ibid p183
3. TNA WO 339/22723
4. *Impressions and Recollections* p184
5. *Brass Hat* p132
6. *Impressions and Recollections* p184
7. TNA WO 95/2607 & *Impressions and Recollections* p187

8. *Impressions and Recollections* p188
9. TNA WO 95/2604 entries for 5–9 February 1917
10. Whitton, Lt Col F.E. *History of the 40th Division* p56
11. TNA WO 95/2592
12. Whitton op cit pp66–7
13. TNA WO 339/69109, Supplement to *London Gazette* dated 25 August 1917, Andrews' Obituary (probably written by Frank) *The Times* 19 January 1923
14. *Impressions and Recollections* pp188–9
15. Report dated 6 May 1917 TNA WO 95/2592
16. *London Gazette* 18 July 1917
17. TNA WO 95/2592
18. *Impressions and Recollections* pp192–3
19. IWM 83/23/1
20. Quoted Van Emden, Richard *The Soldier's War: The Great War through Veterans' Eyes* pp271–2 Bloomsbury, London, 2008
21. Ibid p271
22. Germa archive
23. Supplement to the *London Gazette* 17 December 1914
24. Plunkett, J. F. *Diary of the War* NAM 1994-05-398-1
25. TNA WO 95/2594, 2604 & 2607, *Impressions and Recollections* pp189–191
26. *Impressions and Recollections* pp198–9
27. Ponsonby diary entry 22 November 1917 TNA WO 95/2594 and *Report on Operations carried out by 40th Division during the period November 21st-26th 1917* TNA WO 158/388
28. *Impressions and Recollections* p201
29. Plunkett op cit
30. Starrett op cit pp99,101
31. *Brass Hat* p179
32. Quoted Whitton op cit p101
33. *Impressions and Recollections* p201
34. Ibid p205 and Starrett op cit p101
35. Ponsonby diary entry 26 November 1917
36. TNA WO 95/2607/1
37. Reproduced *Brass Hat* opposite p182
38. TNA WO 158/381 and Plunkett op cit
39. TNA WO 95/2606
40. TNA WO 374/15760, WO 95/2594
41. Plunkett op cit
42. *Impressions and Recollections* pp202–3
43. Medal Index Card found on Ancestry

Chapter Eight
1. Whitton *History of the 40th Division* p158
2. Ibid p158 & *Impressions and Recollections* p212
3. *Impressions and Recollections* pp213–5
4. TNA WO 374/15760
5. *Brass Hat* pp189–90
6. TNA WO 95/2604 & Whitton op cit p163
7. Letter to Sir James Edmonds dated 12 January 1927 TNA CAB 45/184
8. Whitton op cit pp172–3

9. *Brass Hat* pp193–4 & Whitton p184
10. *Batman* p106 IWM 79/35/1
11. *Brass Hat* pp195–7
12. *Impressions and Recollections* p216
13. Ibid p215
14. *Impressions and Recollections* pp209–10
15. *Brass Hat* p201
16. Ibid p200–1
17. TNA WO 95/2606 & *Impressions and Recollections* p221
18. *Batman* op cit p110
19. Quoted Baker, Chris *The Battle for Flanders* p57
20. Quoted Whitton op cit p241
21. Quoted Ibid p246 & Ponsonby diary entry WO 95/2592
22. TNA WO 95/2594
23. *Impressions and Recollections* p221
24. Quoted Grace Crozier *Guns and God* p89
25. Impressions and Recollections p223
26. Entry dated 27 April 1918, IWM PP/MCR/187
27. Lamb Diary op cit entries for 27 & 30 May 1918
28. Divisional war diary entry for 14 June 1918 TNA WO 95/2594
29. *Brass Hat* pp209–210
30. Ibid p214
31. Plunkett, J. F. *Diary of the War* NAM 1994-05-398-1
32. *Impressions and Recollections* pp225–6
33. Sheffield, Gary & Bourne, John ed *Douglas Haig: War Diaries and Letters 1914–18* p423 Weidenfeld & Nicolson, London, 2005
34. Plunkett op cit
35. *Impressions and Recollections* p227
36. Whitton op cit p278
37. Plunkett op cit
38. Tabor, Maj Sidney *History of the 13th Bn The East Lancashire Regiment* p2 TNA WO 95/2606
39. Plunkett op cit
40. *Brass Hat* pp224–5
41. *Impressions and Recollections* p232
42. Tabor op cit p7

Chapter Nine
1. TNA WO 374/16997
2. Quoted Mary Crozier *Guns and God* p101
3. TNA FO 369/1311
4. Lamb Diary IWM PP/MCR/187
5. *Impressions and Recollections* pp234–5
6. *Brasshat* pp236–7
7. TNA WO 339/10200
8. Minute Col P E Lewis DMS to AG2 dated 16 April 1919, TNA WO 374/16997
9. TNA WO 374/16997
10. Ibid
11. *Impressions and Recollections* pp241–2

12. Senn, Alfred Erich *A Conversation with Julius Bielskis* Litanaus Vol 21 No 3 Fall 1975 and found at www.litaunas.org/1975_3_05.htm and Galdis, Henry L. *Lithuanian American Legion History* Legionnaire Sep/Oct 2007, American Legion Lithuanian Post 154

13. Lietvos Centrinis Valstybes Archivos (Lithuanian Central State Archive) (LCVA) F.929 Ap.8 B.31 L.6&8

14. Ibid F.929 Ap.8 B.31 L.12

15. Ltr Maj C Rowland Taylor to Ministry of Pensions dated 15 Sep 23, TNA WO 339/18890 and Surgailis, Gintautas *Draugisku Valstybiu Karinkai LietuvosKarineje Tarnyboje 1919–1920 Metais* (Allied Military Officers in Lithuania 1919–1920), Karo Archyvas XIII, 1992

16. TNA WO 374/16997

17. Letter to FPC dated 2 October 1919, LCVA F.929 Ap.8 B.35 L68–70

18. TNA FO 608/187

19. *Impressions and Recollections* p242

20. TNA WO 339/108203 and letter Crozier to Mr Harvey (Foreign Office) dated 13 October 1919, TNA FO 371/3626

21. TNA WO 339/51016

22. *The VC and DSO Book: Distinguished Service Order 1916–1923* Naval & Military Press, nd

23. TNA WO 339/9821

24. I am indebted to David Grant for the biographical detail, which is on his Cairo Gang website. http://www.cairogang.com/. Details of Macfie's marriage are found at TNA J 77/1761/4866

25. http://www.cairogang.com/other-people/british/castle-intelligence/bowen/lithuania/Pereira/army-record/army-record.html and TNA AIR 76/399

26. TNA WO 339/1151

27. Cairo Gang website op cit. His court-martial papers are found in Library and Archives Canada RG 150 Series 8 File 602-13-13 Microfilm Reel T-8694. I am most grateful to Brent Holloway of Graves Registration, Directorate of History and Heritage, National Defence, Ottawa for copies of these.

28. Ltr dated 5 October 1919 TNA FO 371/3626

29. TNA WO 374/47711

30. TNA FO 371/3627

31. TNA WO 339/82563

32. TNA WO 374/48349. A full list of Frank's officers is given in Lithuanian Army Order No 303 dated 15 April 1920 (I am most grateful to Gintaras Urbanas of Vytautas, The Great War Museum, Vilnius for a copy of this) and in Surgailis op cit.

33. Letter Col Gedgaudas to FPC dated 2 October 1919 op cit

34. TNA FO 371/3626

35. p243

36. *Chums* No 1873, 4 August 1928

37. TNA FO 608/198

38. Woodward, E. L. & Butler, Robin ed *Documents on British Foreign Policy 1919–1939* First Series Vol III, 1919, HMSO, London, 1949 p219

39. Brig Gen Turner in a telegram dated 18 November 1919 reported them passing through Berlin on 11 Nov, Woodward & Butler op cit p231. Hemming's biographical details are from *The VC and DSO Book* op cit

40. TNA FO 371/3626

41. Ibid

42. p244

43. *Chums* No 1877 1 September 1928

44. Report to Earl Curzon dated 3 March 1920 Watt, D Cameron ed *British Documents on Foreign Affairs Confidential Print* Part II Series A Vol 2 p263 University Publications of America, 1984

45. *Chums* No 1873 4 August 1928

46. Zigaras, Doc. Dr. Felkisas, *Lietuvos karo mokyklos istorija 1919–1940 m* Kariunas (Cadet) September 2006

47. Turner's report to the CIGS was dated 3 February 1920 and is found in Watt op cit pp254–7, while Ward's was to Curzon and dated 12 February 1920 and also in Watt op cit p140. The details of Frank's new pay rate are found in his new draft contact with the Lithuanians (LCVA F.929 Ap.8 B.39 L.18).

48. *Impressions and Recollections* p246

49. TNA FO 371/3627

50. Unpublished Mss *The Baltic Military Mission and Lithuania* pp3,5 IWM 04/8/1

51. *The Men I Killed* p113

52. *Chums* No 1885 27 October 1928

53. TNA FO 371/3626

54. Col Ward's report on the revolt dated 25 February is found in Watt op cit pp187–8. His comment on Zukauskas is in his report dated 3 March, Watt op cit pp263–4. Frank's own account of the revolt is in *The Men I Killed* pp114–5, as well as *Chums* No 1881 29 September 1928 and No 1883 13 October 1928..

55. Senn op cit

56. Frank's letter published in *The Times* 12 March 1920

57. Report in *The Times* of 9 March 1920.

58. *Impressions and Recollections* pp246–7

59. Letter Frank to J. D. Gregory (Foreign Office) dated 11 April 1920, TNA FO 371/3626

60. *Impressions and Recollections* p249 and report in *The Times* 22 March 1920

61. TNA FO 371/3626

62. TNA FO 371/3635

63. Ryan Taylor's incomplete biography of Frank, part resulting from interviews with Mary, and contained in the Germa Archive.

64. TNA FO 371/3626

Chapter Ten

1. Leeson *The Black and Tans* p24

2. TNA HO 351/63

3. Ibid

4. TNA CAB 24/109

5. Bowman *Carson's Army* p194

6. *Impressions and Recollections* pp250–1

7. See, for example, *Who Was Who 1929–1940*

8. Andrews left a brief account in his personal file, TNA WO 339/59109

9. *The RIC and the Auxiliaries: Their Organisation and Discipline*, *Manchester Guardian* 28 March 1921

10. *The Times* 13 March 1924, Medal Index Card, and *London Gazette*. Curiously, Kirkwood is not listed as having a personal file in TNA WO 338 and it looks as though it must have been lost during 1918.

11. These memos are in TNA HO 45/20096

12. TNA CAB 27/108

13. TNA HO 45/20096

14. Harvey, A. D. *Who Were the Auxiliaries?* from *The Historical Journal* Vol 35 No 3 (September 1992). This draws on the ADRIC registers contained in TNA HO 184/50 & 51.
15. *Manchester Guardian* 28 March 1921 op cit
16. *The Weekly Summary* 27 August 1920, TNA CO 906/33
17. *Lectures on Guerrilla Warfare, Ireland 1920–1921* p18 Perceval Papers 4/1, IWM
18. Letter to Sir John Anderson dated 25 February 1921, TNA CO 904/188
19. Diaries 1920, 1921, Strickland Papers IWM Documents 2626
20. *Ireland for Ever* pp96–98, Leeson op cit pp121–124
21. Evidence of Macfie recruiting is found in a report on F Company's cash account as at 1 May 1921, TNA HO 351/123
22. *Ireland for Ever* pp161–2
23. This account is drawn from *A Word to Gandhi* pp55–58, with additional material from the Cairo Gang website.
24. TNA WO 35/88B
25. Ibid
26. *Ireland for Ever* p105
27. *Impressions and Recollections* p257, http://www.theauxiliaries.com/companies/g-coy/g-coy.html, and Hopkinson The Last Days of Dublin Castle p91
28. Townshend *The British Campaign in Ireland 1919–1921* pp138–9
29. TNA CO 904/150
30. Diary entry 19 December 1920, Hopkinson op cit p95
31. *Impressions and Recollections* p258
32. *Weekly Summary* 28 January 1921, TNA CO 906/33
33. Leeson op cit p185
34. *Impressions and Recollections* p259
35. Hopkinson op cit p125
36. *Impressions and Recollections* p259–260
37. Ibid & *The Times* 24 February 1921
38. *The Times* 25 February 1921
39. *Impressions and Recollections* pp261–2
40. Frank's version of events is taken from Ibid pp264–7

Chapter Eleven

1. Hansard *House of Commons Debates* Vol 138, Colms 738–42
2. Ibid, Colms 929–33
3. TNA CO 904/188
4. Diary entry 25 February 1921, Hopkinson *The Last Days of Dublin Castle* p132
5. Quoted Townsend *The British Campaign in Ireland 1919–1921* p163 fn192
6. TNA HO 184/52
7. Hansard op cit Colms 1723–68
8. Letters Crozier to Under Secretary, Irish Office dated 14 February 1992 & Private Secretary to Chief of Police Ireland to Head Constable Leary, Holyhead, TNA HO 45/24629 and *Ireland for Ever* p139
9. Issue of 28 March 1921
10. 8 April 1921
11. *Impressions and Recollections* p270
12. TNA HO 45/20096
13. TNA HO 351/63

14. Report by DI3 B. Conlin dated 24 April 1921, TNA HO 351/123
15. *Impressions and Recollections* p272
16. TNA HO 351/123
17. Leeson *The Black and Tans* pp127–8 and TNA HO 351/123
18. TNA HO 351/187
19. *Impressions and Recollections* p267
20. TNA HO 45/24829
21. TNA J 77/1761/4866
22. TNA FO 847/78
23. *Impressions and Recollections* p267
24. Additional information from the Cairo Gang website
25. Memorandum on Crozier's claim for expenses in connection with Trim Inquiry dated 15 April 1926, TNA HO 45/24829
26. Hansard op cit Vol 140 Colms 1276–7
27. Ibid Colms 1867–8
28. Leeson op cit pp185–6
29. Hansard op cit Vol 142 Colms 23–6
30. Memorandum dated 15 April 1926 op cit
31. Ibid, 31 May 1921 Colms 802–4
32. Ibid Colms 1214–8
33. Memorandum by Chief Secretary for Ireland in *Weekly Summary of the State of Ireland* week ending 11 July 1921, TNA CAB 24/126
34. *Impressions and Recollections* pp282–4
35. Ibid p287–8
36. National Library of Ireland, Erskine Childers Papers Ms 48.052
37. Letter dated 25 June 1922, Lloyd George papers, Parliamentary Archive LG/F/97/1/31
38. TNA WO 374/16997
39. Hemming minutes dated 14 & 27 November 1922 and Letter to A. J. Sylvester dated 2 December 1922, TNA HO 45/24829
40. *Cork Examiner* 27 January 1923
41. *Impressions and Recollections* p235
42. *The Times* 19 January 1923
43. Grace Crozier *Guns and God* p141
44. Letter dated 28 March 1923, *Guardian* Archive Part 2 A/C106/1
45. London School of Economics Library Archive M3383/Coll Misc 1155
46. Grace Crozier op cit p141–2

Chapter Twelve

1. *As Others See Us* pp97–99
2. Ibid pp117–118
3. Letter dated 14 June 1924 *Guardian* Archive Part 2 A/C106/3
4. Letter dated 19 June 1924, ibid A/C106/4
5. In letter to Under Secretary of State, War Office dated 28 July 1925, TNA WO 374/16997
6. Letter dated 13 January 1925, ibid
7. This correspondence is also found in Frank's personal file TNA WO 374/16997
8. *The Times* 26 March 1925
9. Letter Mrs Menzies's solicitors to Frank dated 2 June 1925, TNA HO 45/24829
10. All the above correspondence, including the War Office memo, is in TNA 374/16997

11. Hopkinson *The Last Days of Dublin Castle*, diary entry 1 September 1920 p32
12. *HHA: Letters of the Earl of Oxford and Asquith to a Friend: First Series 1915–1922* p172 Geoffrey Bles, London, 1933
13. Winter, Sir Ormonde *Winter's Tale: A Biography* pp336–7 The Richards Press, London, 1955
14. *London Gazette* 19 February 1926
15. Apart from the Worthington-Evans letter (TNA WO 374/16997), this correspondence to Baldwin and Joynson-Hicks is from TNA HO 45/24829
16. TNA WO 374/16997 for War Office and HO 45/24829 for Baldwin.
17. *Daily Mirror* 13 February 1926
18. Hansard *House of Commons Debates* 20 April 1926 Vol 194 Colms 1010–2
19. *The Hope of Europe* p115 Heinemann, London, 1921
20. TNA WO 374/16997
21. TNA BT 34/4119/141564
22. TNA HO 45/24829

Chapter Thirteen
1. *Impressions and Recollections* p308
2. *Scotsman* 8 December 1928
3. Letters dated 13 and 30 May 1929, *Guardian* Archive Part 2 A/C106/5 & A/C106/6
4. *Manchester Guardian* 4 January 1929
5. Ibid 2 August 1929, which advertised Frank's articles
6. *Sydney Morning Herald* 8 October 1929 citing the British *Daily Chronicle*. A good account of the Shearer affair is Moser, John E. *The Man Who Wrecked the Conference* http://personal.ashland.edu/~jmoser1/shearer.html
7. Ryan Taylor interview notes, Carol Germa archive
8. Grace Crozier *Guns and God* p5 and *Manitoba Free Press* 24 April 1930
9. Book contract dated 10 January 1930, FP Crozier file, Random House Archive
10. *Now & Then* Summer 1930
11. 2 May 1930
12. 25 April 1930
13. Quoted Grace Crozier op cit p147
14. 31 March 1930
15. 24 April 1930
16. 25 April 1930
17. 24 April 1930
18. *Dundee Courier & Advertiser* 25 April 1930
19. *Western Daily Press* 26 April 1930
20. *News Chronicle* 25 April 1930
21. Letters dated 28 & 30 April 1930, TNA 374/16997
22. FP Crozier file, Random House Archive
23. 3 August 1930
24. 11 August 1930
25. 24 April 1930
26. *New York Times* 3 November 1930
27. Townshend *The British Campaign in Ireland 1919–1921* p159
28. Letter dated 11 November 1930, Guardian Archive Part 2 A/C106/7A & 8
29. Letter dated 16 May 1930, TNA WO 374/65997
30. FP Crozier file, Random House Archive

31. 30 December 1930
32. 2 October 1930
33. 23 February 1932
34. Letters 4 & 5 February 1932, Lugard papers 9/7 122 Bodleian Library, Oxford
35. Foulkes 3/45, LHCMA
36. http://www.gandhi-manibhavan.org/eduresources/bks_read_by_g.htm#Calthrop
37. *The Mercury* (Hobart, Tasmania) 28 February 1932
38. *Sunday Chronicle* 7 February 1932
39. *The Mercury* op cit
40. 12 July 1932
41. Liddell Hart papers LH 1/207/1, LHCMA
42. Letters dated 11 July, 13 July, 29 August 1932, LH 1/207/2,3,5 ibid
43. Letters dated 12 & 16 May 1932, Jonathan Cape Archive, University of Reading MS 2446/AA56
44. Letter to Cape dated 9 August 1932, FP Crosier file, Random House Archive
45. Letters dated 22 October 1932 and no date, Liddell Hart papers LH 1/207/6 & 7, LHCMA
46. Law Report, *The Times* 22 June 1933
47. *Morning Bulletin* (Rockhampton, Queensland), 29 November 1933 and *The Western Australian* (Perth), 28 November 1933, for instance.
48. Letters dated 3, 22, 24 November 1933, Liddell Hart papers LH 1/207/9–11, LHCMA
49. Ibid LH 1/207/12
50. Agreement with Frank Percy Crozier dated 28 August 1937, FP Crozier file Random House Archive
51. *The Times* 3 January 1934
52. Morrison, Sybil *I Renounce War* p8
53. Ibid pp8–9
54. Letter dated 5 December 1934, Grace Crozier papers
55. 24 April 1935
56. *The Times* 16 July 1935
57. Quoted Hetherington, William *Swimming Against the Tide* p6
58. Letter dated 25 July 1935 TNA WO 374/16997
59. Copy in Grace Crozier archive
60. 16 March 1936
61. *New Statesman and Nation* 4 July 1936
62. IWM Sound Archive, AC 4581 Reels 1 & 2
63. 15 July 1936
64. TNA MEPO 3/3113
65. Liddell Hart papers LH 1/207/14–16, LHCMA
66. *The Times* 28 November 1936
67. Letter to Liddell Hart dated 13 March 1937 LH 1/207/19 Ibid
68. Issue dated 19 July 1936
69. Copy of programme in Crozier file, Peace Pledge Union (PPU) Archive
70. Ibid
71. Quoted in book review *Peace News* 24 April 1937
72. Report in *The Advertiser* (Adelaide) 4 February 1937
73. Speech and subsequent debate are found in Hansard *House of Lords Debates* Series 5 Vol 105, Colms 84–92, 29 April 1937 and Cecil's letter is reproduced in Grace Crozier op cit pp200–201
74. *Authors Take Sides in the Spanish Civil War* Left Review, London, 1937

75. Crozier file, PPU Archive
76. *The Men I Killed* p103
77. 12 August 1937
78. 14 August 1937
79. 21 August 1937
80. Grace Crozier op cit p157
81. *Daily Express* 4 September 1937. No trace of this letter or any other relevant documents can be found in the TNA Foreign Office files.

Chapter Fourteen
1. See, for instance, *The Times* 25, 27, 30 August 1937
2. FP Crozier file, Random House Archive
3. Letter dated 31 August 1937, Grace Crozier papers
4. Grace Crozier op cit p214 and Ryan Taylor manuscript. Taylor states that Frank was buried in Highgate Cemetery, London, but Grace Crozier is surely correct.
5. Draft letter to *Daily Graphic* dated 16 April 1937, which he sent to Grace, Grace Crozier papers
6. Grace Crozier op cit p156
7. Letter dated 6 September 1937, ibid.
8. Letter dated 3 September 1937, ibid.
9. 1 September 1937
10. 16 September 1937
11. *The Times* 4 September 1937
12. Grace Crozier op cit pp208–212. It was reproduced in *Peace News* 11 September 1937
13. 1 September 1937
14. 2 September 1917
15. 4 September 1937
16. *Daily Mirror* 10 September 1937
17. TNA WO 374/16997
18. Ibid and letter Liddell to Liddell Hart dated 7 January 1939, Liddell Hart papers LH 1/204/24 LHCMA
19. *Manchester Guardian* 4 February 1938, *Peace News* 5 February 1938 for example.
20. Agreement dated 1 March 1938, FP Crozier file, Random House Archive
21. TNA WO 374/16997 and Liddell Hart papers LH 1/204/28 op cit
22. Draft letter from Grace Crozier dated 18 February 1948 and reply from Buckingham Palace date 3 March 1948, Grace Crozier papers.
23. Liddell Hart papers LH 1/207/30–35, LHCMA
24. Information held in Royal Ulster Rifles Museum

Select Bibliography

Frank Crozier's own books

A Brass Hat in No Man's Land Cape, London, 1930

A Brass Hat in No Man's Land with new Introduction by Philip Orr, Gliddon Books, Norwich, 1989

Impressions and Recollections Werner Laurie, London, 1930

A Word to Gandhi: The Lesson of Ireland Williams & Norgate, London, 1931

Angels on Horseback Cape, London, 1932

Angels on Horseback Cedric Chivers Ltd, Bath, 1970

Five Years Hard Cape, London, 1932

Ireland for Ever Cape, London, 1932

The Men I Killed Michael Joseph, London, 1937

The Men I Killed: A Selection of the Writings of General F.P. Crozier Athol Books, Belfast, 2002

Primary Sources

The National Archives, Kew

BT 226/2653 – F.P. Crozier bankruptcy papers 1909

HO 45/24829 – Brigadier-General Crozier: dismissed the Army following incident involving Royal Irish Constabulary cadets at Trim; claims libel

WO 95/2502 – War Diary 107 Brigade

WO 95/2503 – War Diary 9th Royal Irish Rifles

WO 95/2592–4 – War Diary 40th Division

WO 95/2604–6 – War Diary 119 Brigade

WO 141/93 – Record of the Rebellion in Ireland in 1921 and the part played by the Army in dealing with it. Volume I – Operations

WO 374/16997 – F P Crozier personal file

Imperial War Museum

Starrett, David *Batman* 79/35/1

Published Works

Hopkinson, Michael ed. *The Last Days of Dublin Castle: The Diaries of Mark Sturgis* British Academic Press, Dublin, 1999

Perry, Nicholas ed *Major General Oliver Nugent and the Ulster Division 1915–1918* Sutton Publishing, Stroud, for the Army Records Society, 2007

Secondary Works

Baker, Chris *The Battle for Flanders: German Defeat on the Lys 1918* Pen & Sword Military, Barnsley, 2011

Bond, Brian *Survivors of a Kind* Continuum, London, 2008

Bowman, Timothy *Irish Regiments in the Great War: Discipline and Morale* Manchester University Press, 2003

Bowman, Timothy *Carson's Army: The Ulster Volunteer Force, 1910–1922* Manchester University Press paperback, 2007

Drooglever, Robin *Thorneycroft's Unbuttoned: The Story of Thorneycroft's Mounted Infantry in the Boer War, 1899–1902* privately, PO Box 42, Bulleen, Victoria, Australia, 2011

Falls, Cyril *The History of the 36th (Ulster Division)* Constable, London, 1922

Grayson, Richard S. *Belfast Boys: How Unionists and Nationalists Fought and Died Together in the First World War* Continuum revised paperback edition, London, 2010

Hammond, Bryn *Cambrai 1917: The Myth of the First Great Tank Battle* Weidenfeld & Nicolson, London, 2008

Haywood, Col A. CMG CBE DSO & Clarke, Brig F.A.S. DSO *The History of the Royal West African Frontier Force* Gale & Polden, Aldershot, 1964

Hetherington, William *Swimming Against the Tide: The Peace Pledge Union Story 1934–2009* Peace Pledge Union, London, 2009

Leeson, D.M. *The Black & Tans: British Police and Auxiliaries in the Irish War of Independence* Oxford University Press, 2011

McCall, Ernest *Tudor's Toughs: The Auxiliaries* Red Coat Publishing, Newtonards, 2010

Middlebrook, Martin *First Day on the Somme* W.W. Norton edition, New York, 1972

Messenger, Charles *Call to Arms: The British Army 1914–18* Weidenfeld & Nicolson, London 2005

Morrison, Sybil *I Renounce War: The Story of the Peace Pledge Union* Sheppard Press, London, 1962

Orr, Philip *The Road to the Somme: Men of the Ulster Division Tell Their Story* Blackstaff Press paperback edition, Belfast, 2008

Stewart, A.T.Q. *The Ulster Crisis: Resistance to Home Rule 1912–1914* Blackstaff Press paperback edition, Belfast, 1997

Taylor, Richard & Young, Nigel ed *Campaigns for Peace: British Peace Movements in the 20th Century* Manchester University Press, 1987

Townshend, Charles *The British Campaign in Ireland 1919–1921: The Development of Political and Military Policies* Oxford University Press paperback edition, 1978

Whitton, Lt Col F.E. CMG *History of the 40th Division* Gale & Polden, Aldershot, 1926

Index

For Frank Crozier's family members, their relationship to him is given in brackets.